TECHNOLOGY OF PERFUMES, FLAVOURS & ESSENTIAL OILS

TECHNOLOGY OF PERFUMES, FLAVOURS & ESSENTIAL OILS

Written By :

EIRI Consultants and Engineers

ENGINEERS INDIA RESEARCH INSTITUTE

4449, Nai Sarak, Main Road, Delhi-110 006 (India)

Ph. : 91-11-23918117, 23916431, 23840361

Fax : 91-11-23916431, 23918117

✶ **E-Mail :** eirisidi@bol.net.in

✶ **Website :** www.eiriindia.org

Sole Distributor :

EIRI PROJECT CONSULTANTS & PUBLISHERS

4/54, Roop Nagar, Delhi-110007

Printed and Published by :

ENGINEERS INDIA RESEARCH INSTITUTE

4449, Nai Sarak, Main Road, Delhi-110 006 (India)
Ph. : 91-11-23918117, 23916431, 23840361
Fax : 91-11-23916431, 23918117
* **E-Mail** : eirisidi@bol.net.in
* **Website** : www.eiriindia.org

Distributed by :

EIRI PROJECT CONSULTANTS & PUBLISHERS
4/54, Roop Nagar, Delhi-110007

ISBN : 978-81-89765-22-4
Printed in New Delhi (India)

Rs. 1175/-

Printed and Published by Sudhir Gupta for
"Engineers India Research Institute", 4449, Nai Sarak, Main Road,
New Delhi-110 006 and Printed at Swastik Offset, Delhi

Preface

The book **'Technology of Perfumes, Flavours & Essential Oils'** covers various methods including Creating a Perfume, Flower Perfumes and Their Formulations, Packaging of Perfumes, Testing a Perfume, Aerosol Spray, Aromatic Perfumery Compounds, Scents and Perfumes, Spray (Perfumes), Floral Oils, Manufacturing Processes of Flavours, Non-Alcoholic Flavours, Flavours Fruits (Whiskey, Vodka, Grape Butter Scotch and Rum), Terpeneless Menthol Crystals, Trends in Trade of Essential Oils, Demand for Essential Oils, Super-Critical Fluid Extraction (SCFE) Technology-For Spice Extraction, Citronella Oil, Clove Oil, Extraction of Essential Oils by Super Critical Fluid (Carbon Dioxide) Method from Flowers, Herbs and Spices, Eucalyptus Oil, Ginger Oil, Jasmine Flower Oil, Production Technology of Jasmine for Essential Oil, Lemon Grass Oil, Palm Oil Crushing Unit, Essential Oils by Steam Distillation, Composition of Essential Oil from Flowers of Keora, Distillation of Eucalyptus hybrid Oil, Turmeric (*Curcuma Longa* L.) Leaf Oil, a new Essential Oil for Perfumer Industry, Essential Oils and Flavours, Technology of Essential Oils, Essences and Ottos : Preparation of Essences, Natural Essences, Marketing of Artificial Essences, Preparation of Ottos, Rose and Keora Water, Toilet Water, Technology of Flavours, Role of Perfumer, Quality Control in Aromatic Plants, Palmarosa Oil, Chemical Composition of Lemongrass Varieties, Kewda Essential Oil and Attar, Palmarosa Oil, Sandalwood Oil, Technology fo Palmarosa Oil, Lemongrass Oil, Patchouli Oil, Rose-Scented Geranium, Basil Oil, Turpentine Oil

The book has been written for the benefit and to prove an asset and a handy reference guide in the hands of new entrepreneurs and well established industrialists.

Director

ENGINEERS INDIA RESEARCH INSTITUTE

Nai Sarak, Main Road,
Delhi-110 006 (India)
E-mail : eirisidi@bol.net.in

CONTENTS AND SUBJECT INDEX

1

Creating a Perfume

INTRODUCTION

To create new thing is satisfactory work for perfumer. Therefore in many panel discussions proposal for producing novel perfume have come forward. Few desired to make a mystery of it, a sort of arcane divination, almost as though they considered the simple truth to be unworthy of such a specialised subject. To produce novel perfume, quality perfume requires perservance, in depth ofknowledge of perfumery chemicals, imagination and trained mind.

Working within a Framework

Price

Perfumery is a very different art from painting and sculpture and commercial craft such as creation of hand jewellery. It operates within relatively strict limits of price. The topmost perfumes having high price ceiling and very low a limit might not succeed the object of pleasing whatever section of public the perfume is designed to reach. Even if perfumer, is working with a reputed organisation or has renowned his work, has to consider the necessity of working out price level acceptable to buyer. One must not exaggerate the importance of cost factor because it will put restriction on the performer's general freedom of action.

The most important difference of perfumery as an art is complete absence of amateurism. In case of sculpture and painting a large number of amateurs or dilettantes are found. As an amateur it is very difficult to learn the art, craft and technique of perfumery. Even if the few amateurs available due to heavy demand they tend to become involved sooner or later as professionals.

Packaging

Packaging is the important activity, that contribute to the acceptance of a fine perfume. It involve the designing of bottles, the choice of casket or carton, the label. the colour scheme, the general ambiance - and, of course, the name. But the utmost importance has to be given to the perfume itself as, even with the prettiest and most luxurious presentation, the perfume must fulfil all the demands made of it in agreeable odour, originality, tenacity, strength etc., or else it will soon disappear from the market.

One has known perfumes that had a strikingly successful impact because of their pack and publicity but which, owing to their inherent defects as perfumes, fell off alarmingly in sales as soon as the initial publicity died down. On the other hand (and this is perhaps more important) there have been many perfumes of considerable merit introduced, over the years, only to rank as failures because of poor packaging, ineffective marketing and insufficient distribution.

Inspiration

The perfumer, in fact. is inevitably one of a team. Like all star performers, he is apt to have his idosyncrasies. His inspiration can come from many sources, not the least of which may be conversations with his colleagues - or even with rival perfumers. On some occasions, it is true, he may be absorbed entirely in his own thoughts and impressions, work out certain basic accords and proceed to devise a perfume that is truly 'himself' - but even then he owes much, like any other artist or craftsman, to the thoughts and teachings of those who have preceded him. On other occasions, however, the inspiration will definitely come from outside.

THE PRACTICAL FOUNDATION

The first important point to remember for obtaining new perfumes is that, one should have complete study of natural and synthetic materials, and their characteristic odours should be fixed in olfactory memory. It is necessary to have knowledge of the differences that exist between high-grade and inferior products and the new products appearing on the market. But how is all this knowledge to be gained?

All that need be added at this juncture is that perfume creation is essentially bilateral: one side is intuitive, aesthetic, imaginative, subjective, while the other is technological. methodical. and to an increasing extent objective and scientific. Neither side can operate successfully alone.

The perfumer's inspiration comes from many quarters, from the laboratory, the perfumery boutique, the garden, the boudoir; from the beach, theatre of fashionable restaurant; even from books. The talented perfumer, not only qualified by technical expertise but also endowed with an imagination, may well have some specially attractive woman in mind when ideas come to him, or he may merely be excited by life in general. But the perfumer at this stage will not be thinking in poetic or musical or literary images: his ideas will come to him as top notes and *accords,* as aldehydes, esters, lactones-a touch of this, a background of that, a hint of something else, something subtle and unusual. and beyond that initial phase the need to improvise, to discover, to round off and perhaps, at last, achieve a new climax of originality and seduction. Yet these are words and he, at that time, will be thinking in odours.

Inspiration: Response to Stimuli

Different perfumers react to different stimuli. Henri Robert of Chanel suggested that odour-diary should be maintained by perfume~ during their travels. On returning back to the laboratory perfumer with the notes in odour diary, attempt to create in memory the various olfactory impressions that has been received. To inspire is to breathe, in and this the perfumer does, receiving his inspiration from all quarters. 'A perfumer should be most concerned with expressing his personality in his compositions. His perfumes should incorporate an ideal - his ideal - and should therefore be characteristic, so that they cannot be confused with any other compositions. Later on, when he has gained more experience, the perfumer must see to it that each perfume combines strength of odour with diffusive power, without dispensing with the fineness and purity of the odour. He will have to devote his special attention to the volume of odour, which is usually more important in use and is often harder to achieve than, say, stability of the odour. This is practically guaranteed if one limits 'oneself to simple compositions and takes careful heed of the reactions of the various ingredients:

Here one notes the essential association of artistic and technological factors. The former may perhaps range, as in painting, from the representational art typified by the simple flower perfume through impressionistic and expressionistic concepts down to those which are almost purely abstract; while the technological side of the perfumer's craft will control the actual form and outcome of his efforts.

Trial and error

Irrespective of source, the perfumer's feelings and ideas must eventually result in action, which can be accomplished by traditional trial-and-error methods. One such procedure consists of forming a nucleus of a few essential oils and synthetics, and to proceed by tentative additions of further constituents. As one can add in this context but not subtract, many false starts and fresh beginnings may thus be involved. There are two ways to carry out trial and error method. In first case one may work up a base suitable for incorporation in an already established composition, so that when it is properly adjusted and added all that is necessary to round off the harmonious finished composition is the addition of a few final touches here and there. Another method is to work on a base, self-made or purchased from outside, by adding different products to it, little by little, in accordance with the type of perfume that one is setting out to create.

This method of making perfumes can only be practised satisfactorily, of course, after the perfumer has acquired a long and intimate experience of the effects of mixing odouriferous substances together. When the mixtures or blends are produced perfumer must observe very attentively and acutely all the little olfactory phenomena which takes place. These were the only methods of producing perfumes and it is still used today.

Colours

Creating a perfume is analogous to painting. A painter knows that if he would like to get certain shade e.g., flame, he just gives touch of yellow to saffron to obtain effect. Similarly the touching effect can be obtained in mixture of odours wherein the part played by induction is enormous. Nevertheless, in the mixture of colours we have the conventional decomposition of light passing through a . prism into the primary colours: violet, indigo, blue, green, yellow, orange and red, that are reduced to three: blue, yellow, red, which by being mixed enable all the others to be obtained. This process is not so complete with odours. Then there is the Chevreuil disc which aids the process of mixing colours. We have nothing comparable for mixing odours.

Until we have a reasonable theory of olfaction, enabling us to conduct similar work, we shall remain more or less subject to the trial-and-error methods of empiricism. That is the reason why so many research workers have suggested practical methods relating to the technical side of perfume composition and paid little attention to the indispensable artistic inspiration. As their views collectively present many points of interest, we attempt to look at them briefly but critically in the paragraphs that follow.

JEANCARD ON COMPOSITION

As per the idea of composition proposed by the Jeancard, the perfume will have a prelude and a finale, which will frame the motif and bring it out. We have here, he added, a distillation at ambient temperature and pressure, where according to their vapour pressure, components will become dissociated and volatilise, undergoing a true fractionation. This evolution, governed by the laws of physics, is a function of the moleqular weights and vapour pressures, which express the volatility of the mixture.

Highly volatile odourants with an evanescent effect can have their action modified and made more tenacious by being admixed with a less volatile component. This has been clearly demonstrated in the cases of methyl amyl ketone and benzyl acetate in alcoholic solution, with and without benzyl benzoate. We must not overlook the formation of azeotropes, i.e., a mixture of substances which distil as though they in fact formed only one single substance. In theory it is possible, when there are only two or three substances, to calculate the formation of azeotropes, but the picture becomes too complicated when there are a considerable number of substances present.

Many years ago, it was noticed that the great perfumes which had a lasting success behaved on evaporation almost always in an identical way. It indicate that there must be, in all of them, a similar azeotropic evaporation that would show up in. an evaporation curve. An experiment was conducted.. First collect considerable quantities of different well known perfumes having the qualities sought and recognised, originality, atmosphere (character), power tenacity, diffusiveness etc. Extract the perfume concentrate using pentane and separate leaving behind a residue which resembled closely that used at the time of making the perfume. Evaporate the solvent separated at the ambient temperature, 15-20°C and relevant curves obtained for temperature against time. It was found that all these curves were almost identical or at least their outlines were very similar.

While in nature, i.e. in the essential oils, azeotropes must undoubtedly exist. the complexity of these phenomena becomes quite formidable when one has to deal with mixtures of many different substances, as opposed to mere binary systems. Here the empirically derived experience of the perfumer has to take over in judging a priori the substances to be associated and the relative proportions that will be required to obtain a desired note.

LIMITATIONS OF FORMULAE

For those who have come into possession of a formula and think they are going to have success with it, they should remember that a formula is only of maximum value, if the person using it knows exactly the origin and name of the supplier of each of the raw materials and it is, moreover, olfactorily necessary for every raw material in the formula to be identical with that used in the creation of the perfume.

As per Felix Cola: 'A perfume is composed like a poem, a symphony. It is a happy inspiration which decides the substances that have to be used and the respective proportions of the constituents which have to be employed.' He also put forward. that the proportions are gradually modified to obtain a better balance. Then, an attempt is made to simplify the formula, while still retaining its special character; for if the number of constituents is unduly increased, the perfume will be deprived of personality. It becomes grey and undistinguished - what a painter calls *grisaille*.

In other words, the finest of the natural essential oils seem to consist of several basic organic substances which form the typical note, but this characteristic basic odour is rounded off by the presence of infinitesimal quantities of a large number of organic substances, related or not to the first ones, which combine to give fineness, distinction and sweetness, which characterise the quality of these essential oils.

Otto Gerhardt, expert seems indispensable that a perfumer should have above all else an artistic talent. experience, and complete knowledge of the development of the composition. He should of course have a full knowledge of the raw materials (natural and synthetic) and way to use them. In this case, an olfactory memory plays a leading part.

THE PERFUMER'S KNOWLEDGE OF CHEMISTRY

A knowledge of chemistry helps perfumer to understand perfume mainly from synthetic products in better manner. There is of course no incompatibility between the fact of having studied chemistry and that of having artistic tastes. Perfumers who have not had scientific training have usually endeavoured later on to acquire at least a minimum of chemical knowledge, after realising that they lacked it and were thus at a disadvantage. This does not mean that any chemist can become a perfumer: far from it. And it is quite certain that very many people who have never studied chemistry have been excellent perfumers.

For perfumer it is necessary to remember the composition of the principal types of perfume, so as to have a comprehensive knowledge of possible combinations. At the same time he should know the majority of the natural and synthetic odourants. He must have an excellent and extensive olfactory memory, which has recorded all the knowledge he mentions and which will enable him to identify and copy each special note, floral or otherwise, just as occasion demands.

Frank Atkins wrote in a series of articles on the Use and Abuse of Fixatives, in which he dealt with fixation as an integral part of perfume composition. Marcel Billot, in a long and heavily documented review of Fixation in Perfumery. also looked at fixation in the general content of composition.

The Russian perfumer, contributed on fixation and other aspects of perfumery. According to him: (i) The persistence of perfumes depends on the coefficient of useful work, i.e., the nature of the evaporation and the value of the threshold concentration; (ii) The stability increases with the coefficient of useful work and with reduction in the threshold concentration; (iii) The change in the rate of evaporation and the proper use of threshold concentration values should be carefully studied by perfumers and research institutes; and (iv) Qualities demanded of the perfumer are the ability to conceive his objective clearly, to persist in his purpose, to have immense patience, and to have the requisite wide knowledge of his medium.

'The perfumer must have an intimate knowledge of a thousand aromatic substances. He must be familiar with the odour value of each. its source, and the characters that determine its quality, as well as its floral type and blending range. Moreover, he must also select and use each one of them skilfully to compose, reinforce and shade his basic note until it becomes a symphony of fragrance. But this is not all; for his creation is to be employed as a perfume for cosmetics and soaps he must also have a profound knowledge of their composition and the effect each of their raw materials will have upon every constituent of his original fragrance. which involves cunning substitution and fresh blending to achieve : ultimately the same finished note.'

Creativity in the Art of Perfumery

Creativity in the Ait of Perfumery is based on the following principles

(1) Chose and work out a harmony or a pleasing combination of harmonies: original. agreeable and carefully completed.

(2) Perfect the top note or depart with light components which harmonise with the base.

(3) Complete the basic note so that it harmonises with the general, characteristic note of the perfume as a whole.

Carles' Method

Jean Carles, a perfumer of high repute opposed to the idea of exceptional nose'. 'There are no doubt people whose sense of smell is naturally keen, but the highly developed olfactory sense can only come from education and training, and particularly from education of the olfactory memory (just as for other memories). No perfumer can, exist without an olfactive memory.

Carles conducted a study of both contrasting and similar odour of each family which suggested that each perfumer should prepare for his own use an empirical classification of this kind, listing all raw materials, natural and synthetic, according to their relative volatility, i.e. as Ii) top notes- or very volatile products lacking tenacity; (ii) base modifying notes - or products of intermediate volatility and tenacity; and (iii) base notes - or products of low volatility and high tenacity.

Carles make a very important point, that the skilled perfumer, like the skilled musician, should be able to 'smell' his perfume by setting it down on paper and thinking about it. The preliminary 'blending' thus goes *on* in the mind, although it obviously has to be put to material proof, tested and modified, before it can be regarded as satisfactory.

The stepwise method of Carles' to produce perfume is (i) First find combination of two or three odourants capable of providing the basic note of a perfume; (ii) Examine them rapidly and make a mixture of -two substances which is possibly an attractive blend or accord; (iii) Perfect them quantitatively. Assume these two odourants as 'A' and 'B'. Prepare series of a trial using different ratio of 'A' and 'B' as under:

Serial Nos.	'A' Parts	'B' Parts	Total
1	9	1	10
2	8	2	10
3	7	3	10
4	6	4	10
5	5	5	10

From these series perfumer can select what seems best to him. In case this series fails to provide best perfumer may prepare series *or* solutions having reverse proportions. i.e.

Serial Nos.	'A' Parts	'B' Parts	Total
I	1	9	10
2	2	8	10
3	3	7	10
4	4	6	10

In many cases he would presumably make less than the suggested five trials. The basic group obtained by this method may consist of two, three, four or even five substances, although the fact should not be forgotten that an .excessive increase in the number of constituents of such a basic accord will involve the risk of 'extinguishing' or 'blanketing' a perfume, leading to the production of *grisaille* or a merely nondescript odour.

After preparing a mixture of odourants, add modifier or modifiers. The modifier is a substance of intermediate volatility and tenacity, chosen to enhance the character of the basic accord and to sweeten, subdue or round off any harshness exhibited by the latter. As Carles points out, most basic accords - and he instances one composed of 6 parts of oakmoss absolute and 4 parts of an ambergris/cistus compound - may have a rather unpleasant top note, which soon gives way to a pleasant, long-lasting note. The chosen modifier in this case, a rose compound - is added for the dual purpose indicated and then is itself surmounted, as it were by a top note that further develops the character of the blend. At each step the perfumer may proceed either by experience or by trial-and-error tests of the type used in his selection of the basic accord. The best example shows that an oakmoss absolute and a certain Ambergris 162 B form a more balanced accord in the ratio of 6:4 than in any other ratio. This simple blend is further improved by the addition of I part of musk ketone. The modifier, Rose d'Orient 2644, is shown to function best in the proportion of 3 parts, while the top note of this highly simplified Chypre perfume consists of 4 parts of sweet orange oil and 1 of bergamot. As a very general guide Carles suggests the following

Top notes (notes de tete)	20-25 per cent
Body notes (modifiers)	20-30 per cent
Base notes	40-55 per cent

These indications are not of course binding, but will be modified according to the character of the materials used and the type of perfume that it is intended to make. Musk ambrette, for example, is one of those basic constituents which also emerge as part of the top note. Nevertheless, as

Carles points out, a perfume containing 20 per cent of bases; 30 per cent of modifiers and 50 per cent of top notes would lack tenacity, since the percentage of bases would be relatively too low as compared with that of the more volatile modifiers and top notes. Therefore, the proportions are selected so as to obtain a balanced evolution during evaporation.

Merit of Carles' System

It enables a balanced nucleus to be formed in a simple, straightforward way, and for that nucleus to be modified or extended at will. Thus he starts by illustrating his theory with a Chypre theme based on a carefully adjusted accord of oakmoss absolute and an ambergris speciality. He subsequently suggests that this might be replaced by accords of oakmoss/patchouli/ vetiver, oakmoss/methyl ionone/vetiver, or oakmoss/ciste labdanum/musk ketone. Any of these basic accords might likewise be modified by the addition of products other than rose, e.g. orangeflower absolute, jasmine, lily-of-the valley or carnation. The top note will naturally be modified accordingly. He suggested modifications as below:

---

1. Chypre modification A

Sweet organge Bergamot Orange flowers 1103 or absolute, colourless Absolute oakmoss Ambergris 162 B Absolute jasmine Musk ketone

2. Modification B

Bergamot

Laurel nobilis

Angelica seeds

Juniper berries

Muguet 113

Absolute oakmoss

Vetiver

Patchouli

Ambergris 162 B

Aldehyde C 14

Absolute Jasmine

Musk ketone

3. Modification C

Contd.

Bergamot Lemon Linalyl acetate jasmine 1103
Geranium African
Orange flowers 1103
Aldehydes C_9, C_{10}, C_{11}
Absolute oakmoss
Gardenia Invar
Styrallyl acetate
Vetiver Ambergris 162 B
Musk ketone

The important feature of Carles' method is that certain odourants are regarded as 'accessories', which in general are products to be used in small quantities and to impart special effects. These products can not be used in large amounts in basic accords or as conventional modifiers. Addition of traces of these products in a formulation results in complete change in the character of the latter and imparts to it unique cachet. e.g., aldehyde C_{12} (MNAI and C_{14} styrallyl acetate, isobutyl quinoline, galbanum, cascarilla and the like. There are sometimes, of course, exceptions to this rule of moderation. We quote: 'Aldehyde C_{12} (MNA), for examples, proves to be an exception and it should be known that some products such as Geranium give most successful blends with as much as 50 per cent of it. The advantages which may be derived from the use of accessory products are therefore readily apparent...'

Carles advised his young pupils against a quest for maximum equilibrium. 'Dominantly effective notes in perfumes should be neither feared nor deliberately avoided. Such "faults" have quite often been responsible for tremendous success.' Sharp contrasts have their place in fine perfumes, as in the other arts. An excess of polish or rounding-off can, at worst, result in a subdued, characterless composition.

The point has been made that Carles' method may overstress the importance of the basic notes, but this need not be so if sufficient interest is taken in the top notes and the accessories.

Raymond Kling, perfumer had some interesting notions about aids to creativity. His ideas were coloured by his early training as an engineer and he never ceased seeking for a methodical mode of procedure. Like Carles he started with the notion of an accord of two, three or four odourants which should together provide a homogeneous base. This basic accord was obtained by creative artistic induction or by trial-and-error tests extended almost 'ad' infinitum with an extraordinary degree of patience.

Kling classified odourants into - top notes, basic notes, exalting or lifting agents and proposed new concept called as "place creators", which is defined as a substance which, in an already established composition, insinuates itself among the constituents and forms a place to enable odourant substances of a different nature from those existing in the composition as originally conceived; to "hang on to" this place creator like touches of bright paint against the grisaille of a background cloth. The substances of relatively mild or moderate odour and having great viscosity, with rather low volatility, such as hydroxycitronellaL nerolidoL benzyl benzoate etc., are included in the class of place creators.

Although our understanding of odours and odour phenomena remains limited, certain factors such as tone, volatility, intensity, volume and tenacity can to some extent be studied.

Tone

Tone is the general character of an odour. If the note is acidulated, acute or 'pointed' (e.g. lemon oil or octyl aldehyde) it is said to be sharp. If mild and even, like the odour of rhodinol or geranioL it is medium. If warm, a little muffled or heavy, like sandalwood oil or Peru balsam, it is described as low.

Volatility

Volatility means evaporation or the more or less rapid sublimation of an odouriferous substance. It is proportional to the vapour pressure of the substance, and inversely proportional to its molecular weight. This factor may be expressed by the formula

$$m = P\sqrt{\frac{M}{2\pi RT}}$$

where m is the rate of evaporation in $g/cm^2/sec.$, P the saturating vapour tension in atmospheres of the substance at T° absolute, M the molecular mass in grams, and R the constant of the law of perfect gases which, in the system of atmospheric units and cm^3 is equal to 82. The formula thus becomes

$$m = P\sqrt{\frac{M}{515\ T}}$$

It has been confirmed that the theoretical figures are matching with practical figures obtained by evaporation in air. It has been found that the classification of the products is the same in both cases. The result is that, to keep to simple practical data, it is sufficient to determine figures that ate proportional to the volatility of each substance and characterise each of them..

The coefficients of volatility is carried out in the following manner. Carles' method is different from this one. In this process evaporation is conducted in similar condition i.e., same room, place, time, day, temperature (about 18°C) and free from draughts. The capsule is weighed with a standard uniform weight for each of the substances whose volatility is to be measured. First of all we observe how evaporation takes place, eliminating for the purposes of measurement the terpene notes and the base or residual notes. Only the characteristic note of the product is taken for effecting the measurement.

Now take dry extract in a small flat bottomed capsule having dimensions about 5-6 cm diameter and 1-2 cm depth. Note the weight and entering time. As soon as no further characteristic odour is perceived, the capsule is re-weighed and the time noted.

With all these figures noted a calculation is made of the weight of the evaporated product and the time necessary for this evaporation. Taking the quotient obtained by dividing this time period by the evaporated weight, we have the 'coefficient of volatility', which must be differentiated from persistence or tenacity. In the composition, the substance of appropriate volatility can be selected as required.

The study of volatility makes it possible to specify and state the three fundamental properties, which are of great importance in perfumery are intensity, volume, and atmosphere.

Intensity

It is the unprovable psycho-physical proposition Weber-Fechner law states that the intensity of the sensation is proportional to the logarithm of the stimulus. It is unprovable precisely because the sensation is not at present capable of being measured. Billot and Appell have both produced variants on this law and thus helped to elucidate the rather complex matter of odour intensity. Appell, indeed, has set out to measure the 'absolute intensity' of odours and as a result has listed over 250 odourants, including natural and synthetic materials, in order of intensities rated from the minimum of 1 (rosacetol or 'rose crystals') to 10 (citronellyl oxyaldehyde, skatole and violet leaves absolute). 12 (2-hexenalj and the maximum 15 (crude nonadienal). We may note that all the aliphatic aldehydes from C_7 to C_{12} are shown in the Intensity 8 or 9 groups. Angelica, bay, cardamom, costus and camomile oils are all to be found under Intensity 9, together with methyl heptin carbonate, rose oxide and some of the paramethyl quinolines. Hydroxycitronellal and ionone are grouped under Intensity 4, in the company of lavender and lemon oils, bergamot. cyclamen aldehyde and musk ambrette. Ylang-ylang and orangeflower absolute come under Intensity 6, jasmine and rose absolutes and styrallyl acetate under Intensity 7; and benzyl acetate under Intensity 2-in the company of benzyl salicylate, guaiacwood acetate and phenylethyl alcohol. Guaiacwood oil is assigned the same intensity rating as lemon oil, and sandalwood oil the same as citral.

It is evident, as Appell states that a distinction must be made between what he terms the absolute intensity, i.e. 'the intensity factor of the substance itself', which' 'must be distinguished from the psychological response'. Elsewhere, in the same series of papers, he observes that 'we must make a distinction between apparent intensity, i.e. the psychological response to odour as perceived by the sense of smell and true or intrinsic intensity of the odourant. The first is the intensity of the sensation; the second is the intensity of the stimulus.' He adds that. whatever we measure or deduce, 'we do not of course know the nature of this (intensity) factor or stimulus' .

Referring to the Purkinje phenomenon, which in the study of colours relates to the great difficulty of comparing, for example, the intensities of red shades with those of blue shades, Billot emphasises the comparable difficulty of comparing equal or disparate intensities of two odours of completely different character.

At the present time the perfumer has no practical alternative, in the matter of judging or estimating comparative' intensities, to prolonged experience based partly on trial-and error. The theoretical approach to the subject is nevertheless well worth pursuing.

Volume

The concepts of 'volume', 'atmosphere' and even 'lift' or exaltation tend to merge into one another and are frequently confused. Volume refers in general to the fullness or amplitude of a perfume. It is analogous to the volume of sound that fills a room. It somewhat resembles the 'body' of a wine. A good perfume has volume; a poor one is tenu or 'thin'. Roudnitska says, volume in this sense is an aspect of form and is not to be confused with strength or effective range (portee). The concept of volume is more applicable to blended perfume compositions than to simple odourants as such, although some of the latter, as for example essential or flower oils, will have more volume than, say, a relatively 'flat' synthetic like linalyl acetate. Billot has suggested that evaporation curves of individual odourants should be plotted as a function of time. The angular coefficient of each curve will, in his view, represent the volume. He adds that the curves of a blended perfume can enable the perfumer to see at what moment its major characteristic portion evaporates, and thus to form a positive idea of the perfume's structure, with a view to making it more homogeneous by suitably filling in any gaps. This would merely serve as an aid to what a skilled perfumer would do almost automatically.

Atmosphere

The 'atmosphere' of a perfume has been described as its more or less pronounced faculty of dispersion. In practice it is the perfumed wake which a woman. using perfume leaves behind her. It is to some extent possible to measure its value comparatively as follows: We measure the rate of propagation of the molecules carrying the odour through a long tube of fairly thin diameter. These different times will provide coefficients proportional to the dispersion, thus characterising the atmosphere, the shortest time representing the greatest atmosphere.

Closely associated with the idea of atmosphere is that of effective range (portee); that of 'lift' or exaltation; and Francis Bacon's division of flowers and plants into those which 'do best perfume the air' and those whose scents are detectable only at close quarters. Bacon mentions the wide ranging fragrance of double violets, wallflower, clove pinks, lime blossom and honeysuckle. To this list E.S. Maurer has added hawthorn, lilac, heliotrope, evening primrose, mignonette and nicotiana. Maurer considers that the aerosol-like, zephyr effect of these natural perfumes must be due not only to the obvious and admittedly potent osmophores which they contain, but also to some kind of 'carrierwave' mechanism which operates simultaneously from the radiating flower centre and may involve the emission of odourous or inodourous volatile materials concurrently with the more potent and characteristic odourants. As carriers or boosters he tentatively suggests certain terpenes, formates, acetates, and simple aliphatic ketones, a preference being given to products of high mineral oil solubility. He adds that a perfumed spray made up on these lines operates best in an atmosphere of high humidity.

An Indian writer has similarly observed that a balanced blend of all the known constituents of a natural jasmine perfume would not in fact exhibit the airborne fragrance of growing jasmine flowers. He thinks that the flowers in the living plant 'generate ...some gaseous lifters or organic compounds of low boiling point and high vapour pressure, which blend with the odour of the flowers and carry it away to a distance'. His thoughts on artificial substitutes for these natural exaltants tend in the direction of ethyl alcohol methyl and ethyl formates, methyl acetate, etc. He also mentions the chloro-fluorinated propellants used in aerosol perfumes.

At the other end of the scale are the tenacious, long-lasting synthetic musks of the cyclopentadecanolide type. A Firmenich booklet. referring to the nomenclature of Exaltone and Exaltolide, states that 'this designation comes from the fact, which was immediately evident. that large-ringed ketones and lactones possess an exceptional power of exaltation on perfumes'.

To predict the 'lift' of a perfume by reference to its individual constituents is very difficult. One may consider, however, the exalting properties of such esters as isoamyl acetate, ethyl aceto-acetate, ethyl oenanthate and pelargonate (nonanoate) and p.tert. butyl cyclohexyl acetate; and such terpenes as myrcene, d-limonene and pure alphaphellandrene. One might note that methyl heptin carbonate, anisyl acetate, methyl nonyl acetaldehyde and other perfumery aldehydes, and of course the synthetic musks are odourants of lower volatility.

The elucidation of the problems involved in ensuring adequate lift or exaltation await further developments in olfactory research. Meanwhile the empiric approach must make what use it can of the simple test that we have described or smelling the sprayed perfume in a spacious smelling chamber, as suggested by Carles. (It must be remembered, however, that a perfume allowed to evaporate from a surface is in a different physical form from that which it assumes when sprayed into space and that different odour effects can be expected from space spraying).

Tenacity

Tenacity, is the ability of a perfume to last a longer or a shorter time on its support. is somewhat complex. The nature of the support plays a significant part. Thus a fur retains perfume well, whereas a silken fabric does not. Wells has investigated the tenacity of perfumes on the human skin. Two aspects of tenacity or persistence have to be considered

(1) Strength of persistence, which is the relative force of a perfume after a limited period of evaporation (2 hours, for example) expressed as a percentage of its original odour; and

(2) The duration of persistence, which is expressed by the number of hours or days which elapse until no further odom is perceived.

In the first case the note remains in general unchanged over the period, whereas in the second case it may have become completely different.

All determinations of this kind should be performed under identical conditions (time, temperature, same paper, same quantity of perfume etc.). A disc of filter paper is taken. On each disc is placed the same standard quantity of perfume. It is allowed to evaporate until nothing more is smelled, and the time taken is noted. This time represents for each substance the total tenacity. It might be possible to note the specific tenacity, which would be the time of evaporation from the start and throughout the time of evaporation, while the characteristic note remains, until it stops and changes to another note.

Fixation

'A fixative is simply a substance whose odour lasts a sufficient length of time. The idea of fixing a perfume in order to retard or prevent the evaporation of its volatile constituents is chimerical. There are no means of fixing the odour of top notes, of linalool for example, whatever the nature of the fixative or mixture of fixatives.' Further it was observed: 'If the evaporation of these volatile bodies Isuch as amyl and propyl acetates) is slowed down a little by tricks of blending, the fact is certain that this slowing down will be of short duration and will not respond to the perfumer's idea of fixation.

The odd fact is that Bassiri outlines some simple experiments with ethyl alcohol, diethyl phthalate and benzyl benzoate, very similar to those with which Picklhall appeared to arrive at opposing conclusions. Poucher had almost simultaneously carried out yet a third series of tests of this kind.

While the traditional high boiling, low vapour pressure 'fixatives' with little or no intrinsic adom (e,g. diethyl phthalate, benzyl benzoate) are undoubtedly useful materials their utility, is strictly limited. Although they exert a retarding action on the evaporation of the more volatile constituents af a perfume, their mere addition to a blend will not necessarily make the desired odour more lasting. Such an addition may in fact unbalance or exert a deadening effect on the entire complex. There is a place for these fixatives in the formulation of perfumes, and especially of those of a volatile, evanescent character, but for a properly constructed formula the perfumer must pay maximum attention to basic accords and graduated persistence. 'If he is a master of his craft: writes Poucher, 'he will .., select his aromatics in accordance with their lasting properties, rather than rely upon dubious additions which might. in effect, impair his work of art.'

Billot's conducted study on the Problem of Fixation which should be noted, and a comparison made of the various fixatives listed by Bassiri. Maurer and Cerbelaud; The last-named divides fixatives into eight separate classes, and these are still worth studying even if the theory uniting them has become rather out of date.

Systematic Recording of Data

The first draft or sketch of a perfume, no matter whence or how the inspiration or creative impulse comes, must subsequently be reinforced by patient and often painstaking technique. It is here that properly recorded information can facilitate the flow of ideas and save both time and effort. Billot's method of card-indexing essential information has been expounded at some length. In summary, each odourant used by the perfumer has a large card allocated to it. The name of the product provides the heading. Then are recorded, in order: its note and the series to which it belongs, its nature (Le. essential oil. absolute, resinoid, synthetic, composite base, etc.); its concentration, tone, volatility, tenacity, colour and dermatological behaviour, etc. The card has also space for 'uses' to be entered and solubilities, as well as 'analogies'.

All these cards are filed in a card index in alphabetical order, separating the natural from the synthetic products by making two different card indexes. A third index could be made with the bases and specialities. To complete this information, however, there are registers which gather together for each fundamental property, as enumerated above, the list of products classified according to their places in these properties. There are five of these registers

(1) Register of the tone of the note - three classes: sharp - medium - basic, and in each of these classes the list of products connected therewith.

(2) Register of volatilities - from -1 to 100, 100 being the figure for the least volatile product. Against each number is inscribed the list of substances having such volatility.

(3) Register of Intensities - in sections from 30 to 120, the greatest intensity being represented by 120

30 - 60 - 90 - 120

in each of the sections a list of substances with intensity corresponding to that section:

(4) Register of volumes - in sections of 15 of the angular coefficients of the evaporation curves up to 90

15 - 30 - 45 - 60 - 75 - 90

In each section a list of substances having a volume within that section.'

(5) Register of Atmospheric Diffusive Values, in sections of proportional coefficients from 10 - 30 - 50 - 70 etc., the lowest figure representing the largest 'atmosphere' or the most marked d,iffusive properties. In each of the sections, a list of substances belonging to that section.

Finally, for tenacity (persistence), the coefficient is indicated on the, card. For this property, it is not deemed necessary to have a register.

By way of illustration the original paper shows models of the index cards, although each firm or individual can easily modify them according to his own ideas. Admittedly the compilation of such indexes and registers involves a good deal of time and effort, but it systematises masses of what would otherwise be heterogeneous and perhaps inaccessible information and, in the long run, can be both helpful and time-saving. It is a task, moreover, that may well be entrusted to an assistant or apprentice, provided that the work is conscientiously carried out and well controlled.

2

Flower Perfumes and Their Formulations

Introduction

For the perfumer flowers and perfume has immence importance. There are three different reasons cited: (i) They are stimulus, a point of reference, pleasure source and provides immense information; (ii) They are irreplaceable even with drawback and higher cost; and (iii) Many flower notes or floral accords have become essential structure. Flowers and their perfumes are still of very considerable and even basic importance to the perfumer. In the first place they are a stimulus, a point of reference, and a source of pleasure and invaluable information. In the second, some of them are still irreplaceable raw materials, despite any disadvantage that may attach to them in respect of scarcity or cost. And, in the third place, many flowers notes or floral accords form part of the essential structure of even the most advanced, and up-to-date fantasy perfumes.

The prime object of this chapter is to obtain the true note of each flower using the various constituents for each flower and provide illustrations of complete formulae. Here it is necessary to point out that such formulae can only be considered as the sum of the actual materials used in preparing them in the first place; and that subsequent reproduction must involve olfactory adjustments in order to give the desired result. Let us begin with the more familiar perfumes based on flower notes.

ROSE

Rose notes differ considerably one from another. Besides the basic constituents for red rose, rose damascena, and rose centrifolia naturally occurring esters, few aldehydes and acetals are required as auxillary notes.

The traces of many other odourants creates significant effect (Table 2.1). Into the composition of specialised rose notes, e.g., those of the tea rose, Banksiana, Zephyrine Drouhin and Marechal Niel types.

Bulgarian rose has played very creative role in almost all rose perfumes. It is often required but due to higher cost pure Bulgarian rose oil's use is restricted. This necessitates research into compositions 'de coupage', i.e. diluents or extenders, .and these must be the best possible for the purpose. By using certain raw materials judiciously one can in fact arrive at some very interesting extenders which will blend well with the natural oil. giving an excellent quality of end product at a reasonable price. The raw materials in question are relatively few in number. -One thinks of phenylethyl alcohol. oil of geranium - such as the Geranium incalore de Grasse, geraniol, rhodinol. 1 citronellol; and very small quantities of nerol and farnesol.

An example is given below in formula 1. This is a convenient point to emphasise that no formula can be better than the type and quality of its individual constituents. It is therefore essential for perfumers to make their

Table 2.1. Effects of some odourants.

S.Nso.	*Type* of *Rose Notes*	*Main Constituents*	*Special effects*
1.	Red rose	RhodinoL phenylethyl alcohol. a-ionone, nerol	Rose absolute, Bulgarian otto Bulgarian geranium oil
2.	Rose damascena	RhodinoL geraniol. ex palmarosa oiL phenylethyl alcohol cinnamic alcohol	Natural oils and esters
3.	Rose centifolia	CitronelloL geraniol. phenylethyl alcohol. rhodinol	Ca aldehyde citral
4.	Tea rose	CitronelloL phenylethyl alcohol. geraniol	guaiyil acetate menthone, tuberose absolute
5.	Rose Marechal Niel	Geraniol ex palmarosa oiL citronellol	isoeugenoL benzoin, sandalwood oil
6.	V/hite rose	RhodinoL phenylethyl alcohol, benzyl alcohol. linalool.	bergamot, phenylethyl acetate

own trials and adjust their final formulae accordingly.

Formula 1

Rose Extender 1	*Parts* by *weight*
Geraniol ex palmarose, 1st quality	1. 50
Oil of Grasse Geranium, incolore	0.50
Phenylethyl alcohol	2.50
Linalool ex bois de rose, 1st quality Brazilian	1.20
Rhodinol ex African geranium oil	1.20
l-Citronellol	3.00
Nerol, pure	0.07
Farnesol. pure	0.03
Total	10.00

With the aid of this 'extender', following blends can be produced.

Formula 2

Odourants

		Rose Blend	
	No.1%	No.2%	No. 3%
Rose Bulgarian	75	50	25
Bulgarian absolute oil of rose	-	4	3
Rose extender 1	25	46	72
Total	100	100	100

The above table shows that three different rose formulae having Bulgarian rose tonality .and different prices can be easily produced. Formulation over a reasonably wide price range is thus facilitated. Some formulae of actual rose perfumes are given in Formulae 3-6.

Formula 3 *(Rose F)*

Constituents	*Parts*
Rhodinol, 1st quality	40.0
lonone alpha	23.0
Rose-2	6.0

Phenylethyl alcohol	12.0
Bois de rose Brazil	12.0
Rose de Grasse absolute	6.5
Jasmine absolute	0.5
Menthone	trace
Total	circa 100

Formula 4 *(Rose H)*

Constituents	*Parts*
Rhodinol, 1st quality	10.0
Phenylethyl alcohol	20.0
Cinnamic alcohol	6.0
Geraniol	20.0
Citronellol	10.0
Linalool	6.0
Hydroxycitronellal	5.0
Linalyl acetate	4.0
Eugenol	4.0
Rose de Grasse absolute	4.0
Geranium (African) oil	10.0
Phenylethyl acetate	1.0
Total	100.0

Formula 5 *(Rose rouge)*

Constituents	*Parts*
Violettone A (Firmenich)	18.0
Rose-I	4.5
Rose de Grasse absolute	13.0
Phenylacetic acid	0.4
Lorena (Firmenich)	4.5
Phenylethyl alcohol	9.6
Rhodinol	50.0
Total	100.0

Formula 6 (Rose blanche)

Constituents	*Parts*
Rose- 1	13.50
Sandalwood oil	6.30
Patchouli oil	6.30
Tuberose	5.50
Tubereuse (Synarome)	5.00
Orris resinoid	5.00
Jasmonis (Givaudan)	3.50
Benzyl acetate	2.00
Geraniol synth, pure	12.00
Lorena (Firmenich)	9.00
Phenylethyl alcohol	11.00
Iraldeine 100% (de Laire)	9.00
Rhodinol P (Rhone-Poulenc)	11.50
Aldehyde C_9	0.10
Aldehyde C_{10}	0.15
Aldehyde C_{12} (lauric)	0.15
Total	100.00

Where specialities are cited under the names of specific firms, this simply means that no firm makes and offers exactly the same end product as the others. In each case one must take into account the fact that chemicals included in a process as trace impurities are not likely to be present in exactly the same pattern or proportions in a competitive product.

JASMINE

Rose and jasmine are the most important flower notes used in perfumery. Singly or together, they provide a conventional floral background for a great diversity of perfumes. A wide range of formulae for 'jasmine artificial' have been resulted after conducting many experiments based on analytical research of jasmine oil. The basic constituents of these formulae include, benzyl acetate, amyl and hexyl cinnamic aldehydes; benzyl alcohol, formate, salicylate. and other esters; indole and derivatives; phenylethyl alcohol. dimethyl benzyl carbinyl acetate, hydroxycitronellal. linalooL linalyl acetate; esters of propionic and butyric acids; Peru balsam etc. The use of jasmine absolute *chassis* may be made to sweeten formulae for artificial jasmines which may be crude and synthetic. Jasmine absolute chassis is the absolute obtained by petroleum ether or benzene extraction from jasmine flowers that have previously been treated by the enfleurage process but which have nevertheless retained some of their perfume. This must not be confused with the actual absolute of jasmine d'enfleurage.

It is a principle in fine perfumery that natural materials should be used to sweeten and soften the odours of synthetic blends. When costing considerations prevent the more liberal use of 'naturals', the result of judiciously incorporating even small quantities will usually prove conclusive.

(Formulae 7-10).

Formula 7 *(Jasmine* 1)

Constituents	*Parts*
Benzyl acetate, pure	28.0
a-Amyl cinnamic aidehyde prima (Descollonges)	20.0
Jasmine chassis absolute ex benzene Schmoller & Bompard), 10% in benzyl benzoate	110.00
Benzyl propionate	4.00
Paracresyl isobutyrate	3.02
Dimethyl benzyl carbinyl acetate	1.06
Benzyl alcohol	9.02
Linalyl acetate	2.00
Methyl anthranilate	0.04
Isojasmone (Descollonges)	0.05
Bois de rose oiL Brazil	6.00
Geraniol Isynth., chern. pure, Firmenich)	1.06
Iraldeine 100% (de Laire)	2.00
Allofloral (Allondon-Firmenich)	6.75
Ylang-ylang oil	2.04
Indole, 10%	2.08
Total	100.00

Formula 8 (*Jasmine* 2)

Constituents	*Parts*
Benzyl alcohol	11
Linalyl acetate ex bois de rose	11
Benzyl acetate	19
Benzyl benzoate	6
Ethyl phthalate	3
Jasmine chassis absolute, ex benzene (Schmoller & Bompard)	6
Laurine (Givaudan)	10
'Phenylethyl alcohol	8
Linalool	9
Bergamot oil, sesquiterpeneless	4
Peru balsam	5
Ylang-ylang oil	3
Benzyl salicylate	5
Total	100

Formula 9 (*Jasmine 22.0,* Fantasy 3)

Constituents	*Parts*
Phenylethyl alcohol	22.0
Benzyl acetate	45.5
Cinnamic alcohol	3.5
Methyl anthranilate	2.0
Diethyl phthalate	5.5
Citronellol	3.5
Geraniol (synth, chem. pure, firmenich)	5.8
Ylang-ylang oil	2.0
Cananga oil	1.0
Isoeugenol	0.5
Benzyl salicylate	2.5
Ethyl salicylate	0.2
Cedrenol (ex cedarwood oil)	3.0
Virginia cedarwood oil	3.0
Total	100.0

Formula 10 -(Jasmine Base 5)

Constituents	*Parts*
Cinnamyl acetate	0.8
p-cresyl isobutyrate	1.1
Methyl anthranilate	0.3
Benzyl alcohol	18.0
Benzyl acetate	18.0
Linalool	4.6
Benzyl propionate	3.1
Terpineol pure (BBA)	3.1
Amyl cinnamic aldehyde	15.3
Methyl eugenol	1.5
Linalyl acetate	7.5
Raldeine D(Givaudan)	3.8
Hydroxycitronellal	3.1
p-Methyl methylsalicylate	1.5
p-Cresyl phenylacetate	0.7
Phenylpropyl aldehyde	2.0
Aldehyde C_{10}	0.15
Indole	0.45
Tolu tincture	15.0
Total	100.40

Formula 11 *(Jasmine base 5a)*

Constituents	*Parts*
Jasmine Base No.5	70.0
Jasmine d'Espagne (Givaudan)	13.0
Jasmine Frutal Wolak's Frutal works)	13.0
Jasmine chassis absolute ex benzene (Schmoller & Bompardl	4.0
Total	100

ORANGEFLOWER AND NEROLI

The difference between Orange flower and Neroli are well known to the perfumers. Both are frequently used, and it could even be said that there are relatively few compositions into which the orangeflower note does not enter. Neroli is particularly valuable in eau de Cologne and related notes. Here are some (Formulae 12-13)

Formula 12 *(Orange flower A)*

Constituents	*Parts*
Linalyl acetate	7.1
Petitgrain oil, terpeneless	33.4
Flonol 160 (de Laire)	14.3
Indole 10%	4.7
Eugenol	2.2
Geraniol synthetic	5.6
Geranyl acetate	3.7
Brouts absolute (Robertet)	19.0
Ylang-ylang oil	1.2
Phenyl ethyl alcohol	4.7
Lentisque (Mastic) oil	0.8
Methyl anthranilate	2.4
Citral	0.9
Total	100.00

From the above example Brouts Absolute is extracted from petitgrain bigarade water or a mixture of this with orange flower water.

Formula 13 *(Neroli A)*

Constituents	*Parts*
Petitgrain oil pays (Grasse)	31.5
Methyl anthranilate	25.0
Eugenol	18.5
Geraniol	6.0
Phenylethyl alcohol	4.25
Linalyl acetate	7.3
Indole 10%	4.7
Aldehyde C_8 10%	2.75
Total	100.00

This formulation is useful for blending with natural neroli, in certain applications, as a diluent. A suggested proportion is 1 part of natural neroli oil to 2 parts of Neroli A.

Flower perfumes such as honeysuckle, syringa, gardenia, and narcissus not only has orange blossom note but also has fruity note of apricot.

VIOLET

The classic note of violet is favourite of ladies. There are two examples of violet perfume. The simple violet (Nice or Toulouse) may be based on a blend of methyl ionone, alpha ionone, orris absolute or resinoid, violet leaf absolute and phenylethyl alcohol. A floral note, projected as it is by a trace of MNA aldehyde, is imparted by jasmine or cassie. The double or Parma, violet is based on varying proportions of beta ionone, alpha ion one and methyl ionone, together with orris resinoid or concrete, a little phenylethyl alcohol, methyl octin carbonate, a trace of vetiver, and a small quantity of hydroxycitronellal and even, sometimes, bergamot. Very small amounts of violet leaf absolute may be included, but the green leafy note of Parma violets is much less accentuated. For imparting the necessary sweetness to the base of Parma violet,. use may be made of a plum or mirabelle note.

Wood violets, with their rather earthy background, may be simulated by the inclusion of very small quantities of a pure grade of amyl acetate, which helps to provide the odour of damp earth and humus. Other humus notes may be similarly employed. (Formulae 14-15).

Formula 14 *(Violet* 1)

Constituents	*Parts*
Ionone alpha	10
Iralia (Firmenich)	10
Irisone extra (Givaudan)	10
Jasmine No.2	20
Ysminia (Firmenich)	5.0
Jasmonis (Givaudan)	2.0
Violet leaf absolute	2.0
Orris absolute or Irophore(Firmenich)	1.1
Ylang ylang oil	1.0
Ylang ylang absolute	0.6
Cassie absolute	0.55

Rose No.1	0.1
Neroli oil	0.06
Phenylethyl alcohol	1.0
Bitter orange oil	0.6
Oakmoss absolute (Robertet)	0.16
Folione (Givaudan)	0.03
Linalool	0.5
Bois de rose Brazil	3.0
Cinnamylal (Givaudan)	4.5
Heliotropin	2.0
Musk ambrette	0.1
Musk ketone	0.5
Vanillin	0.2
Civet tincture	16.5
Peru balsam tincture	8.5
Total	100.00

Formula 15 *(Violet* 2)

Constituents	*Parts*
Violet No.1	60.0
Irisone Beta (Givaudan)	6.0
Iralia (Firmenich)	10.0
Cetone V (allyl ionone, Givaudan)	9.0
Ylang ylang absolute	4.0
Irophore (Firmenich)	1.0
Violet leaf absolute	2.6
Cassie absolute	0.8
Mimosa absolute	1.3
Jasmine absolute	1.2
Mirabelle (Firmenich) 1 %	3.5
Total	100.00

The absolute oil of Parma violets, which had a delightful odour, is no longer commercial. The following formula given in formula 16 yields a product of fine odour which may be utilised as a reconstituted' absolute oil of Parma violets.

Formula 16 *(Parma Violets Absolute Art)*

Constituents	*Parts*
Violet leaf absolute (Schmoller & Bompard)	1.8
Irophore (Firmenich)	4.0
Violettone B extra fine 100°/u (Firmenich)	4.0
Parmanthene (Firmenich)	0.2
Benzyl benzoate	90.0
Total	100.0

The basic formula that follows gives a product of fine quality, which can be used in a multitude of different combinations in order to give effects approaching those of a little violet bouquet. The delicate odour of earth and humus that is so often found in a bunch of violets is mixture of amyl salicylate and pure amyl acetate, etc. (Formula 17).

Formula 17 *(Violet base)*

Constituents	*Parts*
Paracetone (Givaudan)	24
Beta-iso methyl ionone	32
Irisone extra incolore (Givaudan)	24
Beta methyl ionone	3
Boronia absolute	1
Ionone alpha	16
Violet leaf absolute	10
Orris absolute (Robertet)	10
Total	120

The concrete and absolute oils of Boronia, which contain ionone beta in its natural state, are much sought after in violet compositions, where they soften any harshness and add a tendency towards the Parma violet note.

ACACIA

This is not in fact a true acacia. The cassie is true species represented in perfumery. This perfume is widely accepted in warmer climates. It has fragrant and orangeflower like odour of the tree Robinia pseudoacacia. The composition of acacia has basic odourants such as, phenylethyl alcohol. cinnamic alcohol, benzyl acetate, hydroxycitronellal, methyl naphthyl ketone, methyl anthranilate, linalool. terpineol. anisic aldehyde ex anethole, and just a touch of apricot.

BROOM

Broom, genista or genet is a shrub very popular in the south of France and in Spain; particularly in Catalonia, where the hills of Barcelona and the Tibidabo are covered with retama (the Catalan name for broom) at the approach of summer. From the perfumery point of view, the base is one of orange blossom: methyl anthrapilate, fleur d'oranger, etc., associated with methyl paracresol. methyl acetophenone, anisaldehyde and Grasse absolute of genet. Other constituents include alpha ionone, terpineol. linalool. phenylethyl alcohol, heliotropin. synthetic musk and olibanum.

CARNATION

There are three main types of carnation: (i) The carnation of Nice has a rather rosy, honeyed odour; (ii) The garden pink has a spicy odour recalling cloves and pepper; and (iii) The so-called sea pink (not to be confused with Armoria maritima) has the basic odour of carnation plus a note of phenylacetic aldehyde. In all carnations oleo resins are used as fixatives therefore they have slight resinous note.

Types of Carnation

Oeillet de nice

Here the basis is a blend of eugenol, isoeugenol and methyl eugenol, in varying proportions, accompanied by phenylethyl alcohol. benzyl salicylate, and sometimes amyl salicylate, vanilla, vanillin or ethyl vanillin. This base is sweetened with rose notes from rhodinol or rose de Mai absolute, carnation absolute or concrete and, above all, tuberose absolute. Unfortunately, as the latter has become very expensive, it must usually be replaced-as by a blend of synthetic tuberose with the natural material, or by a good ylangylang oil or ylang-ylang absolute. As aids to fixation there are benzyl isoeugenoL heliotropin and so-called heliotropin amorphous (a mixture of heliotropin, vanillin, anisic and benzoic acids).

Garden pink

Garden pink, known as Oeillet mignardise, has a slightly more clove-like odour. This indicate that the. use of more eugenol and less isoeugenol in the base, together with a trace of clove oil. The vanilla base will preferably contain methyl vanillin (veratraldehyde). Oils of pimento, bay or black pepper will add characteristic note.

Sea pink

This small pink, which has a simple flower whose colour is actually mauve, is found growing wild on dunes by the sea. Its strong odour may be imitated by adding to a garden pink formula amyl salicylate, phenylacetic aldehyde and, if desired, a trace of hyacinth absolute.

Carnation notes have a vital role in all kinds of perfumery. Even they can be fully exploited in the area of masculine perfumes. It is not necessary to go for too familiar spiced-cologne complexes. A straightforward carnation note is much better for use. Some such formulae are shown in formulae 18-19.

Formula 18 *(Base Claveline* 1)

Constituents	*Parts*
Eugeno	51.35
Cananga oil	26.7
Ylang-ylang oil	2.55
Rose	5.6
Benzyl acetate	2.55
Orris absolute	4.25
Ceylon cinnamon oil	0.5
Nutmeg concrete	1.5
Nutmeg oil	1.0
Benzyl benzoate	3.45
Heliotropin	1.55
Total	100.00

Formula 19 *(Base Claveline* 2)

Constituents	*Parts*
Eugenol	61.5
Ylang-ylang oil	4.6
Cananga oil	4.0
Rose	4.6
Cinnamic alcohol	16.7
Benzyl acetate,	2.5

Vetiver oil Java type	1.25
Nutmeg oil	0.65
Labdanum absolute (Lautier)	0.20
Heliotropin	4.0
Total	100.00

CYCLAMEN

C persicum and C. europaeum important species of cyclamen are scented. The basic elements responsible for scents are hydroxycitronellaL linalooL phenylethyl alcohoL terpineol. cinnamic alcohol, amyl cinnamic aldehyde, styrallyl acetate, rhodinoL phenylacetic aldehyde, ionone, LiliaL Lyral and, finally. the essential cyclamen aldehyde and some of the classic 'freshness' components.

The interesting variations of the composition of this perfume could result into novel and appreciating formulae. Think. for example. of its association with a group containing cyclopentadecanolide. aldehyde MNA. incense and vanilla. This type of association might well provide a very attractive ensemble. The cyclamen odour and its possible derivatives have not yet. in our view. been fully exploited - especially if the cumin note is one of the elements used in its formation.

FOUGERE (FERN)

The fern or fougere may be one of several thousand species. but in any case it will rarely have an odour other than a mild and vague effluvium of humus. greenery and earth. This perfume has been. created by imaginative perfumers. Most of them have a more or less pronounced note of verdure and moss. Fern perfumes are divisible into two main groups: (i) based on the triad bergamot. Tonka bean tincture or coumarin. and a product of musky odour; and (ii) in which linalyl. terpinyl. geranyl and above all bornyl and isobornyl acetates. give a compound of more or less rustic or woodland character.

Example 20 *(Fougere I)*

Constituents	*Parts*
Tree moss absolute	2.0
Bergamot oil	10.1
Lavender oil	10.1
Rhodinol	10.1
Rose M.S.	6.1

Patchouli oil	3.1
Geranium absolute incolore (Grasse)	4.1
Methyl ionone	12.15
Cyclopentadecanolide	1.0
Petit grain oil, Paraguay	2.0
Coumarin	14.3
Musk ketone	6.1
Heliotropin	6.1
Phenylethyl salicylate	3.1
Methyl salicylate	1.0
Eugenol	1.0
Jasmine No. 1	3.1
Clary sage oil	1.35
Amyl salicylate	2.0
Musk tincture	1.0
Tobacco (I.F.F.)	0.2
Total	100.00

Formula 21 *(Fougere* 2)

Constituents	*Parts*
Musk ketone	0.4
Patchouli oil	1.0
Vetiver oil, Java	1.0
Lavender oil Mitcham type	6.5
Lavender absolute	1.6
Bergamot oil	35.0
Linalyl acetate	2.2
Terpinyl acetate	2.0
Coumarin	31.4
Cyclopentadecanolide	0.2
Tobacco (I.F.F.)	0.2
Oakmoss absolute, Yugoslav	0.8
Mousse de Chene 1026 (Roure-Dupont)	0.2
Alliantone (Givaudan)	1.3
Allofloral (Firmenich) 10%	0.2

Rose No.3	4.3
Palmarose oil Geranium oil	1.1
Neroli A	4.7
Myrtle oil	0.2
Cuir 1073 (Firmenich)	0.8
Bornyl acetate	0.2
Total	100.00

When it is desired to impart a fruity note other than the classic peach, apricot, prune or mirabelle, one such note that can be extremely successful is strawberry, and this has in fact been incorporated in the above formula.

GARDENIA

The gardenia odour is reproduced using several components of tuberose. However, emphasis is given to the rose like tonalities. Thus in the first place consideration is given to ylang, jasmine, benzyl salicylate, phenylethyl alcohol, an orange blossom note, etc. Secondly, one turns to dimethyl benzyl carbinol, acetyl isoeugenol, hydroxycitronellal, rose de Mai absolute, benzyl acetate, terpineol, etc. And, above all, there is styrallyl acetate, which provides the peculiarly green and fruity note of gardenia, and gamma nonyl lactone.

No doubt that gardenia has been considered as a flower but it has prominent role in perfumery. It contributes fragrance to such perfumes as Miliot's Crepe de Chine. Absolute oil of gardenia has been produced and is, when available, a remarkable and attractive product.

Formula 22 (*Gardenia* 1)

Constituents	*Parts*
Dimethyl benzyl carbinol	4.0
Styrallyl (methyl phenyl carbinyl) acetate	9.5
Neroli	2.5
Isoeugenol	4.0
Rose de Mai absolute	1.0
Ylang-ylang oil	7.0
Benzyl acetate	4.0
Jasmine absolute	1.0
Lilol (Givaudan)	6.0
Ionone alpha	10.0
Hydroxycitronellal	20.0

Phenylethyl alcohol	8.0
Phenylacetic aldehyde 50%	1.5
Citronellol	4.5
Cinnamic alcohol ex styrax	7.0
Coumarin	2.5
Heliotropin	7.5
Total	100.00

Formula 23 (Gardenia 2)

Constituents	*Parts*
Musk ketone	2.5
Musk ambrette	1.0
Jasmine de Provence (Descollonges)	1.0
Jasmine absolute	1.0
Rose de Mai absolute	3.5
Jonquil absolute	1.0
Tuberose absolute	3.0
Opopanax L.G. (Givaudan)	16.9
Muguet	10.2
Styrallyl acetate	12.0
Hydroxycitronellal	15.0
Ylang-ylang oil	5.0
Cinnamic alcohol ex styrax	2.0
Phenylethyl alcohol	2.0
Gardenia (Givaudan)	23.9
Total	100.00

At current raw material prices it would obviously be essential to replace most of the natural absolutes with the best 'artificials' available within costing limits.

HAWTHORN

The hawthorn perfume has a base of anisic aldehyde along with anisic alcohol and methyl acetophenone. One can use hydroxycitronellal, cinnamic alcohol, citronellol, linalool, terpineol for middle note and heliotropin and coumarin for lower note.

The noted English horticulturist, Graham Thomas, listed 'Crataegus, all species' (including of course the common mayor hawthorn, G. oxyacantha) among thirty or so flower scents that he considered 'unsuitable for sensitive noses'. The perfumer may here and in similar cases improve on nature by ignoring the methylamine or other off-notes present in the actual flowers and create, as it were, an idealised version of the natural floral odour.·

HELIOTROPE

The heady, delightful and characteristic perfume of the heliotrope (Heliotropium peruvianum and other spp.) is duplicated chiefly with heliotropin and heliotropin amorphous; the latter being a mixture of heliotropin with vanillin etc. With these are associated benzoic and anisic acids, phenylethyl alcoholL ylang-ylang oiL rhodinoL cinnamic alcohol, anisic aldehyde, benzaldehyde (traces) and benzoin resinoid. A synthetic of hazel nut odour, used discreetly, will help to give an impression of the real flower. The slight note of greenery is obtainable with an oakmoss or, better still, a mignonette absolute or base. Another useful constituent is paramethyl hydrocinnamic aldehyde.

HONEYSUCKLE

The delightful fragrant of flowers are honeysuckles, Loincera *fragrantissima,* L. *brachypoda,* L. caprifolium and chevrefeuille species. Their general odour, sweet and diffusive but only slightly honeyed, can be simulated with basic constituents such as: muguet, orange blossom, rose and jasmine odourants; cinnamic alcoholL phenylethyl alcohol, terpineoL citronellol, linalool, hydroxycitronellaL paracresyl phenylacetate and anisic aldehyde. Small quantities of methyl cinnamate, methyl naphthyl ketone, phenylethyl acetate, iseugenol, and ylang-ylang, enter into consideration. To ensure the correct emphasis on the fruitiness of the natural flower odour, use may be made of an apricot note.

Formula 24 *(Chevrefeveuille 1)*

Constituents	*Parts*
Peti tgrain oil Paraguay	5.0
Neroli	6.55
Brouts absolute (Robertet)	1.0
lonone alpha	4.85
Anisic aldehyde	2.5
Linalool	3.0
Terpineol	10.0

Geraniol	5.1
Hydroxycitronellal	3.8
Lilac	5_1
Phenylacetic acid	1.0
Bergamot oil	5_0
Benzyl acetate	5.1
Jasmonone	5.0
Chevrefeuille	35.0
Musk ketone	1.25
Musk ambrette	0.75
Total	100.00

HYACINTH

The odour of the hyacinth flower is often harsh and strident. Variants biased towards the rose or orange blossom are more acceptable. The basic odourants are phenylacetic aldehyde, hydroxycitronellaL cinnamic and phenylethyl alcohols, terpineol and phenylethyl acetate. The piquant note of hyacinth is due to dimethyl benzyl carbinol and its acetate, bromstyrole ltraces), methyl octin carbonate, cinnamyl acetate; and, for rounding off the composition, when costing limits permit, hyacinth absolute. There was at one time, incidentally, an absolute of wild hyacinths lbluebells) available, but despite its remarkabe odour properties it proved too expensive, owing to the high cost of gathering the flowers even before they were treated.

Hyacinth bases have found quite a number of applications in currently popular perfumes.

Formula 25 *(Hyacinth 1)*

Constituents	*Parts*
Lilac	10.0
Jacmthone (Givaudan)	20.0
Cinnamic alcohol	20.0
Neroli	5.0
Jasmonone	10.0
Jasmine chassis ex benzene	4.0
Hyacinth absolute	5.0
Phenylacetic aldehyde 50%	6.0
Hydratropic aldehyde	3.0

Dimethyl benzyl carbinol	2.0
Hydroxycitronellal	10.0
Rose de Mai absolute	5.0
Total	100

If it is found that the peculiarly piquant note of the natural flower. compared with the odour of horseradish, is not sufficiently emphasised, an added trace of bromstyrole will impart the desired effect.

IRIS

The scent of the iris flower is quite different from that of the dried iris (orris) root. and it varies according to species. Sometimes one observes a note of orange blossom, associated with the odour of orris root; sometimes almost the odour of hyacinth. The bases that are usually employed to duplicate this elusive floral scent are the various ionones and methyl ionones, terpineol, orris absolute and resinoid, anisic aldehyde, myristic acid, etc.

Now-a-days iris flower bases are rarely used. However, it is worth to use for producing such compositions that would no longer resemble iris, instead add to the number and novelty of the solid blending notes available.

LILAC

There is a good deal of variation in odour among the different species and forms of lilac. Persian lilac, for example (Syringa persical, resembles hyacinth, while purple lilac comes closer to heliotrope and vanilla; while yet another species recalls hawthorn. The basic components of a lilac perfume are heliotropin, cinnamic alcohol, terpineol, phenylethyl alcohol and hydroxycitronellal. Special notes are given by paracresyl acetate, phenylacetic aldehyde, anisic aldehyde and cinnamyl acetate. To emphasise the floral quality use is made of rose absolute, rhodinol, jasmine, etc. And, to impart 'thrust', benzyl acetate. The green stalk note is always to be observed in a spray of freshly cut lilac; and this may be contributed to the composition by Vert de Lilas notes: phenylacetic aldehyde dimethyl acetal, etc. The special note of Persian lilac is conveyed by means of a natural or synthetic hyacinth.

Since many years Lilac has become an essential element in some of the classic semi-floral, floral bouquet and sophisticated perfumes. Lilac really came into its own after. discovery of hydroxyciaonellal.

Formula 26 *(Lilac base 1)*

Constituents	Parts
Hydroxycitronellai	18.0
Cinnamic alcohol	1.7
Terpineol	7.4
Benzyl alcohol	17.0
Linalool	1.0
Phenylethyl alcohol	18.0
Styrax resinoid	2.55
Jasmine	9.1
Phenylacetaldehyde	0.5
Anisic aldehyde	7.0
Indole 10%	2.55
Heliotropin	15.2
Total	100.00

Formula 27 *(Lilac 2)*

Constituents	*Parts*
Lilol (Givaudan terpineol)	10.0
Phenylethyl alcohol	18.0
Hydroxycitronellal	33.5
Cinnamic alcohol (ex Styrax)	9.0
Menthol	0.7
Phenylacefc aldehyde 50%	0.1
Anisic aldehyde extra	0.5
Peru balsam	1.0
Jasmine	8.0
Heliotropin	11.0
Ethyl phthalate	8.2
Total	100.00

LILY-OF-THE-VALLEY

One may readily distinguish between the odours of *Muguet des* boil and green-house-grown lily-of-the-valley. A somewhat rough-and-ready way of compounding a lily-of-the-valley consists of mixing a lilac with a fresh rose compound. By gradually and systematically altering the proportions of both of these constituents, it is easy to arrive at a note similar to that of lily-of the valley. Two features of the delicious *Muguet des boil,* the variety found in the woods, are difficult to reproduce: namely the sharp and very fresh lemony top note and the slightly green note at the end. The basic muguet constituents are HydroxycitronellaL rhodinoL citronelloL terpineoL linalooL indole. To these must now be added the relatively recent para-tertiary Butyl alphamethyl hydrocinnamic aldehyde (e.g. Givaudan's Liliall and 4 (4 Hydroxy-4-methyl pentyl)-3-cyclohexene-10-carboxyaldehyde (Lyral of I.F.F.). Both have become important additions to the perfumer's shelves. Lilial is particularly notable for its extreme persistence and unusual diffusive properties. Also deserving of mention is citronellyl oxyacetaldehyde (I.F.F.'s Muguet Aldehyde).

The sharp lemony note de *depart* can be obtained with fatty aldehydes, certain lactones, lemony esters, etc. Violet leaf absolutes, some of the 'greener' oakmosses, phenylacetaldehyde and its acetals, and other odourants may be used to give the necessary verdant background effect. Tarragon (estragon) has been suggested for a green note. Some of the carbinols and their. esters are also of interest. To impart the impression of freshness of lily-of-the-valley, use can be made of traces of Ceylon citronella oil as 'citronellyl lactone' .

Formula 28 *(Muguet No. 1)*

Constituents	*Parts*
Citronellol	33.7
Rhodinol (Rhone-Poulenc)	11.3
Phenylethyl alcohol	24.7
Laurine (hydroxycitronellaL Givaudanl	14.6
Benzyl benzoate	6.7
Ethyl phthalate	4.5
a-Amyl cinnamic aldehyde	2.25
Indole 10%	2.25
Total	100.00

Cuminic aldehyde is included in next formula due to typical muguet note touch. This hint of cuminal has contributed to the success of a muguet compound. For a different effect it may be replaced by a good grade of cyclamen aldehyde. Lilia!, Lyral, etc. may also be introduced on an experimental basis.

Formula 29 *(Muguet 2)*

Constituents	*Parts*
Hydroxycitronellal	34.5
Rhodinol	20.7
Phenylethyl alcohol	13.8
Alcohol C" (enic)	2.0
Jasmine d'Espagne (Givaudan)	6.9
Linalyl acetate	3.5
Heliotropin	6.9
Terpineol	3.5
Cuminic aldehyde	1.35
Jasmonone No. 4a	6.85
Total	100.00

LINDEN (LIME BLOSSOM)

The lime (linden, tilleul) blossom has a captivating and powerful odour. A synthetic perfume sold under the name of lime is nothing more than hydroxycitronellal with something of a 'bouquet'. It is, however, quite possible to reproduce the odour of lime blossom, on a basis of hydroxycitronellaL linaloo!, linalyl acetate, ethyl linalool and its acetate, phenylpropyl alcohoL terpineol and farnesol. Small quantities of ethyl anisate, anisic aldehyde, cyclamen aldehyde, p.-methyl acctophenone, phenylethyl phenylacetate, geraniol and orange blossom etc., may be added. Persistence is accentuated with heliotropin, Peru balsam, etc. Aldehyde (lauryl) gives good results in the top note.

Formula 30 *(Tilleul 1)*

Constituents	*Parts*
Hydroxycitronellal	15.0
Linalool ex bois de rose	8.0
Farnesol	6.0
Bergamot oil	6.0
Tilleul absolute (Grasse)	18.0
Nerol	8.0
Geranium absol'ute incolore (Charabot)	3.0
Rose de Mai absolute	4.2
Lavender absolute	4.5

Tonka bean hyperessence (Charabot)	1.5
Petitgrain oil. French	8.5
Orangeflower	2.5
Jasmine absolute	6.15
Jasmine	6.0
Peru balsam resinoid	1.5
Phenylethyl phenylacetate	1.0
Aldehyde (lauric)	0.15
Total	100.00

MANGOLIA

The thick foliage is intensely perfumed with enormous white, fleshy flowers, splashed with a few mauve or pink patches. What is most striking about the perfume of this flower is the contract between the heavy, warm base note and the very lemon and fresh top note. The base note may be simulated with ylang and cinnamic alcohol, together with vanilla, vanillin or ethyl vanillin, with a dash of labdanum or incense. The body consists of hydroxycitronellal, nerol and various rosy notes. Finally, the top note is given by lemon, citral and alpha-amyl cinnamic aldehyde. Mangolia provides a good starting point for the development of new and original compositions.

MIGNONETTE (RESEDA)

The characteristic note of reseda or migonette is obtained with methyl octin or heptin carbonate, methyl nonyl ketone, methyl nonyl acetaldehyde, dimethyl hydroquinone, phenylpropyl acetate, phenylethyl acetate and styrallyl acetate. The components of the body and base are : geraniol, alpha ionone, hydroxycitronellal, rhodinol, cyclamen aldehyde, heliotropon, caumarin and guaiyl acetate. Also of interest are diphenylethyl acetal, phenylethyl isothiocyanate, sweet basil oil and boronia absolute.

The following formula (Formula 31) incorporates some alternative suggestions.

Formula 31 *(Reseda 1)*

Constituents	*Parts*
Reseda (Firmenich)	10.0
Reseda absolute hyperessence (Charabot)	27.1
Cyclamen aldehyde	10.9

Muguet	27.4
Orange flower	0.5
Jonquil absolute (Robertet)	1.0
Rose	1.0
Ylang-ylang oil	3.15
Supercitron 50% (Lautier)	0.8
Superportugal (LaUtier)	1.0
Jasmine	10.9
Jasmine absolute	2.1
Methyl ionone delta	1.5
Violet leaf absolute	0.15
Coriander oil	1.0
Musk ketone	1.5
Total	100.00

The mignonette note, blends well with rose and the already popular 'green' notes, and deserves to be considered for the elaboration of new-style perfumes.

MIMOSA

The base of mimosa is paramethyl acetophenone, isobutyl salicylate, phenylacetaldehyde and anisyl alcohol. These form the characteristic note, together with absolute oil of mimosa. There are three types of absolute oil: absolute from the flowers, absolute from the flowers and leaves, and absolute from the leaves. The body of the note is obtained with hydroxycitronellal and cinnamic alcohol, and the base consists of coumarin. Lemon, alpha amylcinnamic aldehyde and fatty aldehydes contribute to the top note.

NARCISSUS

The white flower of the valley narcissus, is extracted and supplied under the name of *Narcisse des Montagnes:* Benzyl acetate, cinnamic alcohol. hydroxycitronellal. terpineol. methyl anthranilate, ionone, eugenol. aurantiol. ylang-ylang and tuberose is used for producing adour of narcissus. The characteristic paracresylic shading of the narcissus note is then provided by aracresyl acetate and phenyl acetate,.metacresyl acetate and phenylacetate, Actyl acetate and phenylacetic aldehyde.

Formula 32 *(Base Narceine 1)*

Constituents *Parts*

Benzyl acetate	12.0
Phenylethyl alcohol	20.0
p.Cresyl phenylacetate	7.5
p.Cresyl acetate	3.0
p.Cresol	0.5
Neroli	6.0
Phenylacetic aldehyde	2.5
Hydroxycitronellal	20.0
Ylang-ylang oil	19.0
Narcisse des Montagnes absolute	2.5
Musk ketone	5.0
Musk ambrette	2.0
Total	100.00

Formula 33 *(Narcissus 2)*

Constituents	Parts
Isoeugenol	6.0
Eugenol	6.1
Bois de rose oH, Brazil	2.4
Anisic aldehyde	1.2
Base Narpeine	6.0
Phenylethyl alcohol	14.5
Terpineol	7.3
Hydroxycitronellal	14.5
Cinnamic alcohol	3.6
Methyl. ionone	3.9
Bergamot oil	7.3
Neroli	7.3
Benzyl acetate	7.3
Jasmine	7.3
Mastic (lentisque) oil: Robertet	0.5
Musk ketone	1.2
Indole 10%	2.4
Heliotropin	1.2
Total	100.0

The narcissus note has beerk stylised in some well-known and successful perfumes, and lends itself admirably to this type of work.

NARDO

Nardo is a Spanish flower quite similar to the Tuberose. Its perfume is heavier than that of the tuberose from the south of France, and above all its background note is much more fruity than that of the tuberose and the French gardenia. Nardo perfume is very fashionable in all the Spanish-speaking countries. Its bases are the same as those found in the tuberose and the gardenia, with a few lighter constituents than in the first two: benzyl acetate, cinnamic alcohoL linalooL hydroxycitronellaL terpineoL cyclamen aldehyde and, above alL there is more accent on the peach note.

NEW-MOWN HAY

The natural odour of new mown hay. though delightful and exhilarating, is not really a flower perfume, although the small blossoms of such flowers as woodruff and alyssum may contribute to it. In some respects it has points in common with fern or fougere and with clover or trefle. but essentially its odour is that of coumarin and tonka beans. There are several interesting foin coupe absolutes and a foin coupe distilled oil available; and. also of Grasse origin. flouve absolute, extracted from the flowering tops of a special grass. known as flouvre pdorante. Other constituents of newmown-hay perfumes may include lavender. lavandin. clary sage and rosemary oils; acetanisole, dimethyl acetophenone. ethyl anisate anisic aldehyde and alcohoL dimethyl hydro quinone, heliotropin. linalool; and small amounts of sandalwood. patchouli. olibanum.

NICOTIANA

Nicotiana tabacum. known as nicotiana or tobacco flower, perfume is most pronounced in the evening. Its odour may be simulated by introducing variations on the jasmine theme, i.e. by adding to a typical jasmine flowers base such lily components as Lilial or LyraL cyclamen aldehyde, etc., together with small quantities of p.cresol methyl ether or p.cresyl acetate.

OPOPANAX

This is not a flower perfume but is included here because of its general applicability, like many flower perfumes, in forming part of the background structure of a complex composition. In this respect is much resembles the 'Amber Art.', so frequently found as a perfume formula constituent. Opopanax resins and resinoids come in a variety of types and are of diversified and sometim,es unknown origins. Many opopanaxes sold under the name are nothing but mixtures, even though some are exceedingly well contrived.

The following formula for an Opopanax Art (i.e. 'artificial') is for a blend that has given consistently good results in many different applications.

Formula 34 *(Opopanax Art. 1)*

Constituents	*Parts*
Coumarin	9.3
Vanillin	17.6
Heliotropin	5.7
Musk ambrette	3.4
Musk ketone	2.3
Patchouli oil	1.7
Labdanum brun absolute (Lautier)	4.6
Mandarin oil	2.3
Bergamot oil	9.3
Petit grain oiL French	1.1
Castoreum tincture	3.4
Olibanol (Robertet)	1.1
Hydroxycitronellal	4.6
Geranium oil African	1.1
Vetiver Bourbon oil	4.6
Sweet orange oiL Guinea	4.6
Tolu balsam tincture	5.7
Diethyl phthalate	17.6
Total	100.0

ORCHID (ORCHIDEE)

Orchid, poppy and clover (trefle) are examples of perfumes that owe more to the perfumer's imagination than to nature. The base of orchid in perfumery is a combination of the salicylates, formed by. the amyL isobutyl and benzyl esters - the relative proportions varying. Very small amounts of the methyl ester may also be incorporated. Besides these products, there are several others worthy of special mention, i.e. alpha ionone, ylang-ylang, bergamot, neryl butyrate, rose components, cyclamen aldehyde, terpineoL paracresyl phenylacetate, aldehydes etc.

PANSY

Pansy (pensee) represents for thought. Its scent, is light and fresh, reminding one more name heart's-ease. The perfumer chiefly recognises in this lowly member of the violet family, Viola tricolour, a violet odour with a rather special green note.

The foundation of a simulated pansy perfume was essentially similar to that of the violet. It included alpha and beta ionones, methyl ionones, neryl acetate and, optionally, orris absolute. These are associated with phenylethyl alcohoL rose. jasmine; violet leaf absolute, the alkyne carbonate and other green notes; and a sweet persistence is assured by including a bouquet of 'crystallines' harmonising with the general tone.

PEONY

Peony (Fr. pivoine, Germ. pfingstrose) is not such a well known fragrant flower, perhaps, as it deserves to be. Its varieties have in the main two distinct types of odour. One of the red peonies is not very pleasant-smelling and recalls in fact the harsh green scent of the dahlia. On the other hand the white peony, with a few pink.patches, and the completely pink peony, have a deliciously fresh odour. When smelling this perfume one has often had the impression of being in the presence of an excellent citronellol. The basic products for simulating the peony odour are primarily the rose-like odourants: cintronellol, rhodinol, phenylethyl acetate, dimetilyl benzyl carbinol, the butyrate and isobutyrate esters of the rose alcohols, and linalool and ethyl linalool. For the base, there are the derivatives of guaiac wood oil, alpha ionone, styrax, ylang-ylang oiL heliotropin and vanillin. The green note may be given by styrallyl acetate associated with paracresyl phenylacetate and cinnamyl acetate. The peony is yet another of those flower types which could contribute rather more than they currently do to novel odour combinations.

PHLOX

Phlox, a herbaceous plant which has become well acclimatised in Europe. It includes many odourous species and varieties. The typical phlox is the one having scent of violet and heliotrope. This can be simulated by using a violet base rich in methyl ionone, fixing it with heliotropin and adding a touch of a hazel nut or noisette compound. Although the phlox deserves further investigation as a potential flower component in perfumery, the fact must not be overlooked that many people find its perfume disagreeable.

SWEET PEA

The sweet pea odour is highly regarded in Anglo-Saxon domestic circles. Basic odourants for its simulation include: phenylethyl phenylacetate, benzyl salicylate, benzyl isoeugenoL methyl acetophenone, and the various orangeflower notes. HydroxycitronellaL cinnamic alcohoL terpineoL linalool and traces of rose de Mai absolute - are added.

Formula 35 *(Pais de Senteur 1)*

Constituents	*Parts*
Coumarin	2.85
Neroli	2.0
Rose	4.3
Sandalwood oiL East Indian	5.7
Bergamot oil	5.7
Verbena oiL art	0.85
Lavender oil	1.4
Jonone alpha	1.4
Jasmine d'Espagne (Givaudan)	8.6
Sweet orange oil	8.6
Cinnamic alcohol	14.3
Hydroxycitronellal	11.45
Phenylethyl alcohol	11.45
Rhodinol	4.3
Phenylacetic acid	3.4
Methyl anthranilate	2.3
Heliotropol (Firmenich)	2.85
Jasmine enfleurage absolute (Lautier)	5.7
Phenylethyl phenylacetate	2.85
Total	100.00

If this type of compound seems a trifle harsh, a small addition of Rose de Grasse absolute will round off the edges and enhance the desired honeyed note.

Formula 36 *(Sweet pea 2)*

Constituents	*Parts*
Rose	13.2
Sandalwood oil Mysore	2.3

Bergamot oil	10.6
Hydroxycitronellal	13.3
Phenylethyl alcohol	13.3
Benzyl acetate	1.3
Wardia (Firmenich)	5.3
Methyl ionone	4.3
Jasmonone	16.0
Pais de Senteur (Firmenich)	15.6
Vetiver oil	0.8
Benzyl propionate	4.0
Total	100.0

SYRINGA (PHILADELPHUS)

The base of the so-called syringa perfume (the true syringa being lilac) is methyl acetophenone. This syringa or mock-orange, which is in fact Philadelphus coronarius, has an odour that resembles orange blossom and has, in its finer varieties, a fresh lemony top note.

'The components, are methyl acetophenone, hydroxycitronellal. cinnamic alcohol. ylang-ylang, alpha-ionone, phenylethyl alcohol, products with an orange flower note, terpineol. anisic aldehyde, isoeugenol. The freshness of the depart is imparted by lemon oil, fine quality citral and/or octyl or decyl aldehyde.

The perfume of the mock-orange, and particularly the lemon-scented variety, is heady, fresh, very agreeable. This is a floral odour that could be effectively used as the flower bouquet, or part of the flower bouquet, of new and attractive perfumes.

Formula 37 *(Syringa 1)*

Constituents	*Parts*
Phenyl ethyl alcohol	15.0
Folia (Bertrand freres)	2.0
Methyl anthranilate	0.5
Isoeugenol	5.0
Syringa aldehyde (p.-tolyl acetaldehyde)	4.0
Anisic aldehyde ex anethole	0.5
Bois de rose oil. Brazil	2.5
Muguet	2.5

Cassie absolute (Robertet)	1.5
Hydrvxycitronellal	15.0
Jasmonis (Givaudan)	13.5
Jasmonone	15.0
Jasmine absolute	2.5
Amyl salicylate	4.0
Heliotropin	9.0
Indole 10%	5.0
Aldehyde	2.5
Total	100.0

TREFLE (CLOVER)

Trefle or clover. like orchidee (orchid); is one of those important half-floral, half-herbaceous odours founded on the salicylates. One of the famous classic perfumes of the past was the Trefle Incarnat of Piver. Trefle compounds are conventionally based on the saEcylates in association with coumarin, lavender. bergamot; with suitable flower notes and aldehydes.

Formula 38 *(Trefle 1)*

Constituents	*Parts*
Amyl salicylate	20.0
Isobutyl salicylate	22.0
Benzyl salicylate	8.0
Bergamot oil	12.0
Coumarin	17.0
Isoeugenol	2.5
Vetiver oil	1.5
lonone alpha	2.5
Ylang-ylang oil	2.5
Oakmoss absolute	0.5
Methyl nonyl acetaldehyde (1 %)	0.6
Musk ambrette	2.2
Lavender oil	2.0
Rose oil art (Bulgarian type)	1.5
Jasmine absolute art	2.5
Hydroxycitronellal	2.5

Birch bud oil	0.2
Total	100.00

TUBEROSE

The tuberose, has nevertheless found widespread use in perfumery. This applies both to the natural absolute and to 'tuberose artificial'. As a dominant theme it is especially appreciated in eastern countries and in territories under Spanish influence. More generally it finds application as a floral support capable of conferring body and persistence. Its basic component are: Ylang-ylang oiL phenyiethyl or phenylpropyl alcohoL benzyl salicylate and acetate, benzoin resinoid, Peru balsam, tuberose absolute, tuberose pomade absolute and. - this is indispensable - methyl salicylate or oil of wintergreen in very small quantities. To give a flowery touch one uses lauryl aldehyde or other aliphatic aldehydes, in association with orange blossom, jasmine, and a mere suggestion of styrallyl acetate.

Formula 39 *(Base Tuberose* 1)

Constituents	*Parts*
Jasmine absolute ex chassis (benzenel)	1.6
Tuberose absolute	1.2
Wintergreen oiL natural	4.0
Methyl salicylate	8.0
Benzyl acetate	24.5
Benzyl alcohol :	22.5
Methyl anthranilate	22.5
gamma Nonyl Lactone	8.0
Peach synthetic (Givaudan)	8.0
Total	100.00

Formula 40 *(Base Tuberose 2)*

Constituents	*Parts*
Tuberose absolute	1.0
Hydroxycitronellal	29.5
Benzyl benzoate	3.0
Isobutyl salicylate	10.0
Methyl salicylate	3.0
Ionone alpha	20.0

Aldehyde (lauric)	10.0
alpha-Amyl cinnamic aldehyde	7.0
Heliotropin	16.5
Total	100.00

VERBENA

Men pleasing odour is Verbena. It is simple, refreshing and comes midway between what one may term 'hygienic' perfumes. It is used in toilet preparations for personal hygiene, and the more frankly perfumed toilet waters of the Cologne type. Verbena oil, is distilled from the true verbena.

Formula 41 *(Verveine 1)*

Constituents	*Parts*
Supercitron (Lautier)	3.5
Grapefruit oil	15.55
Cassie synthetic (Givaudan)	7.2
Geraniol extra	9.1
Geranium Bourbon oil	6.0
Verbena oil, Grasse, rectified	31.1
Citral extra	15.55
Verbenol (Firmenich)	3.0
Bergamot oil	3.0
Sandalwood oil, East Indian	1.2
Opopanax	4.8
Total	100.00

WALLFLOWER

In nineteenth-century perfumery, especially at the beginning, the wallflower (giroflee) enjoyed great favour. The odour of this flower is fresh and agreeable. The base consists of eugenoL isoeugenol arid acetyl isoeugenoL associated with benzyl salicylate, amyl salicylate and anisic aldehyde, to which there may be added small quantities of oils of cloves, pimento, bay, or even pepper, and a trace of methyl p~sol. The 'filler' consists of terpineol, hydroxycitronellaL cinnamic alcohoL phenylethyl alcohoL linalooL geranioL rhodinoL neroL dimethyl benzyl carbinyl acetate. There may be added an ionone or its derivatives and for the flowery touch, Lilial (Givaudan) and neroli too. The lower notes comprise heliotropin, vanillin, ethyl vanillin, methyl naphthyl ketone, and a little mace or mastic oil or guaiyl acetate.

The wallflower note, orientated towards the basic carnation-salicylateaubepine base, could well contribute to the development of an interesting perfume.

WISTARIA

The wistaria, wisteria or glycine, grown for its climbing habit and its attractive drooping racemes of blossom. It has a sweet and diffusive odour of rather honeyed type, suggesting orangeflower, lily and mimosa. The odourants chiefly entering into the composition of artificial wistarias are hydroxycitronellaL benzyl salicylate; geranioL phenylethyl alcohol and other rose alcohols; ylang-ylang, mimosa absolute, isoeugenol, terpineol, methyl naphthyl ketone, methyl anthranilate, isobutyl phenylacetate, paramethyl acetophenone, p.-methyl totyl ketone, p.cresyl acetate.

YLANG- YLANG

The essential oil of ylang-ylang is one of the most widely used of natural materials in perfumery. In old days, there were three types of natural products: ylang from the Bourbon islands of Madagascar, ylang from Manilla and cananga from the Java islands. To-day ylang from Manilla has almost entirely vanished. It had a very special note, more like ora!lgeblossom than ylang from Reunion and lighter, too, with the base more like tuberose. Ylang is so useful that there have been numerous attempts at synthesising it. Some 'artificials' are in fact quite close in odour to natural ylang. For Bourbon ylang, the basic products are; methyl paracresol and paracresol. These very powerful products are only present in small quantities. Associated with methyl benzoate, benzyl benzoate, eugenol and Isoeugenol. they form the characteristic part of this note. The body consists of terpineol. geraniol. linalool and alpha ionone.

This origmal note has certainly not been fully utilised; it is powerful and heedy, especially in the case of Manilla ylang, which is less violent but otherwise similar. Here must be added an orange blossom note (natural or synthetic), methyl anthranilate, and a tinge of methyl salicylate or oil of wintergreen. As a rule, when it is desired to give a 'bouquet' to a composition, LLis considerably more advantageous to use the natural essential oil .::-an-a, moreover, the finest quality that costing will permit.

There are very few fine quality perfume compositions in which ylangylang does not or could not enter as a valuable constituent. Here is a formula for an artificial version of Ylang-Ylang Bourbon:

Formula 42 (Ylang I)

Constituents	*Parts*
Bois de rose oiL Brazil	10.5
Linalool ex bois de rose	15.7
Linalyl acetate	8.65
Benzyl1acetate	11. 35
Vanilla tincture	10.55
Methyl paracresol	6.9
Palmarosa oil	8.6
Nerol (Lor~na, Firmenich)	2.6
Benzyl alcohol	4.3
Orris concrete (10% in benzyl benzoate)	5.2
Isoeugenol	4.35
Peru Clair (Lautier)	3.5
Coriander oil, Russian	3.5
Methyl benzoate	1.75
Estragon oil (P Chauvet)	0.85
Methyl anthranilate	0.8
Methyl salicylate	0.8
Cananga oil, terpeneless	0.1
Total	100.00

3

Sophisticated/Fantasy Perfumes and their Formulations

Introduction

Perfumes of fantasy (as we may call them for want of a better name) are roughly divisibly into six categories.

(1) Floral perfumes

(2) Aldehydic perfumes

(3) Chypre types

(4) Oriental types

(5) Green types: and

(6) Perfumes with a distinguishing dominant note.

The independent notes that characterise perfumes-in each separate category, and tonality also plays an important part in all these types. This may be, in each group, one of three, namely, light, medium and heavy.

The formulae for general and specific nature can be given. Here is a representative of the very interesting bergamot-vanilla baes

Bergamot Oil	100
Vanillin	5
Aldehydre C_{12}(MNA) 10%	1
Aldehyde $C_{8'}$10%	0.3

In the formula that follows the cadrat oil, once a natural product, may be replaced by the now conventional artificial blend of lemon, bergamot and orange oils.

Formula 1

Constituents	*Parts*
Aldehyde C_8	0.50
Aldehyde C_9	1.25
Aldehyde C_{10}	2.50
Aldehyde C (undercylenic)	1.25
Aldehyde C_{12} (lauric)	2.50
Aldehyde C_{12} (MNA)	1.50
Bergamot Oil	12.50
Bergamot Oil, sesquiterpeneless	6.20
Sperorange (Lautier) 50%	10.00
Supercitron (Lautier) 50%	1.90
Lemon oil	1.25
Cedrat oil	3.75
Nerolic	3.10
Folia (bertrand freres)	0.60
Ylang=ylang oil	37.50
Opopanax L.G. (Gaaundan)	1.25
Costus absolute	0.60
Musk tincture	2.50
Rose	6.20
Sandalwood oil	3.50
	100.00

As orange curacao oil can be contained which have characteristic note hence the following formula is useful.

Formula 2 (Curacao Base)

Constituents	*Parts*
Bitter orange oil (Guinea)	37.50
Bitter orange oil, deterpenated	3.45
Anethole	4.65
Citral	3.70

Coriandrol (from Russian coriander oil)	2.70
Aldehyde C_8	2.00
Aldehyde C_9	5.00
Aldehyde C_{10}	7.00
Aldehyde C_{11} (undercyclinc)	18.30
Aldehyde C_{12} (MNA)	3.00
Aldehyde C_{12} (lauric)	8.70
	100.00

Leather or 'cuir' bases have continued to be popular and are widely utilised in perfumery at the time of writing. They are indispensable in certain fashionable perfumes and are particularly of interest in perfumes for men.

Formula 3 (Perfumes Cuir base 1)

Constituents	*Parts*
Bergamot oil	1.5
Framboisis (de Laire)	7.5
Coromia (Givaudan)	40.0
Corianal (Firmenich)	14.0
beta-Methyl ionone	4.5
Jasmin	2.4
Mandarin oil	1.5
Cedrol	12.0
Lilac	9.0
Musk ketone	1.8
Musk ambrette	1.8
Neroli	0.9
Coriandrol	0.3
Cedrat oil	0.8
Vanillin	1.5
Dimethyl phthalate	0.5
	100.00

The woody note is often employed in association with other notes, not only to confer its owen characteristics but to soften and round off the finished composition.

Formula 4 (Perfume woody base 1)

Constituents	*Parts*
Linalyl acetate	27.00
Bergamot oil	12.35
Rose de Grasse absolute	12.20
Jasmine absolute	6.90
Bois de rose oil, Brazil	6.00
Lilac	5.70
Muguet	5.25
Vanillin	4.95
Coumarin	4.95
Sandalwood oil	3.90
beta-Methl ionone	2.70
Neroli oil	1.95
Bitter orange oil, guinea	1.95
Labdanum absolute	1.20
Patchouli oil	1.05
Vetiver oil, Bourbon	1.05
Hyperessenee oranger (Charabot)	0.90
	100.00

The moss note plays a very importat part in perfumery. It sustains the head notes of 'green' compositions, which are currently fashionable; but long before this it found other applications.

In addition to the newer 'green' odourants marked as pure chemicals, other have been introduced as proprietary bases. In most instances these bases have been well contrived, so as to permit their introduction into standard formulae without causing any undue imbalance or interference. They nevertheless give rise to effects that are quite distinctive and different from those that prededed their introduction. The auxillary notes to introduced may of course be pleasing or displeasing, but the possibility of producing novel and interesting affects cannot be overlooked.

As per taste moss note may be similar to fruity.Moss base M.2 can very easily be reorientated in this fashion.

A certain number of odourants are capable of suggesting the sea and the open air, faintly suggesting the odour of ozone. This type of perfume could well be the subject of tomorrow's success story.

Formula 5 (Perfume QHI)

Constituents	*Parts*
Lilac	50.00
Hyacinth absolute	0.10
Aldehyde C_{12} (MNA) 10%	0.25
Aldehyde C_{12} (lauric) 10%	0.10
Citronellyl lactone (I.F.F.) 10%	0.05
Amyl salicylate	5.00
Sandalwood oil	1.55
beta-Methyl ionone	5.05
Benzyl acetate	3.90
Rose	4.00
Jasmin absolute	2.00
Cedrat oil	7.00
Bergamot oil	5.00
Ylang ylang oil	10.00
Musk ambrette	1.00
Musk ketone	1.00
Vanillin	2.00
Ambrophore (Firenich)	2.00
	100.00

The next flower perfume (A_2o) is characteristic of a kind of bouquet which had a great success at the end of the nineteenth century. Bouvardia, which has a wide acceptance to perfumer, is essential part of flower perfume. Therefore, the example for a base given below in formulae.

Formula 6 (Bourvardia BM)

Constituents	*Parts*
Ylang-ylang oil	20.00
Geraniol extra	5.00
Jasmine absolute	3.75
Base Tuberone	2.50
Neroli	12.50
beta-Methyl ionone	25.00
Bois de rose oil, Brazil	25.00
Hyperessence orange flower (UOP)	6.25
	100.00

Formula 7 (Parfum AO)

Constituents	*Parts*
Mimosa flower absolute	1.7
Rose de mai absolute	3.4
Hyperessence orange flower	5.0
Narcisse des Montagnes absolute (Camilli)	2.0
Base tuberose	4.0
Jasmin absolute	3.4
Jasmonone	1.0
Ylang-ylang oil, Manilla	3.0
Heliotropin	2.0
Acacia (Firmenich)	8.5
Bourvardia BM	4.0
Bouvardia 100% (de Laire)	3.0
Bergamot Oil	10.0
beta-Methl ionone	8.0
Anisic aldehyde	6.0
Methyl anthranilate	1.0
Linalyl acetate	2.0
Ionone alpha	2.0
Ambrophore (Firenich) 3%	20.0
Civet tincture	10.0
	100.00

Formula 8 (Parfum F)

Constituents	*Parts*
Ylang-ylang oil	12.70
Jasmin absolute	3.40
Marsisse des Montagnes absolute (Camilli)	2.10
Lilac	21.50

Paracetone (Givaudan)	22.70
Gardenia 9058 (Givaudan)	10.25
Heliotropol (Firenich)	4.20
Jasmin	4.20
Grapefruit oil	5.10
Bergamot oil, sesquieterpeneless	3.40
Neroli	3.40
Base cuir	2.10
Caumarin	1.70
Boronia absolute oil	1.00
Rose	1.00
Pollenol (Firmenich)	0.50
Hyperessence reseda (Charabot)	0.15
Hyacinth absolute (Polal'c frutal)	0.15
Aldehyde C_{12} (MNA) 50%	0.05
Penhylacetaldehyde dimethylacetal 50%	0.05
Cyclopentadecanolide	0.35
	100.00

Formula 9 (Perfume HB)

Constituents	*Parts*
Jasmin	7.50
Bergamot oil	10.00
Lavender oil	7.45
Opaslaunax (Et. Hasslauer)	7.50
Methyl anthranilate	6.70
Orange oil	4.10
Lilac	3.60
Rose	3.00
Methyl ionone	2.20
Jasmin absolute	2.20
Muguet	2.00
Neroli	1.40
Claveline base	1.30
isoEugenol	1.30

Sandalwood oil	1.30
Heliotropin	1.30
Ambreine (Firmenich)	0.80
Venillin	0.80
Caumarin	0.75
Orangeflower water absolute	0.80
Ylang-ylang oil	0.65
Anisic aldehyde	0.45
Cedarwood oil, Virginia	0.40
Marisia (Descollonges)	0.40
Orris absolute, P.V	0.20
Benzyl acetate	0.20
zdravetz oil, 10%	0.90
Cinnamon oil, Ceylon 10%	0.40
Frambiosis (de Laire) 10%	0.20
Peru balasam tincture	13.00
Civet tincture	13.00
Musk (tincture)	4.20
	100.00

ALDEHYDE PERFUMES

Formula 10 (Perfume VN)

Constituents	*Parts*
Bergamot oil	5.30
Bitter orange oil	4.25
Aldehydric base	3.00
Ambreine (Firmenich)	3.25
Methyl ionone	4.25
Cinnamic aldehyde	3.40
Jasmin de provence (Descollonges)	3.00
Petitgrain oil, French	2.20
Jasmin asolute	2.20
Sophora (Givaudan)	2.80
Lavender	1.40
Neroli	1.15

Jonquil absolute (Charabot)	0.50
Hydroxycitronellal	2.70
Sandalwood oil	0.60
Benzoin gomodor (UOP)	0.60
Opopanax vrai resin (Hasslauer)	3.00
Elami resinoid	2.00
Rose	2.20
Civet tincture	30.60
Musk tincture	12.45
Peru balsam tincture	5.15
Castoreum tincture	4.00
	100.00

Formula 11 (Parfume C)

Constituents	*Parts*
Rose	0.40
Lilac	4.20
Jasmin	6.70
Neroli	0.15
Hydroxycitronellai	6.30
Terpineol	3.20
Clnnamic alcohol ax styrax	0.50
Methyl ionone	3.20
Amarante (Viaudan)	5.00
Oakmoss absolute	1.25
Opopanax	3.75
Base	2.60
Liquidambar	0.10
Mousse de Saxe (de Laire)	5.00
Thyme oil	0.30
Vetiver oil, Java	1.90
Patchouli oil	3.00
Sandalwood oil	3.00
Coriander oil, Russian	4.00
Cedrat oil	1.00

Bitter orange oil	2.00
Lavender oil	3.00
Bergamot oil	10.00
Linalyl acetate	5.00
Ambreine s (Firmenich)	4.50
Dimethyl phthalate	0.60
Ethyl vanillin	0.80
Musk ketone	0.50
Musk ambrette	1.00
Cyclopentadecanolide	3.00
Coumarin	3.00
Aldehyde C_{11} (undecylenic)	0.42
Aldehyde C_{12} (lauric)	0.36
Aldehyde C_{12} (MNA)	0.27
Tincture of civat	1.50
Tincture of castoreum	8.50
	100.00

Fairly frequent reference is made in these formulae to the natural resin, liquidamber. This balsamic product of very dark bituminous aspect is not used as such but is appropriately treated to yield three different fractions. The first of these has the strongly 'gassy' styrene odour; the second has a labdanum odour and an 'animal' note; while the third has the animal note in an even more marked degree. In fine perfumery only the second and the third fractions are normally used and formulae are called as liquidamber II and liquidamber III. The raw material can be suitably treated and used in perfumery.

Formula 12 (Parfume SP)

Constituents	*Parts*
Opopanax	2.20
Opopanax (de Laire)	0.90
Cyclamen aldehyde	0.10
Amyl salicylate	0.25
Costus resinoid (Camilli)	0.15
Bergamot oil	3.20
Patchouli oil	2.40

Grisambrol (Firmenicii)	0.80
Labdanum oil (Schomoller)	0.25
Moss Base	0.40
Oakmoss absolute superessence) (Yugoslav)	0.90
Liquidamber	0.05
Mousse (Roure dupont)	2.15
Musc (Rhone-Poulenc)	0.10
Musk ketone	0.60
Cyclopentadecanolide	0.15
Ethyl vanillin	0.10
Thibetine (Givaudan)	0.60
Animalis (synarome)	0.30
Civette (Rhone-Poulenc)	0.10
Elecampane oil	4.50
Sandalwood oil	0.20
Methyl ionone	3.20
Jasmonone	5.70
Gardenia (Givaudan)	19.70
Gardenia	4.50
Cardamon oil, Naardenised (Naarden)	0.25
Hydroxycitronellal	2.40
Corona (Roure Dupont)	1.70
Hyacinth absolute (Polak's Frutal)	1.60
Phenylacetaldehyde	0.05
Camomile absolute (Schmoller)	0.15
Lavender oil, Barreme (42% esters)	1.30
Linalool ex bois de rose	4.50
Ylang-ylang oil	0.25
Styrallyl acetate	2.10
Aldehyde C_8	0.10
Aldehyde C_9	0.10
Aldehyde C_{10}	0.60
Aldehyde C_{11} (undecylenic)	0.60
Aldehyde C_{12} (lauric) 50%	0.70

Opopanax resin tincture	6.30
Peru balsam tincture	20.00
Vanilla tincture	1.10
Castoreum tincture	2.70
	100.00

CHYPRE TYPES

Chypre perfumes have always found great favour among women and men. The characteristic note of the Chypre is a safrole or isosafrole. Chypre has also conventional notes of bergamot, oakmoss, civet. linalyl acetate, amyl, salicylate, rose, neroli, vetiver, sandalwood, labdanum and the little rustic or herbal notes of red thyme, tarragon and basil.

Many Chypre variants have been prepared, each with its slightly different not or emphasis which distinguishes it from the other members of its class. This can be referred as 'special Chypre', which is safe to produce. During the past few years aidehydic chypres have made headway. The following examples are given as typical of this class.

Formula 13 (Perfume)

Constituents	*Parts*
Rose	1.80
Ysminia (Firmenich)	15.00
Jasmine absolute	15.00
Oakmoss absolute supperessence, Yugoslav (Schmoller0	0.60
Bergamot oil	4.20
Oakmoss absolute (Camilli)	4.35
Jasmine	4.00
Geranium sur rose oil	1.80
Methyl ionone	11.30
Vetiver oil	3.60
Sandalwood oil	1.30
Linalool ex bois de rose	1.80
Dianthine (Firmenich)	7.60
Eugenol	0.75
Hydroxycitronellal	0.75
Gardenia 9058 (Givaudan)	4.00

Costus absolute 10%	2.10
Mace oil	0.15
Florizia (Firenich)	3.15
Tincture of Musk, 3%	7.60
Tincture of Civet, 3%	1.00
Musk ambrette	0.7
Musk ketone	1.40
Coumarin	0.30
Vanillin	0.15
Aldehyde C_{10}, 1%	0.80
Aldehyde C_{11} (undecyclenic) 1%	1.20
Aldehyde C_{12} (MNA) 10%	3.60
	100.00

The following Chypre base is typical aldehyde.

Formula 14 (Base Chypre H)

Constituents	*Parts*
Coumarin	8.70
Vanilin	4.60
Ethyl vanillin	2.90
Heliotropin	1.80
Methyl ionone	1.20
Musk ketone	0.75
Rose	0.60
Orange oil, bitter, Guinea	4.50
Geraniol extra	2.90
Bois de Rhoses oil (Chiris-UOP)	1.00
Noisette (de Laire)	0.20
Sandalwood oil	2.80
Benzoin supergmodor (Chins-UOP)	0.45
Liquidamber	2.90
Labdamm Clair (Lautier)	5.80
Linalool ex bois de rose Cayenne	0.45
Linalyl acetate ex bois de rose	2.90
Terpinyl acetate	8.80

Benzyl acetate	2.90
Vetiver acetate	0.09
Estragon (tarragon) oil 5%	0.54
isoButylduinoline 5%	0.75
Ysminia (Firmenich)	1.20
Bergamot oil, sesquiterpeneless	34.97
Bergamot oil	6.00
	100.00

Mandito chypree perfume formula with a peach type of tap note is given below.

Formula 15 (Perfume V.W.)

Constituents	*Parts*
Ysminia (Firmenich)	3.00
Wardia (Firmenich)	2.00
Benzyl acetate	9.00
Orange oil, sweet	3.00
Jasmine absolute	1.25
Veetiveryl acetate	4.50
Cedryl acetate (Givaudan)	4.00
Sandalwood oil (Mysore)	2.50
Lavender oil, Barreme 42% easters	6.00
IsoEugenol	1.75
Amyl Salicylate	1.50
Bergamot oil	12.00
Lemon oil, Guinea	3.50
Methyl ionone	5.00
Ylang-ylang oil	3.50
Oakmoss decoloree (Robertet)	3.50
Patchouli oil	2.50
Petitgrain Oil, Paraguay	4.00
Indole	0.15
Citral	0.50
Aurantiol	4.00
Dimethyl benzyl carbinol	3.00

Hydroxycitronellal	3.00
l-citronellol	2.00
Geranium extra	2.50
Fennal oil	0.75
Black pepper oil	0.75
Coumarin	2.60
Musk ketone	1.50
Civettone	0.20
Ambrettozone (Haarmann & Reimer)	0.40
Ambrarome Absolute (Synarome)	0.25
Clove bud oil	0.30
Aldehyde (pseudo) C_{18} 10%	0.40
Aldehyde (pseudo) $C_{16'}$ 10%	0.20
Aldehyde C_{14} ('peach'), 10%	5.00
	100.00

Oriental Perfumes

The creation of oriental perfumes is carried basically by using balsam and all kinds of resins, e.g., Peru balsam, benzoin, opopanax, olibanum, labdanum etc., accompnied by musk and civet, etc. natural and artificial. The conventional crystalline 'faxatives' are also used according to taste. The desired objective is to obtain a perfume with warm and even seductive tonalities. the typically oriental base is 'floralised' by means of heady flower odours such as jasmin, tuberose, mangolia, gardenia, honeysuckle, syringa etc.

Due note must be taken of the fact that all the basic raw material are heavy in characters and slow to be released into the atmosphee. It is therefore necessary to use, with them, a sufficiency of citrus type oils etc., acetates and other synthetics of alight nature in order to entrain and disperse them.

By way of formula we give a base that may serve as a starting point for these types of perfume.

Formula 16 (Base S.H.)

Constituents	*Parts*
Tonka beans hyperessence (Charabot)	1.75
Peru balasam rectified (Hasslauer)	3.30
Castoreum anhydrol (Givaudan)	2.55

Ethyl vanillin	2.20
Bergamot oil	51.25
Orange oil, bitter (Guinea)	8.70
Orange oil, sweet	8.70
Lavender oil, Barreme	4.40
Ondatrol (Descollonges)	0.75
Linalyl acetate ex shiu oil	16.40
	100.00

Here is another oriental perfume

Formula 17 (Perfume J)

Constituents	*Parts*
Coriandrol (Robertet)	10.85
Vetyrisine (Firemenich)	7.30
Opasalaunax (Hasslauer)	7.30
Humuscol (Descollonges)	5.82
Vanillin	3.90
Heliotropol (Firemenich)	0.35
Coumarin	3.65
Sandalwood oil	3.65
Lavender oil, Barreme, 42% easters	3.65
Bergamot oil	3.65
Coriander oil	2.91
Gardenia (Givaudan)	3.65
Neroli	2.54
Supercuracao (Lauteir)	2.59
Clary sage (Chiris-UOP)	1.48
Jasmin absolute	1.48
Patchouli oil	0.74
Musk ambrette	0.74
Ylang-ylang oil	0.37
Rose	0.37
Wintergreen oil	0.14
Peru balasam rect. (Hasslauer)	2.50
Cyclopentadecanolide)	0.92

Anhydrol Castoreum (Givaudan)	0.37
Civettone 100%	0.37
Musk tincture	27.71
	100.00

Green Perfumes

For some years there has been a growing demand for perfumes with a more or less pronounced not of greenery or verdure. It could of course be said that the original perfumes with a type of green note were the ferns or fougers. Other fougers wer quick to follow and all helped to popularise the fern note, which is really one of forest trees and undergrowth rather than a truly green leaf note.

Here is a hyacinth-green base which can be considerable service in the creation of green perfume.

Formula 18 (Hyacinth Green Base)

Constituents	*Parts*
Hydroxycitronellal (Cyclosia Firmenich)	3.60
Phenylahyl acetate	1.80
Phenylethyl alcohol	43.00
iso Eugenol	3.50
Cinnamic alcohol	16.66
Phenylacetaldehyde 50%	0.85
Phenylacetaidehyde dimethyl acetal	0.50
Folial (Firemenich)	0.05
Hyacinth absolute	1.25
Benzyl acetate	1.80
Phenylethyl formate	0.50
Terpineol	3.10
Rhodinol	1.20
alpha-Amylcinnatnic aldehyde	0.30
Paracetone (Givaudan)	0.20
Rose	0.06
Jasmin absolute	0.20
Hosaldeine (de Laire)	0.79

Framboise (Firemenich) 10%	0.24
Dimethyl phthalte	20.40
	100.00

Dominant Note types

Dominant notes are perfumes which have a well-defined characteristics note yielded by a specific synthetic odourant or a group of two or three odourants, natural or synthetic. It is easy enough to obtain in perfumery what, in painting, one terms a grisaille; in other words a souless overall tint, which shades off into a heavy and nondescript mist. Here is a formula in which the dominant not is formed by an accord of four principal odourants; ambergis, arthenol, boronia and cassis.

Formula 19 (Parfum)

Constituents	*Parts*
Boronia absolute oil (plaimar)	3.75
Cassis bud absolute incolore	3.00
Oakmoss absolute incolore	2.50
Jasmine absolute butaflor (Robertet)	1.25
Vetiver oil, naardenised (Naarden)	7.38
Carrot oil, naardenised	0.07
Paracetne (Givaudan)	9.80
Benzoin Supergodor (Chiris-UOP)	2.00
Rose	1.87
Cinnamon, oil naardenised (Naardan)	1.25
Clary sage oil, naardenised	3.50
Clary sage oil, natural	3.50
Sandalwood oil	4.00
Hydroxycitronellal	4.50
Arhenol (Firemenich)	4.50
Pollenol (Firemenich)	3.00
Ambrarome (Firemenich)	7.38
Ondatrol (Descollonges)	3.50
Alcohol. C., (undecylenic)	0.62
Aldehyde $C_{10'}$ 10%	0.03
Linallol ex bois de rose Brazil	3.75
Bergamot oil, sesquiterpeneless	15.50

Mandarin oil	0.75
Moskene (Givaudan)	0.25
Ethyl vanillin	2.50
Benzyl acetate	2.25
Opopanax tincture	4.00
Castoreum tincture	3.60
	100.00

The Ambergris Note

When it comes to using this composition for preparing a perfume. of chosen concentration, the quantity of tincture of ambergris diet should be added is calculated in to proportion of 100 parts of the concentrate to 73.5 parts of ambergris tincture with the balance made up of perfumery alcohol. As an example, suppose that what in wanted is a perfume containing 15 per cent of concentrate. Then to 15 parts of the concentrate we add 11 parts of tincture of ambergris, and complete the formula by adding a sufficiency of alcohol at 95° to arrive at a total volume of 100 parts.

Tincture a ambergris at 3 per cent concentration may be replaced by much less expensive synthetic odourants. In this particular case excellent results, possibly even superior to those yielded by the natural product, may be obtained with a 3 per cent tincture of Ambergris synthetique (Givaudan).

Another formula in this category is given below :

Formula 20 (Perfume B.M.)

Constituents	*parts*
Arthenol (Firemenich)	5.40
Sophora (Givaudan)	20.00
Cattleya (Givaudan)	3.60
Jonquille alpha (de Laire)	6.00
Hydroxycitronellal	23.00
Orangeflower	0.30
Folia (Bertrand freres)	2.00
Methyl ionone	1.00
Paracetone (Givaudan)	3.00
Cinnamic alcohol ex styrax	9.78
Benzyl acetate	2.00

Linalyl acetate	4.00
Phenylethyl alcohol	0.80
Rose	3.20
isoEugenol	0.80
Citral	0.40
Orange oil, bitter	4.00
Orange oil, sweet	1.60
Cedrat oil	2.00
Aldehyde C_{12} (MNA)	0.03
Aldehyde C_{11} (undecylenic)	0.02
Patchouli oil	0.27
Coumarin	3.00
Ethyl vanillin	0.80
Jasmonone	3.00
	100.00

The formula for the finished perfume is made as follows, chilled and filtered.

Formula 21 (Perfume concentrate as above)

Constituents	*Parts*
(Parfum BM)	15 Kilos
Tincture of musk	4 Litres
Alcohol at 95°	81 litres

Many simple, small-scale chemical processes may be profitably used by the perfumer or his associates. One thnks of the fractional distillation of Virginian cedarwood oil, for example, or the interested end-product of distilling bergamot oil over oakmoss, just as the larger supply houses have-distilled geranium over rose flowers and petitgrain over orangeflowers. The separation of a determined portion or portions of a known essential oil can also yield an attractive result. Nothing should be overlooked, in fact, that may contribute a novel and perhaps an inimitable note to a new perfume.

Manufacturing Processes

It is necessary to select best quality of formulation as the concentrates prepared should be better. Take utmost care in choosing buying and storage of raw mahxials e.g., Citrus oil, It is deteriorates rapidly. Hence its stock should be used accordingly and note deterisoration. The place of storage should be dry, shaded and ventilated and have fire protection.

Storage should preferably be in glass; although internally lined aluminium cans provide one of the permissible alternatives. some oxidation-prone essential oils are often treated on the production site with traces (e.g. 1 part in 20.000) of antioxidants, but the practices of adding such materials should be kept to the minimum and not knowingly encouraged in fine perfumery. A first grade fresh oil is always superior to a comparable treated oil.

A few odourants, e.g., myristic aldehyde, should not be stored in the cold. The particular aldehyde tends to polymerise if kept below room temperature.

First make types not on Cellophane-wrapped card and clip it on holder having movable wide flat strip specially designed for the actual line to be weighed. The design and material of containers and utensils should be appropriate. It means that they are fabricated from good quality tin plate, with spouts for drip-free pouring and suitable for steam bath or hot plate.

Tie weighing has to be accurate specifically in case of small weights or 10, 5, 1 per cent solution of ethyl alcohol, benzyl benzoate, diethyl phthalate and other diluent. A microprocessor based electronic balance having facility for zero setting, tare weight facility which facilitate direct weighing.

Almost all the mixtures are prepared in cold. In certain cases heat is required to enhance solubility e.g., flower absolutes and fatty aldehydes. In this case heat is applied for dissolving and then blend is cooled.

In olden days mixing is carried out by hand methods. Modern methods of liquid mixers are most efficient. At the beginning that concentrate is matured on storage, then reduced or diluted with alcohol; chilled filtered and filled into bottles.

The finished perfume is prepared by mixing the concentrate with equal quantity by volume of the alcohol and the dilute with proper amount of distilled water. then cool it completely and add concentrate and alcohol with stirring. This process presents colloidal preceipitation of concentrate and easily solubilise all the constituents. After 24 hours, the alcoholis batch is chilled at -0.4 to -0.6°C and filterd, using asbestos wool and diatomaceous earth as filter aid.

Alcoholic Strengths

The perfume content of Colognes, eaux de toilette, eaux de-parfum and other funcifully named 'dilute perfumes' may range from 3 to 8 per cent, although in some few cases this figure has been found to exceed even 10 percent. There seems little point in marketing as a toilet water what is, in fact, a perfume-unless its water solubility has been artificially enhanced for the purpose.

Perfume themselves range from the perhaps old-fashioned 'low' of 10 per cent to 15, 20, 25 and even, quite irritationally. 35 per cent. The alcoholic strength may lie-between 85° and 95°.

Inexperienced perfumes, and some captains of industry in the perfumery would who are not perfumers, seem occasionally to believe that higher perfume concentration means enhanced strength and tenacity. This is not so. Sometimes the tenacitymay be slightly increased but, beyond a certain optimum level, the strength is not increased. Indeed, too high a concentration lowers the tonality of a perfume and flattens it out curtailing its ability to expand. With a very high concentration, dull; non diffusive perfumes result, and one of the most valued properties of a good grade of ethyl alcohol is wasted.

Control

Adequate checking and control methods are of course essential at all stages of perfume production: from the intake and assay of raw materials, through storage and processing to filling and packaging. The variability of certain materials because of batch or climatic deviations, etc., is an additional obstacle in the way of producing a uniform series over a period of time. The perfumer should be closely concerned with the provision and use of standard samples for odour checking and comparison. These standards must be kept in optimum conditions, i.e. where possible in sealed ampoules or under nitrogen. Watch should also be kept on the exact matching of colour shades.

It is frequently necessary to dilute 95 per cent alcohol to 90, 85, 80, 70 per cent or even lower strengths. To determine the amount of proof alcohol required is calculated using following formula :

$$\text{Amount of proof alcohol} = \frac{\%\text{ alcohol desired x Total volume}}{\%\text{ proof alcohol}}$$

$$= \% \frac{\text{alcohol desired x 1000}}{95}$$

e.g., prepared 90% alcohol using 95% proof alcohol.

$$\text{Amount of proof alcohol required} = \frac{90 \times 1000}{95}$$

$$= 947.3 \text{ ml}$$

It means 947.3 ml of 95% alcohol is diluted to 1000 ml using 52.7 ml of water.

90 per cent alcohol results from diluting 842 ml of 95 per cent alcohol to 1000 ml. 70 per cent alcohol is obtained by diluting 737 ml of 95 per cent alcohol; 60 per cent by, diluting 632 ml, 50 per cent by diluting 536 ml, and 45 per cent by diluting 474 ml to 1000 ml with purified water.

Contraction of volume and rise of temperature occur when ethyl alcohol and water are mixed. The final adjustment of volume when preparing these dilutions, is therefore made at the same temperature as that at which the 95 per cent alcohol is measured., i.e. about 20°C.

4

Packaging of Perfumes

INTRODUCTION

The elegant packing makes marketing easier. The essential factor in presenting perfume such as toilet water or cologne is, attractive package. The technology and aesthetic attitude has reduced the problems of packing.

Another important feature of packing is that, the other component parts of pack should also be attractive and have public acceptance. What will the public accept for purchasing and what will they not accept? It is difficult, for example. to get the public to accept a pack in which the bottle is presented horizontally. i.e. is lying down. why is this so? The reason is probably a fear that some of the perfume will spill and be lost, but there are other rejections and predilections for which there is no such ready explanation. One comes up against the imponderables of fashion and taste. Why is it that certain shapes of bottle simply will not sell? No obvious law regulates these' preferences and only experience and flair can guide the designer's choice.

The major disadvantage of the packaged perfume is that the bottle can give no idea of the contents and affords no means of appreciating them until, of course, it is opened. Hence the utility of tiny sample sizes and counter-displays featuring the perfume packed in an atomiser-dispenser. To attract the customer's attention. perfumers throughout the ages have tried to make the outward appearance of the pack as luxurious and conspicuous as the perfume deserves.

Packaging in the Past

In the fifteenth and sixteenth centuries perfumes were contained in cut crystal bottles. which were often encased in precious metal (gold. silver gil, silver). finely enwrought. The whole attached to a wrought chain of the same metal and carried cross-wise or by a short chain on the wrist, with the purse which elegant women also carried.

In the centuries that followed, the bottles were of precious metal or decorated porcelain. Private and public collections contain many objects of this kind, some of them very fine and luxurious.

It was really only in the nineteenth century, however, when the large perfumeries were started, that bottles of original shape were produced for this purpose, each belonging specifically to a certain perfume.

Glass or crystal bottles assumed the most varied forms, following the inspirations of fashion and the general artistic tendency of the times. These shapes were more or less felicitous, although some of them may now appear to us a little tasteless and clumsy.

On these bottles were glued labels showing the name of the perfume and that of the perfumery house which had created the perfume. These labels, sometimes multicoloured, were apt to state the extraordinary properties of the product. Their dimensions varied. Thus for toilet waters, lotions and eaux de Cologne, they were often rather large and covered the whole surface of the bottle. For extracts, where the bottles were of smaller size, the labels were smaller, very luxurious and in most 'cases gilded.

The coffrets or boxes in which the bottles were encased were often quite luxurious, with embroidered materials or printed silk fabrics vying with one another in luxury and sumptuousness.

THE IMPACT OF AÉROSOLS

The presentation was greately influenced due to development in bottle making. Aerosol packs raised the problems of valves, propellant reactions, and the use of metal cans or heavy and plastic-coated glass containers. An attempt was made to use neutral. odourless gases such as carbon dioxide and nitrogen. Labels then began to disappear and give way to printed decorations on the metal cans. With the coming of reduced internal pressures, glass containers with thinner walls became practicable. Concurrently the processes of printing on glass and productive of some fine, decorative effects were much improved.

As regards plastic bottles, due account has to be, taken of their permeability; which is in general unbalancing and sometimes actually denatures a perfume. Even the use in perfumery works of plastic pipes and tanks is often ruled out for this reason.

In case of lables whether they are still used or direct printing takes their place, the tendency has for some time been towards simplicity. This is' partly due to fashion and the streamlining tendency in production and partly, also, to the continual increase in the cost of manpower and man-hours. Jobs that are done by hand simply have to be minimis ed, especially when one is trying to refute the allegation that perfumes are excessively expensive luxuries making fabulous profits for their makers. Here we should add in parentheses that the manufacturing perfumers themselves, by frequently referring to and exaggerating the costliness of their raw materials and, so forth, are largely to blame for this absurd invention.

PERFUME IDENTITY

The packaged perfume can be identified by the name, the bottle, the label, the carton or coffret and the outer wrapping.

The Name

The name establishes the identity. The names of perfumes have been divided into five groups.

(1) Those refer to flowers, e.g., Rose jacqueminot? Vera violetta.

(2) Those refer to love, e.g., Amour-Amour.

(3) Homage to person, a regime or fashion, e.g., Zibeline.

(4) Those which have foreign names or evocative of exotic places or romantic occasions e.g. Nuit de Noel. Quadrille.

(5) Which are more abstract relating to letters and numbers, e.g., No. 5s N, S, Y.

The name must appeal to the class of customer for-whom the perfume is intended. It should suggest the personality of the perfume, be relatively simple, short, original and. easy to pronounce, even by foreigners (if export is to be considered).

Whoever chooses the name should appreciate the fact that the name is the perfume and is of extreme importance. Another fact that has to be faced is that in these days, in most so-called advanced countries, there exists a long list of names already registered as trade marks. The chosen name may not therefore be registrable. If not, another has to be chosen instead and then, perhaps, another and yet another. It is often wise to start with five or six alternatives, no matter how enthusiastic one may be about the name originally selected.

The Bottle

Bottles—are mostly of glass, fitted with metal or plastic closures and, additionally, with either plastic plugs or liners made of cork-and-metal or plastic material. Ground glass stoppers are now-a-days but rarely encountered, this being due to their involving too much hard labour and also to their suffering from the defect of 'rattling', Le. not fitting perfectly. Atomiser packs must also be noted.

In principle every large perfumery house has its own art department, whose function it is to be responsible to and with the management for all aspects of package design. This service involves the preparation of mockups or models of bottles, cartons, coffrets, labels etc. and it is necessarily accompanied by a technical service which pays close attention to all the practical details of presentation: screw threads of bottle necks and closures, dimensions of the boxes, quality control of all accessories, consideration of the quality of the glass. Rules and standards are laid down or devised, and these are then followed in collaboration with the purchasing department and the various supplie's.

Objectionably alkaline glass must in any case be avoided. In warm and humid climates it can result in bottles losing their polish and developing matt or frosted patches. The obsolete practice of packing in straw or contact with some qualities of board or even paper can similarly lead to matt or irridescent patches. Before use, bottles should be vigorously rinsed in demineralised water and thoroughly drained and dried.

Apart from the artistic merits of its line or shape, a perfumery bottle should always be steady on its base and not top heavy. The surprising fact is that this simple rule is sometimes broken.

Atomisers form a separate category. The internal gas pressures which they sustain make it essential for the glass containers to by cylindrical. Fancy shapes are out. Decoration is by printing on glass, this being the only process that can conveniently be used. The stainless metal closures, which are now available in various colour shades as well as in white or gilt, can be embellished with engraved or relief designs.

Labels

Despite the advances made in direct printing on to bottles, fine quality labels are still widely used. Their style and finish have never reached a higher standard than they reach today; and this particularly applies to very small labels meticulously designed and finished to the strictest specifications.

Labels, fabrics, board and paper that are likely to be exposed to daylight in window displays or on the user's dressing-table should be tested for their tendency to fade. This forcibly applies to many colour shades, as well as to gilded and silvered finishes. Such tests can be conducted in a solarium or by using arc lamps with selected electrodes always, of course, under standard conditions.

The adhesive used on metallised labels should be carefully chosen so as not to interact with the metal or varnish. Manufacturers should also beware of varnishes that can be dissolved or made tacky by spilt perfume.

Cartons and Coffrets

Each and every packaging material should be pre-tested and shelf-tested for faults. Some plastics, for example, show a marked disposition to warp when subjected to high humidity. Natural cork has the disadvantage of variability. Every aspect of a package should be studied as a possible source of off-odours. Nothing should be taken for granted: A rubber gasket in an aerosol container may contribute a disagreeable mercaptan note. Residual solvent odours from a label's ink or varnish, or from its adhesive-even the smallest items must be scrutinised as potential troublemakers. A product in a clear glass bottle is subject to the influence of light, and it must be remembered that some perfumery materials, in these conditions, will oxidise, resinify or discolour.

External Wrapping

The perfume coffret containing the precious bottle is often protected by being enclosed in an outer carton fabricated from white or grey chipboard, which in turn is enveloped in a decorated paper outer-wrap. This paper may be suitably embellished with the name of the perfume, the name of the firm, and sometimes a coded reference number. It should be identifiable at a glance, and should in fact be an attractive and recognisable advertisement for both the perfume and its makers.

The instantly identifiable signs such as large letters, bands of different colours are all helpful to the heavily stocked retailer in the management and arrangement' of wares. A good pack is one that inspires confidence in the product; that assures the user that the same perfume or one like it cannot be had under another label at half the price. Eccentric packs make a sensible woman think that the manufacturer takes her for a fool. There is one thing certain, and that is that a perfect pack is as rare as a really good perfume; which means that there are not very many on the market.

PERFUME AND THE WORLD OF FASHION

Whoever decides upon the perfume and the pack ought, in any case, to be familiar with the market, and this particularly applies in the case of an elegant perfume. Hence,. indeed, came -the many successes of the couturier and couturiere. the high-class dressmaking establishments, the trend-setters. The worlds of .fashion and art have to be frequented and appreciated, and their reactions and suggestions carefully taken into account but the immediate interpreter should be the perfumer, not the marketing executive, the advertising accounts man or the industrialist promoter.

The Question of Colour

Most fine quality perfumes are green or yellow, whether artificially tinted or not. At least one well-known perfume is blue, but the former fashion for perfumes and toilet waters in mauve, violet, pink etc. is no longer acceptable. Perfumers with little experience sometimes decide to add no colouring matter, but the fact is that a colourless perfume looks insipid, while a perfume with a natural colour will tend to vary in shade from one batch to another unless it is corrected each time by small additions of a suitable dye. In this way one guards against complaints from customers who see a colour change as indicative of a decline in quality.

THE MEANS OF ADVERTISING

Press Publicity

One extraordinary feature of the selling of fine perfumes is that this has hitherto been achieved almost entirely without the aid of memorable commercial publicity. We say 'commercial' because writers and journalist have more than compensated for that deficiency. Books on advertising and motivation research seem to give very little space" or attention to perfumery marketing.

Samples and Models

All forms of publicity should be considered on their merits for each particular case; the usual media, such as magazines and journals, newspapers, television and commercial radio; window displays, even perfumed cards and theatre programmes. The distribution of small samples of a perfume can provide excellent publicity, but it is costly and can be wasteful unless it is handled with discernment by the retailers.

Finally there is a direct form of showing one's wares to the public which consists of vapourisirig them in theatres, cinemas or other suitable places to the public. A variation of this method is the presentation of a perfume on a female model, just as a gown is presented on a mannequin. This method is particularly suitable for the introduction of a new couturier perfume during a showing of the latest season's fashions, so long as each day is confined merely to the showing of one perfume. This idea can be carried further by suggesting that special rooms or cubicles, or even travelling air-conditioned units, could be devised as a means of perfume advertising or collaborative perfumery, propaganda, the perfume being sprayed into the space on to selected wall or other surfaces and subsequently removed by modern air conditioning in order to prepare the space for the next perfume. In this way, a whole series of perfumes might be presented in sequence. 'During the brief intervals required for deodourisation, music could be played and time allowed for conversation. This might be an amusing as well as a novel way of encouraging the appreciation of fine perfumes.'

5

Testing of Perfumes

INTRODUCTION

The quality of the perfume is adjudged on the basis of analysis of its every constituent. The process involves two basic steps : (a) Sampling and (b) Analysis. The analysis is sub-divided into physical and chemical analysis. The physical analysis include, estimation of colour, specific gravity, viscosity. optical rotation, residue. solubility, melting and boiling ranges, olfactory assessment and freezing point. The chemical analysis include, determination of water content. alcohol and acid values, ester value, carbonyl value, and content. phenol, cineole. petroleum and mineral oil, chlorine and heavy metal content.

SAMPLING

The mode of sampling varies with the physical state of sample and from which it has to be drawn. In case of liquid product the sampling also depend upon number and capacity of containers. The following precautions should be taken while carrying out sampling.

(i) The sampling device should be cleaned and inert e.g. aluminium or glass is most suitable.

(ii) If samples are drawn from different containers of same products. all of them should be properly mixed:

(iii) The sampling container should be completely filled, sealed airtight after sampling with suitable labels.

(iv) Store samples in cool and dark place and if required in inert atmosphere.

(v) Samples should be protected from moisture, dust and spilage.

Sampling Equipment

Three types of sampling equipments are available.

(i) Closed type (divided or undivided) : The closed type of sampling tubes are used for heterogeneous, semi-liquids, free-flowing powders and pastes.

(ii) Open type : The open type sampling tubes are used for homogenous samples.

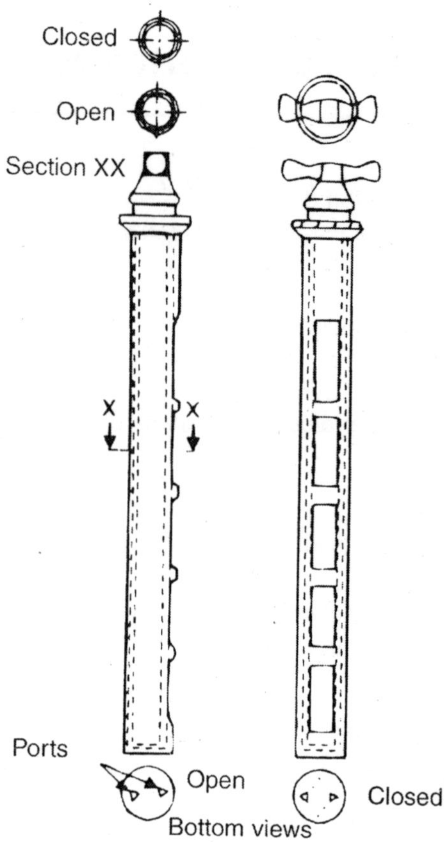

Fig. 5.1 Closed type samplit, tube , undivided

(iii) Sampling scoop : The samples in the form of powders, crystals, tablets and lumps if broken into pieces can be sampled.

Closed type (Undivided)

It consists of two concentric metallic tubes closely fitted into each other throughout their entire length, so that one tube can be rotated within the other. Longitudinal opening of about one-third the circumference are cut in both tubes (Fig. 5.1).

In one position, the openings in the two tubes coincide; the sample tube is open when in this position and admits the material. By turning the inner tube through an angle of 180°, it becomes a sealed container. The inner tube may have a diameter of 20 to 40 mm and. is undivided along its length to serve as a single container.

The two concentric tubes shall be provided with V-shaped ports at their lower ends, so placed that the material contained in the equipment can be drained through them, when the longitudinal openings are in line.

The length of the equipment shall be such as to enable it to reach the bottom of the container being sampled.

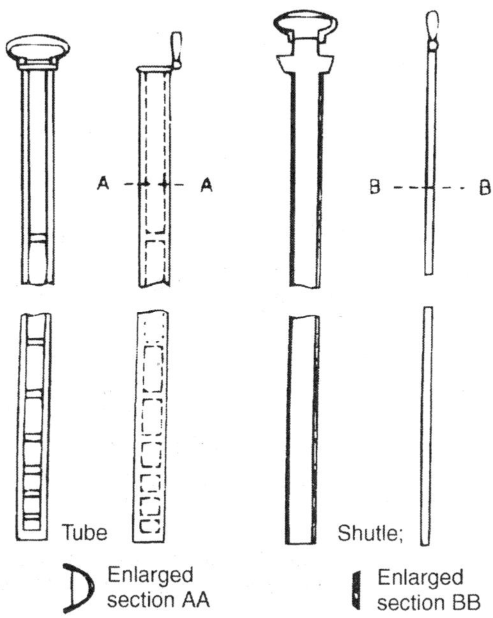

Fig. 5.2 Closed type sampling tube, divided

The equipment is inserted closed. the material is admitted by opening it and finally it is closed and withdrawn.

Closed type (Divided)

It is also of metal and has D-shaped cross-section. It is provided with comments along its length and is opened and closed by means of a closely fitting, shutter which moves up and down throughout the entire length. It may be from 25 to 50 mm wide (Fig. 5.2).

The equipment is inserted closed, the shutter is pulled out to admit the materiaL and the tube is then closed and withdrawn.

Open type

It is made of metal or thick glass, and may. be of 20 to 40 mm diameter and 400 to 800 mm length. The upper and lower ends are conical and narrow down to 5 to 10 mm diameter. Handling is facilitated by two rings at the upper end (Fig. 5.3). For taking a sample. the equipment is first closed at the top with the thumb or a stopper and lowered until the desired depth is reached. It is then opened for a short time to admit the material and finally closed and withdrawn.

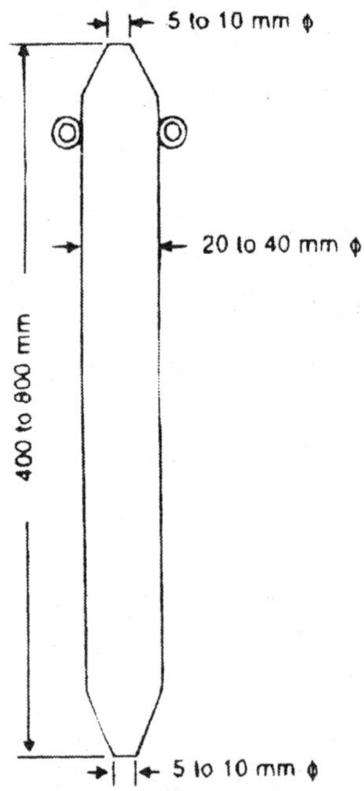

Fig. 5.3 Open type sampling tube.

Sampling scoop

The sampling scoop made of a suitable metal shall be as shown in Fig. 5.4.

Sampling from tanks

First withdraw five partial samples from each container at (a) 10% of the total depth (b) 1/3 of total depth (c) 1/2 of the total depth (d) 2/3 of the total depth (e) 90% of the total depth and mix them to obtain one homogenous sample. From this make three equal representative sample. In case of impurities at the surface of essential oiL sample it separately, mix it and obtain three representative sample.

The composite sample can be obtained by taking equal quantity of material from the three samples obtained and mixed. The quantity of the sample should be sufficient to carry out triplicate analysis.

All the individual and composite samples shall be divided into three equal parts, one for the purchaser, another for the supplier and the third to be used as a referee sample: For packing of individual and composite sample and for referee test samples the procedure are given below in preparation of test samples.

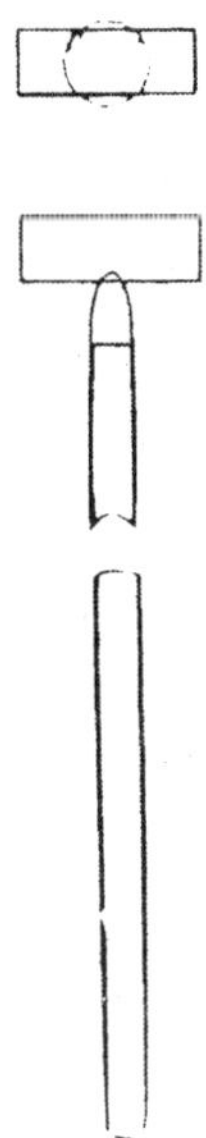

Fig. 5.4 Sampling scoop.

The number of containers to be selected for this purpose (n) shall depend on the size of lot (N) and shall be in accordance with Table 5.I.

The containers shall be selected at random. In order to ensure the randomness of selection, following procedure may be adopted

(1) If the lot consists of individually packed containers, then starting, from any container in the lot. count them in any suitable order as 1. 2, 3 ....

up to, r and so on where r is the integral part of *N/n.* Every rth container thus counted shall be withdrawn till the requisite number of containers is obtained.

(2) If the lot consists of cartons or cardboard boxes each containing more than one container, then a certain number of boxes (not less than '5 per cent of the total number of boxes in the lot wherever feasible) shall be chosen first. From each of the boxes so chosen, approximately equal number of containers shall then be selected so as to obtain the required number of containers specified in Table 5.1.

Table 5.1 Scale of sampling

Size of the Lot (N) (No. of Containers)	Minimum No. of Containers to be selected (n)
1 to 3	Each container
4 to 20	3
21 to 60	4
61 to 80	5
81 to 120	6
121 and above	One is every twenty

From each of the containers selected according a small representative portion of the material shall be drawn with the help of the sampling equipment. The approximate quantity of material to be drawn from a container shall be nearly equal to thrice the quantity required for testing indicated below.

Criteria for conformity

For individual samples

For each of those characteristics, which have been determined on the individual samples the mean (x) and range (R) of test results shall be calculated as follows:

$$\text{Mean } (\bar{x}) = \frac{\text{The sum of test results}}{\text{Number of test results}}$$

Range (R) = The difference between the maximum and the minimum values of the test results.

If the specification limit for the characteristic is given as a minimum, then the value of the expression (x - KR) shall be calculated from the relevant test results. If the value so obtained is greater than or equal to the minimum limit. the lot shall be declared as conforming to the requirement of that characteristic. If the specification limit for the characteristic is given as a maximum, then the value of the expression (z+ KR) shall be calculated from the relevant test results. If the value so obtained is less than or equal to the maximum limit. the lot shall be declared as conforming to the requirement of that characteristic. If the characteristic has bilateral specification limits, then the values of the expression (X. ± KR) shall be calculated from the relevant test results. If the values so obtained lie between the two specification limits, the lot shall be declared as conforming to the requirements of that characteristic. The value of the factor K referred shall be chosen in accordance with Table 5.2. given below, depending upon the acceptable quality leveL namely, the percentage of non-conforming containers that could reasonably be tolerated.

Table 5.2. Values of K for achieving different acceptable quality levels.

Acceptable Quality Level	Value of K
Not more than 3 per cent defectives	0.4
Not more than 1.5 per cent defectives	0.5
Not More than 0.5 per cent defectives	0.6

For declaring the conformity of the lot to the requirements of all other characteristics determined on the composite sample, the test results for each of the characteristic shall satisfy the relevant requirements given in the product specification.

Examples

In case of oil of peppermint total alcohols as menthol (per cent by mass) is to be tested on individual samples and the value of K has been chosen as 0.4. In the case of pine oil 'Specification of pine oil', distillation yield (per cent by volume) and total alcohols as terpineol (per cent by mass) are to be tested on individual samples and the value of K is 0.5. The conformity of the lot to the specification requirement in these two cases shall be judged as follows :

Product	Characteristic	Type	Specification Requirements	Criteria for Confirmity
Peppermint oil	Total alcohols as menthol, per cent by mass	1	75, Min.	$(\bar{x} - 0.4\ R) \geq 75$
	-do-	2	45, Min.	$(\bar{x} - 0.4\ R) \geq 45$
Pine oil	Distillation	Below 185°C	5.0, Max.	$(\bar{x} - 0.5\ R) \geq 5.0$
	yield, per cent	Below 200°C	25.0, Max.	$(\bar{x} - 0.5\ R) \geq 25.0$
	by volume	Below 230°C	95.0, Min.	$(\bar{x} - 0.5\ R) \geq 95.0$
	Total alcohols as terpineol, per cent by mass		70, Min	$(\bar{x} - 0.5\ R) \geq 70$

Packing and labelling

All containers should bear labels showing at least the following information to guarantee the authenticity, indentity of the sample and sealed

(1) Sample number;

(2) Nature and quantity of the product;

(3) Name of the owner or his authorised representative;

(4) Date of sampling;

(5) Number. kind and marking of the containers;

(6) Signatures and names and, if necessary addresses of the interested parties or their authorised representatives; and

(7) Signature and name of the sampling supervisor.

Instructions regarding costly materials

Small containers are generally used for packing costly products. The bulk sampling depends on the number of containers used; the combined partial samplings, however, shall not exceed the quantities necessary for a normal analysis. The interested parties shall agree in advance as to the size of the bulk sample and the manner in which it shall be done.

ANALYSIS

The representative sample obtained using above procedure is brought to the laboratory for physical and chemical analysis ..

Preparation of the Material for Physico-chemical Analysis

Remove as far as possible any visible water present in the sample by decanting, then add about 10 per cent by mass of neutraL freshly ignited and powdered magnesium sulphate and shake the mixture vigorously from time to time during a period of 2 hours. Filter through paper and store if necessary in clean, dry, airtight, opaque, non-absorbent containers, preferably of glass or of metal on which the sample has no action. Fill the sample containers leaving a little air space to allow for expansion and immediately seal after filling. Use only new good quality corks or glass stoppers or screw-lids in the case of glass containers and new good quality corks or sore stoppers in the case of metal containers. To prevent contact with the sample, aluminium foil or other suitable material may be wrapped round corks. Protect samples frbm heat.

In the case of perfumery materials which are solid or partly solid at room temperature (oils of rose and guaiac wood) warm the material just sufficiently to liquefy if and proceed as above, maintaining the temperature so that it remains liquid throughout. The colour of some dark coloured perfumery materials may be lightened by shaking them intermittently for 10 minutes with 1 per cent (mlm) of tartaric or citric acid. Filter and proceed as above.

Physical Analysis

The original containers selected for sampling and the test samples drawn, as the case may be should be opened and the condition of the content noted for colour, clarity and by note. Then the following physical properties of the sample were determined.

Estimation of relative density

Estimation of relative density by Pyknometer

Principle

The relative density of perfume is very important as it plays vital role in the measurement. It is defined as the ratio of the density of the liquid material to the distilled water at 27°C. It is dimensionless.

Apparatus

Pyknometer or specific gravity bottle, water bath and analytical balance, thermometer.

Procedure

First clean and rinse pyknometer or specific gravity bottle with alcohol and dry it. Take weight of empty specific gravity bottle with stopper. Fill the specific gravity bottle with distilled water and weight it. Empty the bottle, dry it and filled it with material under the test, and weight it. Take all weights at 27°C.

Calculation

$$\text{mt The relative density (d)} = \frac{m_3 - m_1}{m_2 - m_1}$$

m_1 - Weight of empty specific gravity bottle at 27°C

m_2 - Weight of specific gravity bottle with water at 27°C

m_3 - Weight of specific gravity bottle with test material at 27°C

Determination of freezing point

Principle

Either the constant temperature, or the maximum temperature, observed when the oil. in a supercooled liquid state, liberates its latent heat of fusion. Slow and progressive cooling of the essential oil. Observation of the variations in temperature as the oil passes from the liquid to the solid state.

Apparatus

Calibrated thermometers, test tube, stout-walled test tube rubber stopper.

Procedure

First fill the container with water. melting ice, or freezing mixture so as to obtain a temperature 5°C less than the freezing point of material. Fit the stout-walled test tube through rubber stopper. Place 10 ml of-essential oil in the test tube, dip thermometer in it and place it in stout-walled test tube and allow the temperature to fall further up to 2°C. (Fig. 5.5).

Seed the oil with a trace of the solidified oil, obtained in the preliminary test, and stir vigorously with the thermometer, taking care to avoid the adhesion of particles to the walls of the tube. Observe the temperature variations as carefully as possible.

Note the observed temperature when the temperature curve in relation to time shows a maximum value, or a constant level for at least 1 min.

Remove the test tube from the apparatus and again liquefy the essential oil. Repeat the determination until two consecutive results do not differ by more than O.2°C. Average the two last readings to obtain final figure.

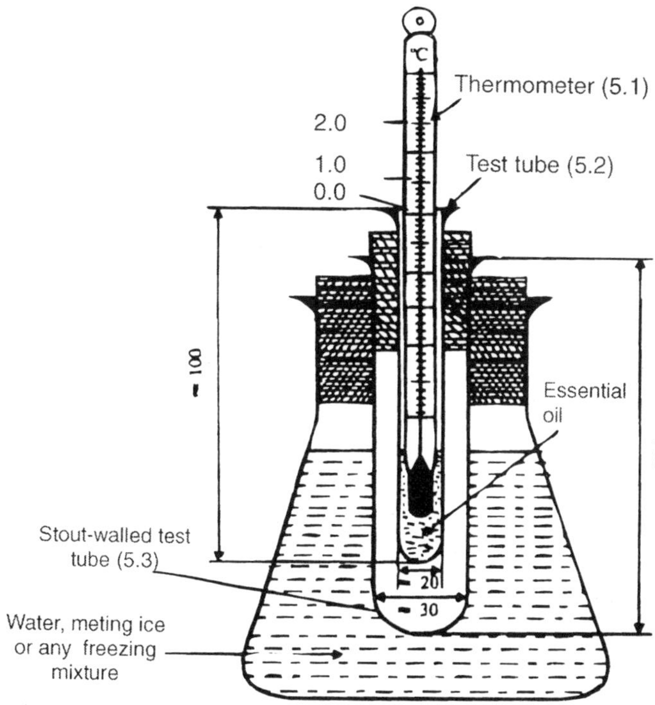

(All dimensions in milimeters)

Fig. 5.5 Suitable apparatus assembly for determination of freezing point.

Results

The freezing point is the maximum temperature observed at the end of the test. It is expressed in degree celsius to one decimal place.

Determination of refractive index by refractometer

Principle

Refractive index is the ratio of the sine of the angle of incidence to the sine of the angle of refraction, when a ray of light of defined wavelength passes from air into the material kept at constant temperature. The wavelength is 589.3 ± 0.3 run corresponding with D_1 and D_2 lines of sodium spectrum. The reference temperature is 27°C except those which are not liquid at this temperature, in which case a higher temperature (say 30°C) depending on the melting point of the material shall be used.

Apparatus

Refractometer, light source (Sodium light).

Procedure

Pass a stream of water through the instrument so as to keep it at the temperature at which the readings must be made. This temperature shall not differ from the reference temperature by more than ± 02°C. Before placing the material in the instrument, bring the test sample to a temperature similar to that at which the measurement must be made. Make readings only when the temperature is stable.

Calculation

Determination of solubility in ethanol

The refractive index n^t_D at the specified temperature is given by the following formula :

$$n^t_D = n^t_D + 0.0004\ (t-t)$$

where

n^t_D is the reading taken at the working temperature *t*.

Principle

An essential oil is said to be soluble in V volumes and more of ethanol of given strength, t when the mixture of I volume of the oil in question with V volumes of that ethanol is clear and stays so after further gradual addition of ethanol of the same strength up to a total of 20 volumes.

An essential oil is said to be soluble in V volumes of ethanol of given strength, t and to become cloudy when diluted in V' volumes, when the mixture of 1 volume of the oil in question with V volumes of that ethanol is clear, becomes cloudy after further gradual addition of (V'-V) volumes of ethanol of the same strength, and remains cloudy after further addition of ethanol up to a total of volumes.

An essential oil is said to to be soluble in V volumes of ethanol of given strength t, and to become cloudy when diluted in Y volumes, when the mixture of 1 volume of the oil in question with V volumes of that ethanol is clear, becomes cloudy after further gradual addition of (V'--V) volumes of ethanol of the same strength, and again becomes cloudy after further addition of (V"-VI volumes of ethanol of the same strength.

An essential oil is said to be soluble with opalescence when alcoholic solution is being diluted shows a bluish tinge, this even being similar to that of the standard of opalescence, freshly prepared.

Apparatus

Burette, Measuring cylinder. constant temperature device, thermometer.

Reagents

Dilute solution of ethanol: Solutions of 50, 60, 70, 80, 90 and 95 per cent (v/v). Standard solution for opalescence : Add 0.5 ml of 0.1 N silver nitrate solution to 50 ml of 0.0002 N sodium chloride solution and one drop of 25 per cent (m/m) nitric acid. Stir the solution and allow it to stand for 5 minutes.

Procedure

Measure 1 ml of the material into the cylinder either with a pipette or by weighing to an accuracy of ± 5 mg. Place the cylinder and its contents in the constant temperature device maintained at a temperature of 27 ± 0.2°C. Using the burette, add the diluted solution of ethanol of known strength, which has previously been brought to a temperature of 27 ± 0.2°C by increments of 0.1 ml until the material is completely dissolved, shaking frequently and vigorously during the addition of the solvent. When the solution is perfectly clear, record the volume of ethanol solution added. Continue to add the solvent by increments of 0.5 ml up to 20 mL and keep shaking after each addition. If the solution becomes cloudy or opalescence before a total volume of 20 ml of ethanol has been added, record the volume of ethanol solution added at the point where cloudiness or opalescence appears and. if applicable. the volume at which it disappears. If a clear solution is not obtained when 20 m1 of solvent has been added. repeat with the next higher concentration of ethanol solution given in Table 15.3.

Calculations

If V is the volume in.m!. of dilute solution of ethanol of dilution t to obtain a clear solution.

If V" is the volume, in m!. of dilute solution of ethanol of dilution t to obtain cloudiness after the clearness, if it occurs; and

If V' is the volume in ml of dilute solution of ethanol of dilution t at which cloudiness disappears; the, solubility of .the material in the dilute solution of ethanol of strength t will be 1 volume in Y volumes, with cloudiness between V' and Y" volumes.

Table 5.3. Dilutions of ethanol by volume and by mass.

Dilutions: ml of ethanol in 100 ml of the mixture (% V/V) to ± 0.1 % (% v/v)	*Volume of distilled water at 20°C to be added to 100 ml of ethanol* 95 % *(V/V) at the same temperature within ± 0.1°C, for the preparation of the corresponding dilutions* (ml)	*Mass of ethanol* 95 % *(v/v)* (g)	*Mass of water to be added* (g)	*Limits of relative density and the apparent specific gravity* d^{20}_{20}	d^{27}_{4}
50	95.8	46	54	0.931 6 to 0.932 0	0.927 9
60	62.9	56.4	43.6	0.910 5 to 0.911 9	0.906 4
70	39.1	67.6	32.4	0.886 8 to 0.881 3	0.882 5
80	20.9	79.6	20.4	0.860 4 to 0.861 0	0.856 0
90	6.4	92.7	7.3	0.830 3 to 0.830 9	0.825 8
95	0.0	100	0	0.812 3 to 0.813 1	0.808 0

If the solution is not entirely clear, but only opalescent record whether the opalescence is 'greater than, equal to' or less than that of the standard solution.

Determination of *optical rotation* and *specific rotation* by *polarimeter*

Principle

The optical rotation. The angle through which the plane of polarised light is rotated by a layer 10 cm thick of the material under test at a specified temperature. The wave length of radiation used should be 589.3 ± 0.3 nm.

The specific rotation. The optical activity of the material in a solution determined at a particular temperature and spectral line of light source.

Apparatus

Polarimeter. monochromatic light source. polarimeter tubes. thermometer.

Procedure

Optical rotation. Switch on the monochromatic light source and wait till - full luminosity is obtained. Determine the zero error of the instrument. Fill the polarimeter tube with the material, ensure that air bubble is absent. Place the tube in the polarimeter and read the dextrorotatory (+) or laevorotatory (-) optical rotation on the scale of the instrument. After carefully adjusting the analyser so that both the. halves of the field when viewed through the telescope. should show illumination of equal intensities.

When the room temperature is outside the limits 17 to 27°C or when the material contains large amounts of highly optically active constituents. use a jacketed polarimeter tube provided with water circulation at 27°C. By means of a thermometer inserted in the central opening check that the temperature of the material in the tube is 27 ± I °C. Record the results as the average of at least three readings; the readings should agree within 0.08°(5'). Make zero error correction if any.

Specific rotation. Dissolve the material in rectified spirit reserving a separate portion of the solvent for a blank determination. Make at least five readings of the rotation of ·the solution at 27 ± I°C Replace the solution with the reserved portion of the solvent. make the same number of readings and determine the average which shall be zero point value. Subtract the zero point value from the average observed rotation; if the two figures are of the same sign or add. if opposite in sign. to obtain the corrected observed rotation.

Calculation

$$\text{Specific rotation (a)} = \frac{100\ a}{1\ p\ d} = \frac{100\ a}{1\ c}$$

where

a = the corrected observed rotation in degrees of the solution at temperature to, using D line of sodium or yellow -green line of mercury as the case may be;

1 = the length in mm of polarimeter tube;

d = the relative density of the material at the temperature of observation (t°C)' p = the concentration of the material expressed as grams of active substance in 100 g of solution; and

c = the concentration of material expressed as the number of grams of active substance in 100 ml of solution.

Determination of melting point and melting range Principle

The temperature at which the material melts and becomes liquid throughout as shown by the formation of a definite meniscus is known as the melting point of the material.- The temperature between which the material collapses against the side of the tube and the temperature at which it is liquid throughout, is known as the melting range of the material.

Apparatus

Capillary tube, thermometer and glass heating vessel.

Procedure

Spread a small quantity of the finely powdered material in a thin layer and dry at a temperature below its melting point/melting range in an oven, or in a vacuum desiccator over sulphuric acid for 24 hours.

Transfer a quantity of the dried powder to a dry capillary tube and pack the powder by tapping the tube on a hard surface so as to form a tightly packed column of 2 to 4 mm in height. Attach the capillary tube and its contents to the thermometer so that the dosed end is at the level of the middle of the bulb, and heat in the heating vessel. regulating the rise of temperature during the first period to 3 deg per minute. When the temperature reached is 10 deg below the expected melting point/melting range, of the material being tested, the heating of the vessel is adjusted so that the rate of rise in temperature is 1 to 2 degree per minute.

Results

For melting point, note the temperature reading at which the liquefaction of the material occurs. For melting range, note the temperature reading at which the material collapses against the side of the tube and material remains liquid throughout.

Determination of boiling (Distillation) range Principle

This -method specifies a method of test for determininu the boiling (distillation) range of perfumery materials.

The range of temperature between which a liquid boils or the percentage of the material that distill between two specified temperatures is determined.

The lower of the two temperatures is the corrected thermometer reading when the first five drops of distillate have been collected, and the upper temperature is the corrected reading when the per centage specified has been collected. This method covers the distillation of aromatic perfumery materials of relatively narrow boiling ranges between 30°C and 250°C.

Apparatus

Distillation flask, water condenser, receiver, asbestos sheet, heating mantle thermometer.

Procedure

Assemble the apparatus as shown in Fig 5.6. Carefully measure a 100-ml sample of the material to be tested in the 100-ml graduated cylinder at room temperature and transfer to the distillation flask, draining the cylinder at least 15 s. This is preferably done before mounting the flask in position in order to prevent liquid from entering the side arm. Connect the flask to the condenser and apparatus, assembled as shown in Fig. 5.7. Do not rinse out the graduated cylinder used to measure the sample for distillation, but place under the lower end of the condenser tube to receive the distillate. Heat the flask slowly, especially after ebullition has begun, so as to allow the mercury column of the thermometer to become fully expanded before the first drop

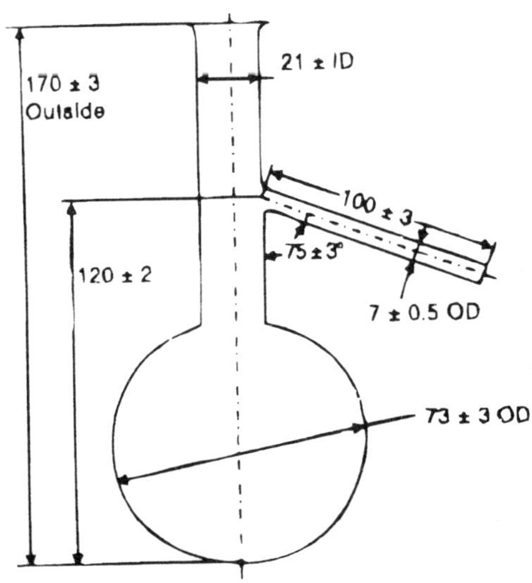

All dimensions in millimetres.

Fig. 5.6 Distillation flask.

distills over. Regulate the rate of heating so that the ring of condensing vapour on the wall of the flask reaches the lower edge of the side arm in not less than 90s, and preferably approximately 120s, from the start of the rise of the vapour ring. The total titre from the start of heating until the first drop falls into the receiver should be not less than 5 nor more than 10 minutes. Avoid major changes in heating rate. Even operation is best gained through experience with the method. When distillation starts, adjust the receiver to allow condensate to flow down its inner wall to prevent loss by spattering; then adjust the heater to continue the distillation at the rate of 5 to 7 ml/min (about 2 drops/ s). Maintain this rate, and continue the distillation to dryness.

Record the temperature reading when the first drop of distillate falls into the receiving cylinder. Take additional readings when 5 per cent, 10 per cent, each additional 10 per cent up to 90 per cent, and 95 per cent of the sample have distilled over. Take a final reading when the liquid just disappears from the bottom of the flask. When testing crude materials, a decomposition point, rather than, a dry point, may be obtained. When a decomposition point is reached at the end of a distillation, the temperature will frequently cease

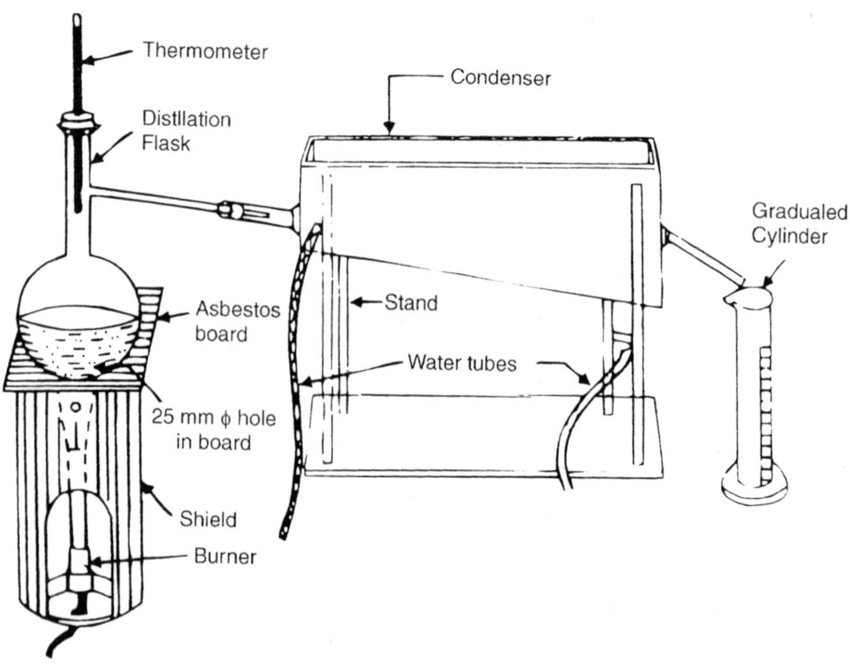

Fig. 5.7 Assembly of apparatus for distillation test.

to rise and begin to fall. In these case, take the temperature at the decomposition point as the maximum temperature observed. The decomposition point may also be indicated by the appearance of fumes in the flask. Should that occur, record the temperature at the time the bulb of the flask becomes substantially full of fumes.

Observe and record the following additional data at the time and place of the distillation test.

(1) Number of degree graduations on the emergent stem from top of cork to the graduation at the observed temperature, and the average temperature of the exposed stem.

(2) Correction for inaccuracy of the thermometer.

Emergent stem corrections: Any convenient mercury. etched glass stem thermometer with a range including 20 to 40°C may be used for determining the temperature of exposed stem of the Distillation thermometer. Calculate the correction for emergent stem of the thermometer as follows :

$$C=KN\,(T-t)$$

where

C = Number of degrees celsius to be added to .the observed thermometer reading;

K = Correction factor for the thermometer = 0:000154 = difference between coefficients of expansion for glass and for mercury;

N = Number of degree graduations on the stem exposed;

T = Observed reading of the thermometer in degrees celsius; and t = Average temperature of the emergent, stem in degrees celsius.

Method for olfactory assessment of natural and synthetic perfumery materials

Principle

Natural, and synthetic perfumery materials, such as essential oils, aromatic chemicals, etc., are used primarily for their odour appeal. Although the analytical. characteristics which are commonly determined may provide some assurance regarding the chemical purity of an odouriferous substance, they do not necessarily indicate the 'purity' of odour. Hence, olfactory evaluation has been practised for centuries and, in.'the perfumery trade, it has been formed the basis of acceptance or rejection of odouriferous materials.

In spite of the importance attached to this subject, there is no uniform method for odour evaluation nor has a standard procedure yet been formulated in any country. This standard was formulated with a View to introduce a uniform method of test for olfactory assessment of natural and synthetic perfumery materials.

This method for olfactory assessment of. natural and synthetic perfumery materials is based on comparison of a given material with its corresponding standard sample.

Terminology

For the purpose of this method the following definitions shall apply.

Top note. The initial and primary odour effect perceived. by the olfactory nerves on smelling a strip freshly impregnated with the material being tested. The top note(s) is (are) usually of a short duration and mayor may not be co-perceived along with the middle note.

Middle note. The secondary overall odour effect experienced by the olfactory nerves on smelling a strip impregnated with the material after the initial top note has evaporated. It lasts for a longer time on the strip than the top note.

Residual note (Dry-out note). The tertiary odour effect experienced by olfactory nerves on smelling a strip impregnated with a material after the top and the middle notes have disappeared. Besides indicating the lasting character and strength of the material, it may also reveal the nature of the lesser volatile materials.

By note. An odour effect, additional to the normal pattern of odours associated with the material, experienced by olfactory nerves on smelling an impregnated strip during any stage of evaporation. It is generally regarded as an index of foreign odour and/or undesirable adulterant and alien.

Odour description. Due to the absence of precise terms, descriptive words which are subjective in nature are commonly used to express the odour sensations perceived in the top, middle, residual and by-notes. Some of these terms are given below but the list is not intended to be exhaustive : acid, acrid, aldehydic, amber, animal, Balsamic, bitter, burnt, camphoraceous, choking, citrus, cloying, cooL dry, dull, earthy, exalting, faecal, fatty, fishy, floral, fungal, fresh, fruity, goaty, grassy, green, heavy herbaL honey, intense, leafy, leathery, minty, mossy, mushroomy, musky, musty, nauseating. orientaL peppery, persistent, phenolic, piney, powdery, pungent, refreshing, sappy, sharp, sickly, smoky, sour, spicy, stem like, still odour, sulphuraceous, sultry, sweet, tarry, tart, woody.

Requirements. The following general precautions are required to be noted.

Selection and training. Better results are obtained if individuals with a keen sense of smell and ability to distinguish between different odours are selected for training in olfactory assessment.

Fatigue. Continuous smelling causes olfactory fatigue and decreases. critical odour perception. To avoid this, the number of samples assessed during a session should be limited as far as is practical. Further, during smelling, the body should be relaxed. Resting for an interval between smelling different samples is also advantageous. If the number of samples to be tested is fairly large, it is advisable to examine last those materials which are known to be pungent or strong in odour. It should be borne in mind that inability to correctly identify certain odours may arise from natural deficiencies such as specific anosmia. For instance, some people are unable to perceive musky odour.

Bias. The necessity of minimising all differences between samples other than that of odour in order to prevent the prejudicing of results is stressed. 'Blind' tests should be conducted by ensuring that the markings on the smelling strip do not dislodge the origin of the samples.

Time of olfactory assessment. The evidence relating to the most favourable time for conducting olfactory assessment is somewhat conflicting. However, the morning appears to be generally favoured.

In general olfactory assessment should be done after a reasonable interval of time has elapsed after a meal or a beverage has been taken.

Freedom from contaminating odours. It is necessary to ensure that the hands. nose and smelling strips are free from contaminating odours as these are likely to vitiate the results. It is recommended that the individual responsible for assessing odour should wash his/her hands several times during a smelling session as well as clear his/her nose.

Material Requirements

The following materials, apparatus and environmental conditions are required

Library of standard samples. For each essential oil, aromatic chemical or other perfumery material, there shall be a standard sample of, approved odour value as agreed upon by the purchaser and the supplier. The standard samples shall be kept in well-stoppered. air-tight, neutral amber-coloured glass bottles and when not in use, they shall be stored in a refrigerator at about 5°C. The odour characteristics of standard samples are likely to change over a period of time however well they may be stored. Some materials improve in odour as a result of maturing while others deteriorate because of minute oxidative changes. An alteration in the odour characteristics of standard samples is not desirable and, in such cases, fresh standards should be adopted. Generally, all perfumery materials have recommended shelf life and the sample should be changed thereafter.

Ethyl alcohol. Perfumery grade.

Diethyl phthalate. Perfumery grade.

Smelling strips. These shall preferably be 1 cm wide and 15 cm long. They shall be made from odourless. thin, absorbent paper and shall be sufficiently stiff so that the strips do not. bend under their own weight when held in a horizontal position. Smelling strips shall be packed in air-tight, odour-free containers and stored in a clean odour-free room. Those intended for daily use shall preferably be kept in a wide-mouthed glass bottle covered by a beaker.

Strip stand. A cruciform patterned 3-clip stand. approximately 21 cm high, or any other suitable device, to hold impregnated smelling strips as shown in Fig. 5.8.

Environment. A well-ventilated room, as free as possible from all outside disturbances. Ideally, the temperature and humidity suited are about 20°C and 80 per cent RH. respectively. The colouring of the room shall be sober and the furnishing restricted: The general environment shall have a restful rather than a distracting effect.

Procedure. One end of each smelling strip shall be clearly marked before use. Dip the unmarked end of one strip (about 0.5 to 1.0 cml in the material under examination and of another strip to the same depth in the standard sample after it has attained room temperature. For certain perfumery materials. such as fatty aldehydes. absolutes and solids. use 1 to 10 per cent solutions in ethyl alcohol or diethyl phthalate -for, olfactory assessment.

For semi-solid materials. The odour of semi-solid materials such as guaiacwood oiL oakmoss resinoid arid absolute. labdanum resinoid and absolute. etc .. should be taken on smelling strips but only after melting the contents completely under controlled temperature below 100°C preferably

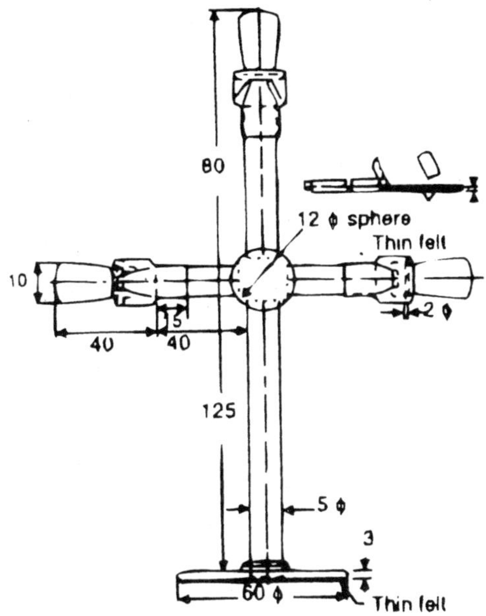

All dimensions in millimetres

Fig. 5.8 Strip stand.

on water-bath.

For solid materials. The odour of solid materials. such as coumarin. musk. ambrette. etc .. should be examined after pouring out some quantity (about 5 g) on odour-free non-absorbent paper (such as glassine). Solids should be smelt both as such. as well as after crushing to enable the occluded impurities to be perceived more easily.

For strong-smelling materials. In order to have a better perception, strong smelling substances irrespective of their physical appearance may also be smelt after dilution to about 1. to 10 per cent such as mdole, fatty aldehydes, etc., using ethanol or digthylphthalate as a diluent.

Hold the strip impregnated with the standard sample at such a distance from the nose that there is incipient yet distinct perception of odour. While smelling, concentrate wholly on the sensations received and make mental observations. Repeat the procedure with the strip impregnated with the test sample. After about a minute's rest, repeat the comparison reversing the order of smelling the two strips. Finally, compare the two strips for their odour in a 'blind' test. If a difference in odour is observed, repeat the 'blind' test on the two strips five times. Record the observations of each 'blind' test.

It is important to note that although the room shall be well-ventilated, the strips kept under examination should not be exposed to a direct draught.

After this initial assessment for top notes, fix the two strips on a stand keeping them sufficiently apart to avoid inter-contamination. Examine the strips periodically by the 'blind' test and note the changes in quality and intensity of odour. Continue in this manner as long as the odour on each strip remains perceptible.

Report. Report the top, middle and residual odour assessment of the test sample as compared with the odour of the standard sample at corresponding stages of assessment.

Criterion for judgement of quality. The odour of the material under examination shall correspond to that of the standard at all stages of assessment. If it does not and the pattern of odour is considered to be inferior to that of the standard, the quality of the material shall be regarded as not satisfactory.

Referee test. In case of dispute, present the individual assessing odour with three suitably coded smelling strips, two of which have been dipped in the material under examination and the remaining one in the standard sample (or vice-versal. If the 'odd' sample is consistently picked five times in a 'blind' test, the material shall be deemed to have a pattern of odour different from that of the standard sample.

Determination of residue on evaporation

Apparatus

Evaporation basin, water-bath.

Preparation of sample

The quantity of the perfumery material shall be taken in accordance with Table 5.4.

Procedure

Weigh the dry basin. Weigh into the basin a suitable quantity of perfumery material- as given in Table 5.4 and place the basin and contents on the vigorously boiling water-bath. Screen from draughts and heat continuously for 5 hours, or for 6 hours in case of bergamot oil. Remove the basin, wipe it and place it in a desiccator for 20 minutes.

Table 5.4. Mass of perfumery material to be taken for the determination of residue on evaporation.

Expected Residue on Evaporation, Per cent by Mass (1)	*Mass of the Material g (2)*
Less than 5.0	4.8 to 5.2
5.0 to 8.0	2.8 to 3.2
More than 8.0	1.8 to 2.2

Calculation

Residue on evaporation, per cent by mass $\frac{100 M_2}{M_1}$

where

M_1 = mass in g of the sample taken, and

M_2 = mass in g of the residue.

Express the results to the first decimal place.

Chemical Analysis

Chemical Analysis is important from the view point of quality of perfume. It provides composition of the perfume. The quantitative estimation of alcohol. water, acid value, ester value, carbonyl value. phenol and heavy metals is des·cribed.

Determination of content of *alcohol Insoluble solid Impurities*

Principle

Extraction of the perfumery materials is done with ethanol and weighing of any residue after filtration.

Reagent. Ethanol - 95 per cent (v/v). *Apparatus.* Hot-air-oven.

Procedure

Weigh accurately about 20 g of the perfumery material into a conical flask. Add about 200 mf of ethanol, mix the contents of the flask thoroughly and filter through a sintered glass crucible (porosity 4 is suitable) which has previously been dried in the oven at 105°C and weighed. Wash any insoluble matter remaining in the flask into the crucible, suck dry and then dry the crucible and its contents in the oven at 105°C until the loss of mass on drying in the oven for an additional 30 minutes does not exceed 1 mg.

Calculation

Content of alcohol-insoluble solid impurities,

$$\text{Per cent by mass} = \frac{100\,(m_3 - m_2)}{m_1}$$

where

m_1 = mass in g of the sample of perfumery material taken,

m_2 = mass in g of the empty sintered glass crucible, and

m_3 = mass in g of the sintered glass crucible and residue.

Determination of water content

Principle

Distillation of the perfumery materials is done with a water-immiscible solvent.

Reagent

Heptane or toluene.

Apparatus

Dean and stark apparatus, electric heating mantle or oil-bath. Procedure Weigh 20 ± 0.5 g of the perfumery material into the distillation vessel. Half fill the vessel with solvent and add a few dry porcelain chips to regulate boiling. Assemble the apparatus. Maintain the contents of the flask at the boil using the heating mantle or oil-bath until the level of the water layer in the receiver remains constant for 30 minutes. Cool the apparatus to room temperature and detach any globules of water from the condenser wall by means of the spray tube.

Calculation

$$\text{Content of water. per cent by mass} = \frac{V \times 100d}{m}$$

where

V = volume in ml of water collected in the receiver,
m = mass in g of perfumery material taken, and
d = density of water at the air temperature (0.997 g/ml at 27°C).

Determination of acid value

Principle

Acid Value - The number of milligrams of potassium hydroxide required to neutralise the free acids contained in 1 g of the perfumery material.

Apparatus

Conical flask, measuring cylinder and burette.

Reagents

Ethyl alcohol, potassium hydroxide solution (0.1 N), phenolphthalein (95%) and phenol red.

Procedure

Weigh about 2.5 g of dried material and dissolve in 20 ml of neutral rectified spirit. Add about 10 drops of indicator (except in the case of phenolic perfumery materiall and titrate with potassium hydroxide solution until the solution remains faintly pink after 10 seconds of shaking. If the perfumery material under examination contains -phenols or compound with phenolic groups, use phenol red as indicator instead of phenolphthalein.

Calculation

$$\text{Acid value} = \frac{56.1 \times V \times N.}{M}$$

where

V = volume in ml of potassium hydroxide solution,

N =normality of the potassium hydroxide solution, and

M = mass in g of the material taken for the test.

Determination of ester value, content of esters and combined alcohols

Principle

The number of milligrams of potassium hydroxide required to neutralise the acids liberated by the hydrolysis of ester present in 1g of the perfumery materials.

Apparatus

Saponification flask, reflux condenser, burette, pipettes.

Reagents

Ethyl alcohoL (95˚% v/v), alcoholic potassium hydroxide (0.5 N), hydrochloric acid (0.5 N), phenolphthalein indicator and phenol red alcoholic solution.

Prepared sample

The material shall be taken for the determination of ester value, content of esters and combined alcohols, with a suitable quantity as given in Table 5.5.

Table 5.5. Mass of perfumery material to be taken for determination of esters value, content of esters and combined alcohols.

Expected Ester Value (1)	Mass of Perfumery Material (2) 8
Less than 50	4.5 to 5.0
50 to 70	3.5 to 4.0
70 to 90	2.5 to 3.0
90 to 110	2.0 to 2.5
110 to 140	1.5 to 2.0
140 to 180	1.2 to 1.5
180 to 220	1.0 to 1.2
220 to 280	0.9 to 1.0

Procedure

Blank determination. To a saponification flask containing a few fragment of pumice stone or porcelain, add 5 ml of ethyl alcohol and 25 ml of 0-5 N alcoholic potassium hydroxide solution and gently reflux on the heater for the period specified in, specification for individual perfumery material. Then allow the liquid to cool, remove the reflux condenser, add five drops of phenolphthalein solution and neutralise with 0-5 N hydrochloric acid contained in the burette. Alternatively under similar conditions gently reflux the contents reserved from the acid value determination after the addition of 25 ml of the 0-5 N alcoholic potassium hydroxide solution and fragments of pumice-stone or porcelain. Then allow to cool and remove the reflux condenser adding five drops of phenolphthalein indicator except in case of phenolic perfumery material and neutralise the liquid with 0-5 N hydrochloric acid as indicated for the blank test carried out separately under identical conditions.

Calculation

Ester value. Calculate the ester value of the material as follows:

$$\text{Ester value} = 56.1 \times \frac{N(V_1 - V_2)}{m}$$

where

N - normality of hydrochloric acid used for titration.

V_1 - volume in ml of hydrochloric acid used for the blank,

V_2 - volume in ml of hydrochloric acid used in determination to neutralise the excess alkali after hydrolysis, and

m - mass in g of the material taken.

Ester content. The percentage of esters present in the material may be calculated as given below

$$\text{Ester \% (by mass)} = \frac{E \times M}{561}$$

where

E = the observed ester value; and

M = molecular mass of the ester.

Combined alcohols. The percentage of alcohols combined as esters in the material may be calculated as follows:

Combined alcohols % (by massl = E56 M where
E = the observed ester value, and
M = molecular mass of the alcohols.

Saponification value. The saponification value is equivalent to ester value plus acid value.

Saponification value = Ester value + Acid value

Determination of ester value after acetylation and free alcohols

Method A - Acetic anhydride method

The perfumery material is acetylated by acetic anhydride in the presence of sodium acetate followed by alkaline hydrolysis. Excess alkali is titrated to determine the, ester value after acetylation.

Apparatus

Acetylation flask and saponification flask.

Reagents

Acetic anhydride, Sodium acetate, Sodium carbonate (2 %), Sodium chloride solution (saturated). Magnesium sulphate or sodium sulphate, Alcoholic potassium hydroxide solution (0.1 N). Hydrochloric acid (0.5 N).

Procedure

Mix approximately 10 ml of the sample of perfumery material, 10 ml of acetic anhydride and 2 g of anhydrous sodium acetate in the acetylation flask. Add fragments of pumice-stone or porcelain and fit the flask with its reflux condenser. Heat the flask by means of any suitable heating device and gently reflux the liquid for 2 hours. At the end of this period, allow the liquid to cool; add 50 ml of water and heat at a temperature between 40 and 50°C for 15 minutes with shaking frequently. Cool to room. temperature, remove the refluk tube and transfer the liquid to a separating funnel; wash the flask twice with 10 ml of water and add these washings to the contents of the separating funnel. Wait until separation of the liquid is complete then reject the aqueous layer. Wash the oil layer by shaking successively ',with

(1) 50 ml of sodium chloride solution;

(2) 50 ml of sodium carbonate;

(3) 50 ml of sodium chloride solution; and

(4) 20 ml of water.

Shake the acetylated pertumery material vigorously with the saturated solutions, and gently with water which, if the washings have been properly conducted, will be natural to litmus paper.

Run the acetylated material into a dry tube and shake intermittently several times with about 2 to 3 g of anhydrous magnesium sulphate or ahydrous sodium sulphate till it is dried.

Filter the dried material through dried filter paper in a covered funnel.

In the saponification flask. about 2 g of the acetylated perfumery materiaL and add 2 ml of water and 0-5 ml of phenolphthalein indicator.

Neutralise the liquid with the ethanolic potassium hydroxide solution using the burette.

Determine the ester value adding 25 ml of 0.5 N ethanolic potassium hydroxide solution depending upon the mass of the sample taken.

Blank determination. Simultaneously carry out a blank determination of the ethanolic potassium hydroxide by the same procedure but omitting. the perfumery material.

Calculation

Ester value after acetylation = $\frac{56.1 \times N \times (V_1 - V_2)}{m}$

where

N =normality of hydrochloric acid used for titration.

V_1 = volume in ml of hydrochloric acid required for the blank.

V_2 = volume in ml of hydrochloric acid required to neutralise the excess alkali after hydrolysis. and

m = mass in g of acetylated material.

Content of free alcohols % by mass = $\frac{M \times (E_1 - E_2)}{561 - 0.42\ E_1}$

where

E_1 = ester value of the material after acetylation,

E_2 = ester value of the material before acetylation, and

M = molecular mass of the specified alcohol.

Method B - Dimethylaniline acetylchloride method (Fiore Method)

Principle

The perfumery material is acetylated by acetyl chloride in the presence of *Dimethylaniline* and acetic anhydride followed by alkaline hydrolysis. Excess alkali is titrated to determine the ester value after acetylation.

Apparatus

Saponification flask, Graduated measuring cylinders. Burette.

Reagents

Dimethylanine. Freshly distilled and,free from methylaniline and aniline. Acetic anhydride, Acetyl chloride, Sodium sulphate solution - 10 per cent (m/v), Sulphuric acid - 2.5 per cent (m/v), Sodium bicarbonate solution - 50 per cent (m/v), Magnesium sulphate anhydrous, neutral, freshly ignited and powdered., Potassium hydroxide solution = 0- I Nand 0.5 N solution in 95 per cent ethanol lv/vl. Hydrochloric acid - 0.5 N, Phenolphthalein indicator solution - Dissolve Or:-2 g phenolphthalein in 100 ml of.95 per cent ethanol.

Procedure

Introduce 10 ml of the sample of perfumery material into the 100 ml glass stoppered conical flask. Add 20 ml of dimethylaniline. Stopper the flask and mix thoroughly. Cool in melting ice and add 8 ml of acetyl chloride followed by 5 ml of acetic anhydride. Keep the flask in the ice-bath throughout the addition and allow it to stand at room temperature for 30 minutes. Immerse the flask for 16 hours in the water-bath maintained at 40 ± 1°C. Cool to room temperature, transfer the contents of the flask to the separating funnel and wash by shaking successively with

(1) Twice with 75 ml of sodium sulphate solution,

(2) Five times at least with 50 ml of sulphuric acid until the washings are free from dimethyl aniline as demonstrated by freedom from turbidity when the last washing is made alkaline.

(3) Twice with 25 ml of sodium bicarbonate solution, and

(4) Twice with 25 ml of sodium sulphate, solution.

Shake vigorously for 30 seconds with each solution and allow to separate. Check the neutrality of the last solution to litmus paper.

Dry the acetylated material with 2 g to 3 g of magnesium sulphate for at least 2 hours with intermittent shaking. Then, filter the material through a dry filter paper in a covered funnel.

Add 2 ml of water and 2 ml of phenolphthalein indicator solution. Neutralise the free acidity 'with potassium hydroxide solution using the burette. Not more than one drop should be required to give a pink colour. Take the first pink colour as the neutral point as certain esters,. namely, linalyl acetate are easily hydrolysed.

Determine the ester value of the acetylated material as described earlier.

Blank determination. Simultaneously with the hydrolysis of the acetylated material by the procedure as described above. Carry out a blank determination on the ethanolic potassium hydroxide by the same procedure but omitting the acetylated materiaL

Calculation

Calculate the ester value after acetylation using the formula given above under ester value after acetylation.

Determination of carbonyl value and content of carbonyl compounds.

Two methods, namely, hydroxylammonium chloride method and free hydroxylamine method are available for determining the carbonyl value of a perfumery material. Anyone of these may be adopted for the determination of carbonyl value of a perfumery materiaL as specified in the individual standard or as may be agreed to between the purchaser and the supplier. The procedure for the two methods have been prescribed as under.

Hydroxylammonium chloride method - Method A

Principle

The carbonyl compounds to be determined are converted into oximes by reaction with hydroxylammonium chloride. The hydrochloric acid liberated during the reaction is determined by an ethanolic potassium hydroxide solution.

Apparatus

Conical flask, Graduated measuring cylinder, burette.

Reagents.

Potassium hydroxide. Approximately 0-5 N solution in 95 per cent (v/v) ethanol.

Bromophenol blue indicator solution. Dissolve, while warming, 0-2 g of bromophenol bluein 3 ml of ethanolic potassium hydroxide, 0- 1 N hydrochloric acid, using bromophenol blue as indicator and running the alkali into the acid.

Hydroxylammonium chloride, ethanolic solution. Dissolve 50 g of hydroxylammonium chloride in approximately 100 ml of water, and about 800 ml of 95 per cent (v/vl ethanoL then 10 ml of the ethanolic bromophenol blue solution and dilute to 1000 ml with 95 per cent (v/v) ethanol. Add the ethanolic potassium hydroxide solution until the solution is green, if the liquid, is observed in a thin layer, or until red, if the layer is thick.

This solution is suitable for use if a lemon-yellow colour is obtained when 0.05 ml of the hydrochloric acid is added to 20 ml of the solution, and a red colour is obtained when 0.05 ml of the potassium hydroxide solution is added to another 20 ml of the solution. The solution is stable for 1 week.

Procedure

Weigh accurately into the conical flask the amount of perfumery material specified in the individual standard. Add from the graduated cylinder 25 ml of hydroxylammonium chloride solution and set aside for the time specified in individual standard. If additional heating is necessary, this will be specified in individual standard.

After the time prescribed, and if necessary after cooling to room temperature, titrate the contents of the flask with the ethanolic potassium hydroxide solution, taking care to avoid going beyond the greenish-yellow colour of the indicator, continue the titration with the potassium hydroxide solution until a bluish green colour persisting for 5 minutes is obtained.

Calculation

The carbonyl value and content of carbonyl compounds are calculated as follows :.

$$\text{Carbonyl value} = \frac{56.1 \times V \times N}{m}$$

where

V = volume in the ethanolic potassium hydroxide solution used in the determination;

N = the normality of the ethanolic potassium hydroxide solution, used;

and

m = mass in g of the sample.

Content : of carbonyl compounds (as aldehyde or . ketone!. per cent by mass

$$= \frac{M \times VXN}{10\ m}$$

where

M = molecular mass of the carbonyl compounds in which the results are to be expressed,

V = volume in ml of ethanolic potassium hydroxide solution used in the determination,

N = the normality of the ethanolic potassium hydroxide solution. used, and

m = mass in g of the sample.

Free hydroxylamine method - *Method B*

Principle

The carbonyl compounds are converted into oxime by reaction with hydroxylamine freed through the action of a solution of potassium hydroxide on the hydroxylammonium chloride. The hydroxylamirie remaining after the reaction is determined by titration with standard hydrochloric acid.

Apparatus

Alkali-resistant glass flask, Pipette, Conical flask, Burette.

Reagents

Hydrochloric acid - 0.5 N, Hydroxylammonium, chloride solution, Bromophenol blue ethanolic solution, Potassium hydroxide solution 0.5 N in ethanol.

Procedure

Weigh accurately into a flask, a mass m of the perfumery material' as prescribed in individual standard. Introduce by means of a pipette, 20 ml of hydroxylammonium chloride into a conical flask. Add 10 ml of potassium hydroxide solution measured from a burette. Mix it well.

Pour the liquid into the' flask containing the perfumery material and reserve the conical flask without washing. In case of aldehydes, allow to stand for 15 minutes at room temperature while for ketones, reflux gently for one hour using a water condenser or an air condenser at least 75 cm long. Cool to room temperature. Where the individual standard specifies, add bromophenol blue indicator (as for dark coloured perfumery materials).

Neutralise with hydrochloric acid contained in the burette till a greenish yellow colour is observed. Transfer the liquid .to the conical flask used to mix the reagent and the alcoholic potassium hydroxide solution, and pour about half back again into the flask. Continue the neutralisation in one of the flask only till the greenish-yellow colour of the indicator chang.es to lemonyellow. The colour obtained in both flasks, shall not alter further when two drops of 0-5 N hydrochloric acid are added.

Alternatively this titration may be carried out by a potentionmetrit: method to pH 3.5.

Blank determination. Simultaneously using above procedure, carry out a blank test with the same reagents and following the same procedure but omitting the perfumery material.

Calculation

The carbonyl value is calculated as follows :

$$\text{Carbonyl value} = \frac{56.1\,(V_1 - V_2)\,N}{m}$$

where

V_1 = volume in ml of standard hydrochloric acid used in the.blank titration.

V_2 = volume in ml of standard hydrochloric acid used in the determination.

N =the normality of the hydrochloric acid used for titration, and

m = mass in g of the sample.

The content of carbonyl compounds expressed in terms of designated aldehydes and ketones is calculated - as follows

Content of carbonyl compounds (as aldehyde and ketone), by

$$\% \text{ by mass} = \frac{M(V_1-V_2)}{20m}$$

where

M = molecular mass of the aldehyde or, ketones specified in the individual standard for the particular perfumery material.

V_1 = volume in ml of standard hydrochloric acid used in the blank titration,

V_2 = volume in ml of standard hydrochloric acid used in the determination, and

m = mass in g of the sample taken.

Determination of phenols

Principle

Phenols react with alkali hydroxides, giving rise to water soluble phenolates, which can be separated from the unabsorbed material. In the case of materials deficient in phenol content which are apt to yield troublesome stable emulsions, 2 ml of xylene may be added to the measured volume of the material to help in breaking the emulsions, and allowance made foi the volume of added xylene in the final volume of unabsorbed residual materials.

Apparatus

Cassia flask with a graduated neck

Reagents

Tartaric acid, xylene, 0.1 N aqueous potassium hydroxide solution.

Procedure

Preparation of test sample. Remove as far as possible any visible water present in the sample by decanting, then add about .15 per cent by mass of neutral, freshly ignited and powdered anhydrous magnesium sulphate or anhydrous sodium sulphate and shake the mixture vigorously by from time to time during a period of 2 hours. However, before drying the material with magnesium sulphate or anhydrous sodium sulphate, shake vigorously a quantity of the material greater than 10 ml in a conical flask with 0-02 g of the tartaric acid per millilitre of the material.

Determination

Pipette out 10 ml of the perfumery material prepared with the pipette into the Cassia flask containing approximately 75 ml of potassium hydroxide solution. Shake the mixture six times at 5 minutes intervals at room temperature.

Raise the unabsorbed portion of the material into the neck of the Cassia flask by the addition of more of the potassium hydroxide solution. Facilitate the separation of the material drops attached to the walls by rotating the flask between the hands and.gently tapping.

After allowing the flask to stand for few hours, read off the volume of the unabsorbed material if all of it is gathered into the neck. If a quantity of emulsion is observed, add 2 ml of xylene measured. with the pipette, agitate the emulsified layer by means of a glass capillary tube and allow to stand. If the emulsion has disappeared, read the volume of the unabsorbed material. If, however, the emulsion persists, repeat the test with the addition of 2 ml of xylene to the portion before the initial shaking.

In the two latter cases, subtract from the reading 2 ml, corresponding to the volume of xylene added.

Calculation

Phenol content, per cent by volume = (10 - V)

where Y = volume in ml of the unabsorbed portion of the perfumery material.

Determination of heavy metals

Place in a test tube 10 ml of the perfumery material and add an equal volume of distilled water to which one drop of concentrated hydrochloric acid has been added. Shake thoroughly and then pass hydrogen sulphide through the mixture until it is saturated. Carry out simultaneously a blank determination to which no hydrogen Sulphide is passed. In the absence of heavy metals, like copper or lead no darkening in colour in either the material or the water layer is produced. A comparison of the colours of the blank and of the determination will aid in establishing the absence of heavy metals, or the presence of traces. The formation of a scum at the surface between the material and the water layers is no indication of the presence of heavy metals, unless the scum is dark in colour. If the dark colour scum is obtained, follow the procedure of lead content.

Determination of Lead Content

Principle. Volatile components of the perfumery material are removed by boiling a suspension in dilute hydrochloric acid followed by extraction with carbon tetrachloride. The lead in the aqueous acid solution is then determined absorptiometrically as lead dithizonate.

Reagents. Carbon tetrachloride (Lead-free), Chloroform, Aqueous ammonia, Hydrochloric acid (Lead free). Nitric acid solution 1 %, Ammonium citrate (Lead free), Sodium sulphite (4%), Ammonical sulphite-cyanide solution, dithiozone solution, Potassium cyanide 10% (Lead free) and Hydroxylammonium chloride solution (20%). Sodium hexametaphosphate solution (Lead free), Lead solution, Thymol blue indicator solution (0.1 %).

Ammonium citrate solution. $(NH_4)\ C_6H_5O_7$, *lead free, prepare* as *follows:*

Dissolve 125 g of ammonium citrate in 400 to 450 ml of water, make faintly alkaline to litmus paper with lead-free aqueous ammonia (5 M) and extract with chloroform and appropriate additions of the stock dithizone solution. Continue extraction until all metals have been removed and the extract is faintly green, then make the solution just acidic by adding lead-free hydrochloric acid (5 M), and extract with further portions of chloroform until the final extract is colourless.

Ammonical sulphite-cyanide solution. Mix 340 ml of the aqueous ammonia, 75 ml of the sodium sulphite solution, and 30 ml of the potassium cyanide solution and 605 ml of water,

Dithizone stock solution (0.1 %)

Dithizone solution. Prepare by shaking 6 ml of the stock dithizone solution with 9 ml of water and one m!. of ammonia. Separate and reject the lower layer. Centrifuge the aqueous layer until clear.

Sodium hexametaphosphate solution lead free. Dissolve 10 g of sodium hexametaphosphate in 90 ml of water. adjust to pH 9 with thymol blue indicator solution by adding (lead-free) aqueous ammonia and extract with dithizone in chloroform until free from lead. Make the solution just acidic and remove the dithizone traces by extraction with chloroform. Finally adjust to the maximum blue colour of the indicator.

Standard lead solution. Dissolve 1.60 g of lead nitrate [Pb (N03)2] in water. add 10 ml of nitric acid. and diluie to 1000 ml. Further dilute one volume of this solution freshly as required to 100 volumes with water. One ml of this solution is equivalent to 10 /1g of lead.

Apparatus

Separating funneL spectrophotometer with cells.

Procedure

Weigh. approximately 5 g of the sample into a 250 ml beaker. Add 80 ml of water and 10 ml of hydrochloric acid. Boil gently with constant stirring for 10 minutes to volatilise most of the materials. Cool and transfer the acid solution to a 250-ml-separating funnel. Add 10 ml of the carbon tetrachloride to the beaker. boiL cool and transfer to the separating funnel. Repeat this procedure. then rinse the beaker twice with 10 ml of water. adding the washings to the separating funnel. Extract with 20 ml portions of carbon tetrachloride until no further colour is extracted. Filter the aqueous layer through a wetted filter paper into a 100-ml volumetric flask. rinsing out the separating funnel and filter with water until 100 ml of filtrate is obtained.

Transfer 10 ml of this solution to a small beaker. add 5 ml of ammonium citrate solution and 10 ml of sodium hexametaphosphate solution. a few drops of thymol blue indicator solution and sufficient aqueous ammonia to give a blue-green colour indicating pH 9-0 to 9-5. CooL add one ml of potassium cyanide solution. one ml of hydroxylammonium chloride solution and adjust the alkalinity to pH 9-0 to 9-5. if necessary. Transfer to a 100 ml separating funnel containing 10. ml of the chloroform. washing in with a few millilitres of water. The volume of the aqueous layer at this stage should be about 50 ml. Add 0-5. ml of dithizone working solution. shake vigorously for one minute and allow to separate. If the lower layer is red. add dithizone working solution until. after shaking. a purple blue or green colour is obtained. Run the chloroform layer into a second separating funnel and rinse the first separating funnel through with one ml or 2 ml of chloroform. Add. to the liquid in the first separating funnel, 3 ml of chloroform and 0-2 ml of dithizone working solution. shake vigorously for 30 seconds. allow the chloroform layer to separate and add it to the main chloroform extract. The last chloroform extract should be green. If it is not, carry out further extractions with chloroform and dithizone working solution until the green colour of the final extract indicates that all the lead has been extracted. Alternatively. repeat the extractions using a smaller portion of the test solution. Reject the aqueous layer. Shake the chloroform extract vigorously for one minute with 10 ml of nitric acid solution. Separate. discarding the chloroform layer as completely as possible.

Add 30 ml of the ammoniacal sulphite-cyanide solution. exactly 10 ml of chloroform and 0.5 ml of dithizone working solution, and shake the· mixture vigorously for one minute. Allow it to settle. If the supernatant liquid is not pronounced orange-yellow. add a further 0.5 ml of dithizone working solution. shake the mixture again for one minute and allow it to settle. Run off a few drops of the chloroform layer. insert a plug of cotton wool into the dry stem of the funnel and, after rejecting the first runnings. fill a one cm cell with the filtered chloroform solution. Measure the optical density of the solution against chloroform and determine the lead content from a standard curve obtained with 0. 10. 2.0. 3.0 and 4.0 ml of the standard lead solution. diluted to a volume of 10 ml with nitric acid solution. using the same procedure. Measure the optical density of the test solution against chloroform.

Reagent blank determination

Carry out a blank determination as prescribed above but omitting the perfumery material.

Expression of results

Deduct the value of the optical density for the reagent blank from that for the test solution and determine from the calibration graph the lead content of the perfumery material. Express the result as milligrams of lead per kilogram of the perfumery material.

Determination of Iron

Apparatus. Nessler cylinders - 100 ml capacity.

Reagents

Hydrochloric acid - 2 N. Ammonium persulphate, Potassium thiocyanate solution - approximately 5 per cent.

Standard iron solution

Dissolve 0.702 g of ferrous ammonium sulphate [FeSo4 (NH_4So_4 $6H_2O$] in 100 ml distilled water, add 10 ml of concentrated sulphuric acid and dilute with water to 1000 ml mark .. Transfer 100 ml of this solution to a 1000 ml volumetric flask and dilute up to the mark. One millilitre of this solution is equivalent to 0.01 mg of iron (as F_6)

Procedure

Add 25 ml of 2 N hydrochloric acid to 25 ml of perfumery compound, shake and boil. slowly for about 10 minutes. Cool and separate the aqueous layer. Add about 30 mg of ammonium persulphate and boil to oxidise the iron. Cool and transfer to a Nessler cylinder, add 2 ml of potassium thiocyanate solution and dilute to 100 ml mark with water. In another Nessler cylinder, take the same amounts of hydrochloric acid. ammonium persulphate and potassium thiocyanate solution and dilute to about 90 ml. From a burette add standard iron solution in small portions so that after dilution to 100 ml the colour obtained matches with that obtained with the material. The iron content of the perfumery material is then equal to the amount of iron added to obtain equivalent colouration as produced by sample solution.

Detection of petroleum and mineral oils .

The saturated paraffinic hydrocarbons, found in the petroleum oils. are chemically very inert; they are not destroyed by fuming sulphuric acid. Other compounds are attacked, giving rise to reaction products which are soluble in sulphuric acid. The material has to be added to the fuming sulphuric acid very, cautiously since too rapid an addition of perfumery materials is apt to cause the liberated sulphur dioxide to carry part of the acid and material out of thc flask. Since petroleum fractions often contain aromatic and unsaturated compounds as well as paraffins. the separation of the paraffinic portion described above does not usually represent the total amount of added petroleum. In general the portion thus separated is usually a small percentage of the adulterant. The test may be rendered more sensitive by preliminary fractionation of the material.

The addition of petroleum fractions to a material causes a lowering of the specific gravity, refractive index and optical rotation. The solubility of the material usually is also affected.

Apparatus

Cassia Flask.

Reagents

Fuming Sulphuric Acid -15 per cent oleum, Concentrated Sulphuric Acid.

Procedure

Place 20 ml of fuming sulphuric acid (15 per cent oleum) in a dry Cassia flask of approximately 150 ml capacity, and cool thoroughly in an ice-salt mixture. Cautiously add 5 ml of the material from a small burette, drop by drop, with frequent shaking and cooling in the ice-salt mixture. After the material has been added, again shake the flask and allow it to stand at room temperature for 10 minutes. Warm on a steam-bath for 5 minutes with frequent agitation, cool to room temperature, then fill to the mark with concentrated sulphuric acid and allow the flask to stand overnight, when the mineral oil will rise into the neck and separate as a colourless or strawcoloured liquid. To confirm the presence of mineral oil, remove a small amount of the separated mineral oil from the Cassia flask, using a glass tube drawn out to a small tip, and determine its refractive index. For petroleum products and mineral oils, the refractive index is expected to be less than 1.440 0.

Estimation of chlorine

Principle

Absence of even a transient green colour when the material is ignited on a copper gauze in a non-luminous flame is used for determining freedom from chlorine.

Apparatus

Copper wire and Bunsen burner.

Procedure

Place the copper strip in the non-luminous flame of the Bunsen burner until it glows without imparting a green colour. Cool the gauze and repeatedly ignite it until an oxide coating has formed. Cool the gauze and add 2 drops of the sample by means of a medicine dropper, permitting it to burn in air. Again cool and add 2 more drops of the test material and burn as before. Continue the procedure until 6 drops have been ignited. Hold the gauze in the outer edge of the non-luminous flame whose height has been adjusted to about 4 em ..

Result

The flame shall be free from even a transient green colour.

Determination of cineole content Principle

The crystallising temperature is measured of a mixture .of perfumery materials and o-cresol. This temperature depends on the cineole content of the perfumery materials. .

Apparatus

Calibrated thermometer. test tube. stout-walled test tube and wide mouth jar or bottle.

Reagents

o-Cresol. Cineole. Cineole-a-Cresol complex.

Procedure

Prepare the sample as per the procedure described in phenol estimation.

Preliminary test. Weigh 3 g of the freshly prepared test sample in the dry test tube. and add 2.1 g of melted a-cresol. Place the tube in the apparatus and allow the mixture to crystallise by cooling. and stirring. When crystallisation takes place. there is a small increase in temperature t_1.

Determination. First assemble the apparatus as per Fig. 5.9."Remelt the mixture. at a temperature not exceeding t_1. by more than 5°C. using the water bath. Place the test tube into the apparatus maintained at a temperature 5°C below t_1. When crystallisation begins. or when the temperature of the mixture has fallen to a value 3°C below t_1 stir continuously. Induce the crystallisation by rubbing the wall of the test tube with the bath of the thermometer. Note the maximum temperature at which the mixture recrystallises. t_2.

Repeat the determination until the two highest values obtained for t_2 do not differ by more than 0-2°C. If supercooling occurs. induce the crystallisation by adding a small crystal of the complex.

If t_2 is below 27.4 °C. repeat the determination after the additiorn of 5.1 g of the cineole-a-cresol complex.

Calculation

The content of cineole corresponding to the highest temperature observed t_2 is given in Table 5.6. If 5.1 g of the cineole-o-cresol complex has been added. the cineole content of the sample is calculated and given below

Cineole content. per cent
by mass = 2 (A - 50)
where
A = percentage of cineole as given in Table 5.6 .
The content of cineole, corresponding to the highest temperature observed t_2, is obtained, where necessary. by interpolation from the values as given in Table 5.6.

Table 5.6. Cineole content as a function of the crystallisation temperature of the perfumery materials-o-cresol mixture.

Crystallisation temperature 0°C	*Cineole Contents, Per cent*									
	0.0	0.1	0.2	0.3	0.4	0.5	0.6	0.7	0.8	0.9
24	45.6	45.7	45.9	46.0	46.1	46.3	46.4	46.5	46.6	46.8
25	46.9	47.0	47.2	47.3	47.4	47.6	47.7	47.8	47.9	48.1
26	48.2	48.3	48.5	48.6	48.7	48.9	49.0	49.1	49.2	49.4
27	49.5	49.6	49.8	49.9	50.0	50.2	50.3	50.4	50.5	50.7
28	.50.8	50.9	51.1	51.2	51.3	51.5	51.6	51.7	51.8	52.0
29	52.1	52.2	52.4	52.5	52.6	52.8	52.9	53.0	53.1	53.3
30	53.4	53.5	53.7	53.8	53.9	54.1	54.2	54.3	54.4	54.6
31	54.7	54.8	55.0	55.1	55.2	55.4	55.5	55.6	55.7	55.9
32	.56.0	56.1	56.3	56.4	56.5	56.7	56.8	56.9	57.0	57.2
33	57.3	57.4	57.6	57.7	57.8	.58.0	58.1	58.2	58.3	58.5
34	58.6	58.7	58.9	59.0	59.1	59.3	59.4	59.5	59.6	59.8
35	59.9	60.0	60.2	60.3	60.4	60.6	60.7	60.8	60.9	61.1
36	61.2	61.3	61.5	61.6	61.7	61.9	62.0	62.1	62.2	62.4
37	62.5	62.6	62.8	62.9	63.0	63.2	63.3	63.4	63.5	63.7
38	63.8	63.9	64.1	64.2	64.4	64.5	64.6	64.8	64.9	65.1
39	65.2	65.4	65 .5	6.5.7	65.8	66.0	66.2	66.3	66.5	66.6
40	66.8	67.0	67.2	67.3	67.5	67.7	67.9	68.1	68.2	68.4
41	68.6	68.8	69.0	69.2	69.4	69.6	69.7	69.9	70.1	70.3
42	70.5	70.7	70.9	71.0	71.2	71.4	71.6	71.8	71.9	72.1
43	72.3	72.5	72.7	72.9	73.1	73.3	73.4	73.6	73.8	74.0
44	74.2	74.4	74.6	74.8	7.5.0	75.2	75.3	7.5.5	7.5.7	75.9
45	76.1	76.3	76.5	76.7	76.9	77.1	77.2	77.4	77.6	77.8
46	78.0	78.2	78.4	78.6	78.8	79.0	79.2	79.4	79.6	79.8
47	80.0	80.2	80.4	80.6	80.8	81.1	81.3	81.5	81.7	81.9
48	82.1	82.3	82.5	82.7	82.9	83.2	83.4	83.6	83.8	84.0
49	84.2	84.4	84.6	84.8	85.0	85.3	85.5	85.7	85.9	86.1
50	86.3	86.6	86.3	87.1	87.3	87.6	87.8	88.1	88.3	88.6
51	88.8	89.1	89.3	89.6	89.8	90.1	90.3	90.6	90.8	91.1
52	91.3	91.6	91.8	92.1	92.3	92.6	92.8	93.1	93.3	93.6
53	93.8	94.1	94.3	94.6	94.8	95.1	95.1	95.6	95.8	96.1
54	96.3	96.6	96.9	97.2	97.5	97.8	98.1	98.4	98.7	99.0
55	99.3	99.7	100.0	-	-	-	-	-	-	-

6

Aerosol Spray

"Attar" the indigenous fragrance held away over India till the arrival of the westernised, alcohol-based scents and sprays.

Attar may no longer hold the pride of place in the elite Indian homes now, but it still reigns supreme in traditional households and the countryside. while the speciality of attar is that its ingredients are entirely natural and, therefore, totally harmless. With the advent of extravagantly packaged spray perfumes, attar has lost its competitiveness. This being the case, imaginative packaging could perhaps not only revive attar's old glory but also make it the rage of the west.

The early Egyptian used perfume in their daily lives for cosmetic purposes, burning incense, in their temples and for embalming the bodies of their Pharoahs with aromatic substances. The Greeks and Romans learned the use of perfume from the Eastern races they conquered and it was only in the mid-10th century that France established her supremacy over the perfume trade.

MANUFACTURING PROCESS

Essence and Perfumery

General Procedure :- The essence and perfumery are generally prepared by the following ways.

1. These can be extracted from flowers leaves and woods. After extraction recovered by vacuum distillation water in cool conditions.
2. Essence and perfumery are prepared generally by blending of pure essence with alcohol blending and mixing is the process of easiests way to be preparation of essence and perfumery.

For the preparation of essence and perfumery it is required to confirm of the formula of which blending operations can be done to give the exact product.

3. Essence and perfumes can be produced by chemical synthetic way.

Present case I am dealing with the formulation and blending cross for the production of essence and perfumery.

The basic formula of perfumes and essence are given.

Synthetic Rose otto No 1056

Citronellol	200
Phenylethyl Alcohol	100
Geraniol Palmorosa	200
Rhodinol	200
Guaiace wood	50
Eugenol	
Innone Alpha	5
Cinnamic Alcohol	50
Phenyl Acetic Acid	40
Phenyl aectic Aldehyde	3
Trichloro Phenyl Methyl Carbinyl Acetate	80
Un decylenic Aldehyde	2

Red Roses. No-1057

		Parts
Phenyl Ethyl Alcohol	-	150
Rhodinol	-	200
Ionone	-	300
Cinnamic Alcohol	-	150
Rhodinyl Acetate	-	100
Trichlor Phenyl Methyl Carbinyl Acetate	-	50
Jasmine Compound	-	50

A finished perfume may be prepared as follows:

Violet. no. 1068

Parma violet compound	100
Victoria violet compound	40
Cassie absolute	5
Rose otto	1
Civet absolute	1
Musk ketone	1
Santal	2
Ambergris tincture, 3 per cent	30
Musk tincture, 3 per cent	20
Alcohol	800
	1000

PLANT ECONOMICS

Rated Plant Capacity = 2400.00 Bottles /Day Aerosol Spray

LAND & BUILDING

(Land Area 200 Sq.mts.) = Rs. 5,30,000.00

PLANT & MACHINERY

1. Different Storage Tanks
2. Mixing Vessel
3. Refrigeration Unit
4. Distillation Unit
5. Liquid Filling Machine
6. Labelling Machine
7. Heater Unit
8. Miscellaneous

FIXED CAPITAL

1.	Land and Building	Rs.	5,30,000.00
2.	Plant and Machinery	Rs.	2,52,000.00
3.	Other Fixed Assets	Rs.	50,000.00
	TOTAL	Rs.	8,32,000.00

RAW MATERIALS

1. Essence Compounds
2. Ethyl Alcohol
3. Glass Bottles and Packaging Materials

TOTAL WORKING CAPITAL/MONTH

1.	Raw Material	Rs.	7,27,500.00
2.	Salary and Wages	Rs.	26,093.00
3.	Utilities and Overheads	Rs.	85,500.00
	TOTAL	Rs.	8,39,093.00

TOTAL CAPITAL INVESTMENT

Total Fixed Capital	Rs.	8,32,000.00
Total Working Capital for 3 Months	Rs.	25,17,279.00
TOTAL	Rs.	33,49279.00

TURN OVER/ANNUM

1. 25 Ml. capacity bottles 360000 Nos.
2. 50 Ml. capacity bottles 240000 Nos.
3. 100 Ml. capacity bottles 120000 Nos.

TOTAL Rs. 1,27,20,000.00

PROFIT SALES RATIO = Profit / Sales x 100 = 14.78%

RATE OF RETURN = Operating profit / T.C.I x 100 = 56.10%

BREAK EVEN POINT (B.E.P) = 41.21%

7

Aromatic Perfumery Compounds

A perfume can be defined as a blend of odourants materials of natural and synthetic origin which gives a pleasant odour impression.

The art of perfumery is of extreme antiquity. The perfumes have been used from time immemorial and have played an important part in daily life of the people. The idea of perfumes was first conceived and technically employed in the East, especially in India, China, Egypt, and persia. The fumes of frankincense and myrrh giving light odours were employed in religion ceremonies and later on balsams, pomades and cosmetics begin to server the needs of mankind.

Progress in the creation of natural perfume industry was made gradually. The first manipulation of perfumes was as therapeutic remedies utilizing immediate resources of nature. Then as time passed on and the experience of mankind accumulated, they.became the basis of secular employment of incencse. The latter established the art of perfumery.

Unfortunately the flourishing position which India had attained in Olden times and medieval periods dwindled down due to the lack of scientific knowledge and the inability of Indian manufacturers to adopt themselves to modern scientific advancements. The application of cheap synthetic pefumes in the manufacture of soaps, cosmetics and confectionery, etc. induced Indian perfumes to import and methods of production couldnot compete with the modern scientific equipments and process. Therefore, improvements in the existing equipments and process are to be introduced early to develop the present state of perfumery industry in the country.

Formulation and raw materials

The formulations of aromatic perfumery compounds are given below :-

Fancy Bouquet:-

A.	Vanillin	168 kg.
	95% Alcohol 30	4 kg.
	Cinna maldehyde	1 kg.
	Gernaniol	1 kg.
	Benzaldehyde	4 kg.
	Amyl butyrate	16 kg.
	Amyl Acetate	16 kg
	Amyl Valterate	30 kg
	Amyl formate	36 kg
	Capronic ether	38 kg.
	Imitation neroli	48 kg
	Ethyl valerianate	88 kg
	Aldehyde C_{14} (gama under calactone)	250 kg
		1000 kg
B.	Lavender Oil, French	40 kg.
	Bergamot oil	100 kg.
	Geraniol	100 kg.
	Ambrette Oil, 10%	5 kg.
	Ylang-ylang oil	25 kg.
	Clang sage oil	5 kg.
	Rosemary oil	25 kg.
	Jasmine, Synthetic	50 kg.
	Benzoin R.	200 kg.
	Ethyl Phthalate	90 kg.
		1000 kg.

MANUFACTURING PROCESS

Manufacturing Process for fancy and Royale bouquet are given below according to their formulations :

1. Fancy Bouquet

Formulation :

Vanillin	168 kg.
95% Alcohol	304 kg.
Cinnamaldehyde	1 kg.
Geraniol	1 kg.
Benzaldehyde	4 kg.
Amyl butyrate	16 kg.
Amyl Acetate	16 kg.
Amyl Valerate	30 kg.
Amyl formate	36 kg.
Capronic ether	38 kg.
Imitation neroli	48 kg.
Ethyl valerianate	88 kg.
Gamma Undecalctone (Peach Aldehyde)	250 kg.
	1000 kg.

Process :

The ingredients according to the above formulations are taken in a mixer cum blender with 150 kg capacity. Alcohol five times the weight of ingredient is mixed in the mixer. The mixer is equipped with stirrer and M.S. Jacket in which cold water is circulated. After proper blending the whole mixture is left for a suitable time to produce the required perfume in the mixture. The inside temperature of blender is kept low with help of cold water circulation. When the required perfume is generated the mixture is packed in small quantities with the help of a packing machine. The packed product is taken to storage, which is now ready for sale.

2. Royale Bouquet :

Formulation :

Diphenyl methane	5 kg.
Vetivert Oil	5 kg.
Clary sage oil	5 kg.
Jasmine absolute	10 kg.
Violet, synthetic	25 kg.
Sandal Wood oil, English	25 kg.

Coumarin	25 kg.
Musk ketone	50 kg.
Heliotropin	50 kg.
Hydroxy-Cironellol	50 kg.
Iso-butyl phenyl acetate	50 kg.
Rose oil, Bulgarian	50 kg.
Amber, Synthetic	50 kg.
Musk extract, 3%	50 kg.
Benzoin R.	50 kg.
Benzyl benzoate	250 kg.
Ambergris extract; 3%	250 kg.
	1000 kg.

Process :

The ingredients, according to the above formulations are taken in a mixer cum blender with 150 kg. Capacity, Alcohol five times the weight of ingredients is mixed in the mixer. The mixer is equipped with stirrer and M.S. Jacket in which cold water is circulated. After proper blending the whole mixture is left for a suitable time to produce the required perfume in the mixture. The inside temperature of blender in kept low with the help of cold water circulation. When the required perfume is generated the mixture is packed in small quantities with the help of a packing machine. The packed product is taken to storage which is now ready for sale.

PLANT ECONOMICS

Rated Plant Capacity = 10.00 Kg/Day Perfumery Compound

LAND & BUILDING

(Land Area 1200 Sq.mts.) = Rs. 21,05,000.00

PLANT & MACHINERY

1. Blender
2. Refrigeration system
3. Packaging machine
4. Miscellaneous equipments like storage for raw materials, pumps etc.
5. Lab equipments

FIXED CAPITAL

1.	Land and Building	Rs.	21,05,000.00
2.	Plant and Machinery	Rs.	7,15,000.00
3.	Other Fixed Assets	Rs.	2,00,000.00
	TOTAL	Rs.	30,20,000.00

RAW MATERIALS

1. Vanillin
2. 95% Alcohol
3. Cinnamaldehyde
4. Geraniol
5. Genzaldehyde
6. Amyl butyrate
7. Amyl acetate
8. Amyl valerate
9. Amyl formate
10. Capronic ether
11. Imitation Neroli
12. Ethyl valerianate
13. Gamma, Undecealactone
14. Diphenyl methane
15. Vetivert oil
16. Clary sage oil
17. Jasmine Absolute
18. Violet synthetic
19. Sandal Wood Oil
20. Coumarin
21. Musk Ketone
22. Heliotropin
23. Hydroxy Citronellol
24. Iso butyl phenylacetate
25. Rose oil, Bulgarian
26. Amber synthetic
27. Musk extract
28. Benzoin
29. Benzyl benzoate
30. Ambergris extract
31. Ethyl alcohol
32. Packaging Materials as Aluminiumcans/bottles etc.

TOTAL WORKING CAPITAL/ANNUM

1.	Raw Material	Rs.	5,01,500.00
2.	Salary and Wages	Rs.	7,26,000.00
3.	Utilities and Overheads	Rs.	3,71,750.00
	TOTAL	Rs.	15,99,250.00

TOTAL CAPITAL INVESTMENT

Total Fixed Capital	Rs.	30,20,000.00
Total Working Capital for 2 Month	Rs.	2,66,541.00
TOTAL	Rs.	32,86,541,00

TURN OVER/ANNUM

Receipt By Sale of 3,000 kgs. of Fancy and Royale perfume		
TOTAL	Rs.	33,00,000.00

PROFIT SALES RATIO = Profit / Sales x 100 = 21.18%
RATE OF RETURN = Operating profit / T.C.I x 100 = 21.27%
BREAK EVEN POINT (B.E.P) = 67.34%

8

Scents and Perfumes

The perfumery Industry can be considered to have developed along many channels. A rich variety of odoriferous materials occurs naturally as products of plants and animal metabolism. A few decades ago perfumes were composed primarily from natural material. Later isolates obtained form them were also used for compounding perfumes for example terpene alcohol and geraniol which have a lose odour, have been obtained from citronella oil.

Today, the variety of available natural perfume and flavouring materials is small compared to several thousands of synthetic materials. However the importance of natural perfume materials have not been lost.

Natural perfumes are mostly products of plant metabolism and they occur generally in the form of volatile oils. The fragrance of flowers is due to the presence in the petals of minute traces of essential oils which may be in the free state as in rose and lavender or in the form of glycosides, under favourable conditions are decomposed by appropriate enzymes with the formation of volatile oils. Fragrant materials frequently exists in leaves, steams, barks, roots, heart woods etc. of various species in the plant. Natural exudations from some plants also contain odoriferous compounds these includes gums balsams and oleores.ins which form valuable raw materials for perfumes because of their soft and tanacions odour. Animal perfumes like musk, ambergris and civet are important in formulations of finished perfumes.

The separation of fragrant principles from plant is by no means an easy matter the process commonly employed are distillations, enfleurage, maceration, expression and solvent extraction.

Process of Manufacture

Distillation:-Distilled oils may lack some component which is not volatile enough or which is lost during distillation. Three types of distillation are in use:-

1. Water distillation.
2. Water & Steam distillation
3. Live Steam Distillation

The plant material containing the odoriferous principles may need cominution before treatment.

Flowers and Leaves do not need cominution as the cell walls are sufficiently thin to permit the removal of oil.

The water distillation method in which the plant materials is brought into direct contact with boiling water in a closed apparatus with the condenser attached at the top is the oldest and is still in use in *same* places as in case of rose petals & orange blossoms.

In the water steam distillation method direct contact of plant material with the still is avoided by supporting the material on a perforated grid or screen inserted at some distance above the bottom of the still.

The lower part of the still is filled with water to a level some what below the grid and the charge is subjected to distillation by passing low pressure steam. The water beneath the perforated grid is discard after the completion of distillation and replaced with fresh water

Steam distillation method differ from the water and steam distillation method in that no water is kept in the bottom of the still. Live steam at 40-100 lv/ego m in injected through steam coils below the change. The pressure within the vessel may be controlled according to the nature of the material handled.

The oils separated by distillation are sometimes rectified or fractioned by hydro distillation at reduced pressure for improving their colour & odour objectionable impurities are removed in the foreruns & late runs during rectification.

The principal odoriferous constituents of most of the essential oils are oxygenated compounds (alcohols, esters, ethers, aldehydes, ketones, lactones, phenols, phelols ethers etc.) They are usually accompanied by terpenses and esquiterpenses which can be separated by fractional distillation in vacuum or by solvent extraction. The usual practice is to separate the terpenses by vacuum distillation and then extract to terpene less oil with dilute alcohol or other solvent to remove in bringing the oil in to contact with solvent partially soluble in each other e.g. pentance and di methyl alcohol. in a tower. The oil flowing counter current to the solvent mixture. One of the solvent (pentane) dissolves the terpens while the other (rnethyl alcohol), the oxygenated compounds.

For water distillation or water-steam distillation the still consists of a tin lined copper vessel fitted with a mashroori shaped lid of the same material. a bent bamboo wrapped with rope and coated with a clay mixture sieve as a condenser.

The shorter end of the bamboo passes through a hole in the lid and the larger end is led to a tin lined copper receiver which is kept cool by immersion in a cold water reservoir or in a flowing stream.

The distillate is transferred to a coper decante and left over night the floating oil is removed and the water transferred to the still with a fresh change of material.

Extraction Process

Enfleurage or extraction of perfume by contact with cold fat is the method used for certain flowers, particularly jasmine and tube rose which continue to elaborates. Their characteristic odoriferous principle even after packing. In such cases extraction with solvents resuls in loss of perfume.

In the "Enflourage Process" batch of fresh flowers are lightly layered over a specially prepared fat base (refined lard or beef suetj known as corps. The fat is spread in a thin layer on both sides of a glass plate supported on a rectangular wooden frame or chases. Several chasis are placed one above the other so that the flowers get sandwiched between two layers of fats which absorbs the perfume as it is given off. Spent flowers are removed and replaced by fresh blooms. The glass slab is reversed (patagej several times that both surface absorb the perfume. Also the absorption surface is increased by cutting furrows by means of a comb. Removal of state flowers and changing of fresh flowers is continued until then fat is saturated with the perfume.

The pomade is scraped from the plates, extruded with 95% Alcohol and the extract cooled to -15°C and filtered. The clear solution, known as, extracts may be marketed as such or the solvent may be removed by vacuum distillation to yield the essential oil. The oil retained by flowers after defleurae is extracted with a volatile solvent to yield the absolute of chasis. In the "Maceration Process" the flowers are immersed in hot (60-70°) fat when the oil cells get ruptured and the contents pass into the fat. The fat is separated from spent material and used for the treatment of further batches of flowers. The fat retained by flowers is recovered by hydraulic pressing. The pomade thus obtained is marketed as such or it may be extracted with strong alcohol to yield extracts.

Extraction Volatile Solvent

It yield concretes and alcohol soluble absolutes with a true to nature odour the process has superseded maceration and is now largely used for the extraction of aromatic substances from flowers, leaves and mosses. In this process, fresh flowers are extracted at room temperature with a specially purified solvent e.g. petroleum ether of low boiling point (75°) or benzene. Both stationary and rotary extractors are in use. The former i.e. stationary on consists of vertical cylinders provided with perforated metal grids arranged horizontally around a central vertical shaft. The flowers are changed on grids. Extraction is affected by successive washing whereby each batch of flowers is brought into contact with the solvent three times. The final extract is distilled to recover the solvent.

The rotary extractor consists of a tinned iron drum rotating on a horizontal axis, the interior is divided into four compartments for holding flowers by means of perforated metal partitions. The solvent remains at the lowest part of the extractor and when one compartment is lifted in the course of the movement of the drum, the liquid seeps through the perforations and drips back to the bottom. Each batch of flowers receives three washing. The extract is pumped to a vacuum still and the solvent distilled off at a temperature about 60°, 90-9.5% of the solvent is recovered. The concentrate is cooled, filtered and further concentrated in vacuum. The floral concrete thus obtained considerable amount of plant waxes and pigments.

For preparing the absolute the concentrate is exhausted with warm alcohol and insoluble wax separated. The clear solution is cooled to -20 to -25°C when more wax separate out. The filtered clear solution can be used as such in perfumes.

N. The yield of perfume per kg of flowers is 4-8 gms generally by distillation cum Rectification process.

PLANT ECONOMICS

Rated Plant Capacity = 10.00 Kgs./Day Jasmine and Lily Flower Oil

LAND & BUILDING

(Land Area 1000 Sq.mts.) =	Rs.	9,30,000.00

PLANT & MACHINERY

1. Feeding Hopper and Bucket elevator
2. Rotary Extractor
3. S.S. Jacketed evaporation tank
4. Condenser
5. Vacuum still (SS)
6. Solvent Storage tank (SS)
7. Baby Boiler
8. Pipes, fittings, vacuum pumps, valves, motor and other miscellaneous
9. Solvent Recycling Unit
10. Laboratory testing Equipments and Instruments

FIXED CAPITAL

1.	Land and Building	Rs.	9,30,000.00
2.	Plant and Machinery	Rs.	6,50,000.00
3.	Other Fixed Assets	Rs.	1,35,000.00
	TOTAL	Rs.	17,15,000.00

RAW MATERIALS

1. Flower Fresh (Jasmine, Lily)
2. Solvent Petroleum ether
3. Glass bottles & Labels
4. Carton made of Cardboard

TOTAL WORKING CAPITAL/ANNUM

1.	Raw Material	Rs.	13,03,250.00
2.	Salary and Wages	Rs.	63,780.00
3.	Utilities and Overheads	Rs.	48,700.00
	TOTAL	Rs.	14,15,730.00

TOTAL CAPITAL INVESTMENT

Total Fixed Capital	Rs.	17,15,000.00
Total Working Capital for 2 Months	Rs.	28,31,460.00
TOTAL	Rs.	45,46,460.00

TURN OVER/ANNUM

By sale of 3000 kgs. flower oil	Rs.	2,40,00,000.00

PROFIT SALES RATIO = Profit / Sales x 100 = 28.19%

RATE OF RETURN = Operating profit / T.C.I x 100 = 132.96%

BREAK EVEN POINT (B.E.P) = 19.94%

9

Spray (Perfumes)

"Attar" the indigenous fragrance held away over India till the arrival of the westernized, alcohol-based scents and sprays.

Attar may no longer hold the pride of place in the elite Indian homes now, but it still reigns supreme in traditional households and the countryside. while the speciality of attar is that its ingredients are entirely natural and, therefore, totally harmless. With the advent of extravagantly packaged spray perfumes, attar has lost its competitiveness. This being the case, imaginative packaging could perhaps not only revive attar's old glory but also make it the rage of the west.

The early Egyptian used perfume in their daily lives for cosmetic purposes, burning incense, in their temples and for embalming the bodies of their Pharaohs with aromatic substances. The Greeks and Romans learned the use of perfume from the Eastern races they conquered and it was only in the mid-10th century that France established her supremacy over the perfume trade.

Manufacturing Process

General Procedure :- The essence and perfumery are generally prepared by the following ways.

1. These can be extracted from flowers leaves and woods. After extraction recovered by vacuum distillation water in cool conditions.
2. Essence and perfumery are prepared generally by blending of pure essence with alcohol blending and mixing is the process of easiest

way to be preparation of essence and perfumery.

For the preparation of essence and perfumery it is required to confirm of the formula of which blending operations can be done to give the exact product.

3. Essence and perfumes can be produced by chemical synthetic way.

Present case I am dealing with the formulation and blending cross for the production of essence and perfumery.

The basic formula of perfumes and essence are given.

Synthetic Rose otto No 1056

		Parts
Citronellol	-	200
Phenylethyl Alcohol	-	100
Geraniol Palmarosa	-	200
Rhodinol	-	200
Guaice wood	-	50
Eugenol		
Innone Alpha	-	5
Cinnamic Alcohol	-	50
Phenyl Acetic Acid	-	40
Phenyl acetic Aldehyde	-	3
Trichloro Phenyl Methyl		
Carbinyl Acetate	-	80
Un decylenic Aldehyde		2

Red Roses, No. 1057

		Parts
Phenyl Ethyl Alcohol	-	150
Rhodinol	-	200
Ionone	-	300
Cinnamic Alcohol	-	150
Rhodinyl Acetate	-	100

Trichloro Phenyl Methyl		
Carbinyl Acetate	-	50
Jasmine Compound	-	50

A finished perfume may be prepared as follows :

Violet No. 108

	Parts
Parma Violet Compound	100
Victoria violet compound	40
Cassie absolute	1
Rose Otto	1
Civet Absolute	1
Musk ketone	1
Santal	2
Ambergris tincture, 3 per cent	30
Musk tincture, 3 per cent	20
Alcohol	800
	1000

PLANT ECONOMICS

Rated Plant Capacity = 2400.00 Bottles/Day Aerosol Spray

LAND & BUILDING

(Land Area 200 Sq.mts.) = Rs. 5,30,000.00

PLANT & MACHINERY

1. Different Storage Tanks
2. Mixing vessel
3. Refrigeration unit
4. Distillation Unit
5. Liquid filling machine
6. Labelling machine
7. Heater Unit
8. Miscellaneous

FIXED CAPITAL

1.	Land and Building	Rs.	5,30,000.00
2.	Plant and Machinery	Rs.	2,52,000.00
3.	Other Fixed Assets	Rs.	50,000.00
	TOTAL	Rs.	8,32,000.00

RAW MATERIALS

1. Essence Compounds
2. Ethyl Alcohols
3. Glass Bottles and Packaging Materials

TOTAL WORKING CAPITAL/MONTH

1.	Raw Material	Rs.	7,27,500.00
2.	Salary and Wages	Rs.	26,093.00
3.	Utilities and Overheads	Rs.	85,500.00
	TOTAL	Rs.	8,39,093.00

TOTAL CAPITAL INVESTMENT

Total Fixed Capital	Rs.	8,32,000.00
Total Working Capital for 2 Months	Rs.	25,17,279.00
TOTAL	Rs.	33,49,279.00

TURN OVER/ANNUM

1. 25 Ml. Capacity bottles 360000 Nos.
2. 50 Ml. capacity bottles 240000 Nos.
3. 100 Ml. capacity bottles 120000 Nos.

TOTAL	Rs.	1,27,20,000.00

PROFIT SALES RATIO = Profit / Sales x 100 = 17.78%
RATE OF RETURN = Operating profit / T.C.I x 100 = 59.10%
BREAK EVEN POINT (B.E.P) = 41.21%

10

Floral Oils

The preparation of floral oils constitutes by itself a big industry distinctly of Indian origin, and their manufacture can easily be traced to many centuries ago. To this day a flourishing industry centres round Jaunpur, Ghazipur, Lucknow, Delhi and other celebrated parts of Northern India.

Selection of Site

Flowers play an important part in the manufacture of floral oils. It may be noticed by the common observer that the industry thrives in places where finest flowers abound and are available in plenty for treatment and manufacture. A place without this natural advantage and where flower cultivation is not in systematic progress, can hardly prove to be the nursery of a successful floral oil industry. There are many places in India where the finest flowers can be propagated or grown but are allowed to go to waste, and it is at these places that a save industry can be founded to the great benefit of the country.

Raw Materials

Any flowers with a decent smell can be utilised for the manufacture of floral oils. But the flowers most employed are bela, chameli, henna, jasmine, gandharaj, kamini etc., etc., and the floral oils obtained from these flowers are most relished and appeal to the general taste.

The common vehicle in the preparation of floral oils is sesamum oil, though sometimes it is replaced by olive oil. Sesamum oil, however, seems to be the most suited basis for the manufacture of floral oils; for, this by itself possesses several meritorious properties. It keeps the hair soft and the brain cool. Over the above this, the oil has got fixative properties which enable it to bind down the fragrance of the flowers for a long time to come, even on exposure to air or on being washed with water at the time of bathing.

Treatment of the Ingredients

In preparing the floral oils, only the full-blown flowers should be selected. These should be as fresh as possible. Special notice is to be taken of the fact that the flowers should be all of the same standard quality and of the same colour, specially in the case of rose. Before being treated the flowers should also be freed from dust and earth and the stalks also removed from them without unduly pressing the petals.

As regards sesamum oil, only the best refined oils should be used for making floral oils. Special notice need be taken of the fact that only earthern, glass, chinaclay, porcelain, enamelled ware and aluminium utensils are to be used during manupulations. No iron, copper or brazen wares should be employed, for, these are very likely to react on the oil.

There are several methods of extracting the odoriferous principles from the flowers though the underlying principles in each case is either infusion, digestion or maceration or a combination of them. The general processes of manufacturing floral oils are put below.

Manufacture by Maceration

The fresh scented flowers are freed from stalks and are steeped in about double their weight of sesamum oil contained in a wide-mouthed bottle or jar, preferably of glass. The ingredients are then put in the sun, taking care to cover up the mouth of the vessel so that no dust or sand can enter the jar. The jar is continually kept in the sun and sometimes in the dew at night for a considerable period of time which may vary from a week to a month. The oil is then filtered through a piece of filannel or sometimes through cloth and the filtrate is collected. Care should be exercised that the flowers do not get mashed during the process. It is evident that some oil adheres to the surface of the exhausted flowers; a successful manufacturer howeve does not allow this oil to go waste. With the object in view the flowers are put in a big glass funnel having a small orifice to allow the settling oil to drip. The dripping oil is carefully collected and mixed with the previously filtered oil. The sesamum oil can thus be made to inbibe the odour of the flowers, yielding the floral oils of commerce. The oil should then be put vessels having mouth closed tightly with stoppers to avoid contact with air.

Concentrating the Preparation

But on many occasion it will found that the sesamum oil is not sufficiently odorous and can be made to absorb further odour. In such cases oil is charged with a fresh lot of new blown flowers freed from stalks. The whole is then placed in an aluminium pan, covered up and heated on the water bath for about half an hour. The pan is set aside for 24 hours is an undisturbed position and the oil is then strained. The soaked flowers are placed on a funnel and allowed to drip, and the oil is collected below. The waste flowers are then thrown away. The two oils are then mixed and filtered once again. Sometimes the filtered oil is given a third charge of flowers and the same operation is repeated before the process is brought to a close.

Hastening the process

It will be observed that the above method to be successful requires strong sunlight for a considerable time, moreover the complete process requires a pretty long time. When, however, the operations are required to be completed within a short measure of time, the flowers are infused in about double their quantity of sesamum oil and instead of putting the two ingredients in the sun continually for a number of days, they are put in an aluminium pan, covered up and heated on water bath for half an hour, and them set a sude for 24 hours. The oil is strained and the exhausted flowers are thrown away after te collection of the adhering oils in a manner described above. When the final product is desired to be of excellent quality the operation of repeated 7 or 8 times.

In lieu of repeated boiling on water bath, sometimes the filtered oil after a single heating on water bath and collection, is given a further charge of fresh flowers and the whole is set aside for a number of days in the sun after closing the mouth of the vessel tightly.

Tier system

A third method is sometimes adopted. Several pieces of white cotton cloth are soaked in sesamum or olive oil and are then wrung out. The cotton cloth thus moistened is spread at the bottom of a suitable vessel and a quantity of flowers is laid over it. This layer of flower is then covered up by a second piece of cloth previously wetted and fresh flowers are again laid over it. This layer in its turn is covered up by a third cotton cloth. A tier of flower may thus be made with seven or eight layers of flowers, each separated by moistened cotton cloths. Finally a quantity of oil is poured on the top of the lier. Generally the oil should be of double the weight of the flowers taken. The whole is then set aside for a number of days; the oil is then strained and collected. The process is repeated several times when oils of excellent quality are required.

Another Tier Arrangement

Essentially the same principle of extraction of the floral oil may be applied in another manner of substituting raw cotton in place of the cotton cloth. In a big-sized aluminium veseel, fresh flowers are first strewn over in a layer and these are then covered over thoroughly by loose and clean cotton. Then sesamum oil equalling the weight of the flowers taken is poured on the flowers. Fresh flowers are again laid out in the same manner and are entirely covered over thickly by loose cotton; and sesamum oil is again pured on the cleaned cotton. Several layers of flowers, cotton and oil are arranged in this manner. Sometimes as many as eight are made. Then the vessel is placed in the sun for a number of days after its mouth is closed duly. Finally the cotton and the flowers are pressed, together to obtain the oil.

The cotton pads are not thrown away. Fresh lots of flowers are strewn in a vessel, then a part of the wet cotton is laid over the flowers and a part of the above extracted oil is poured on the layer. As many as eight layers are arranged in this way and then the whole is placed in the sun after closing the mouth. The cotton and flowers are next extracted as before. This operation is generally repeated 5 or 6 times in order to obtain a good quality oil.

Oil Direct from the Seeds

Sesamum seeds are often employed in place of the sesamum oil for making the floral oils. In such cases, the fresh flowes are strewn over in a layer and are thoroughly coverd by a layer of sesamum seeds. On the layer thus formed sesamum oil is then poured. The vessel is then place din the sun for a certain number of days. Then the exhausted flowers are replaced by fresh flowers and then the operation is repeated over again several times. Finally the mixture of sesamum seeds and oil is cold pressed in *ghanies* or oil mills, to yield a high class oil with pleasing odour.

The sesamum seeds are sometimes ground and brayed on a muller with a roller and the paste is then applied to the flowers. These may be put in the sun and them boiled with sesamum oil over a water bath. Or, the paste may be put in the sesamum oil and flowers may then be steeped in the mixture and heated on a water bath. The whole mass is then strained and the oil is obtained, which may be similarly treated several times for high quality.

Recipes

With these observations we give a number of recipes which may be adopted with slight modifications for the prepartion of other floral oils.

Bela Oil

Procedure : Take 1 sr. fresh Bela flowers and 2½ srs. of sesamum oil. Put the two together into a wide-mouthed bottle; close it up tightly and place for seven days in the sun and in the dew at night.

Then strain through the flannel taking care that the flowers are not mashed. Put the flowers on a funnel and allow to drip. Collect the oil in an aluminium vessel and steep into it another lot of 1 seer of flowers, heat the vessel on the water bath for an hour and set aside for 24 hours. Now filter the oil, steep into it a third lot of 1 seer flowers and heat on the water bath for half an hour.

Finally filter. In this way a highly concentrated oil will be obtained.

Jasmine Oil

Procedure : Take several pices of clean and white cotton cloth; soak them in olive oil, rasp and wring out. Spread a piece of the cloth thus wetted at the bottom of a suitable veseel and layout a quantity of Jasmine flowers on it. Cover it up with a second piece of cotton cloth and again lay out flowers over it. Cover it with a third piece of cotton cloth. Now pour sesamum oil on the top layer. The quantity of the oil should be double that of flowers. Set aside for 24 hours. Then press the soaked flowes and collect the oil. Repeat the process seven times. Finally strain and squeeze the oil and bottle.

Chameli Oil

Procedure :Take 1 sr. Chameli flowers and 1 sr. sesamum. Layout the flowers in an aluminium veseel and pour 1 seer sesamum oil; close up the mouth of the vessel and place it in the sun for 3 days. Now pick out the exhausted flowers and put in afresh lot of 1 sr. flowers into it. cover the mouth again tand place in the sun for 7 days, after which period pick out the exhausted flowers and put a third lot of 1 sr. flowers into the oil. Cover the mouth and place in the sun again for 15 days. Now finally pick out the exhausted flowers and express the mixture of sesamum seeds and oil to obtain a nicely scented oil.

Champaka Oil

Procedure : Put 200 *Champaka* flowers in a jar and pour 2¼ srs. sesamum oil into it. Close up the mouth and place in the sun for 7 days and in the dew at night. Then press out the oil and give a fresh charge of flowers. This process may be repeated eight times when a highly scented oil will be obtained.

Kantali Champaka Oil

Procedure : Take 100 fresh Kantali Champaka flowers and 1½ srs. good olive oil. Put the two together into an aluminium pot, cover up and heat in the water bath for half an hour. Remove the vessel and set aside for 24 hours. Strain through a flannel and put in bottle. Now take the oil again in the vessel, put in a fresh lot of 100 flowers, heat again for half an hour and set aside for 24 hours. Press out the oil, collect it in the vessel, put in a third lot of 100 flowers, heat for half an hour and set aside for 24 hours. Finally strain and bottle. The soaked flowers may be squeezed to yield oil.

Jahuri Champaka Oil

Procedure : Take ½ seer newly blown Jahuri Champaka flowers and 10 srs. almond oil. Reject the green portion and put them in a bottle. Pour in the oil and place in the sun for 15 days in a the dew at night. Then strain the oil and steep in it another lot of ½ sr. fresh flowers, close up the mouth and place in the sun for 15 days. Finally press the oil, filter and bottle.

Dolan Champaka Oil

Procedure : Take 1 sr. of Nageswar Champakas from stalks and 1 sr. sesamum oil into a wide-mouthed bottle and place for 2 days in the sun and in the dew at night. Strain the oil and put it again in the bottle, steep a fresh lot of ½ sr.flowers; set aside for 24 hours and strain the oil. Put in a third lot of flowers in the oil; set aside for 24 hours and finally press out the oil, filter and bottle.

Nageswar Champaka Oil

Procedure :Take 1 sr. of Nageshwar Champakas free from stalks and 1 sr. sesamum oil into a wide mouthed bottle and place for 2 days in the sun and in the dew at night. Strain the oil and put it again in the bottle, steep a fresh lot of ½ sr. flowers; set aside for 24 hours and strain the oil. Put in a third lot of flowers in the oil; set aside for 24 hours and finally press out the oil, filter and bottle.

Henna Oil

Procedure : Take 2½ srs. sesamum oil in an aluminium vessel, cover up and heat on a water bath for an hour. Then put 1 sr. *Mehndi* flowers into it and set aside for 24 hours. Then press the oil from the flowers. Take the pressed oil in the vessel and heat it again on the water bath for half an hour. Now steep into this oil a fresh lot of 1 sr. flowers, set aside for 24 hours and then press out the oil. Put the oil in a wide-mouthed bottle; steep in it 1½ srs. flowers, cork at air tight and place the bottle in the sun for a fortnight. Finally filter the oil though a piece of flennel and mix the drippings with the original oil.

Gul Henna Oil

Procedure : Take 1 sr. mehandi flowes ½ ch. saffron and ¼ sr. sesamum. First bray the saffron and sesamum together into a fine paste, on a stone with a muller. Now pour into the paste 1½ srs. of sesamum oil. Soak the flowers into the mixture. Cover up and heat on the water bath for half an hour. Set aside the vessel for 24 hours. Strain the whole mass through a flannel, squeezing it into press the oil. Put the pressed oil in a wide mouthed bottle and steep in it another lot of 1 sr. flowers. Place the bottle in the sun for 20 days. Finally strain through a flannel and store in jars.

Musk Henna Oil

Procedure : Take 2 seers of Mehandi flowers 2½ srs. of sesamum oil and 1/8 tollah of musk. Macerate the musk in a stone mortar in 1 ch. of oil thoroughly. Put the colate in an aluminium vessel with the flowers and heat it on the water bath for an hour. Then put the oil in a wide-mouthed vessel, close up the mouth tightly and place it for seven days in the sun and in the dew at night. Finally strain through a flannel and store in bottles or jars.

Janti Oil

Procedure : Take 1 seer fo dry Janti flowers and add 1 seer olive oil. Put the two together into a bottle and place in the sun for a month. After that press the oil and collect it in an aluminium vessel. Steep into it a second lot of 1 sr. fresh flowers. Cover up and heat on the water bath for 24 hours.

Mallika Oil

Procedure : Take 2½ srs. Mallika flowers and 2 srs. of sesamum oil. Put the two together into a wide-mouthed bottle and close air-tight. Place the bottle in the sun for a month. Then strain through a piece of flannel. Put the soaked flowers in a funnel and allow to drip. Mix the two oils together.

Tuberose Oil

Procedure : Take 3 srs. pure olive oil and 1½ srs. tuberoses. Put the two together in an aluminium vessel. Cover up and heat on the water bath for half an hour. Remove, set aside for 24 hours, and press gently to squeeze out the oil. Collect it in a wide-mouthed bottle and steep in the oil another lot of 2 srs flowers. Close air-tight and set aside for a month. Finally express the oil, filter it and bottle.

Rose Oil

Procedure : Take ½ sr. of sesamum oil in a suitable vessel and throw into it 1/8 sr. petals of fresh roses of the same colour. Cover up and heat on the water bath for half an hour. Set the vessel aside for 24 hours. Poar out on a piece of clean cloth and wring to press out the whole oil. Again steep a fresh lot of ½ sr.rose petals in the expressed oil and follow the above directions.If process be repeated 7 or 8 times, the final product will be of excellent quality and command high price.

Bakul Oil

Procedure : Take 1 sr. Bakul flowers and 1 sr. sesamum oil. Put the two together into a jar, close up the mouth and put it in the sun for a month. Then express the oil.

Ketaki Oil

Procedure : Take 1 sr pollen of Ketaki flowers ½ sr. minced petals (white and tender), and 2 srs. of sesamum oil. Put these ingredients together in a jar, close up the mouth and place it for a month in the sun and in the dew at night. Then pour out into a cloth and express the oil. Finally filter and bottle.

Kamini Oil

Procedure : Take 2 srs. of Kamini flowers (free from stalks) and 4 srs. of sesamum oil together in an aluminium an and cover up and heat on a water bath for half an hour. Then pour the mixture in a wide-mouthed bottle, cork it tight and place in the sun continually for 15 days. Finally strain through a piece of flannel, and put the oil in air-tight bottles.

Lemon Flowers Oil

Procedure : Take 1 seer fresh Lemon flowers, free them form stalks; also take 2½ of sesamum oil; put the two together in a jar and place in the sun continually for a month. Then strain a mixture and drain the flowers. Now take another seer of fresh flowers and put them in the above filtered oil. put the mixture in a pan, cover up and heat on the water on the water bath for half an hour. Set the pan aside for 24 hours and then strain the oil.

Gandharaj Oil

Procedure : Grind thoroughtly 2½ srs. of sesamum and mix with the paste 2½ srs. of Gandharaj flowers. Put the mixture in a suitable vessel, cover up and place in the sun for 7 days. Then mix 2 srs. sesamum oil into it and heat the mixture on the water bath for one hour. cover up and set aside for 24 hours. Then strain and the put the oil in a bottle. Squeeze the soaked flowers and mix the oil so obtained with the above. Finally filter the whole quantity of oil.

Madhumalati Oil

Procedure : Procure 1 sr. Madhumalati flowers free from stalk and 1 sr. sesamum oil. Take a big sized aluminium vessel and strew at its bottom 2 ch. flowers. Lay out over them loose cleaned cotton thickly so as to cover thoroughly. Pour on the cotton 2 ch. oil and strew another layer of flowers. Lay out on it another pad of cotton, pour of 2 ch. oil on it and strew flowers. Repeat in this way to make 8 layers. Close up the mouth of the vessel and place in the sun for 24 hours. Now press the cotton and flowers together to obtain the oil.

Do not throw away the cotton pads. Take a fresh lot of flowers; strea a quantity at the bottom of the vessel; lay on it the wet cotton; pour the above extracted oil and arrange in 8 layers. Place in the sun for 24 hours and press the cotton and flowers as before. If this process be repeated for 5 times, an oil of good quality will be obtained.

Khus Oil

Procedure : Take 2 srs. Khus root and 1 sr. sesamum; grind the two together into a paste on a clean stone slab with a muller. If the materials are too dry they may be moistened with a little sesamum oil. Put the paste in a jar, pour into it 2 srs. of sesamum oil and bury the vessel in the earth for one month. The mouth of the jar should be covered with a lid and platered with mud. After the lapse of the period, bring up and extract the oil to the drop by pressing hard. Collect the oil in a wide-mouthed vessel. Now take another seer of Khus, clean it thoroughly from dirt, and proud it fincly in a dhenki (country made rice huller) or in an iron mortar and pestle. Throw the powder thus obtained into the oil already expresed; cover up the mouth of the bottle, place in the sun for 16 days. Finally extract the oil by pressing hard.

Lotus Oil

Procedure : Procure 5 srs. of white petals of Lotus and 5 srs. sesamum oil. Put the two together into a vessel and heat on the water bath for an hour. Remove the set aside for 24 hours. The operations should be carried on under cover. Extract the oil by pressing the soaked petals. Again put 2½ srs petals in the oil; heat on the water bath for half an hour. Set aside for 24 hours and extract the oil by pressing. Steep a third lot of 1 sr. flowers in the extracted oil, heat on the water bath for half an hour, set aside for 24 hours and extract the oil. Steep again and place in the sun for 15 days. Extract the oil by pressing; filter and bottle.

Storing

After the preparation of the floral oils, these are stored carefully in vases in cool but not damp places. On many occasions they are stored in pot-boiled vessels made of the mambrances from the intestines of sheep, goat, etc. These vessels can be transported from one place to another as they are immune from breakge of leakage, very common in cases of glass or earthern vessels. Apart from the advantages of transport, these vessels are considered to be the beat so far as the keeping quality of the oils is concerned. In fact in centres of floral oil manufacture these vessels are much in vogue and are recommended strongly for packing oils.

11

Manufacturing Processes of Flavours

Introduction

Flavours may be produced by a large variety of methods, from the purely synthetic approach, to the extraction of volatile components from materials of botanical origin. Science and technology have let us to more sophisticated ways of creating flavours.An area of knowledge that has developed into a major commercial venture for the flavour industry is the production of process flavours. The term " process flavour" has been used to define a group of flavours or flavouring ingredients that are produced from precursor materials via some type of processing technique(s). The major processing techniques in use today are thermal processing and enzyme modification. Both techniques have been in commerical use for approximately 25 years and currently represent a significant part of the flavour industry's commercial and research activities. A summery of the general types of process flavours is geven in Table 11.1.

What makes this area of flavour chemistry different from the traditional methods is the relationship of the development of the aroma profiles to knowledge of natural, chemical or biochemical pathways that are known to create aromas. The difference between the occurrence of the flavours in a natural system (e.g., meat, nuts, cheese and butter) and in a process flavour is the intelligent selection of precursors and processing conditions that allow for the optimum production of the aroma profiles. These flavours have a close relationship to their natural food derived counterparts.

Three major factors that support the success of these flavours and flavouring ingredients are inherent in process flavour technology. First, because the creation of the process flavour is based on chemical and biochemical knowledge of the original food, its flavour profile is very close to that of the food is duplicating. The use of synthetic chemicals to produce a flavour generally exaggerates the flavour profile.

Second because of flavour is produced from selected precursors and not necessarily the total food, a great degree of control on its production and economy of manufacture may be gained. Typically, less than 0.1 per cent of a powerful aroma is necessary to be present in a food to act as a flavour. This is particularly true in the savory/meat flavour area where some of the flavouring components have odour threshholds in the part per bilion and trillion level The definition of a flavour captures the notion that it is a powerful material whose significant function is flavour and not nutrition or functionality.

Table 11.1

Summary of the types of process flavours

Mechanism	*Flavour type*
Thermal generated	Processed (reaction) flavour
Chemical hydrolysis	Hydrolysates
Controlled of oxidation	Fat flavours
Autolysis-Enzyme	Autolysates
Conversion with endogenous enzymes	
Enzymolysis	Enzyme modified
Fermentation	Flavour

Third because the materials are produced via'natural' mechanisms such as roasting, fermentation and enzymolysis, the final flavour may qualify as a natural flavour or flavouring ingredient. This is particularly true if the precursor is a traditional food or food component, and the processing conditions are those used in traditional food preparation and the resulting product qualifies as a flavour. Newer, more nontraditional uses of process flavour technology come under more discussion when the term " natural" is to be applied. Both the industry and the regulatory groups have been considering a new definition of the term "natural". As of this publication, there has been no resolution of the issue.

During the last 20 years, several hundred patents on process flavours have been granted around the world. However, no single patent has provided a rigid specification for the thermally processed flavour. Recently, the international Organization of Flavour Industries (IOFI) has established a guideline for the manufacture of process flavours. As noted in their guidelines and in the patent literature, the basic compounds used to create a process flavour are amino acids (particularly the sulfur containing ones), reducing sugars, thiamine (vitamin B1) and known synthetically produced components from the Maillard reaction (i.e., dialhyddes) Many of the resultant components of the reactions have been isolated and identified. These compounds were then synthesized and patented for use as synthetic flavouring ingredients. Major compounds are pyrazines, thiazolines, furanones, furans, polysulfide copounds (thianes) and thiophenes.

The two major divisions of process flavours are the thermally processed flavours and flavours produced by enzymatic modification.

THE THERMALLY PROCESSED FLAVOURS (MEAT AND SAVORY FLAVOURS)

The use of thermal methods for flavours development is nearly as ancient as man himself. The use of fire is preparing food has been estimated to be upwad of 10,000 years old. However, it is only in recent, history that the chemistry of thermally induced flavour development has become well understood.

The first thermally produced flavouring material can be traced to the production of a product called hydrolyzed vegetable protein or, more commonly, HVP. It was developed by Julius Maggi, a Swiss chemist, during the last century. The first chemical understanding of the development of flavours by heat is associated with the work of Dr. Louis Camille Maillard of the University of Nancey (France) from 1912 to 1936. Significant symposia have been held on the subject of the "Maillard reaction" mechanism (appropriately named for its discoverer, but some 15 yeas after his death) in the development of aromatic materials from precursors consisting of amino acid and reducing sugars. A fundamental discussion of these mechanisms can be found in one of the more recent symposia on the subject.

The basic challenge to the scientific in producing thermally generated flavours is in the understanding and selection of the precursor materials and processing conditions. Although the "Maillard reaction" is a major pathway for aroma development, other chemical pathways also make significant contributions to aroma formation. Table 11.2 reviews the types of thermally driven chemical mechanisms that make significant contributions to aroma production. The major literature cited will help in understanding the chemical mechanisms and, to some degree, the usefulness of the aroma profile generated.

Although there is a very diverse amount of chemistry related to thermal processing, it is reported that the heterocyclic aromatic generated during the reactions are the most interesting and useful in the preparation of a flavour. These compounds are also, generally the most difficult to produce by chemcial synthesis.

Although the patent literature is full of reference on the manufacture of thermally produced flavours, only approximately 45 are used in commercial production. Table 11.3 indicates the more significant patents protecting the manufacture of process flavours.

The key aromatic compounds of value in creating meat-like, cooked and roasted flavours are the heterocyclic in nature. Table 11.4 lists the types of compounds, their typical aroma character and their ranges of threshold values. Many of these chemicals have been produced by synthetic chemistry and have been approved as GRAS (Generally Recognized As Safe) by FEMA' (Flavour and Extract Manufacturer's Association) Expert Panel or by the FDA. The variety of materials are numerous and their odor thresholds have a very dynamic range. Fors (1981) has prepared a fine review of many of the sensory properties of the volatile maillard reaction products.

These are various types of process flavours used either singly or in combination with other similar materials to produce the final commercially available flavour. The major types are discussed below.

Table 11.2

Mechanisms for thermal development of flavour

Reaction Types	Major precursors(s)	Typical aroma resultant	Major litreature review
"Maillard"	Amino acids and reducing sugars	Various	Waller 1983
Strecker degradation	Amino acids and reducing sugars	Aldehyde	Parliament 1989
Condensation	Dicarbonyl compounds from sugar and amino acids of ammonia	Pyrazines	Mega 1982
Sulfur addition	Furanonone compounds +5 Nucleotides w/sulfur containing material	Thiaziles thiazolines	Van den Ouweland 1975 Shu 1989
Decomposition	Thiamine (vitamin B1)	Thiazoles Thizzolines Thiofurans	Werkhoff et. al. 1980 Guntert et. al. 1980
Oxidation	Unsaturated fatty acids	Unsaturated aldehydes	Nawar 1989
Hydrolysis	Vegetable and animal protein	Pyrazines (+) plus complex mixture	Manley 1981
Cyclo-Dehydration	Sugars	5 Hydroxy+Furfural+	Hodge 1967

Table 11.3
Major thermal process flavour patents

Processing Major Reactant	*Type of (Temp/Time)*	*Flavour*	*Patent Cited*
1-Crysteine	130°C/3hrs.	Meat-Like	May 1960* USA 2,934, 435
Furaneol	100°C/31 min	Roasted meat	Van den Ouweland USA 3,904, 655
Chicken Protien/thiamine	130°C/30 min	Chicken	Chuy USA 4,081,565
2-hydroxy Ethylammonium Hydroxy butanol	80°C/5 min	Bacon	Weiner USA 3, 645, 754
Xylose 1-cysteine HVP	60-180°C 3 min	Roast beaf	Baugher USA 3,930,380
HPV 1-Crysteine xyloxe Malic acid Guanylate	100°C/2 hrs	Beaf	Van Pottelsbughi USA 3,716, 380
Yeast autolysate HVP, lactic acid		Beaf	USA 2,109,084
Fried onion	115°C 40 min	Onion	Huth USA 3,424,592

Table 11.4
Threshhold ranges of key aromatic compounds in process flavour

Key aromatic compounds	*Range of flavour types*	*Range of thresholds (in water)*
Thizolines	Roasted Cooked onion Meaty	3 ppm to 0.003 ppb
Pyrazines	Roasted Green Popcorn Nutty	25 ppm to 0.006 ppb
Furanones	Caramel Meat-like	1 ppm to 0.03 ppb
Furans	Sweet-burnt Rum-like Green	5 ppm to 6 ppb
Aldehyde	Fruity Green	15 ppm to 0.2 ppb
Poly sulfide compounds- e.g., thianes	Onion/garlic	50 ppb to 2 ppb
Thiophens	Fried onion Mustard-like	200 ppb to 1 ppb

Protein Hydrolysates

As mentioned earlier, hydrolyzed vegetable proteins (hydrolysates/ HVP) were the first process flavours. These materials are products of acidhydrolysis of proteins (usually of plant origin, but can be from animal protein). They acquire their flavour from the acid hydrolysis of the protein to amino acids and from the heating steps. During the processing, the residue carbohydrate in the protein sourse is reacted and also generates some aroma. The manufacturer of HVP is also to adjust the flavour profile of the resulting material by the degree to which the material has been processed, the substrate used (protein source) and resultant cleanup of the raw hydrolysate. These steps include the use of activated carbon, to remove some color and harsh flavour notes, and the precipitation of hydrophilic amino acids (biter amino acids) and the general aging of the material.

The Umami (taste enhancing) properties of MSG are well known and, in fact, early hydrolysates (particularly produced from wheat) were produeced specifically to isolate the MSG for use as flavour enhancer in foods. This was the industry practice until the late 50's when fermentation methods proved to be more economical.

Yeast and Autolyzed Yeast Extract

Yeast products and, in particular, their autolyzed extracts (generally referred to as autolyzed yeast extract AYE) are ingredients quite similar to HVP. In a sense, these are the earliest of process flavourings based on the use of enzymates to create a flaour profile. In the case of AYE, the endogenous enzymes are used to break down the yeast components (proteins, nucleotides, vitamines, and carbohydrates) to substrates useful in creating aromas during heating. More recent practice by manufacturers of AYE and process flavours is to add enzymes, not native to the yeast, to develop specific flavour and taste profiles.

The substrates available in a yeast make it an ideal candidate for processing into meat or savory flavourings. The protein content is high, and it contains certain other components, such as thiamine (vitamin B1) nucleic acids and sulfur- containing amino acids, all of which can generate strong flavour profiles when heat activated. One such components of a thermal reaction in yeast is big (2-methyl-3-furyl)-disulfide.

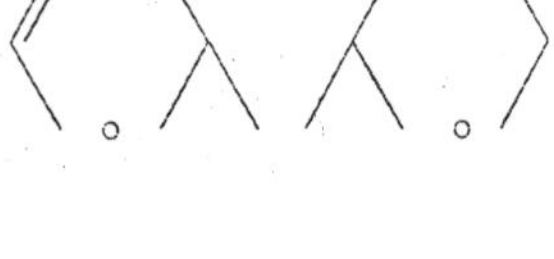

It has been found to have an aroma threshold of 2 parts in 10 parts of water.

The nucleic acids themsalves are useful as flavour enhancers in savory flavours. The flavour-enhancing properties of these materials are well documented.

Yeast and AYE find use directly in compounds flavours for their inherent flavour profile, as well as being used in complex process flaovur systems where amino acids, thiamine and nucliec acids are reacted to produce strong aromas.

Basic Process Flavourings

The early process flavourings were based on the reaction of selected components such as thiamine, amino acids, reducing sugars and hydrolysates. The first commercialy available process flavours were essentially sophisticated hydrolysates. These mateials are still the "workhorses" of the industry. They are materials used to bring more characters to a savory flavour. They usually produce a generally meaty, roasted, or cooked note. They are considerably more intense than the basic HVP or AYE and deliver more aroma characters.

Complex Process Flavourings

The simple process flavours are useful in generating nonspecific aromas. The more recent generation of process flavour development has focused on the production of species specific aroma profiles. The use of very specific precursors and thermal profiles allows for the generation of specific chemicals known to be necessary for creating the aroma of a certain species of cooked animal meat. Chemical, such as the dienals, generated from the thermal breakdown of unsaturated fats and fatty acids, create strong chicken aroma. High amounts of the amino acid proline allow for the generation of breed and/ or cracker notes.

This technology requires the chemical knowledge of the actual foods and their processing conditions. The substrates and processing conditions may be very complex. It is an area of development that is very close to food itself. In fact, the development of gravies, roux and many basic sources are the classical analogy in the food preparation area to the process flavour. Much of the knowledge in this ara is not covered in patents, but is maintained as trade secrets by companies manufacturing the flavours. Because of their complexity, it is generally very difficult to reproduce these flavours without specific knowledge of the formulation and processing steps. In some cases, in the final products use meat, meat and vegetable protein, or fat that has been enzymatically converted to thermally reactable precursor materials prior to the thermal processing step(s).

As noted above, many of the aromatic materials used in creating meat and savory ingredients noted above with the addition of carriers, antioxidants, solvents, other flaours, flavours adjucnts and flavour enhancers. These materials are noted in Table 11.5

Table 11.5
Optical materials used in the manufacture of reaction flavours

Soduim chloride	Antioxidants
Monosodium glutamate	Modified starch
Ribotides (5'nucleotide)	Gums Maltol and ethyl maltol

Table 11.6
Food products using meat and savory flavours

Soups	Sausages
Gravies	Syrups
Souces	Pot pies
Snacks	
Meat Products	Bevarages
Boullions	Toppings
Broths	Confectionery products

These flavours have seen significant sales growth in the past 15-20 years. The estimated sales volume of these materiȧl in1980, including HVP and AYE, is estimated to be in the $250 million range (Manley 1991). They find use in the great array of final food products as noted in Table 11.6.

Now let us turn our attention to the use of enzymes and microorganisms in the production of dairy flavours.

ENZYME MODIFICATION AND FERMENTATION-THE DAIRY FLAVOURS

Dairy products are some of the oldest of man's foods and are certanly one of the most important classes of food for nutrition. There is a great array of dairy products based upon the species of animal used for the milk, the processing conditions and the enzymes and/or microorganisms used to develop the desired texture and flavour character. Table 11.7 notes the types and some of the specific dairy products available around the world. It is intrersting to note that the types of dairy products available are strongly to national and ethnic references. In many cases, that reference is specific to the geographic or ethnic niche. For example, Yakult in Japan and Kifur in Russia are dairy products which are little known outside their principal area of consumption, whereas, butter, Cheddar cheese and yugurt have found nearly world-wide consumer acceptence.

Table 11.7
Types of dairy products available on the world market

Milk

- Fresh
- Pasturized
- UHT
- Canned

Cream

Butter

- Ghee (Buffalo milk)
- Margarine

Cultured Products

- Yogurt
- Butter Milk
- Acidophilus Milk
- Bulgarian Milk
- Yakult
- Leben
- Kifur

Ice Cream

Cheeses

- Fresh Soft Low-Fat Cheese
- Cream/Neufchatel
- Gauda/Nunster
- Port du Salut (Flavoured)
- Brie/Camembert
- Blue Ceeses
- Goat Cheeses
- Emmental
- Emmental
- Cheddar
- Parmesan/Romano
- Whey/Ricotta

The creation of dairy flavours has bee closely related to the understanding of the precursor chemistry (substrate) and processing (biochemical conversion) to create desirable aromatic chemicals. The universal substrate for dairy products is milk. Although milk may come from any of the many mammals, its most common sources around the world are the cow, goat, water buffalo, and sheep.

Milk is a very complex natural material containing fats, sugars (mainly lactose), proteins (such as lactalbumin) and salts (such as calcium phosphate). The taste and aroma of fresh milk is minimal, with most of the taste coming from the fat and salt system. The aroma is faint, but is due to a combination of feed notes inhaled by the cow and directly transferred to the milk and cookd notes coming from the pasteurization process.

Milk fat is the major source of flavours particularly when the milk is processed further or is treated with enzymes of micro organism.Table 11.8 notes the types of fats and lipid material contained in milk fat. The fatty acid composition of milk lipids is also very complex and unique among food products. Over 60 fatty acids have been reported in cows milk. Quantities of butyric caproic, caprylic and capric acids fatty acids with 4,6,8 and 10 carbon atoms respectively) are unique to milk and of great importance in the development of dairy flavours. For oxidation of unsaturated octadecadienoic acid (linoleic acid) leads of the formation of 4-cis-heptenal that has been reported as a cream like flavour component in milk and butter. Small amounts of free butryc acid are important to butter flavour as well as to most cheese flavours. One should also note that milk fat contains a small amount of bounds hydoxy and keto acids, which are readily hydrolyzed by either microbial lapses or thermal treatment. Free hydroxy acids readily cyclize into lactones and the keto acids degrade into methyl ketones.

Table 11.8
Fats and lipids in milk

Type of fats	Range of occurrence (%) in cow's milk
Triglycerides	97.0-98.0
Diglycerides	0.25-0.48
Monoglycerides	0.015-0.038
Keto and glycerides	0.85-1.28
Aldehyco glycerides	0.011-0.015
Glyceryl ethers	0.011-0.023
Free fatty acids	0.10-0.44

Phospholipids	0.2-1.0
Carebrosides	0.013-0.066
Sterols	0.12-0.4

The mechanisms of flavours developments are reviewed in Table 11.9. This table is an indication of the complexity that was noted above. a number of comprehensive reviews on these machanisms exist in the literature.

In order to get a better understanding of the nature of dairy flavours, it is best to review castegories that relate to specific profiles or route of flavour development.

Milk and Cream Flavours

These flavours representatives of dairy products that are minimally processed. Typically, they are heat treated in either a pasteurization step (15 seconds at 72°C) or ultrahigh temperature treated (UHT-a few seconds at 135°C to 150°C). This thermal exposure gives rise to flavours development from :

Table 11.9
Mechanisms of dairy flavour formation

Thermally Directed Reactions

- Maillard reactions
- Sulfur release
- Tiglyceride hydrolysis
- Oxidation of unsaturated fatty acids
- Caramelization (high temperature)

Enzymatically Directed Reactions

- Lppases-release of fatty acids and hydroxy fatty acids for lactone formation
- Esterases-same as lipases
- Proteases-releases of peptides of aged taste of cheeses

Microbiologically Directed Reactions

- Lactic-producing organisms lactic acid taste-pH change
- Molds-Roqueford-blue cheese with methyl ketones.

Table 11.10

Components	*Flavour Note*
Fatty acids	Milk taste components
4-cis-heptenoal	Cream-like
Methyl ketones	Low-levels (below threshold) together give cream-like; also cause state off-flavour at higher levels
Lactones (high carbon # 8-12)	Cooked-butter notes
Coconut flavour character	
Maillard reaction products notes	Heated milk produces caramel
Dimethyl sulfide (from s-methyl methionine sulfonium salt) from cow's diet	Malty or cowy flavour detect in milk
Oxidation of Lipids (Aldehydes and Ketone e.g., hexanal and 1-octen-3-one)	"Card-boardy" off odor-defect
Degradation of methionine producing methional, methyl sulfide, dimthyl sulfide and dimethyl disulfide	Sunlight defect
Sugars	Sweeteners
Diacetyl	Buttery notes
Lactic acid	Sourness
C10 and C12	Sweet
Fatty acids	Cream
Butryric acid	Higher level give rancidity note and character

- Degradation of thermallyliable precursors found in milk.
- Products of sugar/protein (amino acid) reactions.
- The release of sulfur-containing components.
- Degradation and milk oxidation of triglycerides final flavour.

Table 11.10 outline the aromatic components generated that are related to a specific flavour profile in creating milk or cream flavours. This is one of the most delicate of flavours profiles, and one needs that needs the skilled flavour chemists to blend the chemical components or materials from processing to achieve an acceptable final flavour.

Cultured Dairy Flavours

Cultured products are some of the first products developed from milk. Originally, fermentation occurred naturally to milk set aside for later consumption. The spoilage organisms in the milk produced the proper conditions for presentation of the final cultured products. The basic fermentation is due to lactic acid bacteria. Originally, the fermentation was peformed with a mixed or " unknown" culture or : back-slop:, modern technology has developed the pure cultures with their predictable performance potentials.

The major flavour and taste component in these products is the lactic acid produced by the fermentation of the sugar by the bacteria. The preferred metabolite, in flavour terms, is the L(+) Lactic acid (Kielwein). The D(–) enantiomer has a harsh off-flavour note. The acid note is the most significant one is this category. One exception is product from Russia, called Kifur, which undergoes a secondary fermentation is create ethyl alcohol. This producet is often called, with good reason, the "Champagne of Milk".

The flavour is yogurt is also influenced by the amount of another fermentation product, acetaldehyde. There is no agreement on the acetaldehyde values that give optimum flavour effect. Levels from 13 to 41 ppm have been reported as optimum.

The last compound of flavour interest in cultured milk product is diacetyl: a metabolite of citrate by the action of Streptococci or Leuconostoc organisms. This component contributes strongly toa buttery type flavour at levels of 1-2 ppm.

Butter Flavour

Butteris product of the concentration of the fat in the milk by mechanical separation. The resultant product is a water in oil emulsion with a reasonably milk characteristic flavour. During the process, a small portion of the fats are broken down to fatty acids byenzymes. Lactones are also formed from the small amount of γ-hydroxy acids occurring in the milk fat. The g-lactones may also form the unsaturated C_{18} fatty acids via hydration and ß-oxidation.

The major flavour components used to create butter flavours are diacetyl, lower carbon number fatty acids and higher carbon number lactones. Some of the flavour notes in sweet cream butter may be due to the deca and dodecanoic acids and methyl ketones.

Margarine, an imitation butter, is one of the major uses for butter flavours. Because margarine is used in cooking, it is desirable to create a flavour that generates a butter flavour upon heating. The heated butter flavour is due to the thermal generation of certain flavour components (usually lactones). Certain lactone precursors have been synthesized so that margarine may have the same flavour profile as butter after heating. A number of patents have been issued that cover butter flavour; some significant ones are summarized in Table 11.11.

Table 11.11
Recent butter/cheese flavour patents

Brief description	Patent citation
Butter oil/lipase-blue cheese-like	Shay et al. 1990 EP 357812
Lactones from lipids for margarine	Haring 1989 EP 321055
Diketone precursors as a butter-like flavour	Doormbos 1988 EP 293957
Heated fatty acids at 150-475°C to give a dairy flavour	Chen 1988 EP 295509
Hydrozlyzing butter and coconut oil with lipases	Shukunobe 1988 J 63240755
Butter/cream/cheese flavour from fat treated with lipases from Chrombacterium	Tojo 1988 J 64002549
Green notes from soybean with lipases	Kanisawa 1988 USA 4769243
Acetayliacetic acid is converted to diacetyl during baking	Uniliever 1987 NL 8601078
Lipolyzed butter fat by Leuconostoc cremoris	Chang 1987 USA 4670267
Sugar and butter heated at 150-250°F to produce aqueous soluble butter flavour	Izzo 1967 USA 4684532
Omega-alkenyl methyl ketone for butter flavour	Mei ji Foods J 59039822
Lipipolyzed cultured cream	Bakal 1983 USA 4684532

J = Japan EP=Europe NL=Holland

Cheese Flavours

The many varieties of cheese represent centuries of cultivation of the art of cheese making, with its creation of many different flavours, tastes of textures. The different types of cheese are the result of many types of microorganisms (yeast, bacteria and mold) working together with the basic milk sources (which are typically cow's goat's or sheep's milk).

The basic families of cheeses are noted in Table 11.12 with their corresponding flavour character noted and the major components contributing to their aroma profile. By far, the most popular cheese in the USA is Cheddar cheese . It is an English invention that use a unique process, "cheddaring," introduced to repress the growth of the spoilage organisms by pilling and repilling blocks of warm cheese curd in the cheese vat, leading to rapid increase of lactic acid. During this period, the rapid increase in acid destroys the caliform (spoilage) bacteria.

Aged cheese, particularly Cheddar, owes most of its taste character to the peptides formed during curing. These components contribute to the bitter and umami taste of the aged product. The sharpness is generally related to

Table 11.12
Components related to specific cheese flavour character

Componet	*Cheese Variety*	*Flavour Note*
Small peptides	Swicc Gouda/Munester	Sweet taste
Fresh Milk components	Cream Cheese Neufchatel	Milk milk
Small peptides, proponic acid	Emmental	Sweet taste low level (<1%)
4-mercapto-4methyl pentanope-2	Gouda	Fatty note as defect
Bitter-hydrophilic peptides	Aged Cheddar	Higher amount of peptides related to character
Acetic acid	Sharp Cheddar	Sharp character
Medium chain fatty acids (C6 to C-18)	Mild Cheddar	Overall cheddar Character
Methanethiol	Aged note Cheddar	Aged note (threshold at 0.02 ppb)
Acetylpyrazine 2-methoxy-3 ethyl Pyrazine	Aged Cheddar	Aged note-nutty (microbial origins)
Relatively alrge amount of C8 and C10 saturated fatty acids	Blue	Background aroma
Methyl ketone	Blue	Characterizing aroma

the release of acetic acid during the ripening process. The medium-chain have also been shown to be important in cheddar cheese flavour character.

Creation of Dairy Flavours

The significant aroma and taste components discussed above may be blended to produce various dairy flavours. These components may be generated by chemical synthesis, extraction from natural material or produced by biotechnology (enzymolysis or fermentation).

The major chemicals found in dairy flavours have been synthesized and placed on the FEMA or FDA GRAS List. Other materials such as starter cultures (concentrated diacetyl), enzyme modified cheese and other fermentation products are allowed. All of these materials allow the flavour chemist to create the specific dairy flavour profiles for use in a variety of food products.

Regulatory Issues

General regulatory issues related to flavours are covered in another section; however, the specific issue related to savory flavours and dairy flavours need some discussion in this section. These flavours are generally regulated, over all, by the Food and Drug administration under either the GRAS (21 CFR section172.510-172.590) or the natural flavour section (21 CFR section 101.22). Natural flavour claims can be made when the flavour is made from natural substrate by methods indicated in the regulation.

When the savory flavours are produced with amounts of meat or meat by-products exceeding 2 per cent of the flavour, their production comes under the supervision of the US Department of Agriculture's Meat Inspection Department (MID). Flavour manufacturing facilities that produce flaourings with meat/poultry or their by-products must have their plants qualified as a USDS inspected plant and have USDA field inspection.

A flavour not containing the maximum allowed meat /poultry or by product may also come under USDA's regulations when the flavour is used by a meat-or poultry producing plant that is under USDA MID inspection. As an aid to having the flavour qualified for use in such plant, it is useful to have the formulation reviewed by the Proprietary Mix Committee (PMC) of USDA in Washington, D.C. A standard form for submission of information for review of the flavour's formula can be arranged by writing the chairman fo the Proprietary Mix Committee, Food Safety and Inspection Service of the United States Department of Agriculture at 300 12th St. SW, Washington, D.C. 20250-3700.

There are specific ingredients used to make savory and dairy flavours that must be identified to the PMC during the formula review procedure. Table 11.13 indicates those ingredients that need to be acknowledged in a formula disclosure to the PMC. The basis of the disclosure is to indicate to the consumer the presence of any of the following materials: (1) materials of religious or ethnic interest (Kosher); (2) materials of health concern in terms of allergic activities (proteins); (3) materials that are personal aversions (MSG); and (4) materials that have water binding capabilities or make a significant nutritional contribution to the final food.

Table 11.13
Materials used in process flavourings that must be labeled

- Proteinaceous materials
- Food Materials
- Functional (in final product) ingredients
- Materials that are under religious review

The new regulation regarding labeling of flavours for USDA products was issued in 1990 (US Department of Agriculture 1990). At the time of this text's publication, the FDA had not made changes to its regulation regarding these products. It is believed that such changes will be made shortly so that one should review the regulation regarding the current rules for making and labeling these flavours.

Appendix 11.1 IOFI Guidelines for production and labeling for process flavours

I. Introduction

Process flavourings are produced by heating raw material that are foodstuffs or constituents of foodsfuffs in similarly with the cooking of food.

The most practical way to characterize process flavourings is by their starting materials and processing conditions, since the resulting composition is extremely complex, being analogous to the composition of cooked foods. They are prodcced every day by the hosuewife in the kitchen, by the food industry during food processing and by the flavour industry.

The member associations of IOFI have adopted the following Guidelines in order to assure the food industry and the ultimate consumer of food of the quality, safety and compliance with legislation of process flavourings.

II. Scope

1.1 These guidelines deal with thermal process flavourings; they do not apply to foods, flavourings extracts, defined flavourings substances or mixtures of flavourings substances and flavour enhancers.

1.2 These guidelines define those raw materials and process conditions that are similar to the cooking of food, and which give process flavourings that are admissible without further evalution.

III. Definition

A thermal process flavouring is a product prepared for its flavouring properties by heating food ingredients and/or ingredients permitted for use in foodstuffs or in process flavourings.

IV. Basic Standards or Good Manufacturing Practice

Chapter 3 of the Code of Practice for the flavour industry is also applicable to process flavourings.

V. Production of Process Flavourings

Process flavourings shall comply with national legislation and shall also conform to the following :

A. Raw Materials for Process Flavourings

Raw materials for process flavourings shall consists of one or more of the followings :

4.1.1 A protein nitrogen source :

- Protein nitrogen containing food (meat, poultry, eggs, dairy products, fish, seafood, cereals, vegetable products, fruits yeasts) and their extracts.

- Hydrolysis products of the above, autolyzed yeasts, peptides, amino acids and or their salts.

4.1.2 A Carbohydrate source :

-Food containing carbohydrates (cereals, vegetable, products and fruits) and their extracts.-Mono, di-and polysaccharides (sugars, dextrins, starches and edible gums).

4.1.3 A fat or fatty acid source :

- Food contaning fat and oils

- Edible fat and oils from animal, marine, or vegetable origin.
- Hydrogenated, transesterified and/or fractionated fats and oils
- Hydrolysis products of the above.

4.1.4 Materials listed in Appendix Table A11.1.

4.2 Ingredients of proces flavourings.

4.2.1 Natural flavourings, natural and natureidentical flavouring substances and flavour enhancers, as defined in the IOFI Code of Practice for the flavour industry.

4.2.2 Process flavour adjuncts

Suitable carriers, antioxidants, preserving agents, emulsifiers, stabilizers, and anticaking agents listed in the lists of flavour adjuncts in Annex II of the IOFI Code of Practice for the flavour industry.

B. Preparation of Process Flavourings

Process flavourings are prepared by processing together raw materials listed under 4.1.1 and 4.1.2 with the possible addition of one or more of the materials listed under 4.1.3 and 4.1.4.

4.3.1 The product temperature during processing shall not exceed 180°C, with correspondingly longer times at lower temperature.

4.3.2 The processing time shall not exceed ¼ hour at 180°C.

4.3.3 The pH during processing shall not exceed 8.

4.3.4 Flavourings, flavouring substances and flavour enhancers (4.2.1) and process flavour adjuncts (4.2.2) shall be added only after processing is completed.

C. General Requirements for Process flavourings

4.4.1 Process flavourings shall be prepared in accordance with the General Principles of Food Hygeine (CAC/Vol A-Ed. 2(1985)) recommended by the Codex Alimentarious Commission.

4.4.2 The restrictive list of natural and nature-identical flavouring substances of the I OF I Code of Practice for the flavour industry applies also to process flavourings.

D. Labeling

The labeling of process flavourings shall comply with national legislation.

5.1 Adequate information shall be provided to enable the food manufacturer to observe the legal requirements for his products.

5.2 The name and address of the manufacturers of the distributor of the process flavouring shall be shown on the table.

5.3 Process flavour adjuncts have to be declared only in case they have a technological function in the finished food.

Appendix Table A11.1
Material used in processing

Herbs and spices and their extracts
Water
Thiamine and its hydrochloric acid salt
Ascorbic acid
Citric acid
Lactic acid
Fumaric acid
Malic acid
Succinic acid
Tartaric acid
The sodium, potassium, calcium, magnesium, and ammonium salts and the above acids
Guanylic acid and inosinic acid and its sodium, potassium and calcium salts
Inositol
Sodium, potassium- and ammonumsulfides, hydrosulfides and polysulfides
Acids, bases and salts as pH regulators:
Acetic acid, hydrochloric acid, phosphoric acid, sulfuric acid
Sodium, potassium, calcium and ammonium hydroxyde
The salts of the above acids and bases
Polymethylslloxane as antifoaming agent (not participating in the process)

12

Non-Alcoholic Flavours

Among the synthetics in common use for certain applications; as indicated are anethole (anice licorice for cough drops and chewing gum; Benzyl acetate (fruit rasberry and cherry) for candies and soft drinks, cinnamaldehyde (cinnamon) for leaked goodes. Chewing gum, and leaked goods. Methyl anthranilite (comcood grapse) for candies and soft drinks.

Compounding

The flavour chemist is responsible for the basic knowledge of sensory and application properties of each of this large number of raw materials. The tremendous number of possible combination of these flavoured finished compounds is readily apparent. It is not uncommon to develop a flavour that combines essential oils, plant extractives, fruit juices and synthetics.

Simple flavours are those containing a single ingredient alone of diluted in appropriate neutral carrier; compound flavours are blends of several ingredients either as mixture of them alone or diluted in carriers (solvents). The presence of alcohol as solvent is of very important significance, therefore alcohol should be substituted whenver feasoble with carbitols, Glycerine or other approved functional carriers. Flavour ingredients may also be classified as solid, liquid, paste etc.

Formulations of Non Alcoholic Flavour

Vanilla Flavour (Artificial)

Vanilla	28 gm
Glycerine	1.0 ltr
Sugar syrup	0.5 ltr
Water Hot	To make 4.0 lit
Caramel	28 gm

Vanilla Flavour (True)

Vanillin Oleoresin	120 gm
Glycerine	2 lit
Water	2 lit

Lemon Flavour

Lemon oil	5%
Monoethyl Glycerine	95%

Orange Flavour

Sweet Orenge Oil	5%
Diethyl Glycerine	95%

Vanilla Flavour

Vanillin	40 gm
Coumrin	14 gm
Monoethyl Glycerol	280 gm
Caramel	25 gm
Water	To make 4 litre

Vanilla Bean Flavour

Monoethyl glycerol	30 parts
Water	70 parts

Vanilla beans are percolated in this solution

Imitation Rasberry Flavour

Monoethyl glycerin	96 parts
Orris Concrete	2 part
Benzyl Acetate	2 part
Vanillin	4 part
Rohodinol	4 part
Gonone	4 part
Amyl Butyrate	2 part
Ethyl Pelargonate	12 parts
Ethyl Benzoatte	2 parts
Amyl Acetate	4 parts
Raspberry Juice	40 parts

Plant Economics of Non-Alcoholic Flavours

Rated Plant Capacity = 100 kg./Day

Land and Building (Land Area 200 sq.mt.)= Rs. 1,40,000.00

Plant and Machinery

1. Mixing Machine
2. Storage Tanks
3. Various containers for handling chemicals
4. Weighing scale
5. Pouch filling machine
6. Other accessories, motors, pumps

Other Fixed Assets

1. Electrifiction and Erection
2. Technical Know How
3. Preoperative expaneses

FIXED CAPITAL

1.	Land and Building	Rs.	1,40,000.00
2.	Plant and Machinery	Rs.	5,30,000.00
3.	Other Fixed Assets	Rs.	90,000.00
	Total	Rs.	7,60,000.00

Raw Materials

1. Various essence and concentrater
2. Modifiers
3. Solvents Glycerine

Total Working Capital/Month

1.	Raw Materials	Rs.	9,50,000.00
2.	Salary and Wages	Rs.	36,250.00
3.	Utilities and Overheads	Rs.	13,000.00
	Total	Rs.	9,99,250.00

Total Capital Investments

Total Fixed Capital	Rs.	7,60,000.00
Toal working Capital for 2 Months	Rs.	19,98,500.00
Total	Rs.	27,58,500.00

Turn Over/Annum

By sale of 30000 kgs of various flavour per annum Rs. 1,50,00,000.00

Profit sales Ratio = Profit/Sales X 100=17%
Rate of Return = Operating Profit / T.C.I. X 100 = 92%
Break Even Point (B.E.P.) = 22%

13

Flavours Fruit (Whiskey, Vodka, Grape, Butter Scotch and Rum)

Fruit flavours/essences are synthetic mixtures made to stimulate, as closely as possible, the aroma of pure fruits and their juices. They are composed chiefly of ethers, esters, volatile oils and odorous substances. The fruit ethers are an intermediate product in reinforced the final flavour with alcohol, glycerine, sugar and other flavour and carriers.

Flavour is that property of substances (commonly a food or one used in food) that causes a simultaneous reaction or sensation of taste on the tongue and odour in the olfactary centre in the hose. Thus defined, taste and odour are descriptive of a sensation, whereas taste in its coloquial meaning is practically synonymous with flavour.

Flavour has been defined as "a memory" and "an experience" and it is indeed both of these. The preferred definition of flavour is proposed by the society of flavour chemist. "Flavour is the sum total of those characteristics of any material taken in the mouth, perceived principally by the senses of taste and smell and also the general senses of pain and tectile receptors in the month as perceived principally by the senses of taste and smell and also the general senses of pain and tectile receptors in the month as perceived by the brass".

Artificial Flavourings

The largest group of flavourings materials is composed of hundreds of isolates from natural materials and synthetic materials e.g., aldehydes, ketones, acids, esters, phenols, phenols ethers, lactores, organic derivatives of sulfur, and aliphatic aromatic and terpene alcohols. More than are of these chemically active or osmophoric groups may be contained in a single chemical compund, as in vanissin (4-hydroxy-3-methoxybenzaldehyde) with phenolic, aldehydic and ether groups and in methyl authromilate (methyl 2-aminobenzoate) with ester and amine group and in ethylmetal (2-ethyl-3hydroxy-4H-Pyron-4-one) with hydroxy and ketone groups etc.

PROCESS FLOW DIAGRAM OF RUM FLAVOUR

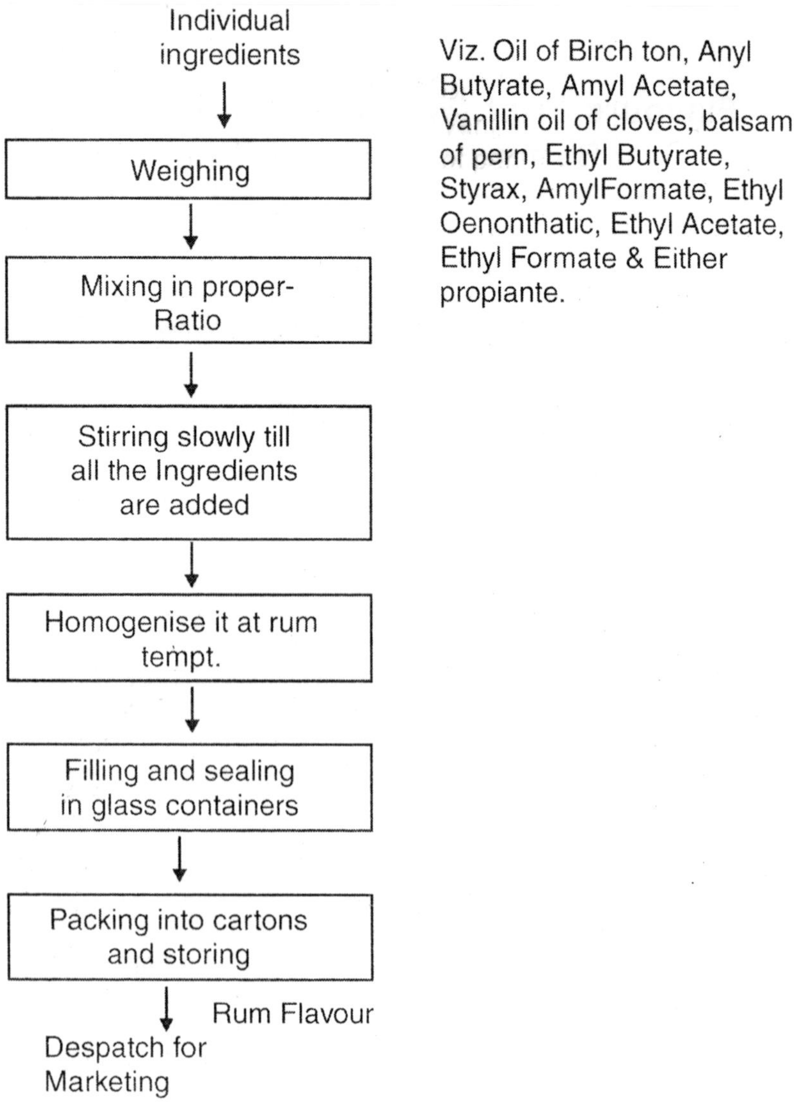

Manufacturing Process

1. For Rum Flavour

First of all, take the various raw materials as specified in the formulation of Rum Flavour in proper quantity of pure good quality. i.e. weigh calculated quantities of oil of Birch tar, Amyl Butyrate, Amyl Acetate, Vanillin, oil of cloves, Balsam of pern, Ethyl Butyrate styrax, Amyl Butyrate, Styrax, Amyl formate, Ethyl oenanthate, Ehtyl Acetate, Ethyl Formate and Ethyl Propionate.

Then blend each ingredient with proper stirring and agitation in the stainless steel mixer fitted with stirror and motor. Add all the components one by one with slow stirring till all the ingredients are completely added.

Subsequently, after homogenising it completely, it is filled in dark glass containers or bottles or other suitable locks by filling and sealing machine and then dispatched for marketing.

Plant Economics of Fruit Flavours

Rated Plant Capacity = 500.00 Kgs./Day

LAND & BUILDING

(Land Area 600 Sq.mts.) = Rs. 9,70,000.00

PLANT & MACHINERY

1. Stainless Steel Mixer
2. Stainless Steel Vessel
3. Packing machine (Filling and Sealing Machine)
4. Lab. Testing Equipments Viz. Beakers Flasks.
5. Miscellaneous

FIXED CAPITAL

1.	Land and Building	Rs.	9,70,000.00
2.	Plant and Machinery	Rs.	4,10,000.00
3.	Other Fixed Assets	Rs.	1,45,000.00
	TOTAL	Rs.	15,25,000.00

RAW MATERIALS

1. I. FOR RUM FLAVOUR :
Oil of Birch tar (rectified)
2. Amyl butyrate
3. Amyl Acetate
4. Amyl Vanillin
5. Oil of Cloves
6. Balsam of pern
7. Ethyl butyrate
8. Styrax
9. Amyl formate
10. Ethyl Oenanthate
11. Ethyl Acetate
12. Ethyl formate
13. Ethyl propionate

14. II. FOR WHISKEY FLAVOUR :
Ethyl Acetate
15. Ethyl Nitrate
16. Caraway oil
17. Anise oil
18. Juniper Oil
19. Worm wood oil
20. Ginger Oil
21. Coriander oil
22. Calamus oil
23. Bitter Almond Oil
24. Ethyl Alcohol

25. III. FOR GRAPE FLAVOUR :
Green Cognac Oil
26. Methyl Anthranilate
27. Ethyl Cinnamate
28. Propyl Cinnamate
29. Ethyl Butyrate
30. Ethyl Alcohol

31. IV. FOR BUTTER SCOTCH FLAVOUR :
Ethyl Oenanthate
32. Ethyl pelarganate
33. Butyl butyrate

34. Amyl acetate
35. Ethyl butyrate
36. Butyric acid
37. Orange oil
38. Ethyl Alcohol
39. Packaging

TOTAL WORKING CAPITAL/MONTH

1.	Raw Material	Rs.	17,79,901.00
2.	Salary and Wages	Rs.	56,625.00
3.	Utilities and Overheads	Rs.	50,000.00
	TOTAL	Rs.	18,86,526.00

TOTAL CAPITAL INVESTMENT

Total Fixed Capital	Rs.	15,25,000.00
Total Working Capital for 3 Months	Rs.	56,59,579.00
TOTAL	Rs.	71,84,579,00

TURN OVER/ANNUM

1. By sale of Rum Flavour 30,000 kgs.
2. By sale of Whiskey Flavour 30,000 kgs.
3. By sale of Vodka Flavour 30,000 kgs.
4. Grape flavour 30,000 kgs.
5. Butter scotch flavour 30,000 kgs.

TOTAL	Rs.	2,91,00,000.00

PROFIT SALES RATIO = Profit / Sales x 100 = 19%
RATE OF RETURN = Operating profit / T.C.I x 100 = 75%
BREAK EVEN POINT (B.E.P) = 23%

14

Terpeneless Menthol Crystals

Manufacturing Process

Put 20 kgs of pudina herbs on dry basis distillation plants, Added to it around 40 litres of water in the distillation plawn, heat the distillation plawnt at 100°C initial 2 hours. Then cool down and heat the contents to 80-95°C about six hours. At this time piperment oil will be distilled away through the jacket, on cooling of the piperment vapour to produce piperment oil and collect in the reciever. Now produce piperment oil around 13.6-14 kgs.

This piperment oil contents around 70-80% of menthol. Now piperment oil is cool down to 15°C to separate out Methol crystal. Now centrifuge the precipited crystal to separate out menthol crystal and menthol oil. By first stage it will separate out around 60-65% of menthol crystal.

Now residual oil is taken and added 0.01 of Boric Acid to it and cool down the oil to 50°C to residual methol crystal separate out. It will be around 10-12%.

It has been found that the 9.8-10.5% kgs of menthol crystal will be obtained. Pack it in a close container. Store it in a cool place for long preservation.

FRACTIONAL DISTILLATION OF D.M.O. FOR REMOVAL OFTERPENE

The properties and chemical composition of pepper mint oil are dependent on the type of the oil. The % of each constituent varies according to the place where the herb is cultivated and the methods of extraction of the oil from the herbs. In India itself the composition and properties are different for the different regions of their procurement. For example, sp. gr. of oil from Jammu is 0.9165 and that of Kanpur mint oil is 0.8966 and 20°C.

Extraction of Menthol

The Principle of menthol extraction consists of three steps, viz.

1. Formation of menthol crystal of freezing of the complete oil.
2. Removal of the crystals from the residual oil by centrifuging, and
3. Drying of the crystals.

The complete natural oil, after arrival from the interior, should be clarified prior to cooling (freezing), as it usually contain some water and mucialaginous impurities which prevent ready formation of the menthol crystals. For this purpose, some producers filter the oil, other centrifuge it in sharples of delaval supercentrigfuges. whereas other rectify it in vaccum stills. The latter process offers several advantages. The crystal of menthol from easier if a part of the complex oil is removed of foreruns, and the menthol crystals will possess a finer odour and flavour, not being contaminated with the bitter tasting, high boilng constituents of the complete oil, furthermore, the remaining oil can be sold as rectified dementholized oil.

(A) Crystallization

The purified oil is slowly and gradually cooled to progressively lower temperature whereby menthol crystals from in each operation. For this fractional chilling is done. The freezing process comprises three steps; first at + 14°C, the second + 10°C and the third at -5°C. Every producer follows his own ideals in this respect and uses certain modifications; this applies equally to the equipment.

The freezing plant proper consists of three tanks cooled with brine solution, or of numberous ceels, such as used in the making of ice blocks, immersed into three tanks in which cold brine solutions of different temperature circulate. However, some manufacturers employ large refrigerator compartmets, usually three, and therein freeze the oil in tin cans. The larger plants are equipped with regular freezing rooms each cooled to the proper temperature.

Gradual and slow cooling permits the formation of larger and more regular crystals, otherwide it would be difficult of separate. The residual dementholized oil from the intricate mesh work of crystals. There are many methods for crystallization by chilling. Every producer follows his own ideas in this respect and uses certain modifications.

Separation of the menthol Crystals from the Dementholized Oil

Separation of dementholized oil from crystals is performed by first decasting the remaining liquid oil from the crystals in large centrifuge rotating at a speed of about 1200 r.p.m. Washing with water during the operation can also be done. For this same operations wash the crystals during the process by pouring small quantities of water into the centrifuge.

Drying the Menthol Crystals

The centrifuged crystals are spread upon trays in large compartments of special room and for approximately 36 hours and dried in a slow current or air at a temperature of about 26°C up to 45% of the menthol can be recovered from fractional chilling.

The above drying operation must be undertaken very carefully, as a too fast air current or too high temperature would result in considerable losses of menthol by evaporation; whereas insufficient drying would elave the crystals too wet. Traces of adhering oil may lower the m.p. the menthol crystals below that prescribed by the US pharmacopoea for l-menthol (41° to 43°C)

Some brazillain menthal producers recrystallise their menthol, which process yields a product of very pure odour, free from traces of adhering oil, but considering of only small needle-like crystals.

Yield of Menthol & Dementholized Mint oil

The yield of menthol evidently depends upon the menthol content or the original complete oil and upon the efficiency of the freezing operation. Most manufacturers aim at a maximum yield of menthol, without much consideration for the menthol content of the residual partly dementholized oil. Yields of menthol by mere freezing vary from 40 to 50%. They are usually 50% of the total oil.

Higher yields of menthol can be obtained by first saponifixing the menthol esters in the complete (natural) oil and by reducing the menthone to menthol with metallic sodium, or by other methods.

A few of the larger and better equipped factories respot to such chemicals means in addition to the regular freezing and thereby obtain dementholized oils which are chemically quite differently composed than those resulting from mere freezing. It is, therefore, not surprising that the dementholized Brazillian oils offered on the market are of widely different quality.

The residual oil which contains menthone, menthl acetate, terpens, water and very small amounts of other ingredients is sent to a fractionator from which all the ingredients are separated because of their boiling differences.

These different fractions are collected separately and stored for packing.

Also, regarding menthol, neomenthol + l-menthol in D.M.O., the separation may be effected by fractional distillation, although the differences between their boiling points, are small, their boiling points (in °C) are as follows :

Neo-menthol	211.7°C
Menthol	216.5°C
l-menthol	218.6°C

The process makes use of a distillation plant, fractionation column operating under vaccum distillation.

The charge is fed into the fractional distillation (rectification) column or still the serving for vaccum distillation is spherical, made of copper and heavily tinned on the inside, with gooseneck condenser tubes and D.M.O. receivers are also tinned. A jacket around the lower half of the retort forms on oil bath or steam bath for heating with high pressure steam (for at least 75 lb jacket working pressure). A column directly above the still equipped with plates provides for better fractionation of the boiling liquid. The oil receiver consists of two closed, strong vessels with vertical glass tubes, through which the level of the liquid within each receiver can be gauged.

These receivers are tightly connected with the condenser outlet through a three-way stop cock, which permits are receiver to remain under 'vacuo' and to collect the fraction distilling over at a given temperature, while the other receiver may be opened to draw off the previous fraction. Pressure monometers on the column and on the oil receivers indicate the pressure within the column and within the oil receivers. An air tight suction line connects the receivers with the vaccum pump which should be of high efficiency.

Heating is achieved by a steam jacket. Provision is also made for the rectification or fractionation of the oil by the use of direct steam at atmospheric pressure.

All the different fractions of various constituents of D.M.O. as listed under 'composition of D.M.O.' based on their difference in boiling points are collected separately in individually receivers and packed in suitable containers and despatched for marketing.

PLANT ECONOMICS OF TERPENELESS MENTHOL CRYSTALS

LAND & BUILDING

(Land Area 4050 Sq.mts.) = Rs. 63,00,000.00

PLANT & MACHINERY

1. Mentha leave Crushing machine
2. Distillation Unit
3. Condenser
4. Filter Vacuum type
5. Stainless Steel tank
6. Refrigeration Unit
7. Boiler
8. Centrifuge
9. S.S. Storage Tank
10. Pipes, Pumps, Valves and Water tanks, and Other miscellaneous equipments
11. Laboratory testing equipments
12. Process Control equipments
13. Fractional chilling unit with three step freezing
14. Decanter S.S.
15. Washer S.S. fitted unit with three step freezing
16. Tray drier
17. Chemical treatment unit
18. Precipitation unit fitted
19. Filter
20. Fractionating column plates
21. Vacuum pump
22. D.M.O. storage tank
23. Finished product stroage tank
24. Miscellaneous viz. fitting, valves, motors etc.

OTHER FIXED ASSETS

1. Office eqipment, furniture plus other equipment & accessories
2. Installation costs for water, electricity, fuel etc.
3. Pre-operative & preliminary expenses
4. Technical know-how & consultancy
5. Miscellaneous

FIXED CAPITAL

1.	Land and Building	Rs.	63,00,000.00
2.	Plant and Machinery	Rs.	54,40,000.00
3.	Other Fixed Assets	Rs.	7,20,000.00
	TOTAL	Rs.	1,24,60,000.00

RAW MATERIALS

1. Mentha leaves
2. Boric Acid
3. Packaging materials Cartons, Glass bottles, Polyethene Pouches, labels.

TOTAL WORKING CAPITAL/ANNUM

1.	Raw Material	Rs.	4,75,000.00
2.	Salary and Wages	Rs.	2,66,665.00
3.	Utilities and Overheads	Rs.	4,04,000.00
	TOTAL	Rs.	11,45,665.00

TOTAL CAPITAL INVESTMENT

Total Fixed Capital	Rs.	1,24,60,000.00
Total Working Capital for 3 Month	Rs.	11,45,665.00
TOTAL	Rs.	1,35,05,665.00

TURN OVER/ANNUM

1. By sale of 51000. Terpeneless Menthol Crystals
2. By sale of Neo-menthol 1950 kgs.
3. l-menthol 3000
4. Menthol-1, 7380 kg
5. Piperitone (1-p-menthaon-3-one) 750 kgs.
6. Pulengone 150 kgs
7. Ethyl Amyl carbinol 450 kgs
8. Cineole 825 kgs
9. 2-hexenyl benyl acetate 450 kgs.
10. Menthyl acetate 2850 kgs.

11. Limonene 450 kg.
12. 1-alpha -pinene (terpene) 345 kgs.
13. Caryophyllene 300 kgs.
14. Cadinene 450 kgs.
15 Sesquiterpene 150 kgs.

TOTAL	Rs.	4,99,08,300.00

PROFIT SALES RATIO = Profit / Sales x 100 = 17%
RATE OF RETURN = Operating profit / T.C.I x 100 = 53%
BREAK EVEN POINT (B.E.P) = 46%

15

Trends in Trade of Essential Oils

Introduction

Essential oils remain the basic raw materials for perfumery, flavour and cosmetic industries. They are used in a wide range of products like soaps, detergents, cosmetics, agarbattis, disinfectants, deodrants, mosquito repellants, flavouring of foods, soft and hard drinks, pharmaceuticals, tobacco, variety of perfumery products, and also used as fixatives and for blending purposes (Fig.). Apart from these know applications in various industrial products the essential oil have become popular in aroma therapy in Japan. The applicaton of essential oil in agriculture as antifeedants, repellants, bioinsecticide, natural herbicide and growth boosters are still open. In this paper an attempt has been made to present an overview of the essential oil industry.

Indian Scenario

India is one of the few countries in the world having varied agroclimatic zones suitable for the cultivation of a host of essential oil bearing plants. Due to increased awareness of health hazards associated with synthetic chemicals coupled with the increased cost of petroleum products, the use of essential oil has been gradually increasing. The consumers are showing increasing preference for natural material over the synthetic. During the last few years with the spurt in the production of essential oil it is emerging as a potential agrobased industry in India. At present in India about 30 per cent of the fine chemicals used annually in perfumes and flavour come from essential oils.

USES OF ESSENTIAL OILS

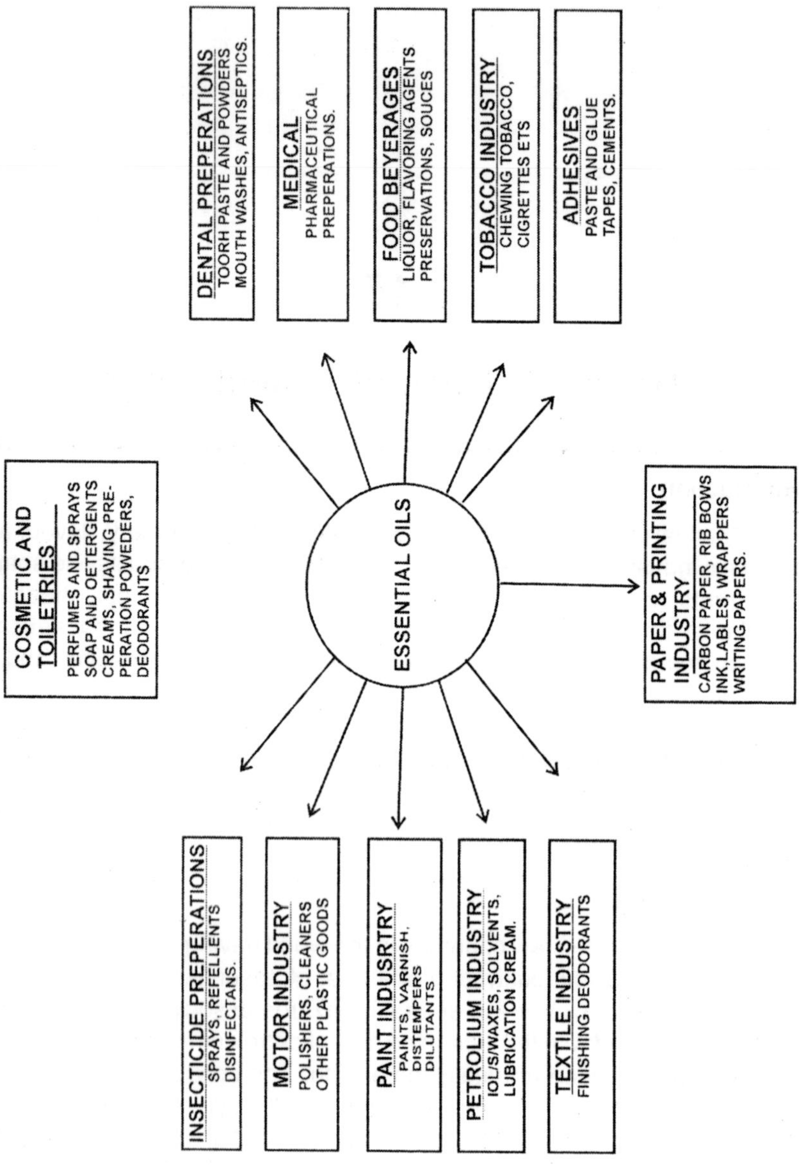

The major items of export are ginger oil, sandalwood oil, lemongrass oil, jasmine, tuberose, concrete and the other essential oils. The major buyers of Indian essential oils being U.S.S.R, U.S.A., France, U.K., Netherlands, U.A.E., Saudi Arabia, Spain, Morocco, Germany, Australia, Korea, Taiwan, Pakistan, etc. Table 15-5 give the export earning, estimated area production, foreign exchange saved from some selected essential oils, productivity of major tropical essential oils, imports and exports of minor forest products in India. Similarly citronella oil production has reached 500 tonnes when it was totally imported 35 years ago. Also jasmine and tuberose concretes from South India have created a mark in the world market. Thus in interesting scenario in the development of natural essential oils in India has emerged.

16

Demand For Essential Oil

In India the demand for essential oil is from few consumers industry products broadly grouped under fragrance, flavours, aromatic chemicals :

Type	Product
Fragrace	*Toiletries*
1. Soap	(a) Shampoo
2. personal care products or cosmetics	(b) Tooth paste/powder
	(c) Cream
	(d) Mouth wash
	(e) Talcum powder
Flavour	
1. food stuff	(a) Soft drinks
	(b) processed food
	(c) Chocolates
	(d) Confectioneries, beverages, and ice creams
Aromatic chemical	
Pharmaceutical	(a) Formulations
	(b) Drug other than bulk

There are about 400 blenders in India. They buy natural essential oils from distillers and prepare industrial perfumes and aromatic chemicals by either mixing one variety with the other or blending the essential oils with fine chemicals. Half of the blenders are in the western zone and the rest in the other zones. There are 20 to 25 manufacturing units of large scale, majority of these are classified under the three main groups; fragrance, flavour, and aromtic chemicals.

17

Super-Critical Fluid Extraction (SCFE) Technology-For Spice Extraction

Abstract

The basic working principle and advantage of the SCFE process, reasons for use of SC carbons dioxide as an extractant, parameters to be determined in the designing of SCFE plant, such as (i) required rate of production, (ii) mode of operation (continues or batch-type) (iii) bulk density of the solids fed (iv) the form (v) consistency and (vi) moisture content of the material (vii) Ratio of solvent mass flow-rate to the mass solids treated (vii) the extraction time, etc. have been briefly discussed, and based on these factors, as illustration of a plant for extraction of pepper (the most important spice of the world and so also, of India) has been provided Later, the R & D work done on some important Spice Essential Oils and Oleoresins and their dominant chemicals constituents using SCFE process, is reviewed and briefly discussed. The commercial SCFE plants in use in some of the development countries like Germany, Canada, Australia, etc., and other commercial SCFE activity areas have also been reviewed. At the end, the future scope of the SCFE process and R & D needs in the area have been highlighted.

Introduction

Spices, which are consumed mostly in flavouring of innumerable foods, are gaining considerable economics/commercial importance as is evident from world trade (Table) in spices (256,000) tons worth about 1.5 billion $ US (1-3) India is one of the major spice producing and exportng countries of the world as is evident from the exporting countries of the world as is evident from the export earnings of over Rs 600 crores (Rs. 6000 millions) during

1994-95 (4-6). Because of the several built-in defects in the use of whole or ground spices in processed foods, such as : (a) Varibale flavour strength, (b) presence of polyphenols which could discolour some manufactured food products, (c) slow release of flavour, (d) microbial contamination, etc., Spice oleoresins, Spice Essential Oils, and other spices extractives are now being used commercially in sophisticated food products in place of ground spices.

India, again, is one of the leading countries producing the exporting about a dozen important spice oleoresins (about Rs. 80 crores worth, but these oleoresins are being produced by use of chemical organic solvents, the use of some of which is now prohibited in spice importing countries like UK, USA, Germany, etc. Likewise steam-distillation too adversely affects the basic quality of essential oils, notably the low boiling volatiles. To overcome these built-in defects, Super-Critical Fluid Extraction (SCFE) Process" provides an excellent new and versatile alternative for the extraction of spices as discussed in this book.

Scope of this presentation

This book presents (a) the basic working principle and advantages of the SCFE process (b) reasons for use of SC carbon dioxide as an extractant and (c) parameters to be determined in the designing of SCFE plant, such as (i) required rate of production, (ii) mode of operation (continuous or batch type) (iii) bulk density of the solids fed, the form, texture or consistency and moisture content of the mateial (iv) Ratio of solvent mass flow-rate to the mass of solid treated (v) the extraction time etc. have been discussed and based on these factors, as illustration of a plant for extraction of peper) has been provided. Later, the recent R & D work done in India and abroad on some important. Spice Essential Oils in India and abroad on some important chemical constituents using SCFE process, is highlighted and briefly discussed. The commercial SCFE plants in use in some of the developed countries like Germany, Canada, Australia, France, Austria, etc. and other related commercial SCFE activity areas have also been reviewed. At the end, the future scope of the SCFE process and R & D needs in the area have also been highlighted.

SUPERCRITICAL FLUID EXTRACTION SYSTEM (SCFE)

Supercritical fluid (SCFE is a versatile separation technology which is receiving increasing attention in view of the selectivity of the extraction from a mixture of components. The pressure -temperature dependent solubility in the solvents with excellent mass transfer characteristics are being utilized in wide range of food processing industries including spice processing. The

SCFE technology has received considerable attention as is evident from a number of standard works/books and reviews given at the end of this presentation.

TABLE : WORLD TRADE IN SOME IMPORTANT SPICES

Sr. No.	Spices	'000 tons'
1.	Pepper (black, white, green)	125-130
2.	Capsicums	55-60
3.	Spice seeds (6 Spices)	55-60
4.	Cinnamon/Cassia	33-34
5.	Turmeric	15-20
6.	Ginger	15-16
7.	Nutmeg/Mace	12-15
8.	Cardamon (Small)	9-10
9.	Curry Powder	5-6
10.	Cloves	3-4
11.	Pimento (All Spices)	3-4
12.	Vanilla and	2-3
13.	Saffron (Tons)	3-5

WORKING PRINCIPLE AND SCFE PROCESS DESCRIPTION

For the extraction of spices or essential oils, the process (Schematic), described in Figure, is generally employed. The spice material loaded in the extractor is brought in contact with the supercritical solvent at a relatively high pressure ranging from 60-300 bar and at temperature of 35°-70°, The supercritical solvent after getting enriched with the solute, is passed through a micrometer valve or pressure reducing valve, where the pressure on the separator side is around 4-60bar and temperature is lower due to a sudden diabetic expansion of the supercritical solvent. This results in lower solubility of the solute. Once the material separation occurs. the gas is again compressed back to extract the material. Thus, solvent recycling is also possible, by means of the compressor or liquid pump.

Carbon Dioxide as SC Solvent - Its Plust Point

SC carbon dioxide is used as a solvent for extraction of food materials such as spices, *coffee,* hops, etc., because it is (i) cheap, (ii) abundant in nature, (iii) non-toxic, (iv) non corrosive (v) inert, (vi) non-inflammable, (vii) devoid of environmental contamination, (viii) the boiling point and heat of evaporation are low and hence, it is easy to separate it from solute mixture

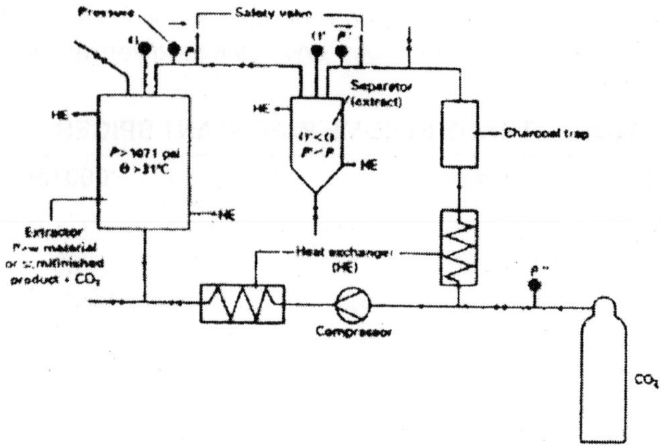

Fig. A typical Super Critical (SCA) CO_2 Extraction System for Spices and Flavour etc.

with less heat energy, (ix) due to lower critical temperature, the extraction of the material can be carried out at near ambient temperature : (x) it can be especially used in extracting thermo-labile compounds, (xi) lesser energies are needed for compression due to its lower critical pressure, (xii) further, separation of the extract can be *effected* by expanding the carbon dioxide, where the temperature of the separation can be low. The above 12 plus points have made SC carbon dioxide quite popular all over the world.

Advantages of the SCFE Process

There are several advantages of this process. Some of them are mentioned here (2-3) :

(i) **Low temperature separation** : It produces extracts from natural products where the heat-sensitive components remain undamaged.

(ii) **No Solvent residue:** The extracted solute can be made almost solvent free, i.e. the residual solvent content can be reduced to almost 0 ppm.

(iii) **Solubility Variation:** The solubility variation of the active constituents can be achieved by simply increasing or lowering the extraction temperature and pressure.

(iv) **Fractionated Extraction and Fractionated Separation:** The different constituents of natural products may be fractionally extracted and the extracted solutes may be fractionally separated.

(v) **Cheap Solvents and their Recycling:** Solvents can be completely recycled and also gases like carbon dioxide which are cheap may be used. This gives lower cost of solvents compared to convention all liquid extraction.

(vi) **Low Energy Process:** The SCFE is a low energy intensive process requiring low utilities consumption.

(vii) **Fast diffusion :-** The diffusivity of supercritical liquids is higher than that of liquids and viscosity is lower than that of liquids and viscosity is lower than that of liquid~. This gives higher mass transfer rates.

(viii) **Easy Solvent Recovery:** Due to high volatility of solvents, they can be easily recovered.

(ix) **No Environmental Risks:**

(x) **No Fire Hazards** are there when carbon dioxide is used as the solvent.

PARAMETERS TO BE DETERMINED IN SCFE PROCESS DESIGN

NEED FOR BASIC PROCESS DATA

As a basis for selecting dimensions of the plant and of individual items of equipment, a prior knowledge of some basis process data is necessary such as: (i) the required rate of production (ii) mode of operation of the plant (Whether continuous or batch-type), (iii) bulk-density of the solids fed (iv) the form, texture or consistency of the material and its moisture content; (v) ratio of solvent mass flow rate to the mass solids treated, and (vi) the extraction time (3) These parameters must, therefore, be determined during the course of a few preliminary experiments.

Of these parameters, the required rate of production is first specified. Depending upon the rate, the mode of operation i.e.whether batch or continuous type is decided. Bulk-density of solids fed must be determined experimentally. These three parameters enable the volume of the extraction to be calculated.

The quantity of solvent to be introduced into the plant is determined precisely from the required operating temperature and pressure. Then, by knowing the time of extraction, the mass flow rate of solvent can be calculated. Hence, the cross-sections of pipelines can also be calculated accordingly.

Eggers and Tschiersch have given extraction of spices as an illustration of the initial prediction of the order of magnitude of a plant.

Important Parameters of the SCF Extraction Plant for Spices (19)

(i) Producton rate:	(i) 500 tons of the spice p.a.
(ii) Min.no.of working days:	(ii) 200 working days p.a.
(iii) Mode of operation/shifts day:	(iii) Three shifts per day
(iv) Bulk density :	(iv) 500 kg/m^2
(v) Mass flow rate/mass ratio	(v) 20 kg CO_2/hr kg of spice
(vi) Time of extraction:	(vi) 7 hr/batch inclusive of filling and emptying of the plant

These values indicate a volume of V = 1.67 W for the extraction vessel and nominal diameter of 50 mm for the pipelines in the plant.

SCF EXTRACTION OF SPICE ESSENTIAL OILS, OLEORESINS AND MAJOR CHEMICAL CONSTITUENTS PRESENT THEREIN

The standardization in the food industry has led to spice extracts or oleoresins to be used in place of ground spices, Extracts of spices such as pepper, nutmeg, and chillies were obtained. The volatile oil of pepper, commonly called pepper oil obtained as the first fraction followed by the oleoresins and piperine. The extraction of ginger was also carried out by using supercritical carbon dioxide. For all oleoresins extractions, the temperature range was 40-55°c and pressure was varied from 200 to 400 bar. The degree of extraction of piperine from black pepper was almost 98% and that of essential oil, 81 % . The extract was yellow as compared to the olive green extract with methylene chloride as solvent. Similarly, the extraction of Capsaicin from Chillies was 97%. These results confirm earlier findings.

SCFE OF PEPPER OIL

A large number of products have been extracted with SC carbon dioxide. Extracts of spices/essential oils or oleoresins are commercially important. Extraction of pepper for pepper oleoresin using SC carbon dioxide of ginger using carbon dioxide has been reported mostly from India.

SCF CO_2 EXTRACTION VERSUS CONVENTIONAL SOLVENT EXTRACTION

Conventionally, black pepper is powdered and subjected to steam distillation and solvent extraction in a two-stage process. At CFTRI. volatile oil was of pepper was extracted with SCF carbon dioxide without contamination with non-volatile compounds. The oil obtained was of excellent quality and had monoterpene to sesquiterpene ratio much less than that in the steam distilled oil. The recoveries of volatile oil have been higher than those in steam distillation. The essential oil obtained by SCFE had excellent fixative character. This can also be seen from table on higher yields and lower time of extraction by SCFE process than that by steam distillation technique.

Table : Analysis of Pepper, Nutmeg ans Chillies-Co-extraction

19 Particulars	Material Before CO²	After CO²	CO² Extracted	Degree of Extracted (%)	Extract commercial (Usually)
					CH, CL₂
		I	PEPPER BLACK		
Piperine (%)	10.1	0.3	44.0	97.7	41.2
Essential Oil (%)	3.5	0.1	12.7	81.1	15.0
Water (%)	9.3	0.1	12.7	81.1	15.0
Colour of extract			Yellow		Olive Green
		II	NUTMEG		
Essential Oil (%)	7.4	0.1	19.0	99.0	20.0
Hexane - soluble matter (%)	46.0	1.7	100.0	98.0	100.0
Water (%)	4.9	4.4	1.6	0.1	
Colour of extract			Whitish yellow		Yellowish brown
		III	CHILLIES		
CAPSAICIN (%)	0.86	0.03	4.9	97.0	4.7
Water (3)	3.2	1.8	1.3	0.1	
Colour of extract	-	-	red	-	red

Table : Physical and Chemical Characteristics of Papper Oil (26)

Physico. Chemical Characteristics	**Steam distillation**	**8 MPa**	**SCFE (CO^2) 8MP a**	**10MP a**	**10MP a**
		40°C	60°C	40°C	60°C
Yield of oil (%)	2.42	2.10	2.25	2.83	2.62
Refractive Index	1.479	1.483	1.475	1.483	1.483
Specific Gravity	0.8834	0.8844	0.8864	0.8859	0.8759
Optical Rotation	-6.74	+0.76	-1.11	+0.13	+0.35
Total Hydrocarbons	84.32	80.40	87.65	82.70	78.60
Monoterpenes (%)	73.19	58.83	68.82	61.01	51.45
Sesquiterpens (%)	26.7	41.17	31.17	38.99	48.55
Oxygenated Compounds	3.24	7.69	4.02	6.69	7.90
Caryophyllene (%)	16.49	18.53	13.05	15.04	24.01

Table : Physio- Chemical Characteristics of Papper Oleoresin (17)

Physico-Chemical Characteristics	**Supercritical Carbon dioxide extracted (SCFE)**	**Conventional Oleoresins (Solvent Extracted)**
Appearance and Odour	Yellow, consisting of upper oily layer and lower crystalline layer	Dark green, Olive green or olive drab extract: usually consist of an upper oily layer and a lower crystalline layer
Volatile oil content	18-35 ml/100	15-35 ml/100
Optical rotation	-15	-1 to -23
Refractive index	1.4872	1.4790 1.4890
Piperine (spectro photometry)	45.55%	35 - 45%
Residual	oil	as per FDA

Table : Physico-chemical characteristics of Ginger Oleoresins

Physico-Chemical Characteristics	Supercritical Carbon dioxide extracted (SCFE)	Conventional Oleoresins (Solvent Extracted)
Appearance and Odourq	A dark yellow to brown viscous liquid with characteristics odour and flavour of ginger	a dark brown viscous to highly viscous liquid with characteristic odour and flavour of ginger
Volatile oil contact	20ml/100 gm	18.35 ml/100 gm
Specific gravity	0.8672	
Refractive index	1.49	1.4880-1.4970
Optical rotation	-54.17	-30 to - 60
Oleoresin content	22%	
Residual solvents		need FDA regulation

Table : CO[2] Extraction of the active Principle (Piperine) from Pepper (19)

Active Principle to be separated	Extracting Agent	Entrainer	Operating Extraction	Conditions of : Spearation
Piperine from Black Pepper	CO_2 N_2O. SF_6 CHF_3SF_2SI CHF_2CI $CF_3 = CH_2C_3F_8$	H_2O	35°to 80° C 80 to 300 bar	Decrease of of pressure

Table : The Comparative Yield and Extraction Times for 11 Spices Extracted by Liquid Carbon Dioxide and Prepared by steam Distillation

Material	Liquid carbondioxide		Steam Distillation	
	Yield (% w/w)	Time (Hrs)	Yield (% w/w)	Time (Hrs)
Cardamom	9.4	2.5	9.0	5
Chilli	4.9	2.5	-	-
Clove	20.0	2.0	15.0	6
Cumin	4.5	2.0	2.5	4
Cumin Black	4.5	2.0	1.0	-
Fennel	5.8	2.0	3.0	5
Ginger	3.7	2.5	1.6	6
Mace	18.5	2.5	13.1	-
Pasley	9.8	2.0	2.7	5
Poppy Seed	2.5	2.0	-	-
Turmeric	3.5	2.0	3.5	-

SCFE OF BLACK PEPPER OLEORESIN

Table shows the physico-chemical composition of the oleoresin obtained by conventional extraction and SC carbon dioxide extraction. The Piperine content of carbon dioxide extracted was better.

SCFE OF GINGER OIL

As in the case of Pepper, ginger oil also can be extracted without the contamination of non-volatile Compounds by supercritical fluid extraction. The ginger oil extracted at the institute at 8-10 MPa at temperatures of 40° to 60° C was found to be of excellent quality and had hinger sesquiterpene content than that in steam-distilled oils. The gas chromatograms indicated that the monoterpene content was less than 12% and the content of compounds like zingiberene, curcumene and humulene was greater in SC carbon dioxide extracted oils than in distilled oils. The quality characteristics of the ginger oleoresin obtained by SCF carbon dioxide are presented in table.

SCFE (CO_2) OF PIPERINE PEPPER

Typical data on piperine are presented in table which are self explanatory.

ECONOMICS OF THE SCFE PROCESS

It is estimated that an extractor with volume 1 m³ may cost about Rs. 7.75 crores, the cost break - up is: the carbon dioxide loop (40-50%), carbon dioxide recovery system (20-25%) and the pressure vessels (25-40 %). The operating cost per shift is around Rs. 50,000-Rs 60,000. The economics of the plant are dictated by a number of factors such as (i) the operating cost per cycle, (ii) the number of cycles per day (iii) the capacity of the cycle and (iv) the unit value added by the product. In case of pepper oleoresin, a plant of 3 tons/day capacity can produce the product at a cost of Rs 450/Kg as against Rs 300-340/Kg of conventional product. Adopting a number of cost reduction steps like (a) power recovery during decompression, (b) reduction in dead time cycle, (c) multistage countercurrent extraction, etc., the cost of the product can be reduced substantially - SCFE processes will be viable for production of only high value and stable priced products required for specialized use in food and drug industry. The IIT, New Delhi Scientists and Engineers based on their fabrication experience in SCFE opined that the cost can be reduced to Rs 20-50 lakhs depending upon plant specification and nature of raw materials etc.

COMMERCIAL-SCALE SCFE PLANTS IN U.K. AUSTRIA, GERMANY, AUSTRALIA & FRANCE

SCFE plants working successfully on commercial scale in Germany, U.K., Austria, France, Canada And Australia and the extracts obtained from the liquid and SC carbon dioxide are finding their way into the international market. Hence there is an urgent need for development of design of a cheaper and efficient indigenously made SCFE plant in a developing country like India.

FACTORS AFFECTING PLANT DESIGNING

The major points to be considered in plant design are: (i) output major capacity, (ii) mode of operation, (iii) bulk density of the raw material, (iv) solvent of material ratio and (v) extraction time. The pressure vessels have to be designed for pressures of 10-30 MPa with an allowance for increasing stress. The steel vessels should be corrosion-resistant and easy to decontaminate. In addition, counter-current extraction for higher efficiencies and multi-tube high pressure heat exchanger for heating the liquid to SC carbon dioxide are essential.

OTHER COMMERCIAL SCFE ACTIVITY AREAS

In addition,. commercial activity or interest has been reported by over 30 companies including some end-users of the technology, equipment suppliers and engineering companies. The activity is generally in the areas of spices extraction, essential oils extraction, oilseeds extraction, flavours extractions, extraction of pharmaceutical materials, extraction of coal, coal tar and crude oil, for the separation of mixtures including separation of isomers, for effluent treatment, and in supercritical fluid chromatrography.

FUTURE SCOPE FOR SCFE PROCESS

SCFE is a capital intensive process requiring high-pressure vessels and pumps. The low cost of carbon dioxide and the low energy cost of separation do not offset the high capital costs. However, where the cost of the products is more than $2.5/kg (Rs75/Kg), the extra cost that supercritical extraction adds to the product, may be acceptable because of the better quality and higher shelf-life of the products. In food industry, the supercritical extraction is likely to be extensively used for products like spices, coffee, tea, etc.

18

Citronella Oil

Planting and Cultivation

Prior to planting and land must be cleared, plowed and harrowed. Citronella is propagted by means of rooted crown division of mature grass of time of planting being the rainly season from June to December. For this purpose clumps of mature plants are pulled from the grounds trimmed of all but 5 or 6 inch of their tops and divided into single or double stalked root segments which should be kept wet until planting. The root segments are set out by intervals of 3 ft. in rows 2 ft. apart. The roots of the new plant must be fixed firmly in the ground and well covered with soil. In the first three months i.e. until the grass fills the rows monthly cultivation is necessary. After the first harves one cultivation will be sufficient. No fertilizers are used. Shortly before each harvest all weeds should be eradicated. Citronella flowers acre a year usually at the end of November in the rainy season each flower grows on separate stalk. Neither the flower not the stalks contains any essential oil.

Harvesting

In actual practice the grass is harvested before it reached the flowering stage the leaves can usually be cut for the first time six months after planting and subsement harvest may take place at intervals of four months which permits three harvest per year. The grass should then be permitted to reach the flowering stage. The grass harvested when the blades reach a height of approximately 3 ft.. It is cut by hand with matchets just above the first node and collected in bundles of about 50 lbs. Dry leaves may be hauled to the stills immediately wet leaves should be left in the field for one day to dry partly and to loose excessive moisture.

Distillation

Prior to distillation the leaves are reduced to 4-inch pieces by means of twin power cutters placed opposite each other. the material is then fed by gravity into the still and packed tightly. Live steam of 15 lbs pressure (measured at the steam inlet gauge) is injected but as soon as the first vapours appeas at the condenser outlet (usually after 10 minutes) the steam pressure is raised gradually to a maximum of 25 lbs and kept up as long as to vapour appears at the condenser outlet distillation is completed when an appreciable amount of oil can no longer be separated from the condensate. The flow of oil may be checked by drawing sampler periodically at the condenser outlet. Depending upon the condition of the leaf material distillation of one charge requires from 3 to 5 hour at the most. The oil collected after hrs. contain very little citronellal, the chief constituent which determines the price of each lot of oil. It is therefore, preferable to stop distillation provided, of course, that a normal yield of oil has been obtained. It has been found that the yield of oil is influenced chiefly by two factors the age of the planting and the amount of rainfall. The condensing system consists of a simple copper or aluminium spiral tube immersed in cold water. The spiral tube is connected to the tapering end of the digester (top) and the other end of the tube projects into the receiver which is a copper or aluminium vessel. In the receiving vesselcitronella oil takes the top layer and water lower layer. On one side of the receives just above the bottom there is a bent tube which allows of the water of the lower layer to flow out.

The upper layer in the oil.is now decanted into the drying unit where an hydrous sodium sulphate is added to the old and mixes. The mixture is now filtered in a small filter. The anhydrous sodium sulphate is added for dehydration of the oil is for removing the moisture from oil.

The dehydrated oil is filled in can or drums and sealed air tight. The oil should not be exposed to light frequently and should be kept in a dark and cool place. Coloured glass, stainless steel or aluminium are preferred to copper container for storage.

Distillation Process Erection and Distillation of Suitable Type of Still

Even though stem distillation is a harsh treatment, citronella oil is prepared in this way. At present three methods of distillation are practised. They are water disitllation, water and steam distillation and steam distillation, water distillation is the crudest methods of separating oil from lemon grasses. This is a simple process in which the plant material is placed into the still, water added and the vessel is fire heated. Water and oil distill together. They are condensed in a simple condenser. The oil takes top layer. This process of water distillation has the disadvantage of exposing the delicate estential oil to a prolonged distillation in the presence of water which results in the unnecessary hydrolysis of esters and oxidation and resentification of unsatuated compounds.

The distillation methods of water and steam type is better than above described method. Here the stills fitted with a horizontal perforated plate upon which the lemon grass rests.The lower part of the still is filled with water to a level some what below the grid and the charge is subjected to distillation by passing low pressure steam. This avoids direct contact of plant materials with distillation by passing low pressure steam. This avoids direct contact of plant materials with distillation water below. This method provides lower yields.

Now the modern method practised is steam distillation. This method is suggested for the preparation of citronella oils.

THE ELECTION AND OPERATION OF SUITABLE TYPE OF STILL

Apart from the question of capital cost, the prospective producer of citronella oils will be guided by several consideration, both technical and practical, when deciding what type and size of still is to be installed. From technical view point, steam distillation gives the best and quickest result but some people are using water and steam stills also.

Practical consideration are mainly bound up and with the question of whether the still is to be portable or a fixed installation. If the cop is cultivated a fixed steam-heated still should be erected in the area of cultivation, the still being provided with means of rapid charging and discharging to ensure rapid distillation and quick turn-over. Where the crop is not cultivated, but has to be collected from a wide area of "difficult" country, it should be brought to a fixed distillery if transport can be arranged, but if it is not practicable, it will be necessary to use a portable still. It might be possible to mount a small steam-heated still on a lorry or trailer. It is of the atmost importance to have an simple water supply for the condenser, whatever type of still is used. The still should, therefore, be situated near to steam, river to lake, when a piped supply is not available.

Water and Steam Still

These are more expensive than water stills, largely owing to the necessity of providing a steam generator, but are better than water stills for the small producer. The feature of this type of still is that the plant charge does not come into contact with the boiling water; it is, in fact, a step towards the steam still. The distillation rate is much faster and providing and still is well lagged to prevent excessive condensation in the still, the charge burn, Consequently, spoilage due to hydrolysis and decompostion is greatly reduced. So that the , yield of oil is higher and its quality better than it obtained by water distillation.

Water and steam stills give good results with most types of plant material, than about 2°C (say 5°F) above the temperature of the water entering the condenser. If the condensate does run warm, the rate of distillation should reduce and, if possible a large condenser substituted.

A coil condenser is economical in the use of cooling water, it also allows water to be heated for the next still charge in the case of water distillation. Patent tubular-type condenser have certain merits they occupy little space, and prevent the escape of steam into the open air-but they may be difficult to repair.

Inactive metals should be used in the construction of a condenser tinned copper, stainless steel, pure tin or aluminium. With tinned copper the plating does not last and is not early repaired. Aluminium is suitable for most essential oils, but not those containing appreciable quantities of phenols, which react with the metals. Aluminium is also subject attach by water of certain hardness.

Fuel

As far as possible, the spent charges, after suitable drying in the sun should be used as fuel for subsequent distillation. Those crops of relatively including citronella oil. The charge should be reduced to regular size, but should not be too finely powdered. It should be packed firmly and evenly, otherwise the steam will not permeate the whole charge but will form channels through the more loosely packed parts, greatly reducing the rate of distillation and increasing the risk of decomposition. The operation of these stills, except that a basket must not be used, as much as the steam would probably escape round the basket, rather than through the charge. The flatter should be packed directly on the grid above the water. The grid may be fitted with chains so that the entire charge may be lifted out by tackle after distillation.

Steam Stills

While the most expensive to install, steam stills gives better result than water-end-steam stills, The rate of distillation of high and the chances of hydrolysis of the end decomposition very small. The charge should be finely powdered as this leads to "channelling" and firm and even packing of the charge is essential. Whereas in the other two types of stills, the temperature within the still does not exceed 100°C, of the pressure rise above atmospheric pressure can be varied in steam stills. Hence, they are essential for the distillation of leaves, seeds roots and wood containing high boiling constituents, they are frequently used in large distillation units for her baccous plants.

The plant material should be placed on a removable grid placed above the steam coil, the grid placed above the steam coil, the grid being fitted with chains for use with lifting tackle, the whole charge being lifted out after distillation. A basket must not be used. it is necessary for the charge to be fairly finely chopped or ground except where it consists of thin walled tissue through which the oil present in the free state and dry out the plant charge. Diffusion will cease and it will be necessary to alternated with, saturated steam in order to maintain the yield of oil. Prolonged distillation with wet steam may cause excessive condensation in the charge, with consequent lumping and "channelling".

Condenser

With all type of stills, condensation should be as rapid and efficient as possible. The distillation not be allowed to run more low value, will not bear the cost of alternative fuel.

Storage of Citronella Oil

The care taken to produce an essential oil of good quality can be entirely vitiated by subsequent faulty conditions of storages. Under certain conditions, citronella oil deteriorate rapidly and it is essential first to free the oil from water and then to transfer it into suitable airtight and light proof containers, stored in a very cool atmosphere.

The oil drawn from the separator, can be cheaply and adequately dried by means of anhydrous sodium sulphate, which can be prinkled on the surface and stirred in for about 15 minutes. This salt absorb as the water associated with the oil, and settles down in a compact layer, leaving the oil clear and bright. It may then be decounted or filtered.

Determination of Aldehyde and Ketones

Of the many procedures which have been suggested for the determination of aldehyde and ketones only four general methods have attained practical significance.

These are :

These are :

(1) Bisulphite method
(2) Neutral sulphite method
(3) Phenyl hydrazine method
(4) Hydroxylamine method

(1) Bisulphide method :- The bisulphide method is an absorption process based upon the general reaction.

$$RCHO + NaHSO_2 - \begin{matrix} OH \\ RCH \\ SO_3Na \end{matrix}$$

Upon shaking a measured quantity of oil with hot aqueous solution of sodium bisulphite, an addition compound forms which is generally water soluble and which dissolves in hot bisulphite solution; the non aldehyde portion of oil separate as an oily layer which can be measured conveniently in the graduated neck of a carria flask. The bisulphite method is perhaps the most convenient and simple of the four general methods. As such it is frequently use us the trade because it requires no standard solution, analytical balance, or special skill.

PROCESS FLOW SHEET

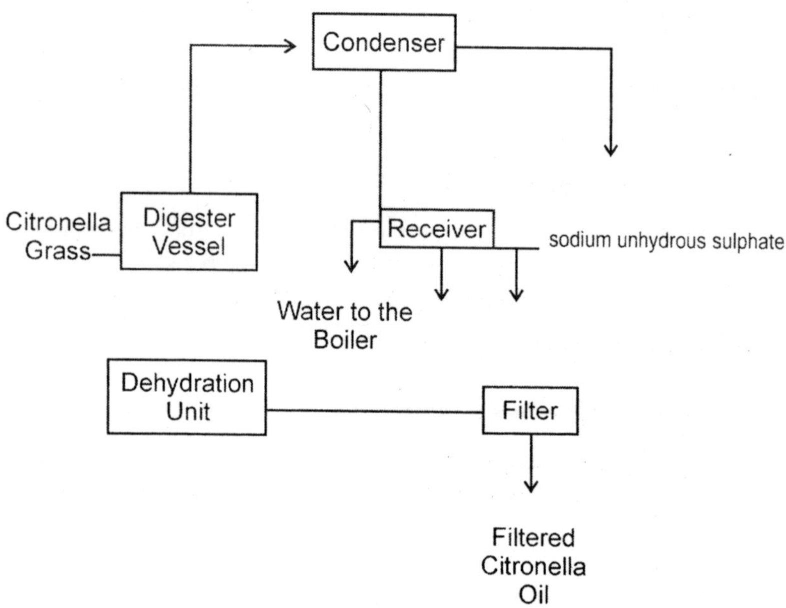

Procedure :-We will introduce 75 cc of a freshly prepared saturated, aqueous solution of sodium bisulphite into a 150 cc flask, Having a thin neck iraduated in 0.1 cc divisions. Then droping 10 cc of the oil into the flask by the use of tripetle. Upon through shaking a semi solid mass frequently will results.

After this immersing the flask in a beaker of boiling water and occasionally shake until the solid addition compound has gone completely into a solution. A further addition of 25 cc of bisulphite solution is made, and the flask is again repeatedly shaken. After standing undistur bed in the beaker of boiling water for 10 minutes to per unit the unreacted oil to rise to the surface, adding sufficient sodium bisulphite solution to force the unreacted oil into the neck of the flask. any drophts of oil into the neck of the flask. Any drophts of oil adhering to the sides are made to rise into the neck of gently tapping of flask, and by rotating rapidly between the palms and the hands. After cooking the flask to room temperature, measure the amount of unreacted oil. The aldehyde content may then be calculated by means of following formula :

Percentage of aldehyde = 10 (10 No. of c.c. of unreacted oil)

2. Natural Sulphite Method :-

This is also an absorption method using a neutral sulphite solution, sodium hydroxide is liberated as the reaction proceeds.

Procedure :-Introducing 75 cc of freshly prepare, aqueous solution of sodium sulphite into a 150 cc flask, having a thin neck graduated in 0.1 cc division. Then adding few drops of a 1% alcoholic phenolphthalein solution and neutalise the free alkali with a 50% queous solution of acetic acid solution. Then pippetting exactly 10 cc of the oil into the flask and shake thoroughly. Immerse the flask in a breaker of boiling water and shake repeatedly. Neutralizing the mixture from time to time 50% acetic acid. Continuing this procedure until no further pink colour appears upon the addition of a few more drops of phenols phthalein solution. Permitting the flask to remain the boiling water for an additional 15 minutes to assure complete reaction. Then adding sufficient neutralized sodium sulphite solution to raise the lower limit of the only layer within the graduated portion of the neck. Any droplets of the oil adhering to the sides are made to rise the neck by gently tapping the flask and ley rotating it rapidly between the palm of the hands. After cooling the flask to room temp. measure the amount of unreacted oil the aldehyde content may be then calculated by means of the formula given under bisulphite method.

PLANT ECONOMICS OF CITRONELLA OIL

Rated Plant Capacity = 90.00 Mt

LAND & BUILDING

1. Land 1000 area	Rs.	55,10,000.00

PLANT & MACHINERY

1. Dozing excanator and tiller equipment
2. Earth digging grass cutting and plaining equipments
3. Steam distillation still with condensers and oil separators
4. Disintigrator
5. Centrifugal filtration unit
6. Air conditioner for storage of Oil
7. Boiler
8. Lab testing equipments
9. Depolluting equipments
10. Electrification and installation

FIXED CAPITAL

1. Land and Building	Rs.	55,10,000.00
2. Plant and Machinery	Rs.	11,70,000.00
3. Other Fixed Assets	Rs.	1,85,000.00
TOTAL	Rs.	68,65,000.00

RAW MATERIALS

1. Citronella grass
2. Manures & irrigation
3. Miscellaneous chemicals

TOTAL CAPITAL INVESTMENT

Total Fixed Capital	Rs.	68,65,000.00
Total Working Capital for 3 Months	Rs.	3,15,847.00
TOTAL	Rs.	71,80,847.00

TURN OVER/ANNUM

Return of sale of 27000 kgs. Citronella Oil pure

Rs. 54,00,000.00

PROFIT SALES RATIO = Profit / Sales x 100 = 46.70%
RATE OF RETURN = Operating profit / T.C.I x 100 = 35.12%
BREAK EVEN POINT (B.E.P) = 44.77%

19

Clove Oil

Process of Manufacture

Oil of clove is the valuable oil obtained by steam distillation of dried flower buds, dried leaves or dried stems respectively of clove tree botanically known as eugenia caryopuyllus.

This process of obtaining clove oil from aromatic plant is a batch process, but specific condition such as temperature pressure length of the cycle and amount of pretreatment of plant material are the most important factors.

Firstly all the plant materials must be broken up to some extent before they ae changed to the still. This process called communication exposes some of the plants oil glands, and reduces are thickness of material to be handled in the still. The overall effect is to greatly increase speed of vaporization and distillation of the oil during steam distillation three things happen at once; oil and hot water diffuse through the plant membrance, some components of the oils hydrolyze, put of the oil is decomposed by heat. The ideal distillation, there is one in which diffusion rate is as high as possible while hydrolysis and thermal decomposition are kept to a minimum. During distillation some part of the oil dissolves in the water present within the plant cell, this solution is carried by osmosis through the cell membrance, and at the surface the oil is vapourized by passing steam. The rate at which the oil becomes available for distillation is related to its solubility in water. For this reason the higher boiling but more water soluble oil component occasionally distill over lover before boiling, less soluble parts.

When steam passes through the still containing the plant material, the clove oil is carried over with the steam into a shell and to be condenser mounted horizontally. The condensed oil and steam flow into an oil separator where they are separated by means of the difference in sp. gravity between the two liquids. Since large amounts of water are collected in proportion to the amount of clove oil, the water is recycled to the still along with fresh steam.

The usual distillation takes about 24 hours. From the charge of about 4,000 lb of clove spice yields about 600 lbs of clove oil.

PLANT ECONOMICS OF CLOVE OIL

Rated Plant Capacity = 300.00 Kgs/Day

LAND & BUILDING

1. Land 1500 sq.mt.	Rs.	10,60,000.00

PLANT & MACHINERY

1. Steam distillation unit.
2. Shell and tube condenser
3. Receiver
4. Separator
5. Baby boiler
6. Storage Tanks
7. Filling and Bottling

FIXED CAPITAL

1. Land and Building	Rs.	10,60,000.00
2. Plant and Machinery	Rs.	6,30,000.00
3. Other Fixed Assets	Rs.	3,00,000.00
TOTAL	Rs.	19,90,000.00

RAW MATERIALS

1. Cloves
2. Packing material

TOTAL CAPITAL INVESTMENT

Total Fixed Capital	Rs.	19,90,000.00
Total Working Capital for 3 Months	Rs.	58,40,910.00
TOTAL	Rs.	78,30,910.00

TURN OVER/ANNUM

By Selling 90000 kg/annum of Clove Oil Rs. 3,15,00,000.00

PROFIT SALES RATIO = Profit / Sales x 100 = 21.04%

RATE OF RETURN = Operating profit / T.C.I x 100 = 84.63%

BREAK EVEN POINT (B.E.P) = 22.95%

20

Extraction of Essential Oils by Super Critical Fluid (Carbon Dioxide) Method from Flowers, Herbs and Spices

MANUFACTURING PROCESS FOR EXTRACTION OF ESSENTIAL OILS FROM FLOWERS, HERBS, SPICES BY SUPER CRITICAL FLUID (CARBON DIOXIDE)

A. Extraction of Essential Oil from Flowers :

Solvent Extraction Process using super critical Fluid (CO_2) :-

Extraction using super critical fluid instead of solvents viz. hexane, benzene etc. is a much beneficial.

From Flowers :-

Extraction of Essential oils from flowers by super critical fluids (SCF) is first carried out in an extraction unit with jacketed reactor convected with condenser system. In the jacket steam is passed impart requisite temperature to the contents in the jacketed vessel, containing the charge comprising of various flowers viz. Jasmine, lavender, etc. using SCF and the vaporization of the essential oils is conducted out under vacuum separately from individual flavers based on their boiling points. These essential oils in the form of vapors rise from the main distillation unit and get condensed in the reflux condenser from which they are taken to their respective storage tanks, packed in suitable containers and despatched for marketing.

The super critical fluid used in the above operation is carbon dioxide. This super critical carbon dioxide at temperatures and pressures above the critical point of 31.06°C and 7.38 m pa (73.8 bar) may be employed.

After the extraction of essential oils, which are volatile oils, the remaining soft is withdrawn and transferred to the solvent extraction unit fitted with heating system using oleum ether for extraction of oleoresins.

After the extraction unit the stuff is well stirred which the solvent is introduced into the system. When the extraction is complete, the solution is filtered and the solvent distilled off. In more upto date equipment, counter-current extraction may be affected through a series of percolators which are fitted; with trays packed with the remaining floral stuff. The solvent after passing through the plant material passes to a vacuum still (vacuum distillation system with condenser, etc.), where it is distilled of and returned for fresh extraction i.e. the recycle of the solvent is accomplished. The relatively less volatile perfume oils remain in the still. The product is usually a solid mass and consists of a mixture of oleoresins plant waxes, pigments, etc. which is known as concrete on treatment with alcohol the insoluble plant waxes can be filtered off, removal of alcohol from the solution yields obsolete.

There are two types of extractors i.e. stationary & rotory extractors. The former consists or vertical cylinders provided with perforated metal goods arranged horizontally around a vertical shaft. The floral stuff is well changed on grids extraction is affected by successive washings whereby each batch of floral stuff is brought into contact with the solvent three times. The final extract is distilled to recover the solvent.

The rotory extractor consists of a tinned iron-drum rotating on a horizontal axis. The interior is divided into four compartments (loading flowers) by means of perforated metal partitions. The solvent remains at the lowest part of the extractor and when one compartment is lifted in the course of the movement of the drum the liquid seeps through the perforations and drips back to the bottom. Each batch of flowers receive three washings. The extract pumped to a vacuum still and the solvent distilled of at a temperature below 60° 90-95% of the solvent is recovered. The concrete is cooled filtered and further concentrated in vacuo. The floral· concrete so obtained contains the odoriferous principles and a considerable amount of plant waxes and pigments. For preparing the absolute the concrete is exhausted with warm alcohol and insoluble wax separated. The clear solution is cooled to -20° to -25° when more wax separates out.

PROCESS FLOW DIAGRAM
FOR EXTRACTION OF ESSENTIAL OILS FROM FLOWERS USING SUPER CRITICAL FLUID METHOD

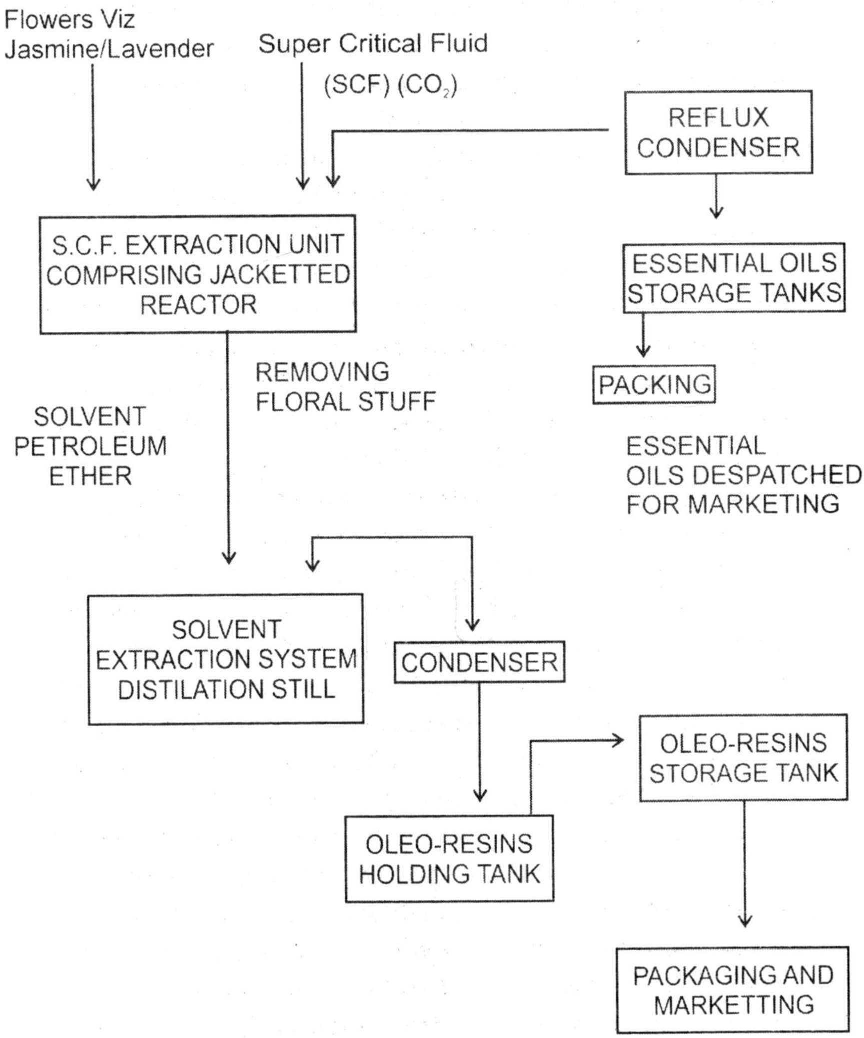

B. FROM HERBS

(Spikenard (Jatamansi)/Cinnamon/Zeodary (Kachur)

The process of extraction of respective essential oils from Herbs comprises the following steps:-

1. Cleaning of the Herb Rhizome,
2. Washing,
3. Drying,
4. Disintegration into small chips,
5. SCF Extraction for Essential Oils using super critical Fluid (CO_2)
6. Condensing of Essential oils,
7. Bottling of Essential Oils & despatch,
8. Solvent Extraction using petroleum ether for extraction of oleo-resins,
9. Bottling of oleoresins & despatch.

1. Cleaning :-

Individually the respective herbs viz. spikenard (Jatamansi)/Zeodary (kachur) etc. of rhizomes are cleared off the adhering soil.

2. Washing :-

The herbs rhizones are then washed with water to wash off the remaining adhering dust or any other impurities.

3. Drying

Then these rhizomes from which the respective essential oil is to be extracted, are dried.

This process of drying of Herbs rhizomes is carried out in the sun for economical reasons.

However, precautions are to be observed that the place where these items are kept for drying in the sum should be such that dust or dirt and any other foreign matter shouldn't get contaminated with them during drying.

4. Disintegration into small chip :-

Prior to the SCF extraction of essential fluid, the cleared and dried rhizomes are disintegrated into small chips, rather caused to coarse powder.
5. Rest of the process is similar to that described under section (A) for extraction of essential oils from flowers.

PROCESS FLOW DIAGRAM FOR EXTRACTION OF ESSENTIAL FLUID METHOD

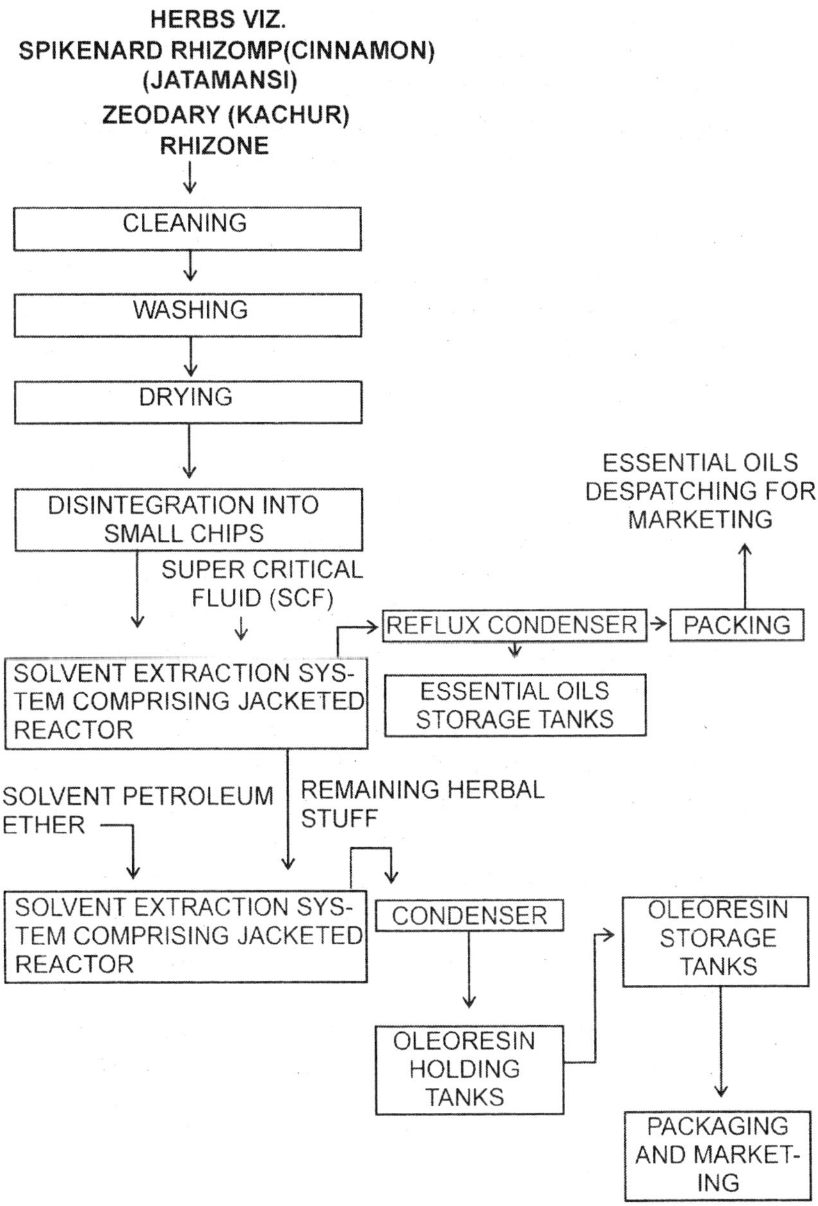

PROCESS FLOW DIAGRAM FOR EXTRACTION OF ESSENTIAL OILS FROM SPICES USING SUPER CRITICAL FLUID (SCF) METHOD

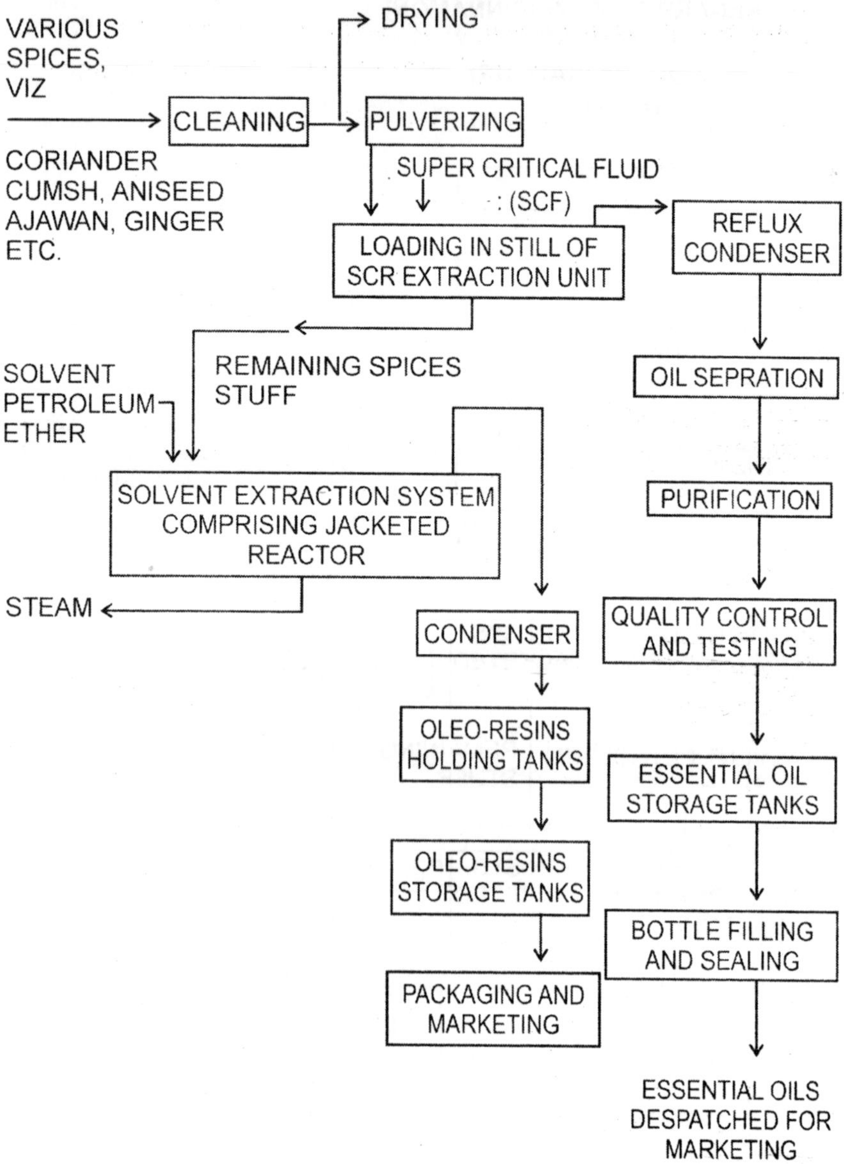

6. FROM SPICES:-

Viz. Coriender, Cumin, Aniseed, Ajowan, Ginger, etc.

The process of extraction of essential oil from spices using super critical fluid involves the following major step.

1. Cleaning of spices,
2. Cutting the item into small pieces/pulverising,
3. Loading of the still of SCF Extraction Unit,
4. Extraction of Essential oils from respective spices,
5. Bottling of Essential oils,
6. Solvent Extraction using petroleum ether for extraction of oleoresins,
7. Bottling of oleo-resins and despatch.

1. Cleaning :-

Individually, the respective spices viz. coriender, cumin, Aniseed, Ajowan, ginger, etc. are cleared off the adhering soil of impurities.

2. Drying :-

The item whose oil is to be extract is dried. This process is proposed to be carried out in sun, for economic reasons. The place where these items are kept for drying in sun should be detected such that the dust and dirt water or any other foreign matter shouldn't get contaminated during drying. One most suitable place is the roof of the working shed. The side walls of the roof should be of sufficient height.

3. Cutting into Prices :-

The items like Cardamom, Cumin seeds and King's Cumin are not need to be cut into pieces for they are naturally present in small size. But for Ginger, it is need to be cut into small pieces.

Plant Economics

LAND & BUILDING

(Land Area 3000 Sq.mts.) = Rs. 44,75,000.00

PLANT & MACHINERY

1. Extraction Unit, using Super Critical Fluid (SCF) Jacketed Reactor for condenser

2. Solvent Extraction system with complete accessories and heating system
3. Vacuum distillation system with condenser
4. Automatic washing machine
5. Cabinet dryer electric operated
6. Disteingrator complete with motor
7. Automatic sieving machine
8. Pulverizer
9. Centrifugal Separator
10. Bottle filling and sealing machine
11. Boiler steam generating
12. Carton sealing machine
13. Storage tanks,
14. Storage tank for SCF & solvent
15. Instrumentation and process control
16. Lab. equipments

FIXED CAPITAL

1.	Land and Building	Rs.	44,75,000.00
2.	Plant and Machinery	Rs.	1,84,10,000.00
3.	Other Fixed Assets	Rs.	40,90,000.00
	TOTAL	Rs.	2,69,75,000.00

RAW MATERIALS

1. Flowers/Jasmine/Lavender/etc.
2. Herbs spikenhard(Jatamansi)/cinnamon zeodary (kachur)
3. For Spices :- Coriander
4. Cumin (Jeera/Seeds)
5. Aniseed
6. Ajowan (Bishop seeds)
7. Ginger (Green)
8. Eucalyptus leaves
9. Garlic
10. Neem leaves
11. Tej patta
12. Turmeric
13. Orange Peel (Dried)
14. Super Critical fluid (SCF) (Carbon dioxide)

15. Petroleum Ether Solvent

TOTAL CAPITAL INVESTMENT

Total Fixed Capital	Rs.	2,69,75,000.00
Total Working Capital for 3 Months	Rs.	2,66,30,475,00
TOTAL	Rs.	5,36,05,475,00

TURN OVER/ANNUM

1. By sale of : (A) Essential oil from Jasmine/Lavender/etc. Flowers
2. (B) Essential Oils from Herbs Spike nard (Jaamansi)/Cinnamon/ Zeodary (Kachur)
3. (C) Essential Oils from Spices : Coriander Oil
4. Cumin Oil
5. Aniseed Oil
6. Ajavan Oil
7. Ginger Oil
8. Eucalyptus Oil
9. Garlic Oil
10. Neem Oil
11. Tej Patta oil
12. Turmeric Oil
13. Orange Peel Oil
14. II. (A) Oleoresins from Flowers Jas-mine/Lavender
15. (B) Oleo-Resins from Herbs (Spikenard (Jatamansi/Cinnamon/Zeodary (Kachur)
16. (C) Oleo-Resins from spices :- Oleoresins from Coriander
17. Oleoresins from Cumin
18. Oleoresins frum Aniseed
19. Oleoresins from Ajawan
20. Oleoresins from Ginger
21. Oleoresins from Eucalyptus
22. Oleoresins from Garlic

23. Oleoresins from Neem
24. Oleoresins from Tejpatta
25. Oleoresins from Turmeric
26. Oleoresins from Orange Peel

Rs.14,49,67,200.00

PROFIT SALES RATIO = Profit / Sales x 100 = 16.52%

RATE OF RETURN = Operating profit / T.C.I x 100 = 44.68%

BREAK EVEN POINT (B.E.P) = 39.65%

21

Eucalyptus Oil

Process of Manufacture

Eucalyptus oil is obtained in India by the distillation of leaves and terminal branches of E.globulus (Blue Gum Tree), which grows on Niligiri, Ammamale and Plain Hills

The leaves are collected from trees filled in fuedl to the towns hills. Nature leaves from trees of 15 years or above are preferred. They are dried in shade for 3 days and subjected for distillation in stills. The crude oil is separated distillation in stills. The crude oil is separated from the distillation in stills. The crude oil is separated from the distillated, filtered and then refined from the distillation, filtered and then refined by distillation after adding caustic potash. The refined oil is filtered and then bottled for marketing. Hydrogen peroxide is used for decolouring the oil. The oil can be marketed as

I. Double Distilled (pale yellow colour)

II. Double distilled & extra refined (colourless)

DISTILLATION

Even though distillation is a harsh treatment a great many oils are produced in this way. In these cases, the perfume bearing part of the plant is cut down or picked up and taken to the distillation unit where it is distilled to separate the perfumery material from the plant part.

These methods of distillation are in use viz water distillation, water and steam distillation and live steam distillation. Water distillation is the crudest method of separating oils from plant parts. This is the simple process in which the plant material is placed into the still, water added and the vessel is fire heated. Water and oil distill together. They are condensed. The oil and water layers are separated subsequently. The process of water distillation has the disadvantage of exposing the delicate essential oil to a prolonged distillation in the presence of water, which results in the unnecessary hydrolyres of esterlic. The tendency now is to use more modern distillation equipments of the water and steam and type in where the still fitted with a horizontal perforated plate upon which the product material rests. The one material rests. The lower part of the still is fitted with water to a level somewhat below the grid and charge is subjected to distillation by passing low pressure steam. This avoids direct passing low pressure steam. This avoid direct contact of plant material into the distillation water below. The water beneath the perforated grid is described after the completion of distillation and replaced with fresh water.

Steam distillation method differs from the water and steam distillation method because no water is kept in the bottom of this-still. Live steam at 40-000 lbs/sq.in is injected through steam coils below the charge, the pressure within the vessel is controlled according to the nature of material handled. A modern distillation unit may also incorporate other refinements such as solvent extraction of the water distillation waters. This enables the water soluble portions of the essential oil to be recovered. The oils separated by distillation are sometimes rectified or factioned by hydro distillation at a low pressure for improved colour and odour. The odours and objectionable impurities are removed in the folreruns and late-runs during rectification.

Distillation Processes :

In the batch distillation a batch of material is charged to the still. Heat is applied and the vapours are removed continuously with no partial condensation of the vapours or refluxing of the condenser. It is chiefly confined to small scale operations which are intermittent and in which efficiency of operation and heat is sacrificed for simplicity. In the continuous distillation process, the efficiency is better but the cost of operation. In this type of distillation, the still is fitted with a fractionation column and reflux condensus. In this cases still may be heated wither by steam or electricity.

Operation :

The method of working is to place sufficient quantity of water in each still and to pack the leaves tightly upon the grid supported upon the bottom. Before the lid is put in position a thick mixture of mud or clay is placed along the ilange. On top of this is placed a strip of horrian or similar packing material and second layer of clay is applied. The lid is then lowered on the flange and fastered by meand of cross timbers, wooden wedges and iron stirrups, which are attached to the tank. The still is built upon a support of bricks or stones and a wood fire is placed beneath. When the water boils the steam passing up through the leaves separates the oil from the plant allows and carries it over, in a caporous state into a condenser where oil and water condenser and flow out into a suitable receptacle where the oil floats upon the surface of the water and is ultimately separated. The time of distillation variety from 3-18 hr. according to the species.

Refining :

Crude medicinal grade Eucalyptus oil is subjected to redistillation. Small quantities of water, objectionable volatile aldehydes (principal isovaleric aldehyde) and some prene, are removed is this way. The main or middle fraction, constituting about 85 to 90% of the oil and containing not less than 70% cineole, is marketed as a rectified eucalyptus oil. The residue in the still, consisting of x-terpineol, sesquiterpenes, sesquiterpene alcohols, p-isopropyl phenol, cumminal or phellondral, cryprone etc. is used as a source of these substances, in the manufacture of commercial disinfectant. The phenolic, aldehydic and ketonic substances passes marked germicidal properties.

Yield :- The oil yield depend on

1. Type and age of Leaf, Randomless of sample, composition of sample is objective leaf selection etc.
2. Storage of Samples: Changes in oil central and constitution during storage, Moisture content of sample preventions of sweating etc.
3. Steam distillation technique: Technique & Time of distillation etc.

Location Conditions :

This plant is based mainly on the agricultural product. So the economics of the plant will much depend on the location of the plant. The factor influencing the plant site selection and economics are discussed below:

Raw Materials

Raw materials for the product is only eucalyptus leaves which is a natural product and hence plant will be seasoned. In order to avoid this dependency sufficient stock of leaves should be done. It is advisable that the plant should be located near the raw material source.

Market

Market is the second major point which affects the economics of the plant very much. So the plant should be located adjacent to the market as well.

Water Position :

Water is used in huge quantities in this plant. In order to meet the requirement of water, sufficient water should be available on the selected site. If water, arrangement is not available, then it is better to more own tube well.

PROCESS FLOW SHEET

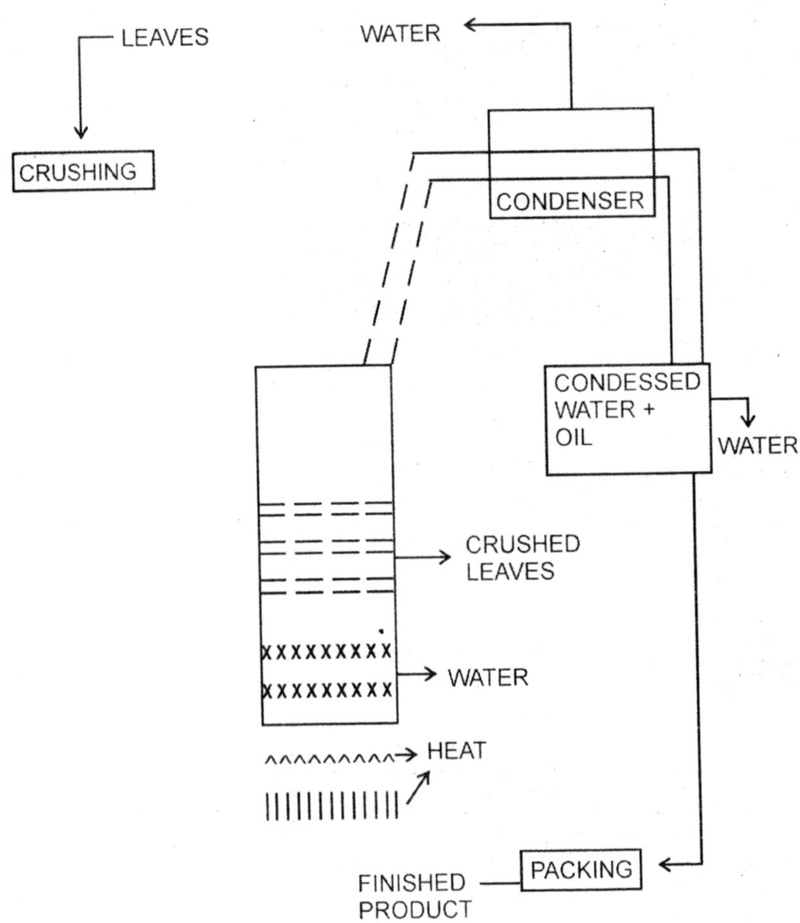

Transportation Facilities :

Transportation is used in all the industries at two stages. One is for transporting raw material to the factory site and other is for transporting the finished product to the market. So it should be carefully studied that the selected site is connected to the desired placed by roads and trains well.

Labour :

Labour required for this units is very less. Hence it does not affect the economists very much. But still the labour availability is kept in view while selected the site.

Power and Fuel

There is not much need of electrical power for this industry. Only fuel is used in bulk quantity Furnace Oil is the best fuel. It is easily available everywhere in India. Therefore this does control the production and economics.

All the above factors are studied carefully while selecting the site. Few factors are contradictory and therefore a compromise is made sometimes.

Plant Economics of Eucalyptus Oil

Rated Plant Capacity : 100.00 Kg/day

LAND & BUILDING

(Land Area 2 Acre) = Rs. 1,50,000.00

PLANT & MACHINERY

1. Distillation (mild steel) equipped with grill etc.
2. Crushing Machine
3. Condenser /Condensing column
4. Separator
5. Rectifying column
6. Filter press
7. Motor, Pumps
8. Boiler
9. Storage Tank
10. Cost of electrification piping

FIXED CAPITAL

1.	Land and Building		Rs.	12,37,500.00
2.	Plant and Machinery		Rs.	6,07,000.00
3.	Other Fixed Assets		Rs.	12,000.00
		TOTAL	Rs.	18,56,500.00

RAW MATERIALS

1. Eucalyptus Leaves
2. Steel containers, glass bottles

TOTAL CAPITAL INVESTMENT

Total Fixed Capital		Rs.	18,56,500.00
Total Working Capital for 3 Months		Rs.	7,36,125.00
	TOTAL	Rs.	25,92,625.00

TURN OVER/ANNUM

1.	Receipt from sale of 30000 Kg. Eucalyptus Oil	Rs.	40,00,000.00

PROFIT SALES RATIO = Profit / Sales x 100 = 16.90%
RATE OF RETURN = Operating profit / T.C.I x 100 = 29.34%
BREAK EVEN POINT (B.E.P) = 63.52%

22

Ginger Oil

MANUFACTURING PROCESS PREPARATION OF RAW MATERIAL

Distillation of ginger oil On an industrial scale does differ some what from distillation of essential oils in general.

Cleaning

Prior to any combination, the spice must be freed from extraneous matters, such as dust, dirt, pebbles and metallic objects. For this purpose salting machine with a magnetic screen and screens of different diameters are used.

Milling

For the grinding of ginger, mills of different type are used, some are equipped with rotating tooth disk, some are hammer mills and for some special purposes, triple- roller mills are used. Both the rotating tooth disk mills and the hammer mills have a considerable airflow, which causes a certain loss of volatile oil from the ground ginger.

The rotating disk mill may be adjusted to the desired grain size of the milled product, but frictioned heat develops during grinding and therefore they are with a cooling device. Hammer mills are not practicable when the material is small and contains a relatively high percentage of fats. For such case crushing in triple roller mills, which rotates at different velocities and have ribbed rollers is the appropriate method of comminution.

Soaking

Ames and Mathews mention the desirability of soaking of some plant material for instance, cinnamon bank and also of grinding the spice prior to distillation.

Loading or Charging

Ground ginger must be loaded into the still and distilled without any delays otherwise, losses of Essential oil and deterioration through oxidation are inevitable. The oil distiller must realize that this valuable product will some day be used in food without any further preliminary purification. Contamination of essential oil with rust, dirt, salt of copper or water can not be tolerated. Therefore, the distillation apparatus should preferably be made of stainless steel. As a minimum requirement the lid of the still, the gooseneck, the condenser and the flerentine flask or oil receiver should be made of this material.

Bleaching of Ginger

The peeled ginger hands are washed in water and kept steeped in plain water for 2 to 3 hours. Thereafter, they are takenout and steeped in about 1.5 to 200% lime (Cao) Solution for about 6 hours. They are then drained and sun dried on mats, barbecues, or a clean cement floor. This liming or bleaching of ginger not only improves its colours but also helps to preserve it better. Care should be taken to use the best quality slaked lime in order to get better whiteness.

Application of these chemicals requires proper control especially in the bleaching of ginger.

Distillation

Ginger Oil is obtained by the steam distillation of the dried ginger. The best raw material is African ginger. It is not only lower priced than other qualities but also gives a higher yield of oil. In general the yield varies from 1.5 to 3 per cent of volatile oil. averaging 2%. Prior to distillation the dry material should be comminuted, then charged into the stills immediately. Care must be taken to distribute the mass evenly on several trays. Within the still Distillation is Carried out with direct steam depending upon the charge in the still and the steam depending upon the charge in the still and the steam pressure applied, distillation of one charge may require up to 20 hour. The distillation water may require cohobation.

Peeling and shaving of the rhizomes constitute an excellent material for distillation, giving a good yield of oil, provided distillation is carried out immediately after peeling.

Practice of Distillation

Steam Distillation

Recovering of the Oil dissolved or suspended in the distillation water consists in saturating latter first with salt and then extracting the solution with volatile solvents - as highly purified petroleum there or Benzene. This is usually done twice. The drawn off and united solvent solutions are there concentrated in still by driving off the solvent first at atmospheric pressure and later in vacuo, until every trace of solvent is eliminated from the oil.

FLOW DIAGRAM FOR GINGER OIL

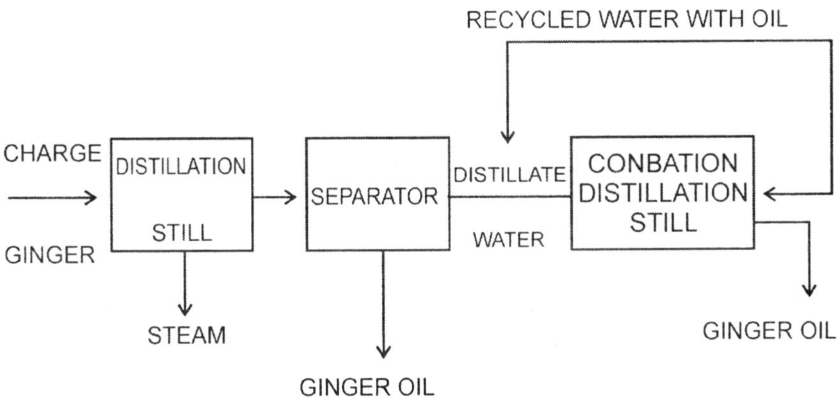

Plant Economics of Ginger Oil

Rated Plant Capacity	:	200.00 Kg/day
LAND & BUILDING		
(Land Area 1400 sq. mtr.) =	Rs.	7,35,000.00

PLANT & MACHINERY

1. Boiler
2. Distillation Still
3. Condenser

4. Storage tank
5. Piping system etc.
6. Accumulator
7. Pulveriser
8. Pumps
9. Electricity Installation erection & commissioning
10. Weighing & Testing equipments

FIXED CAPITAL

1.	Land and Building	Rs.	30,10,000.00
2.	Plant and Machinery	Rs.	6,50,000.00
3.	Other Fixed Assets	Rs.	37,500.00
	TOTAL	Rs.	36,97,500.00

RAW MATERIALS

1. Ginger
2. Lime
3. Nacl

TOTAL CAPITAL INVESTMENT

Total Fixed Capital	Rs.	36,97,500.00
Total Working Capital for 3 Months	Rs.	16,24,695.00
TOTAL	Rs.	53,22,195.00

TURN OVER/ANNUM

1.	By sale of 6000 Kg.	Rs.	1,02,00,000.00

PROFIT SALES RATIO = Profit / Sales x 100 = 21.72%
RATE OF RETURN = Operating profit / T.C.I x 100 = 41.63%
BREAK EVEN POINT (B.E.P) = 50.48%

23

Jasmine Flower Oil

MANUFACTURING PROCESS

There are two modern methods used for manufacturing of Jasmine & other flower oil which are delicate in nature which are thermally unstable and chiefly separated by either solvent extraction using volatile solvents. Another method used for extraction of flower oil is super critical fluid extraction method.

EXTRACTION WITH SOLVENT:-

CONSTRUCTION OF APPARATUS:-

Until some years ago the extactors and stills were constructed of copper, because this metal retains its value after rapping the apparatus, and the pliable copper can be hammered and retirs are easily made. Lately, however, the extractors are constructed are often of heavily tinned sheet rion which is much cheaper and, therefore offers the advantage flower investment and quicker amortization.

The apparatus must be of solid construction of stand wear and tear; all extractor pipes and valves should be within easy to save time and exclude mistakes on the part of the operators. Pipes and valves must be sufficiently wide to prevent formation of pressure by air and petroleum ether apors, one of the principal causes for loss of the solvent and solutions to and from the apparatus, and considerably speed up operation. Pumping of solvents and solutes is done by air pressure created by air compressors.

The extractors are mounted on elevated metal platforms along the inside walls of the building. The platform runs even with the ground outside of the building, so that arriving flower material may be changed directly into the extractors and the exhausted flowers discharged with equal ease.

Loss of solvent during the operation presents one of the most serious problems. These losses are usually caused by incomplete distillation of the solvent from the exhausted flowers, by insufficient condensation in the contensers, or by too narrow pipes and valves creating pressure and blowing off a mixture of air and solvent vapour. To avoid this as much as possible the whole system of extractors, evaporators and solvent tanks is arranged as a closed circle, with only one outlet where escaping solvent vapours can be condensed. The society carbonisation et Carbons Actifs some years ago developed an efficient, rather small sized apparatus in which solvent vapours are absorbed by activated carbon and recovered by blowing live steam through the saturated carbon. A current of hot air then rectivates the carbon. The apparatus is simple and permits considerable economy in factories where large amounts of solvent are in circulation.

The latest model consists of a heavily tinned iron drum rotating around a horizontal axle. Four perforated metal partitions, rectangularly and horizontally arranged arount the central axle, divide the interior into four compartments into which the flowers are charged through four manholes. While the whole system rotates slowly, the flower materials moves, tumbles and disp into the solvent lying on the bottom of the extractor. The liquid seeps through the perforations and drips back to the bottom when one compartment is lifted out of the solvent in the contineous movement of the whole frum. Thus, the solvent does not fill the extractor but only the lowest part, the flowers dipping slowly and continuously into the solvent and rising again in the rotating movement.

Three successive washings are usually made, carried out similarly to the systematic extraction method described under stationary apparatus. The first, i.e. the most saturated washing, is then pumped into the evaporator and concentrated by distilling of the solvent. After the third washing has been drawn off the exhausted flower material, live steam is blown into the extractor to distill over and recover the petroleum ether still adhering to the extracting flowers.

The advantages of the rotatory extractors as compared with stationary apparatus are evident. Through the movement of the flower material in the solvent, its action becomes more penetrating and more effective, resulting in a somewhat higher yield. Figured as concrete, it is about 8 per cent higher in the case of the rotatory apparatus. Since the solvent covers only the bottom drum and not the whole flower material, as in the stationry apparatus, much less solvent is in circulation and, therefore, evaporation losses are reduced. Only 160 to 170 liters are required in the rotatory apparatus to extract 100 kg. of flowers. The loss of solvent for 100 kg. of flowers is less than in stationary extractors; it may be 8 to 12 liters but can be reduced by using the previously described solvent recovery apparatus.

One rotatory extractor does the work of three or four stationary extractors arranged in one battery. Although superior in many ways the rotatory extractors suffer from several disadvantages and cannot altogether replace the stationary type; for example, the latter is better adapted to voluminous plant material, such as lavender, which cannot be so easily charged and discharged through the manholes of the rotating drum.

Concentration of Solutions:- The first, i.e., the most concentrated, washing is filtered through a fine screen and pumped into the so-called evaporator in which the greater part of the solvent is driven (distilled) off. These evaporators are of varying construction, representing basically a modified water or steam bath. In other words, the heating is done by indirect steam blown into a steam jacket beneath the still. The solvent, however, should not be completely driven off In this operation. Most manufacturers stop operation when the temperature in the still (evaporator) reaches about 60°, because any higher temperature at atmospheric pressure would be harmful to the delicate flower perfume. The first washing contains, of course, only a small percentage of flower oil. Therefore, concentrating of this washing in the evaporator means driving off 90-95 per cent of the solvent. (The recovered solvent serves as tresh solvent tor a thırd washıng) I he concentrated solution remaining in the evaporators is permitted to cool, is filtered, then transferred into a special, smaller vacuum still, and there completely concentrated in vacuo.

Final Concentration.: Vacuum stills of small capacity (50 to 100 liters) serve for this purpose. The final concentration represents a most delicate operation and requires much experience and constant attention on the part of the operator. The concentrating has to be done at as low a temperature as possible, yet any trace of solvent must be eliminated. Every manufacturer has his own, often secret, methods of purification. The completely concentrated and purified products represent the so-called floral concretes, which contain the odoriferous principles of the natural flower perfume, plus a considerable amount of plant waxes, albuminous material and colour pigments. The concretes are, therefore, usually of solid consistency and only partly soluble in 95 per cent alcohol.

Concrete Flower Oils:- Although these insoluble concretes are more difficult to work with, some perfumers prefer them to the alcohol soluble absolutes, which are obtained by precipitating and eliminating the insoluble waxes with strong alcohol, and concentrating the filtered alcoholic solutions. Distilling off the alcohol from the solutions when making these absolutes undoubtedly entails the loss of some of the most volatile and delicate constituents of the natural flower oil. It is' often claimed that an alcor"";::: washing of a concrete is superior and more true to nature than a sirt,. I alcoholic solution of the ecorresponding absolute. On the other hand, the processing of concretes requires special equipment and considerable time; therefore, the absolutes represent a more convenient form of flower oils than the concretes.

Conversion of Concretes into Absolutes:- The alcohol soluble absolutes are prepared from the concretes by the following general method:

The concrete is either thoroughly rubbed down in a large mortar with a quantity of high-proof alcohol or, as some manufacturers prefer, melted and dissolved in warm alcohol. Subsequently eight to ten times the amount of alcohol is added and the mass stirred for a prolonged period in batteuses, as described under enfleurage. Usually five to six washings of the concrete are made in a systematic way, i.e., a third washing serves as a second one for a following batch of concrete; the second is used as first for a batch of new concrete, the first washing consequently representing the most concentrated solution. After standing and drawing off the clear solution from the alcohol insoluble waxes, the first washing is then thoroughly cooled in a refrigerator or in a special room, at temperatures ranging from -20° to -25°, when more wax precipitates and is filtered off in the cold. This resulting clear solution can be used as such in alcoholic perfumes.

Most perfume houses have neither the time nor the facilities to carry out their own washing of concretes, and prefer using alcohol soluble floral oils. For those, the manufacturers in Grasse offer the so-called liquid absolutes as the most concentrated form of natural flower oils. These liquid absolutes of extraction are obtained by carefully concentrating the first alcoholic washing of the corresponding concrete at low temperature in a good vacuum still. This process of concentrating involves a loss of several liters of alcohol per kilogram of absolute.

The absolutes are usually viscous oils with a more or less pronounced color, according to the degree of final purification (for which each manufacture employs his own process). The absolutes are soluble in high-proof alcohol,

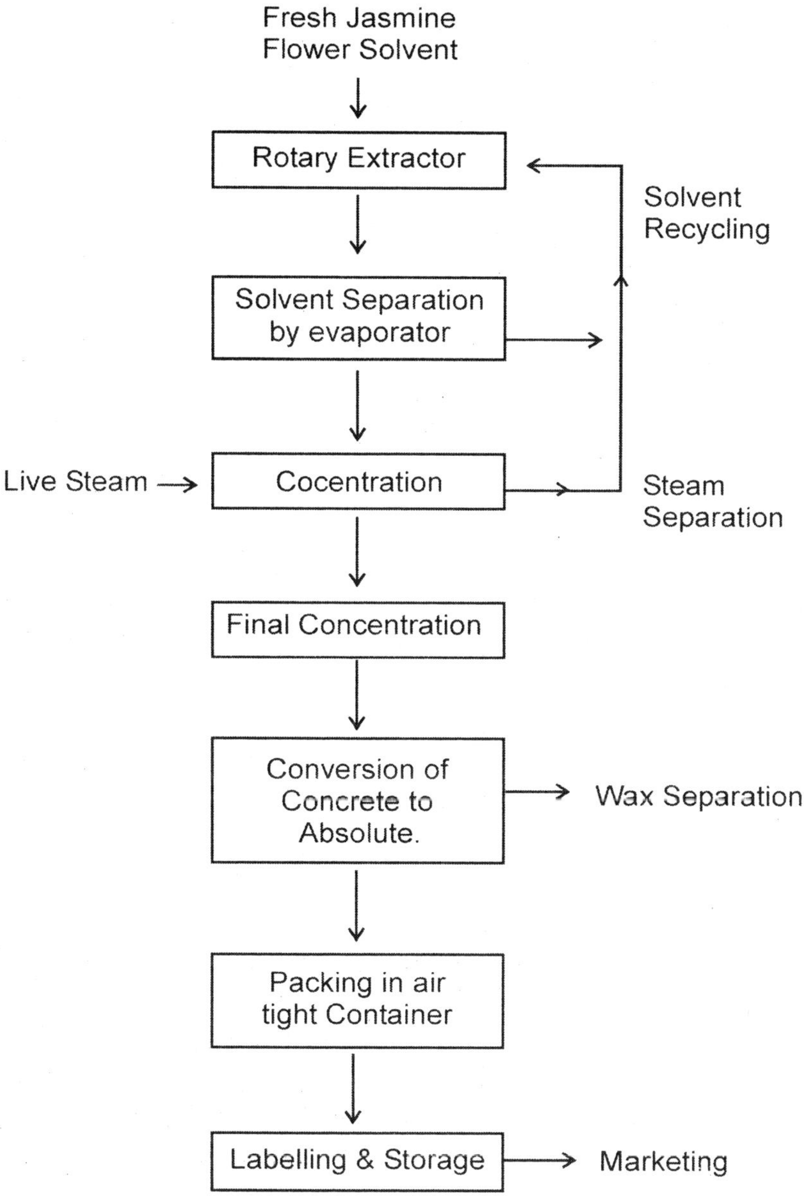
Fresh Jasmine
Flower Solvent
Rotary Extractor
Solvent
Recycling
Solvent Separation
by evaporator
Live Steam
Cocentration
Steam
Separation
Final Concentration
Conversion of
Concrete to
Absolute.
Wax Separation
Packing in air
tight Container
Labelling & Storage
Marketing

and represent the most concentrated form of natural flower oils used in practical perfume work. However, they must not be confused with actual volatile flower oil in the scientific sense. The absolutes usually contain from 50 to 80 per cent of alcohol soluble waxes, and only 20 to 25 per cent volatile oil, which can be isolated from the absolute by steam distillation. However, these volatile oils from the absolutes are not offered on the market because of their excessively high price, and because they completely lack the high fixation value of an absolute, which is due to the presence of alcohol soluble natural waxes, etc., in the absolute.

PLANT ECONOMICS

Rated Plant Capacity = 10.00 Kgs/Day

LAND & BUILDING

1. Land required 1000 sq.mts.	Rs.	4,00,000.00

PLANT & MACHINERY

1. Feeding Hopper with Bucket elevator
2. Rotary Extractor to extract, Jasmine Flower Oil
3. S.S. Jacketed evaporation tank with vacuum system.
4. Condenser
5. Vacuum still (SS) for final concentration
6. Solvent Storage Tank (SS)
7. Baby Boiler
8. Pipes, fittings, Vacuum pumps, valves, motor
9. Solvent Recycling Unit
10. Laboratory testing equipments and instruments.

FIXED CAPITAL

1.	Land and Building	Rs.	15,00,000.00
2.	Plant and Machinery	Rs.	13,45,000.00
3.	Other Fixed Assets	Rs.	2,65,000.00
	TOTAL	Rs.	31,10,000.00

RAW MATERIALS

1. Flower fresh (Jasmine)
2. Solvent petroleum ether
3. Glass bottles and labels
4. Carton made of cardboard

TOTAL CAPITAL INVESTMENT

Total Fixed Capital	Rs.	31,10,000,00
Total Working Capital for 3 Months	Rs.	58,11,300.00
TOTAL	Rs.	89,21,300.00

TURN OVER/ANNUM

1. By sale of 3000 kg. Jasmine Flower Oil	Rs.	3,00,00,000.00

PROFIT SALES RATIO = Profit / Sales x 100 = 15.47%
RATE OF RETURN = Operating profit / T.C.I x 100 = 52.03%
BREAK EVEN POINT (B.E.P) = 40.04%

24

Production Technology of Jasmine for Essential Oil

The delightful fragment essential oil of jasminum grandiflorum is appreciated all over the world. It is an export oriented agro industry in Morocco, France, Egypt, Tunisia, Italy, Sicily, Algeria, India and China. In India there are 16 jasmine essential oil agro industry units located in Tamilnadu, Karnatka, and to some extent in Andhra Pradesh & Maharashtra. Looking up its significant commercial importance. Indian Institution of Horticultural Research, Bangalore has developed its production technology. It is presented here.

Jasmine may be grown in wide range of soils, but the land must be well drained. Duraction of flowering is longer and yield is higher in sunny warm humid weather of Southern India. Flower picking needs many labourers, hence availability of cheap labour is an important consideration taking up its plantation.

Commercial varieties of Jaji are CO-I Pitch and Arka Surabhi. Arka Surabhi is a superior strain having 0.35 per cent concrete with a potential yield of 35 kg concrete /ha in Karnataka.

Planting material is raised in mist chamber from shoot tip cutting treated with 4000 ppm IBA. Recently a low cost and water saving method i.e. closed media Sahcet Technique has been devised by the Laboratory of aromatic crops, IIHR, Bangalore, which eliminate need of power operated mist chamber. It saves large amount of water.

A month before planting, pits measuring 45 cm x 45 cm x 45 cm should be dug at spacing of 2m x 1.8m. The pits should be filled up with 2:1 mixture of soil and farm yard manure. Planting is done in the beginning of monsoon. With proper management the plantation remain reproductive for above 12 years.

For good yield irrigation is required once in 10 to 20 days depending upon season. However the crop has remarkable quality of drought resistance. An experiment at Indian Institute of Horticultural Research, Bangalore, revealed that despite elimination of irrigation for as long as three years, the plants remained healthy. Of course yield was less by about 50 percent.

Regarding nutritional requirement the recommendation per grown up bush is 100 gm N, 150 gm $2P_2O_5$ and 100 gm K_2O in 3 slipt doses. Research on use of growth regulations doses. Research on use of growth regulators have indicated that CCC and B-Nine (1000 ppm) induce early flowering and extend blooming period.

Pruning is necessary to get high yields and to keep the bushes to manageable size. It should be done during mid December. Nine to eleven well spread branches should be retained and pruned at 90 cm height. Chemical defoliants such as penta chlorophenol 3000 ppm, potassium iodide 4000 ppm also have been reported to be effective alternatives.

Flower yield /ha from Jaji (Var. Arka Surabhi) is about 500 kg in 1st year, about 5000 kg in 2nd year and 10 tonnes from 3rd year. For extraction purpose flowering are harvested before sunrise. Therefore, proper light should be provided in the field. Instead of flowers, fully manured buds may be harvested and spread up in specially made trays. The buds bloom by 8 pm and then extracted.

Extraction of Jasmine Concrete and its Economic Prospect

Solvent extraction method is most common flower. Flowers are placed in extactor and dipped in the food grade hexane. The extractor is operated first for 30 minutes, second and third time for 20 minutes. The solvent is drained each time. The first miscella is distilled directly while second and third miscella are combined and used for the extraction of the next batch of flowers. The solvent is removed by distillation and reused. To remove the last traces of solvent, the concentrator is finally connected with a vacuum pump.

The residue left after the removal of solvent is known as 'concrete'. It has semisolid consistency with yellowish brown colour and fragrance of fresh jasmine flowers. It may be stored at 10 to 15°C for over one year. Price of Jasmine concrete ranges from Rs. 14,000/- to Rs. 18,000/- per kg. For use in perfume industry, the concrete is further processed by treating with pure alcohol at 0°C. Final product is called "Absolute". It is viscous, clear, yellow-brown liquid, soluble in 95 per cent alcohol. Price of Jasmine absolute is more ethan double of concrete. It indicate bright economic prospect of this agro industry.

Besides Jaji Jasmine, now a days Jasminum sambac and jasminum auriculatum flowers are also used to produce essential oil. Hence research work is also underway on these species.

25

Lemon Grass Oil

Manufacturing Process

Though steam distillation has been considered as an heat treatment for extracting some thing but still lemon grass oil is extracted from steam distillation. At present three methods of distillation are practices. They are water distillation, water and steam distillation and live steam distillation. Water and steam distillation is the oldest method of separating oil from lemongrass. This process is single in which the plant material is placed into the still water added and the used is fire heated. Water and oil distill together. They are condensed in a simple condenser. The oil takes top layer. The process of water distillation has the disadvantage of explosing the delicate essential oil to a prolonged distillation in the presence of water, which results in the unnecessary hydrolysis of esters.

The distillation method of water and steam type is better than the one described. Here the still is fitted with the horizontal perforated plate upon which the lemon grass reacts. The lower part of the still is fitted with water to a level somewhat below the grid and the charge is subjected to distillation by passing low pressure steam. The avoids direct contact of plant materials with the distillation water below. This method provides lower yield.

Now the modern method is steam distillation. This method is suggested for the preparation of lemon grass oil.

Here lemongrass harvested is chopped into size of 1/4". It is now charged into the digested vessel. Live steam at a pressure 40 to 100 psig from the boiler units, is directly injected through steam coils below the charge. The pressure within the digester is controlled. Due to the pressure and the heating lemon grass oil distills out. The distillate containing lemon grass oil and steam are withdrawn through a pipe, copper and aluminium and is condensed.

The condensing system consists of a simple copper a aluminium spiral tue immersed in cold water. The spiral tube is connected to the tapering end of the Digestor (top) and and other end of the tube projects with the receiver which is a copper or aluminium vessel. In the receiving vessel lemon grass oil takes the top layer and water the lower layer.

On the one side of the receiver just above the bottom there is a bent tube which allows only the water of the lower layer to flow out.

The upper layer i.e. the oil is now decanted into the drying unit where anhydrous sodium sulphate is added to the oil and mixed. The mixture is now filtered in a small filter. The anhydrous sodium sulphate is added for dehydration of the oil i.e. for removing the moisture from oil.

The dehydrated oil is filled in cans or drums and sealed airtight. The oil should not be exposed to light frequently and kept in a dark and cool place. Coloured glass, stainless steel or aluminium are preferred to copper containers for storage.

PROCESS FLOW DIAGRAM

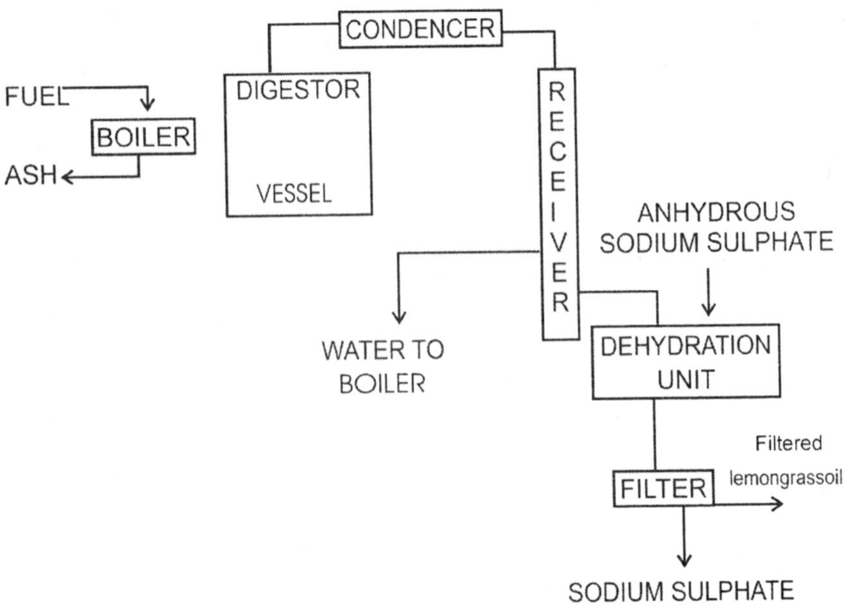

Raw Material Position

The raw material is lemon grass. It is grown in Tirunelveli in Tamil Nadu and in Kerala state. The main lamon grass growing areas in the latter states are Thioderphazha, Muvatupuzha, Meenachil and kumathand Trichur District in Central Kerala in Kozhikode. Tellichery, Morantwadi, Milambut, Sranad, peravoor etc. in North Kerala. Besides, the grass is grown in southern district of Kottayam, Trivandrum in Kerala state, Kanyakumri and Nilgiris in Tamil Nadu state and coorg and south kerala in Mysore state.

There are two types of lemon grass in Kerala differing in appearance and readily distinguishable by the colour of the stem. The so called red grass leaves yields the normal East Indian Lemon grass oil containing 75% or more of aldehydes (chiefly citral). The bulk of Indian lemon grass oil is produced from the red grass.

The ochar variety, the white grass, is produced in small quantities. The oil derived from theplant has a low aldehyde content. The area under lemon grass cultivation was estimated to be 69000 acres in 1956 out of which 66000 acreas are in kerala state, 1000 acres in Tamil Nadu and 2000 acres in Mysore state.

The other chemicals needed for production of lemon grass oil is anhydrous sodium sulphate. It is indigenously available in abudance.

26

Palm Oil Crushing Unit

MANUFACTURING PROCESS

The palm oil is produced by extraction from the reddish to orange pulps of the oval shaped fruits which grow on stalks in fresh fruit bunches (FFB) on the oil palms. Pure oil and kernel are the main final product besides minor quantities of solids are used for animal feed and fertilizer shell and dry fibers are used neither the plam oil processing line for fuelling the steam boiler.

Technology and Process Description

1. Reception of Raw Material :

The fresh fruit bunches are brought from the field to the mill by means of trailors of trucks which pass through weigh bridge (for quality control for the in coming FFB and theout going product as well).

After weighing the bunches are dumped on the storage area which is either a concrete floor or a raised unloading ramps in (small scale plant). Depending upon the type of sterilizer and the capacity of the plant filling of sterilizer baskets or cages is carried out by hand or by suitable system (gravity, loader's etc.) In large plants unloading hopper or specially designed reception system are applied.

2. Sterilizing

In this section in the fruit bunches are submitted to direct steam at a pressure of approx 3 bar over a period in the range of 3-60 minuted depending on the weight/size of the bunches.

- Prevention of any further rise in FFA (free fatty acid content) due to enzyme action by inactivation of these lipolytie.

- Facilitation of mechanical stripping Toloosen the fruits from the bunches, sufficient most heat must penetrate to the point of attachment of the fruit to the stalk.

- Modification of the colloids of the pericap and stalk in a way that deoiling of the fruit solids is favoured in the following pressing phase. This applies both to the fibre solids and to the solid in crude oil which are deoiled in the clarification.

- Pre-conditioning the nuts to minimize Kernel breakage during both pressing and nut cracking.

- Adequate sterilization permits sufficient heat penetration to cause a high percentage of the kernel to become detached from the shell. The process of loosening the kernels is continued in the nut silos and must be completed before the nuts are cracked if " split nuts" are to be avoided.

- Vertical type sterilizer used in small plant are with a limited volume while for large scale plants sterilizer employed are big and of horizontal type and in continuous sterilization process.

3. Stripping

After sterilization of the complete FFB, the fruits are separated from the bunch stalks in the stripping station no palm oil is contained in the colyx leave and the stalks of the FFB, but during sterilizing and stripping some oil is absorbed by them. As for as calyx leave ae concerned the absorbed quantity is unimportant since they will be pressed along with the fruits.

They could be screened oil before, however, their presence have been found helpful to improve the press fibre de-oiling. The bunch stalks. On the other hand, cannot be pressed and it is important, therefore, to keep amount of oil transferred to them to a minimum and to care that no significant quantity of residual fruit remain attached.

4. Digesting

After the bunches have been stripped the sterilized fruit are reheated together with the accompanying calyx leave and these are pericarp is loosened from the nut and prepared for pressing. This is achieved in steam heated vessel (digester) provided with a rotating shaft to which stirring arm's are attached.

5. Pressing/Oil Extraction

Pressing is the most usual method of extracting erude palm oil from

PROCESS FLOW SHEET FOR PALM OIL

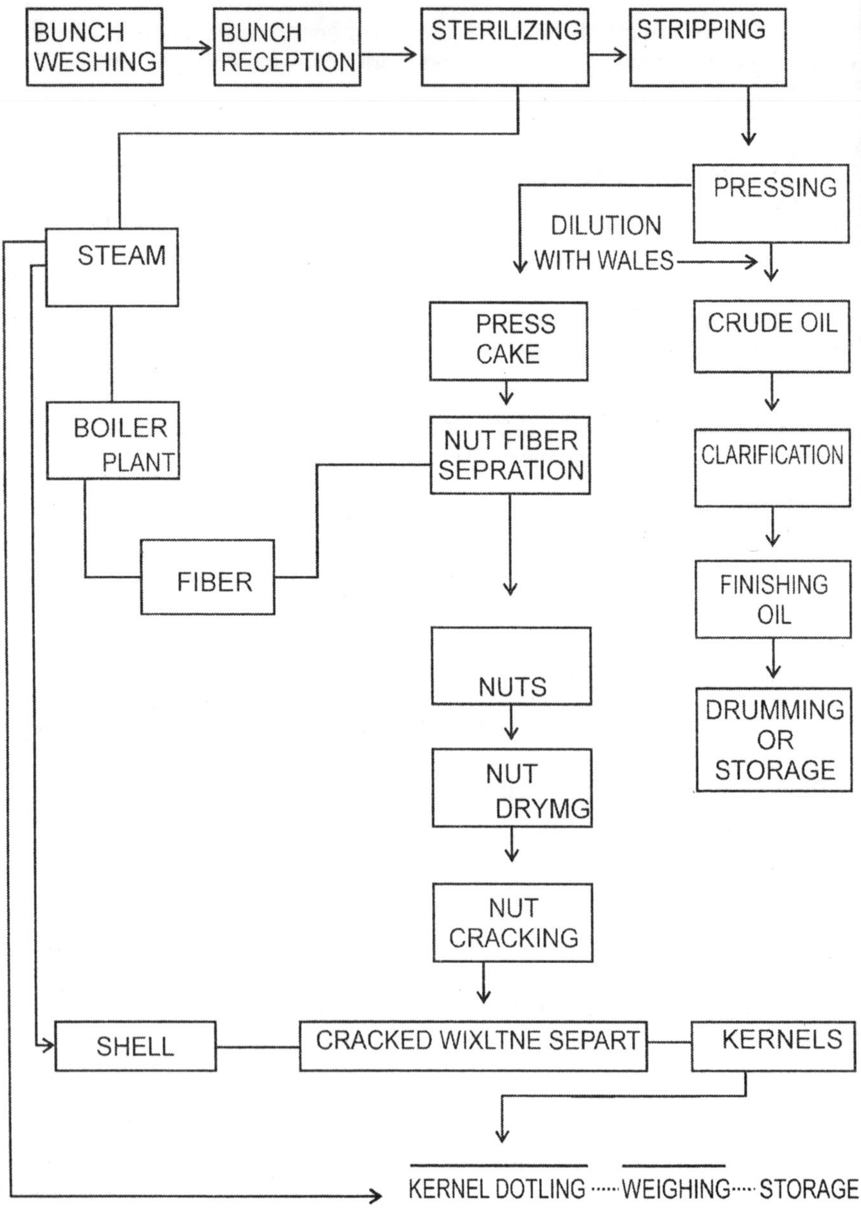

digested palm fruit other methods are centrifuging and the wet processing. Modern types of Presses with highest efficient are continuously operating double screw presses, in which two parallel screw are running siole by side in a common perforated press cage.

The position of a double cone is controlled by drautically in order to achieve constant cone pressure applied to the fruit. Such presses can be rated for different through puts at different screw speeds depending upon the various type of fruits. During the pressing operation, the press cylinder will be flushed with hot water the rate of which is determined by the vate of crude oil usually the water to oil ratio in 1:1

6. Clarification and Storage

The crude oil obtained by pressing centrifuging or by the wet process contain varying amount of water together with empurities consists of vegetable matter which is partly dissolved in the water and partly form's insoluble solids. Oil is now pumped through direct steam heater to a settling tank water contents are reduced to 0.2% and then oil moves to pure oil storage tank simultaneously the kirnel recovery is carried out by various steps such as

Nut Drying   Nut cracking   Kernel separation drying

* The suggested capacity of the plant for producing palm oil is crushing 24 tonne of FFB per (8 hour) shift which is ideal for extracting palm oil.

The yield of pure palm oil in 21% and kernel 4%.

PLANT ECONOMICS

Rated Plant Capacity = 24.00 Ton (F.F.B.)/Day

LAND & BUILDING

1. Land 5000 sq.mt. Rs. 10,00,000.00

PLANT & MACHINERY

1. Fruit bunch Elevator
2. Sterilizing Plant
3. Stripping plant including stalk in cinerator
4. Extracting Station including digester & screw press
5. Clarification plant including settling tank and reheater
6. Oil storage tanks with drum and lorry filling equipment
7. Weight Bridge
8. Kernel plant with equipment for nut/fibre separation

9. Steam Boiler
10. Oil filling machine

FIXED CAPITAL

1.	Land and Building	Rs.	37,70,000.00
2.	Plant and Machinery	Rs.	1,00,00,000.00
3.	Other Fixed Assets	Rs.	25,00,000.00
	TOTAL	Rs.	1,62,70,000.00

RAW MATERIALS

1. Fresh fruit bunches of Palm tree
2. Packing material mild steal drum

TOTAL CAPITAL INVESTMENT

Total Fixed Capital	Rs.	1,62,70,000.00
Total Working Capital for 3 Months	Rs.	1,09,98,375.00
TOTAL	Rs.	2,72,68,375.00

TURN OVER/ANNUM

1.	Sale of Palm Oil (Pure) 1512 Ton	Rs.	4,83,84,000.00
2.	Sale of palm kernel 288 ton	Rs.	1,29,60,000.00

PROFIT SALES RATIO = Profit / Sales x 100 = 15.82%
RATE OF RETURN = Operating profit / T.C.I x 100 = 35.58%
BREAK EVEN POINT (B.E.P) = 55.24%

27

Essential oils by Steam distillation

Introduction

In the process of distillation, the temperature of the bottom layer of the charge rises first as the steam condenses on the herbaceous mass and in this process its latent heat is utilized in raising the temperature of the mass and subsequently, in vapourising the oil droplets. The temperature of the successive layers of the mass inside the still, gradually starts rising till the temperature in the still equalizes. Any further addition of heat to such a heated mass, will assist in vapourizing the oil droplets which are located on the surface of the herbs or somewhere in the ducts located well below the outer surface.

Before the temperature of the top layer reaches the stage of evaporation, addition of further heat to the bottom layers, causes the oil to evaporate which, in turn, condenses on to the successive layers where the temperature attained is not sufficient as needed to sustain the evaporation. This accumulation of oil goes on till the top layer or any other layer near the top gets saturated with oil. This will depend upon the absorption capacity of the herb which will be discussed later on. Any further addition of heat to such a saturated layer, will cause the release of oil. Oil vapours with steam will pass through the still on to the condenser where these are condensed and then oil is separated by virtue of its being insoluble in water and the difference in specific gravity assists in separation of these two liquids.

Thus, two points, although quite elementary, should be clear at this stage.

1. Steam imparts its latent heat to the mass by way of condensation on the surface of herb which, ultimately, causes the evaporation of oil.

2. Steam and oil vapours rise to the top of still & then to condenser together or in other words the necessary current to lift the vapours of oil from the surface of herb is provided by steam.

Principle of Distillation

All volatile compounds emit vapour molecules from their surfaces. These vapours exert a pressure on their surrounding space which increases with the rise of temperature. When the pressure exerted by the vapour, known its vapour pressure, becomes equal to the surrounding pressure and additional heat is applied to the liquid, the temperature will rise no further. The addition of heat will be absorbed by the liquid as latent heat and it will start vaporizing at a certain rate. The temperature at which this phenomenon takes place is known as boiling point of the liquid under the prevailing pressure.

The same criteria applies to the state where two mutually insoluble compounds, like oil and water, are present. Both will exert the pressure equivalent to the concentration of its own molecules, as though the other was not there. The total pressure exerted by the mixed vapours then becomes the sum of the partial pressures exerted by each one. It follows that a liquid mixture will boil when its temperature is raised to the point where the combined vapour pressure becomes equal to the surrounding pressure.

Thus, the vapour pressure determines not only the temperature at which the mixture will boil but also the composition of the saturated vapour rising from the boiling surface at the point of contact between the two immisible liquids. In the case of a mixture of essential oil and water, the oil's vapour pressure will always be much less than water's.

Let us consider an example of a mixture of Mint oil and water at 99.3° C. In saturated mixed vapours of Mint oil and water, at atmospheric pressure, the vapour pressure exerted by Mint oil would be 19 mm & vapour pressure exerted by water vapours would be 741 mm i.e. their ratio is 1:39. On multiplying with their molecular weights, the ratio of vapours by mass would be around 1:4.5.It indicates that, theoretically, every 4.5 kgs of steam can vaporise 1 kg of mint oil. Further, it follows that under normal atmospheric pressure Mint oil can be boiled away in the presence of water at. 99.3° C in spite of the fact that the boiling range of mint oil is 195- 235° C. Generally essential oils donot boil at a constant temperature & there is always a specified boiling range. But the effect of this factor has been ignored while citing above example.

The basic principle of steam distillation, therefore consists in bringing the two mutually insoluble liquids into contact at a temperature very close to the boiling point of the more volatile liquid of the two i.e. water. At this stage small addition of vapour pressure by the vapours of oil, will make the combined pressure equal to the surrounding pressure. The mixture will then boil and the oil will vaporise into the passing steam as fast as its requirement of latent heat can be fulfilled.

Thus, the rate of delivery of latent heat to the boiling mixture will be one of the prime factors governing the speed and efficiency of distillation.

The rate of delivery of latent heat to the boiling mixture will depend upon the factors

1. **Temperature Gradient** i.e. difference of temperature between general vapour space and the point of evaporation of oil on the herb surface.

2. **Heat Transfer Area** where steam particles can condense in order to surrender their latent heat to vapourise the oil.

Efficiency of Distillation

How an efficient distillation system can be defined Broadly, any system capable of extracting and recovering maximum quantity of oil in a shortest possible time utilizing minimum steam, will be considered as efficient distillation system.

Extraction of oil is one parts of the system and recovery is another. Recovery of oil can be 100% in case there is no escape/conversion of the extracted oil by way of reflux or hydrophyllic effect or poor condensation/ separation or otherwise. Further, it should be understood that one particular system may be termed as efficient for one type of herbs but may prove inefficient for another type of herbs. Even the system can behave differently under the varying conditions for any particular herb.

Factors affecting efficiency

The factors which affect efficiency of a distillation system can be summarized as under.

1. Nature of herb surface
2. Quality/quantity of steam
3. Density of charge
4. Size of still
5. Pressure of still

Practical Distillation of Herbs

For the purpose of establishing the most efficient system of distillation for various herbaceous oils, it would be worthwhile to divide these into two categories.

1. Surface born oils
2. Centre born oils

1. Surface Born Oils

Surface born oils are those which are entirely born on the outer surface of the herb. These oils are secreted in glandular hair reservoirs which are even visible with an ordinary microscope. mints, lavender, basils etc. are typical of this class. Broadly herbs of families, like Labiatae Verbenaceae, Geraniaceae, Myrterceae and Rutaceae belong to this category.

Some of the herbs under this class, are absorptive by nature while others can be made absorptive by air drying/wilting in shade. Distillation of these herbs is rather simple operation. Unless the herbs are of highly absorptive type, such as, lavender, it is always advisable to dry the herb under sun for few hours & then under shade for 10-12 hrs till at least 50% of the moisture is evaporated. The practice adopted by farmers of Uttar Pradesh can be followed whereas they leave the herb in open field after harvesting for the rest of the day and then collect the same next day morning before the sun rises. Thus leaves get semi-dried and shading of leaves is also avoided.

Too much drying of herb in field or under the sun or at distillation site is also not recommended as it results in losses of oil by evaporation into air which may go up to 20 to 30% . Subsequently, distillation also becomes tough as it becomes impossible to pack the material inside the still uniformly & at the desired density. As a result, possibility of channeling of steam increases, losses due to hydrophillic bonding increases & the time in extracting the oil is prolonged.

Further it should be remembered that the formation of oil in herbs belonging to this category is most affected by extrinsic factors, such as, air temperature, relative humidity, cloudiness and rainfall etc. Moreover, the plant tissue are alive and continue their biological activities to some extent even after a few hours of harvesting the plant. Some metabolic transformations of glycosides take place during the stage of drying when the plant is under dying stress and hence any loss by evaporation of oil is more than compensated by the gain in oil formation by metabolic transformations.

Both types of stills i.e. direct fired (fitted with calendria on the bottom) and also fed by a separate boiler, are suitable for distilling herbs of this category. For efficient distillation, the following parameters should be maintained.

1.	Height of still	>	1.3 meters
2.	Density of packing		300 to 350 kgs/m3
3.	Condition of herb		Semi-dried
4.	Flow rate of steam	>	120 kgs/hr./m2

Steam should not be used for packing of charge and also the distillation of fresh herb should be avoided. (except for lavenders) because of the following reasons.

1. Yield of oil would be low.
2. Steam consumption would be high
3. Time taken for exhaustion would be long.

Further, it would be nearly impossible to distill a fresh herb or rainsoaked herb in a direct fired still which produces wet steam. Distillation of fresh herbs require dry stearn or even superheated steam in the beginning to evaporate the extra moisture available on the surface of the herb.

Packing a fresh herb inside the still may also cause tight spots and give rise to channeling.

Moisture balance of Still

An operator has to decide on various parameters while planning to distill a herb. Many of the parameters are fixed and once the condition of charge is decided, he has to decide on the quality & quantity of steam. His decision should be governed by the factor called the "moisture balance of the still".

As the moisture is present in both herb as well as steam used for distillation, a balance has to be maintained in order to obtain the best results.

In case the quantity of moisture in herb is more i.e. herb is wet, the quantity of moisture or cloud particles in steam should be quite low i.e. steam should be dry or superheated. Similarly in case the moisture in herb is low i.e. its condition is dry, then the moisture in steam should be high i.e. wet steam should be used.

This adjustment of moisture content in the still is termed as moisture balance of the still and operator has to be conscious of this at stages. For highly absorptive type of herbs this balance can be maintained on plus side for better results.

2. Centre Born Oils

So far we studied the distillation of surface born oils which was easier than herbs having centre born oils. Centre born oils are those which are found in schizogenous ducts occurring in the leaves calyces and stems (e.g. Lauraceae and Compositae) & also oils found in secondary ducts called vittae which are schizogenously formed on the fruits & roots (e.g. Umbelliferae & Zingiberaceae). Thus oils found in many seeds, roots and wood species are classified under these headings. The formation of oil in these materials is least affected by changes in meteorological conditions. Thus it is possible to store them for a certain period depending upon the nature of individual herb.

Centre born oils are secreted deep below the outer surface of the herb and are not exposed on the surface. So, their distillation becomes a two step process.

1. To bring out the oil from centre to the outer surface.
2. To evaporate the oil from the outer surface (as in the case of surface born oils)

Before undertaking the distillation of any centre born oil, the strategy should be defined as to how the oil has to be forced out of its centre i.e. place of location. An usual process which assist this process of movement is comminution of the herb material. This may best be done by crushing in between rollers so that the material is reduced to flattened surfaces similar to a coin placed under the wheel of a passing train woods can be reduced to chips and some of the seeds / roots can also be pulverised to a coarse size. In many cases the purpose is to break the outer casing only. Hard leaves can also be chopped suitably which will assist in packing charge more uniformly.

Water Distillation

Water distillation is the most ancient system of distillation of herbs. In modern times this practice is only occasionally adopted. However there are several plant materials which are unsuited to steam distillation and can only be distilled while immersed in water.

Steam has a tendency to coagulate the petals of flowers, like, rose and neroli etc. andm as such, vapours cannot pass through coagulated mass.

Similarly materials which have been finely powdered will also coagulate and form lumps thus giving rise to channeling. Water distillation is the only choice for such materials.

Let us consider various factors which affect the vaporisation of oil from the surface of herb when water distillation is adopted.

1. Effect of oils affinity for water

Some of the components of the oil have affinity for water. Such compounds, generally oxygenated are water soluble, such as, phenols and phenyl ethyl alcohol in Rosa damascena. Such compounds get dissolved in water & their recovery becomes quite slow as the mixture boils like an azeotropic mixture whereby the proportion of oil is vapours is quite small.

At the end of distillation, these dissolved compounds can be recovered by fractional distillation or in some cases by adding salt and separating on settlement.

In such cases, it is always advisable to reuse the mother liquor left in the still for subsequent distillations.

2. Effect of Hydrolysis

Another phenomenon accompanying water distillation of plant materials is hydrolysis. Hydrolysis can be defined as a chemical reaction between water and certain constituents of essential oil. In the presence of water particularly at elevated temperatures esters tend to react with water to form parent acids and alcohols. In case the amount of water is large, the amounts of alcohol and acid will also be large and hydrolysis will proceed to a greater extent. As a result, yield as well as the quality of essential oil will go down.

In case of steam distillation, the degree of hydrolysis is much less.

Another important characteristic of hydrolysis reaction is that these are not rapid and hence their degree of reaction depends upon time of contact between oil and water which is much more in the case of water distillations.

3. Effect of temperature/Pressure Differential

Another factor which has got considerable bearing on the recovery of essential oil in water distillation is the difference of pressure & temperature on the bottom of the still and the top of herb/water surface. Temperature/pressure on the bottom of still are higher than on the top.

Under such conditions, when the bubble of steam rises from the bottom layer of herb it has a capacity to carry higher proportion of oils vapour which gradually decreases as it approaches the top. Generally, it does not affect the extraction of oil unless the bubble is exceptionally rich in oils vapour or the charge has a greater depth.

However, in case the bubble is saturated, the decline in pressure & temperature with the rise of bubble is quite sufficient to condense some portion of the oil which was vaporised at a lower level in the still. When the oil is less dense than water, the condensed oil will float on the top surface and will tend to form a film.

Recovery of such lighter oil is always very slow and is a major cause of poor economy in water distillation. The reason for this is simple to understand. The top surface of water in a still is never at boiling temperature & supply of heat to this surface is quite slow. Thus, rate of vaporisation is also slow.

As the major part of essential oil recovered by water distillation is vaporised in the form of saturated bubbles of mixed vapours, the proportion of the oil that will condense internally is directly proportional to the depth of the charge. It follows that, when oil is less dense than water, the depth of the charge should be as minimum as possible.

4. The effect of Turbulence

Immediately after its being vaporised, oil must the liberated from the herb surface. In steam distillation, this is being done by the current provided by steam. This suggests that some kind of turbulence may have some effect on the recovery of oil.

In this connection, the test carried out by Mr. Phillip Capell of Wynyard, Tasmania (Australia) is worth mentioning. Mr. Capell was carrying out trial distillations (water) of fresh Huon fine saw dust. As the supply of steam was very limited, he was getting poor yield. At this stage he installed an agitator in the still & in spite of keeping the same supply of steam, the yield improved. The prime significance of these observations were that, even after the initial use of the propeller had ensured that the whole charge was in motion an additional increase in agitation greatly improved both yield & speed of recovery. Thus, the liberation of vapourised oil from the surface of the herb is basically a mechanical operation which can be performed much more conveniently with a small amount of mechanical energy than by burning more fuel to generate steam.

As the performance of water distillations are improved by enhancing the turbulence required to scrub vapour bubbles from surface of herb, it also tends to cause splashes which can carry fine particles through to the condenser. As such, as a rule, the equipment should be designed to have sufficient head by inserting a 4 to 5 ft. long pipe in between the still and the condenser to enable the splashed particles to loose momentum and return back to the still.

5. The effect of Cohobation

The technique of returning distillate water to mother liquor at the point of steam generation is known as cohobation.

It has a two fold purpose.

1. To maintain the fluid level in steam generator.
2. To minimise the loss of compounds of oil dissolved in distillate water.

However, it should be understood that the loss of only those compounds can be minimised which are soluble in water to a certain extent by adopting cohobation. For example, recovery of phenyl ethyl alcohol & some phenols can be improved while distillating roses.

On the other hand, there are oils which create problem in separation and sometimes even form emulsion with water as being very close in specific gravity. In such cases, the recovery of oil can be increased by adopting a better design of oil separator or by settling the distillate at a certain temperature for 20/24 hours rather than going for coholation which will prolong the distillation without much gain.

Design of Equipment

The primary objective of design of distillation system is to determine the size & shape of equipment that will perform satisfactorily under varied circumstances of herbs to be distilled.

The selection of distillation equipment will depend upon the size of the operation and the type of distillation to be carried cut i.e. steam distillation, boiler fed or direct fired or water distillation.

Basically there are two types of distillation set ups prevalent in India.

1. Direct fired stills fitted with calendria.
2. Stills fed with steam from a separate boiler.

Recently, as the size of the distilleries is becoming smaller as run by growers & design of calendria has also improved, the tendency is towards setting up direct fired stills.

However, when volume of work is large, it is always advisable to utilise a boiler for raising steam. At the same time, boiler is more useful while distilling herbs containing high boiling oils.

Generally big distilleries depend upon boilers and also possess 2 to 3 direct fired stills fitted with calendria. These stills are made use of during lean period or when the load is in excess.

Before, the design of equipment is discussed a short note on the system of loading & unloading of stills and moving the spent herb to the desired place would be worth mentioning.

Stills are installed in a battery 4 to 5 together, leaving a clear space of about 20' on each side for movement of cart/trolley etc. It is advisable to install the stills well above the ground with a slope extending up to 3/4th height of the still to facilitate loading of herb. The following advantages are visualised in such a system.

1. Condenser can be kept vertical without raising the height of connecting pipe from still to condenser.
2. Reflex water can be discarged from the bottom at ground level.

Loading of stills is done manually and its a time consuming job. Arrangements for quick unloading of stills is very much required. The most suitable arrangements for unloading of stills & moving the load of spent herbs to an allotted place, either for compo sting or burning as fuel after drying, is to have the overhead gantry with trolley and chain pulley block of right capacity.

In case the number of stills are four or more than four, it is advisable to have an electric chain pulley block to facilitate easy & quick lifting of spent herbs.

It is not necessary to pack the charge on single grid or set of strings. The charge can be divided into two or three compartments while packing into the stills by placing intermediate grids or strings in between. This will facilitate lifting of spent material in two or three parts causing less load / stress on the overhead system.

The overhead gantry beam is always kept extended by 5 to 6 ft. on one side where these loads of spent material can be off loaded on a cart.

Generally a 3 ton capacity chain pulley block is sufficient to use and, in case, stills are of one ton capacity, these can be unloaded in one stroke otherwise, for bigger stills, loading and unloading is done in two steps by dividing the charge in two compartments.

Besides a suitable arrangement for emptying stills and carrying the spent herbs to an allotted place, there are four main parts which form the base for all types of distillations.

1. Still
2. Condenser
3. Receiver
4. Steam Generator

a. Boilers or
b. Calendria

Let us discuss these four parts of the distillation equipments in order.

1. Still

In the simplest form, the still consists of a cylindrical container or tank with diameter equal to or less than its height. The still is equipped with an arrangement to lift the cover quickly and conveniently as this is required to be performed after every two hours or so. In some of the cases, such as, stills needed for distillation of seeds/roots, only manhole is provided & cover is not made removable. The height of the still should not be less than 1.5 meters in any case.

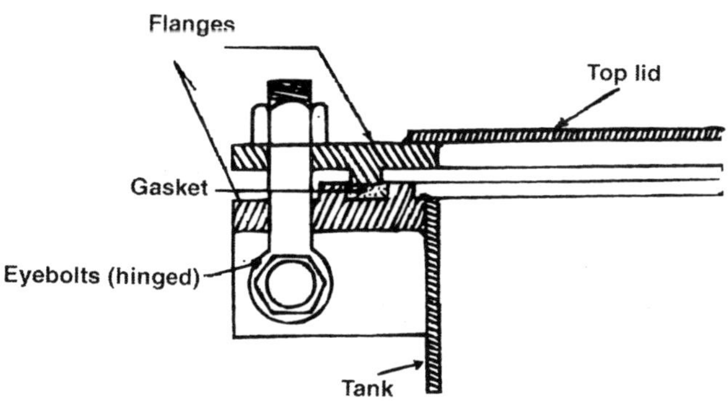

Fig. 27.1 Clamping arrangement of a still

Fig. 27.1 Show one of the designs of clampin cover with tank with use of eve bolts and keeping a gasket in between.

In many installations particularly stills fitted with calendria for generation of steam, provision of water seal is made which dispenses with clamping arrangement of the cover.

The cylindrical section of the still can be made slightly tapered to facilitate removal of spent plant material.

A false grid or steel frame is placed about 8 to 10 inch above the bottom of tank to support the charge. Below this false grid, either a perforated coil of steam pipes duly connected with steam line is placed or the cylindrical tank itself is bolted with a calendria having baffles in between for control of splashing of water.

It is advisable to insulate the stills up to the top to conserve heat and minimise condensation of vapours inside the still.

2. Condenser

Condenser is the second major part of distillation equipment. The purpose of condenser is to convert all the steam and accompanying oil vapours into liquid and bring down the temperature of condensed vapours to a desired level.

The most commonly used condensers are these in which a bundle of pipes, either straight or zigzag, are placed inside a vessel supplied with running cold water, entering from below & exiting from top. Vapour flows inside the pipes in a counter current mode.

Various configuration of pipes are possible and, in fact, are in use. However condensers with straight vertical tubes have more advantages in comparison to others.

From the point of view of efficient heat transfer, it has been found that a more rapid a turbulent flow of cooling water results in more efficient cooling. Similarly turbulent flow of vapours inside the tube will also add to this factor. Both these effects can be created in straight tube vertical condensers. These condensers not only offer saving in space but they are more convenient to clean also.

To create turbulence inside the tubes swirl strips are inserted which help in breaking up the tendency to laminar flow. Similarly baffles are placed outside the tubes in such a fashion so as to create turbulence in the flow of cooling water.

A condenser should always be designed for an overload so that the temperature of the distillate can be controlled more precisely. A condenser is said to be operating on maximum efficiency when the condensate has been cooled d ow n to a desired temperature and the temperature of cooling water at exit is approaching that of the incoming vapours. Usually a temperature of 80° C is attained.

To calculate the surface area required for transfer of heat in a condenser, a simple guide to follow is.

A=1/k x flow rate of steam (kg/hr./sq.m) *X* top area of still (sq.m) A=Area in sq.m.

Generally, the value of 'K' varies from 50 to 70 depending upon the design of condenser, temperature & quantity of cooling water available for circulation.

Assumptions are made that cooling water is available to the extent of 15 times of distillate flow & temperature of cooling water is about 30° C. The distillate is required to be cooled to a temperature of 40-45° C.

3. Receiver

The third essential part of distillation equipment consists of a receiver, decanter or oil separator. Its function is to achieve a quick and complete separation of the oil from the condensate water.

In condensate, quantity of water is always much larger. The lighter one floats on the top because of non solubility as well as the difference in specific gavities. Design of the receiver should permit the removal of water whether oil is heavier or lighter than water.

Oil and water often does not separate immediately in the 'oil separator' especially if the differential between the specific gravities of oil and water is small. The distillate must not, therefore, flow too rapidly and any turbulence in the liquid should be avoided. In other words, separator should be large enough to permit water and oil to separate as completely as possible.

The principle which causes separation of oil and water is the difference in their densities. are interesting. He has shown that the oils specific gravity decrease more rapidly than does that of water over any chosen rise in temperature.

Table below shows the speeds of rise or fall through water of small oil particles at different temperatures.

Table : Speed of rise or fall through water of small oil particles.

Oil	Speed of Particles in mm/min at temp in °C			
	30°	40°	50°	60°
Lavender	4.5	7.0	12.0	17.0
Peppermint	-	5.2	7.5	11.0
Sandalwood	fails	fails	6.0	7.4

For example, take the case of Peppermint oil. Small particles of oil rise at a speed of 5.2 mm/min at 40° C while the same rise at 7.5 mm/min at 50° C. This clearly demonstrates the effectiveness of separation of oil from water when temperature of the distillate is more.

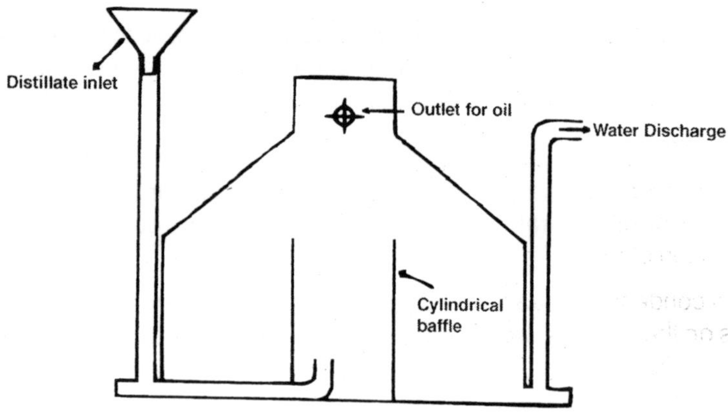

Fig. 27.2 Receiver for oils lighter than water.

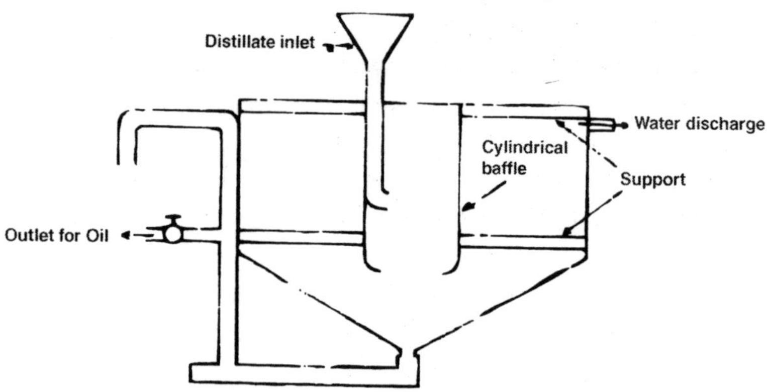

Fig. 27.3 Reciever for oils heavier than water

Even when the oils density is quite close to that of water, a large proportion is separated & floats at the top (when oil is lighter than water) very quickly. This should not be taken for granted that separation is complete as there is always a possibility of oil going in distillate water. Most of these losses of oil can be avoided in case necessary steps are taken to ascertain the speed at which smaller particles of oil rise through water at a given temperature. In the case of peppermint oil we have observed that oil particles rise at a speed of 7.5 mm/min at 50° C the dimensions of receiver can be chosen so that distillate water passes through it downwards at a speed below 7.5 mm/min.

On the other hand, in case the specific gravity of an oil at room temperature is slightly higher than that of water (oil is heavier than water), the distillate should run as cold as possible.

Figures 27.2 & 27.3 are drawn to suggest some outlines for the basic design of oil separator. Separate designs are suggested depending upon oil is lighter than water or oil is heavier than water. However, for oils which comprise of two parts, one less dense and the other more dense than water, it is suggested to utilise two oil-separators in series.

Guenther has suggested to use multiple receivers in series when single is not large enough.

Further, it should be remembered that condensate water always carry some dissolved portion of oil. In some cases, this may go up to 20% of the recoverable oil and, hence, should be considered as a potent source for the recovery of oil.

Recently efforts are being made to separate the dissolved portion of oil by storing the condensed water & treating it by any solvent or by any other physical means.

Steam generator can be either boiler or in case of direct fired stills "Calendria". The size of boiler will depend upon steam required. A general guide can be used which is based on the following formula.

4. Steam Generator

$A = \alpha\, n \times s$

A = Sq. meter rating of boiler

n = no. of stills

s = top area of each still in sq.m

= factor depending upon the flow of steam desired material of construction & efficiency of boiler. Generally, it varies from 3 to 4.

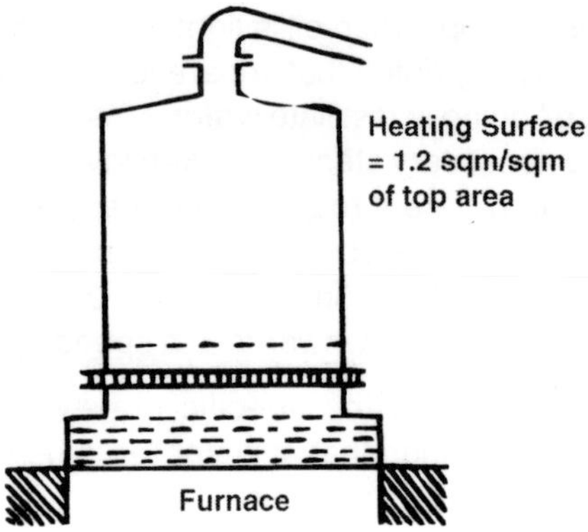

Fig. 27.4 A Flat Bottom

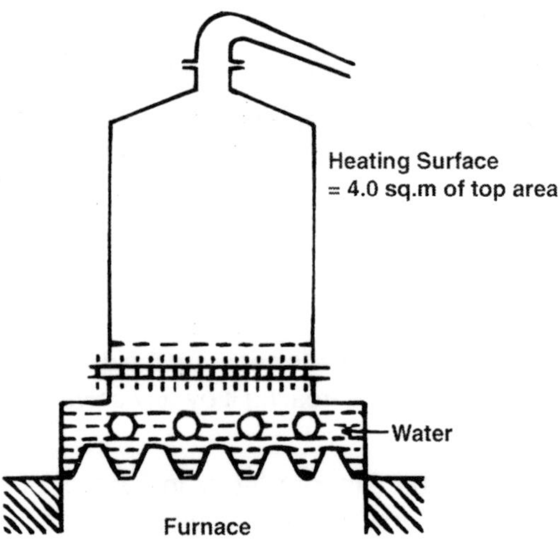

Fig. 27.5 B. Existing Design of Calendria having two pass system

The capacity of the boiler should be calculated based on the assumption that all the stills will be in operation at a time. In actual practice it is not possible as one or two stills are always being unloaded and refilled.

The boiler should be capable of generating steam at 7 kgs/cm2 (100 psi). Although, it may not be required to produce steam at this pressure but while selecting a equipment it should be done for any eventuality. Generally a pressure of 2 to 3 kgs/cm2 is maintained.

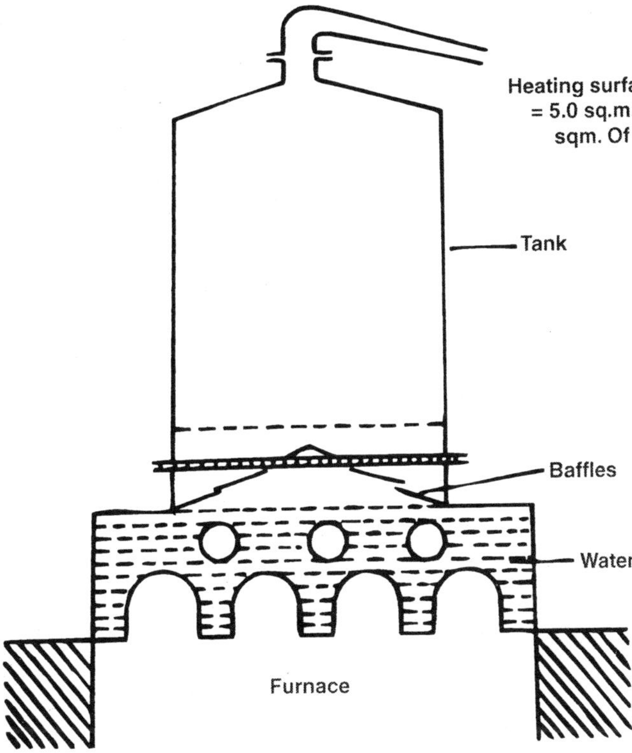

Fig. 27.6 C. Improved Design of calendria with two pass system + baffles (designed by author)

Whereever it is not feasible to use boiler, as the size of operation is small, steam generation is done below the stills by direct firing & the equipment which performs this function is known as "Calendria".

It is quite important to have a proper size and design of calendria to obtain as good results as with a steam boiler or in some cases better.

Taking into consideration the basic principles of steam generator, the design of calendria is based on the following factors.

1. Heating surface area and
2. Temperature gradient (between flue gases and water)

As far as, temperature gradient is concerned, in a direct fired, two pass system, the maximum possible gradient is attained which is also dependent on rate of firing. From the design point of view, heating surface area is all important for obtaining the desired rate of evaporation inside the still. Other factors which affect the performance are design of furnace & height of chimney. Design of calendria is also important as it also governs the movement of flue gases which is the transferring media of heat.

Figures 4 to 6 show various ways of designing a 'calendria' or bottom part of direct fired still. A flat surface can generate only 36 to 48 kgs of steam per hour per sq.m of still area. So, it would be impossible to distill any herb efficiently. Calendria with an improved dt'sign contains about 5 sq.m heating surface area and thus can very well generate 150 to 200 kgs. of steam per hour per sq.m of still area which is generally desired flow rate of steam for most of the herbs.

Storage

This improved still was designed by the author in the beginning of 1992 specifically for distillation of semi-absorptive type of herbs and seeds.

Various aspects of steam distillation of herbs have been discussed. Right from theoretical angle, many of the problems faced in distillation have also been discussed. A distillers choice of equipment mainly depends upon various types of herbs he intends to distill and also the size of his operation. Most efficient use of energy and the maximum recovery of oil in the shortest period should be the aim of the operator. Remember, every drop of oil is costly and at the same time, fuel is also scarce.

At the end, the last but not ofleast importance, is the proper storage of oil after distillation. It should be stored in dry, clean drums, epoxy coated or galvanized steel depending upon the oil. Filtration of oil should be perfect and there should not be traces of dissolved water which is highly injurious to the quality of oil. To remove the droplets of water, oil can be treated with anhydrous sodium sulphate & then filtered. The drums should not be packed half full & there should not be any air left inside the drums which may react with the oil to form resinous substances. Further oil should always be stored in a cool place and away from heat and light.

28

Composition of Essential Oil from Flowers of Keora

ABSTRACT

Capillary gas chramatography of essential oil from "Keora" inflorescence (Pandanus odoratissimus Linn.) showed presence of five major components methyl ether of phenyl alcohol (~70%0, terpinen-4-ol (~17%), terpineol (~1.8%), y-terpinene (~1.5%) and cineole 1:8 (~0.8%). Out of 55 peaks, 43 have been identified and 28 are reported for the first time. Two major components-phenyl ethyl alcohol and phenyl ethyl acetate earlier (16.2% & 2.76% respectively) have been now found to be present only in traces.

INTRODUCTION

The male infloresence of "Keora" (Pandanus odoratissimus Linn. family-Pandanaceae) are valued for the fragment smell emitted by the tender white spathes covering the flowers. " Keora" plants are found growing along sea shore, banks of rivers, ponds, canals etc. Essential oil ('Ruh' or 'Otto') and 'Attar' (essential oil collected over sandalwood oil) are prepared on commercial scale in Ganjam district of Orissa. "Keora Ruh and Attar are very old products used in India since ancient times for flavouring and perfumery purpose.

There are only a few reports about chemical composition of essential oil ("Ruh Keora"). in fiftees, Dhingra and coworkers 2,3 distilled flowers (0.015% to 0.035 yield) collected from Ganjam and Ghazipur regions and identified compounds methyl as given in table-28.1. Sadgopal 4 reported major compounds as follows : dipentene, linalool, phenyl ethyl alcohol, citral and some phthallic acid esters. Nigam and Ahmad reported chemical composition of "Keora" oil by gas chromatography on packed column (Cabowax 20M) using Thermal Conductivity Dectator as shown in Table -28.2.

In the present study two typical genuine samples of essential oil of "Keora" have been analysed on Perkin-Elmer Auto System Capillary gas Chromatograph using polar and non polar capillary columsns (L:50m, I.D. 0.25 mm, film thickness 0.25u), Flame ionization Dectator and Digital Computer DEC Station 320 SX, Oil composition has been identified by comparing with CGCs of authentic compounds.

Major compounds reported by Nigam and Ahmad are phenyl ethyl methyl either (74.67%), phenyl ethyl alcohol (16.23%) and phenyl ethyl acetate (2.76%) CGC of number of essential oil samples of "Keora", during the present study has shown the range of phenyl ethyl methyl ether from 65% to 80%. Other two major compounds phenyl ethyl alcohol and phenyl ethyl actate reported earlier are hardly present in the oil. Other next major compounds reported now are terpinen-4-ol-(~17%) terpineol (~1.8%), y-terpinene (~1-5%) "Ruh Keora".are marked with asterick (28 compounds) in table-28.3. Presence of compene, terpinene, carvone, perillyl alcohol,l citronellyl acetate nerolidol and farnesol have not been observed in the present study as reported earlier. This is first report on CGC of essential oil from "Keora" infloresence.

Table 28.1: Composition of Essential oil of Keora flowers

S.Nos.	Compound	%
1.	Methyl ether of ß-phenyl ethyl alcohol	65.97
2.	Dipentenr	8.31
3.	d-Linalool	18.70
4.	Phenyl ethyl acetate	3.48
5.	Citral	1.82
6.	Acids as caroic acid	0.49
7.	Steroptene	0.20

Table 28.2 -Chemical Composition of Keora Oil.

S. Nos.	Constituents	%
1.	α-Pinene	0.091
2.	Camphene	0.005
3.	ß-Pinene	0.063
4.	α-Phellandrene	0.302
5.	α-Terpinene	0.060
6.	Limonene	0.480
7.	γ-Terpinene	0.492
8.	p-Cymene	0.311
9.	Benzyl alcohol	0.019

10.	Benzyl acetate	0.222
11.	Geranial	0.122
12.	Neral	0.139
13.	Phenyl ethyl methyl ether	74.670
14.	Neryl acetate	0.148
15.	Gernyl acetate	0.235
16.	Phenyl ethyl alcohol	16.233
17.	Phenyl ethyl acetate	2.758
18.	Citronellol	0.398
19.	Carvone	0.197
20.	Perillyl alcohol	0.001
21.	Nerol	0.146
22.	Geraniol	0.055
23.	Citronellyl acetate	0.305
24.	Farnesol	0.554
25.	Nerolidol	0.012

Table 28.3. Composition of essential oil from "Keora" flowers

S. Nos.	Components	Sample 1(%)	Sample II
1.	Ethyl acetate*	0.03	tr.
2.	Ethanol*	0.30	0.18
3.	a-Pinene	0.80	0.59
4.	Unidentified	0.10	0.07
5.	ß-Pinene	0.06	0.05
6.	Sainene*	0.48	0.36
7.	Mycene*	0.23	0.26
8.	a-Phallandrene	0.48	0.75
9.	Limonene	0.29	0.25
10.	Cineole-1:8*	0.93	0.87
11.	ß-Phallandrene*	0.04	tr.
12.	g-Terpinene	1.41	1.87
13.	trans-ß-Ocimene*	0.03	0.04
14.	para-Cymene	1.19	0.45
15.	Terpinolene*	0.48	0.58
16.	Nonanal*	0.11	0.13
17.	Iso-menthone/pentadecane*	0.04	tr.
18.	Methyl ether of ß-phenyl ethyl alcohol	69.81	71.08
19.	Unidentified	0.07	0.06

20.	Unidentified	0.05	0.06
21.	Banzaldehyde*	0.03	tr
22.	Linalool	0.24	0.26
23.	Iso-pulegol*	0.47	0.51
24.	ß-Caryophenllene*	0.03	0.02
25.	Terpinen-4-ol*	17.57	17.72
26.	trans-ß-Terpineol	0.36	0.39
27.	Unidentified	0.06	0.06
28.	Neral	0.10	0.11
29.	Unidentified	0.09	0.09
30.	a-Terpineol*	1.79	1.79
31.	Ceranyl formate*	0.06	0.07
32.	Piperitone*	0.16	0.16
33.	Geranial	0.03	0.03
34.	Unidentified	0.27	0.30
35.	Citronellol	0.25	0.04
36.	Phenyl ethyl formate*	tr.	tr.
37.	Nerol	0.10	tr.
38.	Citronellyl butryate*	tr	0.11
39.	Phenyl ethyl acetate	tr.	tr.
40.	Octadecane*	0.02	tr.
41.	Geraniol	0.48	0.23
42.	Phenyl ethyl alcohol	0.02	tr.
43.	Nonadecane*	0.13	0.10
44.	Eicosane*	0.03	tr.
45.	Unidentified	0.06	0.06
46.	Eicosene*	0.03	tr.
47.	Heneicosene*	0.09	tr.
48.	Unidentified*	0.06	tr.
49.	eugenol*	0.07	0.04
50.	Vanillin*	0.04	tr.
51.	Tricosane*	0.07	0.09
52.	Unidentified	0.16	0.08
53.	Unidentified	0.12	0.09
54.	Unidentified	0.06	tr.
55.	Unidentified	0.04	tr.

* Compounds not reported earlier

tr. : Traces

29

Distillation of Eucalyptus hybrid oil

ABSTRACT

A portable distillation unit working on fuelwood was designed and fabricted for yield distillation of eucalyptus hydried foliage. Under optimum conditions 1-1.8% (average 1.43%) of oil was distilled with this unit, which is higher than that obtained with stationery stills of larger dimensions. More than 95% of oil could be distilled out in the first two hours of distillation of which the first hour collection (about 75%) was found to contain more of cineole than the second hour collection. This unit could be used with advantage for distilling oils from plant materials.

INTRODUCTION

Eucalyptus hybrid is a multipurpose tree yielding good pulpwood, fuelwood and charcoal. Large scale plantations were raised in different States of India mainly to meet the demand for pulpwood and fuelwood. According to latest available statistics Eucalyptus hybrid has been raised in about 5 lakh hectares are in India, of which more than one lakh hectares in Karnataka. Since there is large yield of foliage due to large extent of land under its cultivation, utilisation of foliage needs urgent attention.

With the exception of E. globulus (blue gum) of Nilgris and E. citriodora (lemon scented gum) not much attention has been paid to other species of Eucalyptus as a source of essential oil so far. Though 'cineole-rich' oil yielding trees were found to exist among Eucalyptus hybrid trees (containing more than 65% cineole) they cannot be distinguished from other morpholigically. If leaf from all the trees are mixed and distilled, the resulting oil is a mixture of several constituents in which cineole is generally less than 10% 2. This oil has not been put to any use so far. According to a modest estimate, the potential availability of oil will be about 5000 kg per 100 hectare assuming an yield of about 50 kg of oil per hectare of about 1200 trees 3,4.

Portable field distillation units working on fuel-wood available in the forests can be utilised for distilling the oil at the site of felling, avoiding costly transport of bulky foliage to distillation units stationed at one place.

The experiments carried out are given below.

Materials and Methods.

A portable field distillation units of 300 litres capacity made of mild steel was fabricated as per our design with demountable parts for easy transport in jeep trailer.

It consists of a still or kettle with a lid on the top and vapour outlet at the side of instead of the conventional gooseneck type. The still has a perforated false bottom inside and is heated from a fire box below, with the helpo of fuelwood. The firebox an outlet for smoke to escape through a chimney. The condenser is domountable vertical type made of mild steel with inlet and outlet for water circulation. It contains five parallel stainless steel tubes inside, through which the vaoupurs from the still enter and get condensed. The receiver can be any vessel of suitable size (glass or stainless steel) to collect the distillate (oil and water).

Eucalyptus hybrid leaves separted from branches and twigs are loaded into the still from the top. Depending on the moisture content of the leaf (fresh or aird-dried) the load varies from 25 to 50 kg per batch. About 50 litres of water is required per charge. the top cover and flanges of the unit were securely fastened bymeans of bols and nuts to rpevent any leakage of vapours. Initially about 10 kg of fuelwood (Eucalyptus or any other locally available wood) cut into small pieces were charged in the firebox and lighted. Actual distillation starts after about one and half hours of initial firing. After that 5-10 kg of further fuelwood was added as and when required to maintain the distillation rate. The actual distillation lasted for 2-2½ hours when more than 95% of the oil could be distilled out. However, it was observed that more than 75% of the total oil distilled out in the first hour itself if optimum heat was provided. Leaves collected from two different localities in Bangalore dist. (Jarakabande and Nellal plantations) were distilled in 9 batches, 5 from the former and 4 from the later localities, excluding the trial run.

The oil in the distillate was separted from water by means of a separting funnel and dried with the help of anhydrous sodium sulphate and decolourised using tartaric acid crystals. The resulting clear light yellow coloured oil was filtered and stored in dark coloured bottles. This oil was analysed by GLC using AIMIL-NUCON Dual column Gas chromatograph Modal 5580 with Flame Ionization Detector and Repolex 400 SS column. Argaon was the carriers gas at a flow rate of 30 ml/min. The analysis was initially isothermal for 5 min. followed by programming @ 4°C/min upto 200°. Peaks were identified and quantified in the usual manner by tringulation method.

Discussion

From the table-1 giving details of each distillation it is clear that the oil yield was foun to vary from 1.0-1.8 (average 1.43%) on air dried weight basis depending on the operating conditions, such as rat and efficiency of fuel, amount of water and leaf material charged per batch, efficiency of condensation and local weather conditions. About 450-500 ml of E. hybrid oil could be distilled per batch of about 30-40 Kg of leaf material under optimum conditions in about 4 hours using this unit. The yield obtained is quite encouraging and high when compared to staionery stills of larger dimensions. The oil yield was measured every thirly minutes from the commencement of distillation till completion. The average oil yield of five batches from Jarakabande plantation and four from Nellal plantation were plotted versus time (Fig. 3) from the figure it is evident that irrespective of the source of the foliage, more than 75% of the oil distilled out in the first hour itslf and it is not worthwhile continuing the distillation of E. hybvrid beyond two hours with this unit when more than 95% of the oil distilled out. Thus by proper planning two batches can be run everyday with one attendant using lesser quantity of fuel. Alternatively, two such units can be operated simultaneously by one person in the field. The major inputs are the cost of fuel and wages of one labourers besides the capital investment on the unit. The twigs and small branches available after removing the leaves can also serve as fuel. However, the exhausted leaves when used as fuel burn out quickly. Hence they may also only serve to maintain the distillation rate in the final half in hour. The cineole content of the oil collected in the first hour and second hour of distillation was estimated by GLC separated for the two localities (Table 2). Through the cineole content of the oil was found to vary between the two localities as expected, it is interesting to note that the first hour collection contained more of cineole than the second hour collection from the same locality.

Conclusion :

Portable distillation units working on fuelwood availabe in the forest are useful for field distillation of Eucalyptus hybrid, avoiding costly transport of bulky foliage to distillation units stationed at one place. Trials with one such fabricated unit indicated that more than 95% of oil could be distilled within the first two hours of distillation, of which 75% of oil distilled out in the first hour hours itself. I was also noted that the first hour collection of oil contained more of cineole than the second hour collection. Depending on the operating conditions 1-1.8% (average 1.43%) of oil could be distilled from Eucalyptus hyrbid leaf using this unit under optimum condition, if the actual distillation of carried out for two hours from the time the distillate started coming out of the condenser.

It is hoped to achieve further economy by insulating tne still. This being a pilot unit an optimised unit with commercial viability can be achieved with slight modifications.

Table 29.1 (a)

1.˙Field distillation of Eucalyptus hybrid laves (front Jarakabande Plantations.)

Batch	Quantity of			Duration in hrs.	Qty. of oil ml	% of oil	Remarks
	Fuel kg	Foliage kg	Water L				
1	20	50	50	4	625	1.25	i. More than 75% oil distilled out in
2	20	35	50	$4\frac{1}{2}$	520	1.50	the first hour and 95% oil distilled
3	25	35	50	$4\frac{1}{2}$	580	1.65	out in two hours after the commence-
4	25	35	50	$4\frac{1}{2}$	550	1.57	ment of distilla- tion .
5	25	41	50	$4\frac{1}{2}$	540	1.32	ii. More fuel con- sumption due to weather conditions.
Range	20-25	35-50	50	4-$4\frac{1}{2}$	520-625	1.25-1.65	
Avarage	23	39	50	$4\frac{1}{2}$	563	1.46	

Table 29.1 (b)

1. Field distillation of Eucalyptus hybrid laves (from Nellal Plantations.)

Batch	Quantity of			Duration in hrs.	Qty. of oil ml	% of oil	Remarks
	Fuel kg	Foliage kg	Water L				
1	20	38	50	$3\frac{1}{4}$	560	1.47	i. More than 75% oil distilled out in
2	20	27	40	$3\frac{1}{2}$	490	1.81	the first hour and 95% oil distilled
3	20	26	40	$3\frac{1}{4}$	340	1.31	out in two hours after the commence-
4	20	40	50	4	400	1.00	ment of distillation-
Range	20	26-40	40-45	$3\frac{1}{2}$	340-560	1.01-1.81	
Avarage	20	33	50	$3\frac{1}{4}$	448	1.39	

Table :29.2

Percentage of Clineole in the oil

	Nellai		Jarakabande	
	I hour	II hour	I hour	II hour
1	41.90	27.36	36.62	21.19
2	43.96	29.40	32.54	18.42
Average	42.93	28.36	34.58	19.81

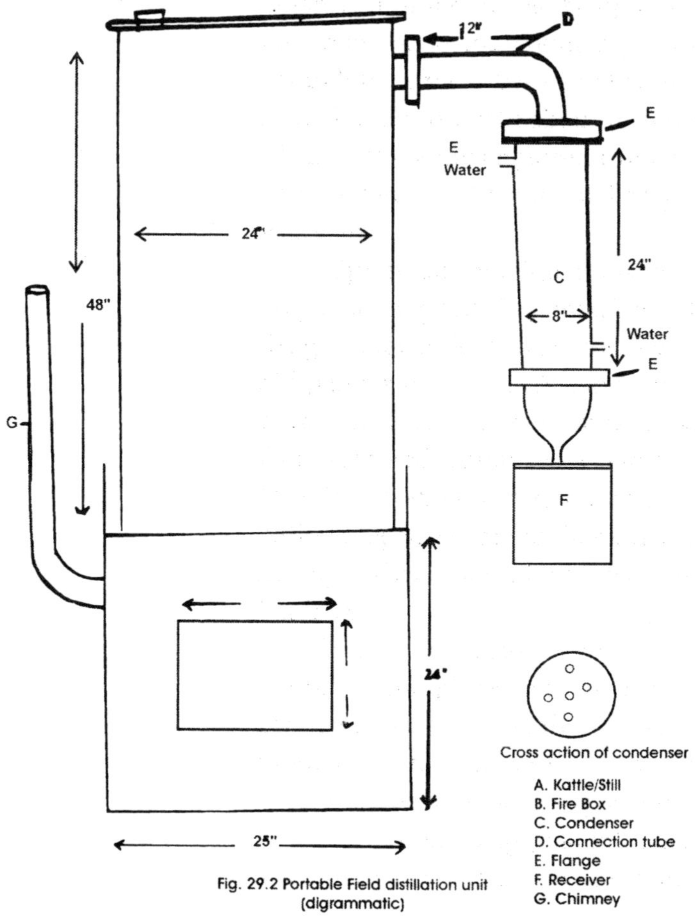

Fig. 29.2 Portable Field distillation unit (digrammatic)

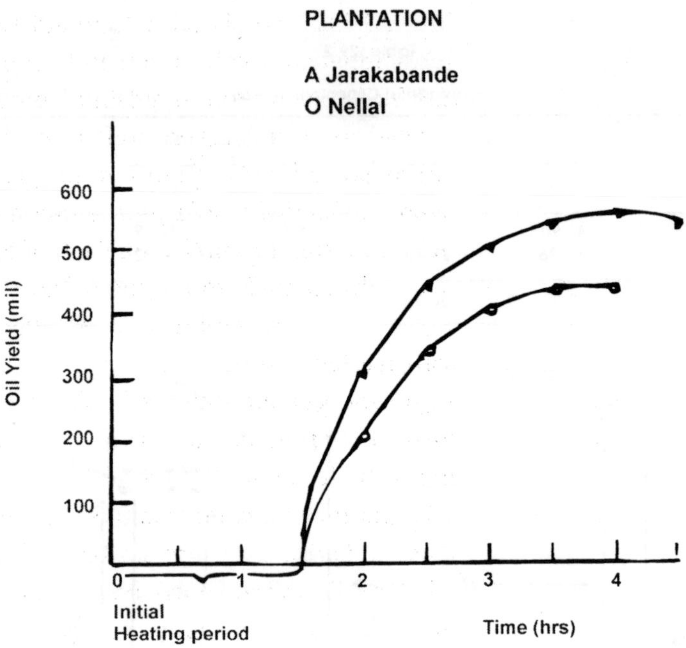

Fig 29.3. Relationship between yield and duration (irrespective of the quality of foliage charged in the still)

30

Turmeric (*Curcuma longa* L.) Leaf Oil, a New Essential Oil for Perfumery Industry

ABSTRACT

The essential oil of dry turmeric leaf (Curcuma longa syn. C. domestica) was investigated for its chemical composition by capillary gas chromatography. Twenty compounds representing 94.16% of the oil were identified. The major constituents of the oil are α-pinene (2.57%), ß-pinene (2.42%), mycrene (2.83%), α-phellandrene (47.14%), P-cymene (11.35%), limonne+1,8-cineole (11.15%) and terpinolene (9.12%). The oil was found to be useful in healing cut wounds.

INTRODUCTION

Curcuma longa : (Syn. C. domestica L; family : Zingiberaceae) is a perennial commercially grown throughout the warmer parts of the world, especially in India, China and South East Asia. In India the plant is commercially cultivated in Andhra Pradesh, Tamil Nadu, Karnatka, Kerala, Bihar and Assam for the production of turmeric, the rhizomes of theplant which is used as a spice. The herb grows to a height of 2-3 feet with short stem and tufted leaves. Turmeric is a condiment used chiefly as a food colouring matter. It has a fine chracteristic aroma too. It has been reported to posses several medicinal properties andis used since times immermorial for the treatment of several ailments. The chief colouring matter of turmeric is curcumin which is present to the extent of 3.2-8.7% in the rhizomes. The rhizomes also contain essential oil (4.8%). India has been exporting turmeric and the oleoresin of turmeric since a ling time, the major purchasers being USa and some European countries. There are several cultivars of turmeric known with different essential oil and curcumin contents.

The essential oil of turmeric rhizomes was extensively studies and the main constituents were identified as ar-turmrone, turmerone, turmerol and atlantone. The leaf of turmeric plant is a waste product generated during post harvest operations of turmeric crop. It is usually used to a small extent as a fuel used in the conversion of fresh rhizomes to commercial grade turmeric and also as green manure. The leaf is aromatic and contains essential oil which was hardly investigated. Recent investigation of the turmeric leaf from Vietnam by GC and GC-MS analyses led to the identification of 22 constituents, the main ocnstituents being ß-pinene (8.9%), mycrene (3.0%) ß-phellandrene (24.5%), p-cymene (13.2%), 1,8-cineole (15.9%) and terpinolene (5.5%). As thee is no report on the oil of turmeric leaf from India, investigation the leaf oil for its chemical composition was under taken.

Materials and Methods

Plant Material

The air-dried leaf material of turmeric plant after harvesting the turmeric rhizomes was procured from M/s Association for Sarva Seva Famrs (ASEFA) Madurai, Tamil Nadu.

Distillation of Essential Oil

The air-dried leave (500g) were cut into small bits and hydrodistilled in glass apparatus for 2 hrs to obtain the essential oil in 1.5% yield. The oil was subjected to physico-chemical analysis (Table-30.1). On Pilot plant scale the yield was found to be 1.0 to 1.2%.

GC analysis

GC analysis of the oil was performed on Perkin Elmer GC-8500 equipped with FID and GP-100 Printer Plotter using capillary Column BP-1 (dimethyl siloxane) (25m x 0.5 mm). Nitrogen was used as carrier gas at a flow rate of 10 psi inlet pressure. Temperature programming was performed from 60°C-200°C@5°C/min. The sample was injected by splitting, the split ratio being 1:80.

Identification of the compounds

The compound wer identified by comparison of the relative retention indices of the peaks on BP-1 column. With those of standards reported in literature ad by peak enrichment on conjection with authentic standards where ever possible. The peak area percentage were computed by FID response without applying correction factors.

Results and Discussion

Turmeric leaf which is a post harvest agro-waste product gave the essential oil yield (1.5-1.7%) on hydrodistillation. GC analysis of the oil shwoed 35 peaks out of which twenty constituents representing 94.61% of the oil were identified b comparing the Kovat's retention indices of thepeak with those reported in literature and by peak enrichment on coinjection with authentic standards. The indentified compounds are presented in Table-30.2.

The major constituents of the leaf oil are a-pinene. 2.57%) ß-pinene (2.42), myrcene (2.83%), a-phellandrene (47014%), 3-carene (2.12%), p-cymene (11.35%), limonene+1,8-cineole (11.15%) and terpinolene (9.12%). The composition of the turmeric leaf oil is quite different from that of turmeric rhizome oil while monoterpenes are predomenant in the leaf oil constituting nearly 80% of the oil, the sequiterpenes and sesquiterpene ketones are the main constituents of the rhizome oil.

The comparison of the composition of the turmeric leaf oil in the present study with that of the oil from Vietnan showed significant difference in the main constituents, a-phellandrene and terpinolene are present in higher amounts in the oil of the present study than in the Vietanmese oil, ß-pinene, p-cymene, 1,8-cineole are present in higher concentration in the Vietnamese oil. These differences may be due to the geographical and climatic conditions and also due to the specific cultivar of turmeric. Studies on the antifungal and antimicrobial and other biological activities of the oil are on progress. Turmeric leaf oil may find application in perfumery, cosmetic and soap industries as well as in aroma therapy.

Table 30.1. Physico-Chemical Characteristics of turmeric leaf oil

Characters		Values
Colour and apperance	-	Pale yellow liquid
Specific gravity at 30°C	-	0.8630
Refractive index at 30°C	-	1,4720
(a)D (Solvent concentration)	-	-18°
Solubility	-	Soluble in 95% athanol
Acid Value	-	0.3
Ester Value	-	6.2
Saponification Value	-	6.5
Evaporation residue (%)	-	2.5

Table 30.2. Composition of the essential oil of turmeric leaf.

Compound	RI	Area %
α-tujene	927	0.16
α-pinene	935	2.57
sabinene	970	0.34
ß-pinene	974	2.42
mycrene	984	2.83
α-Phellandrene	1000	47.14
δ-3-carene	1005	2.12
α-terpene	1010	0.59
P-cymene	1014	11.35
limonene+ 1,8 Cineole	1025	11.15
(Z)-ß-acimene	1028	0.07
(E)-ß-ocimene	1041	0.50
γ–terpene	1053	1.99
terpinolene	1083	9.12
linalool	1087	0.47
bomeol	1156	0.34
terpinen-4-ol	1167	0.42
myternal	1180	0.29
cis-sabinol	1190	0.73

R1= Retention indices

31

Essential Oils and Flavours

Essential oils, aromas and flavours represent a highly complex class of natural product chemistry having a well defined role in the economic development of a country. These aromatic materials are evaluated on the basis of their organoleptic properties, particularly their odour and flavour. However, the evaluation by organoleptic tests is not complete as it lacks the quantitative assessment. With the growing knowledge of organic chemistry and the increasing power of analytical techniques, increasingly difficult takes such as the estimation. isolation and purification of less stable or less abundant aromatic components have been achieved with success.

In this regard the role of physico-chemical constants introduced by Otto Wallach and his contemporaries can be judged from the fact that these are being used in essential oil and flavour industry for more than hundred years and will continue to be used in future as well.

The physical and chemical techniques introduced by Otto Wallach include boiling point, refractive index, density, optical rotation, solubility, acid value, saponification value, hydroxyl value, carbonyl value and the like. These methods have proved to be of great value in the oil industry because of their simplicity, rapidity and reproducibility.

Unfortunately, these routine methods are insufficiently selective when it is desired to determine the actual concentration of a particular constituent in the essential oil or an aroma. Therefore, this aspect of analysis, relating only to totai essential oils, can in no way give information about thp. constituents present in the essential oils.

Therefore, the analysis and evaluation of fragrances and the raw materials used to manufacture them is an inseparable combination of art, chemistry and instrumental techniques.

Gas Liquid Chromatography

The fragrance and essential oil industries were among the pioneers in applying the techniques of gas chromatography which has undergone a tremendous change since its inception. All the components of a fragrance material can be analysed by the application of GC. In addition to its wide applicability, GC is rapid, sensitive, amenable to reasonable quantitative accuracy and possesses high resolving power.

The constituents of essential oil and aromas belong to a variety of chemical substances, such as hydrocarbons, alcohols, aldehydes, ketones, acids, esters, oxides and ethers of monoterpenes and sesquiterpenes. Thus to obtain best results one has to search for the best resolutive conditions. In fact the problem is for a given stationary phase and a given temperature, to use the desired column at its maximum efficiency which depends upon the number of theoretical plates. The choice of the stationary phase is quite important in separating a given mixture in its simplest form, "like to separate like," i.e., non-polar columns are suitable for non-polar sample and vice versa. Apiezon L and silicone oils are quite suitable for separating oils of ginger, pepper and celery seed, but less suitable for oils such as oxygenated materials. However, columns of intermediate polarity like Carbowax- 20M, Reoplex-400 etc. can give good separation for both oxygenated and nonoxygenated materials.

Capillary And Chiral Gas Chromatography

Capillary columns made from fused silica have been found to achieve much needed increase in resolving power for the complex mixtures that make up the essential oils. For example, more than thousand components have been detected in the coffee aroma and many other complex oils. Capillary columns have been successfully used for separation of isomers of menthol etc. Recent advances into the stationary phases has resulted in the separation of even enantiomers. In flavour and essential oil chemistry, many aroma compounds have chiral structures and it is known that different enantiomers may exhibit differences in organoleptic properties.

Many chiral monoterpene alcohols, monoterpene ketones and pheromones could be separated into enantiomers on chiral stationary phases.

In gas chromatography, enantio differentiation can be achieved in two different ways.

1. The preliminary chemical derivatization of chiral molecules with optically pure reagents with the formation of diastereomers followed by their separation on a chiral stationary phase.
2. The direct separation of optically active molecules into enantiomers by injection on a chiral capillary column/packed column.

When reacting a racemic mixture with an optically pure derivatizing agent, the purity of the reagent is of primary importance as small impurities may give rise to more than two diastereomers. The other important conditions to be borne in mind are:

(i) The adduct must be volatile for GC separation.

(ii) The two chiral centres of the molecule and of the derivatizing agent must be as close as possible to each other, in orderto maximize the difference in chromatographic properties of the molecule.

In a recent work, derivatizing of chiral secondary alcohols with different enantiomerically pure reagents has been achieved on OB-21 0 fused silica column. Recently adducts of chiral 2-alkanols with (R)-1-phenylethyl isocynate were separated on OB-210 fused silica column. It was observed that resolution increases with the molecular weight of the alcohol and the adduct with the 8 enantiomer is always eluted before the R enantiomer.

The gas chromatographic separation of the enantiomers of volatile compounds constituents an indispensable modern instrumental technique

If a stationary phase A employed in GC possesses a chemical affinity for substance B, then the retention behaviour of B is not only determined by normal physical equilibrium between the gas and liquid phases but also by chemical equilibrium A+B~AB. If A is Chiral and present in optical active form while B is a recemic mixture, then it is possible to achieve a gas chromatographic enantiomer resolution without isolation of diastereomers, because energetically different diastereomeric associates A (R) B (R) and A (R) B(8) are formed rapidly and reversibly. Enantiospecific hydrogen bonding plays an important role in resolution of enantiomers, but other intermolecular forces, or combination there of, can be considered for the resolution of enantiomers by GC, e.g. charge transfer interactions, and ionic dipole-dipole interaction and host guest inclusion complexes. The resolution of enantiomers by complexation gas chromatography based on enantiospecific coordination interaction often yields high separation factors. Chiral polysiloxanes and low molecular weight siloxanes have been developed and are commercially available under the name Chirasil-Val or its variants and can be operated in the temperature range of 70-240°C.

Three types of chiral stationary phases are used in GC for enantiomer separation:

1. Amino acid derivatives and polymeric siloxanes which form hydrogen bonds (e.g. commercial Chirasil-Val and XE-60 -L-val (R)α-pea).
2. Carbohydrate derivatives notably cyclojlextrins with a propensity to form inclusion complexes.
3. Metal complexes ("Complexation gas chromatography"). Cyclodextrins with six (α) seven (ß) and eight (a) glucopyranose units are commercially available although cyclodextrins with upto twelve glucopyranose units have been observed. Cyclodextrins are used in many chromatographic procedures, for selective separation of enantiomers and achlral compounds. These chromatographic procedure includes TLC (as station8.ry or mobile phase), GLC, GSC, HPLC, Gel-inclusion chromatography (GIC) and Affinity chromatography.

Enantomeric separation of bicyclic alkenes (α-pinene, ß-pinene and carene) and bicyclic alkenes (cis- and trans-pinene) was achieved on packed column in which supporting material (celite) was coa!ed with a solution of a -cyclodextrin in formam ide.

For high resolution and operations at higher temperately various acyl and alkyl cyclodextrins were developed. But alkyl cyclodextrins (hexa, hepta and octa) were preferred as these were less polar and more stable and could be used over a wide range of temperature.

The low concentration of peralklated cyclodextrins in moderately polar polysiloxances (like polydimethylsiloxane OV-1 01 (100% methyl groups) or in OV-1701 (with 5% cyanopropyl group, 7% phenyl group and 885 methyl group) give short analysis time without affecting separation factors and enantiomeric separation of cyclic ethers, cyclic and acyclic ketons, ylactones, terpene ketones (e.g. pulegone), secondary alcohols, aromatic alcohols, terpene alcohols (e.g., 3-menthanols) aliphatic dials, esters, oxiranes, bicycloalkanes (α- and ß-pinane) and bicycloalkanes (α-and ßpinene) has been achieved.

The perfect separation of enantiomers of camphor, isomenthone, menthone and fenchone was achieved on y-cyclodextrin-18 (octakis (3-

Obutanoyl-2,6-di-0-n-pentyl)- cyclodextrin) at 100°C (2°C/min, capillary column 45m 0.25mm carrier H2 bar).

Enantioselective Inclusion gas chromatography has found wide application in the detection of synthetic adulterants in fruit flavours. a-lonone is found in raspberry fruit juice concentrate with *ee* of 90%.

Some commercial juice samples with racemic ionone clearly indicated the adulteration with synthetic products as the synthetic material is racemic in nature.

Preparative Gas Chromatography

Preparative gas chromatography involves the use of columns with greater capacity and the injection of large samples for the isolation purposes. Columns used in a preparative GC, range from wide bore glass capillaries to larger packed columns. Such columns require samples from few µl to few ml. Preparative GC columns are heavily loaded (-20% liquid phase) to increase their sample capacity. Large quantities of essential oil components could be handled by the use of adsorption column chromatography.

Column Chromatography

Adsorption column chromatography is a routine technique for the separation of oxygenated fractions from the hydrocarbons by the use of adsorbents like silica gel or alumina. The adsorbed components of the essential oils are eluted by running solvents ranging from nonpolar to polar. However, normal column chromatography is a slow and laborious process and may require several days if step wise gradient elution is employed. Recent advances in this technique have quite changed this slow process into a fast technique requiring only few hours. Techniques of Flash column chromatography (Chromatotron) have become a common laboratary tool for quick separation of compounds.

Since terpene hydrocarbons are themselves a mixture of saturated and unsaturated hydrocarbons of monoterpenes and sesquiterpenes series, they pose problems in their separation by normal adsorbent chromato-graphy. Argentation chromatography, in which the adsorbent contains a silver salt is a valuable tool for the separation of saturated from the unsaturated or the geometrical and positional isomers of unsaturated components.

Thin Layer Chromatography

The commonly used technique is that of thin layer chromatography which is essentially an adsorption-cum-partition chromatography. This is a highly convenient technique and has the advantage of simplicity and rapidity, of not giving rise to artefact formations. It has an added advantage of colour reaction of essential oil components with different detection reagents which can be utilized for the detection of adulterants in essential oils. A thin layer chromatogram is obtained by spotting the given oil (diluted in suitable solvent) on a silica gel or alumina plates and developing the chromatogram in a suitable solvent. Most commonly used solvents are benzene, ethylacetate. di-ethylether, n-hexane, chloroform, etc. After a chromatogram is obtained, it is first examined under visible and ultra-voilet light. Then the plates are subjected to detection with spray reagents which give different colour reactions with the constituents of essential oils. The most commonly used reagent in the essential oil analysis is vanillin dissolved in sulphuric acid. This is a highly sensitive reagent and in visible light, gives colours which are mostly blue, green, red, purple and orange. However, there are some specific reagents which give colour reactions with particular type of grouping only; for example, 2, 4-dinitrophenyl hydrazine solution giving colours with carbonyl compounds only, while ortho di-ansidine reagents react with aldehydes only. Identification of the spots on the chromatostrips is done by the comparison of the Rf values with those of the reference samples and also by matchings the colour of the spots. Thus two different compounds having similar Rf's can be differentiated by view of their different colour reactions on TLC plate and even compounds which are not separated by GLC can then be detected.

A modified technique in TLC comprises of using silica gel plates impregnated with silver nitrate, for the purpose of forming complexes between Ag+ ions and olefinic linkages, thus, favouring the separation of unsaturated hydrocarbons of essential oilsand for the separation of many sesquiterpenes. Another development in this field is functional group modification right on the TLC plates. in this way, geraniol was separated from citronellol by preepoxidation, the former giving a diepoxide and the later a mono epoxide. Another interesting feature of thin layer chromatography was the separation of four stereoisomers of menthol. The epimers having OH groups equatorial (menthol-isomenthol) are strongly adsorbed on silica gel and in this way menthol-isomenthol pair was separated from neoisomenthol-neoisomenthol pair by using benzene as the solvent.

From the experiments conducted during the screening of industrially important essential oil bearing plants at Regional Research Laboratory, Jammu. It is apparent that silica gel TLC is a technique of choice for the study of essential oils because of its rapidity and simplicity. With the help of TLC, hundreds of oils of different chemical races of Cymbopogon, Ocimum,

Eucalyptus and Juniper have been screened and the results concluded. Also with TLC alone we were able to identify the type of adulterants commonly used in Umbelliferae seeds. Thus, the common adulterants of *Carum* carvi were identified as *Bunium cylindricum, Bunium bulbocastanum and carum* gracile. The supperiority of TLC has also been demostrated by coupling GLC and TLC together, where single peak on the gas chromatogram was actually a mixture on a TLC plates. The citronellol peak in Java citronella on the TCl plate. The similar results were obtained with *Mentha arvensis and* M. *piperita.*

Instrumental Thin-Layer Chromatography (High Performance Thin Layer Chromatography-H PTLC)

Modern TIC methods offer high automation, improved repeatability of chromatograms and accurate quantitation of separated components and has turned into an instrumental technique. Modern TIC & HPTIC are complementary separation techniques. For separation both rely on distribution of the sample between a stationary phase and a liquid mobile phase and on different migration rate of the sample components along the stationary phase. However, TLC system provides simultaneous sample clean up and separation, because the stationary phase is used only once. On each plate several samples and standards.are separated simultaneously hence high sample throughput is obtained and the costs associated with a large -scale screening programme, are significantly reduced.

Precoated plates for high-performance, conventional and preparative TLC are available with consistancy at affordable price and therefore are being used on large scale in germplasm selection to check counterfeit extracts, adulterants and detection of crop protection agents etc. For enantiomeric separation in TLC, mobile phase additives such as substituted cyclodextrins and amino acid derivatives have been used as chiral selectors. Chromatograms are recovered in the UV-V is region or by fluorescence using scanning densitometry. Some researchers have been also coupled TLC with MS for quick identification.

Supercritical Fluid Extraction (SFE)/Fractionation/(SFF)/ Chromatography (SFC)

SFE, SFF & SFC techniques can be used to extract, fractionate and analyze a broad range of compounds. When a substance is above its critical temperature and pressure. It is said to be in its supercritical state. A supercritical fluid has both gas like mass transfer and liquid like solvating properties and sometimes referred as a "super solvent."The solvating power of supercritical fluids approaches that of liquid solvents only as the density of the supercritical fluid is increased, and is easily controlled by adjusting temperature and pressure.

Many supercritical fluids are gaseous at ambient conditions and are comparatively inert, non-toxic, pure and inexpensive.

Their gaseous nature also simplifies the concentration procedures. The combination of these gas and liquid-like properties with other characteristics has made SAF & SFC attractive. Various commercial SFE instruments are available, but for successful application one has to truely understand the technique and develop experimental conditions according to need.

SFC may be considered as a hybrid between GC and LC as it combines the advantages of both and therefore adds a great deal of control and flexibility in developing separations. In density (or pressure), temperature and composition of the supercritical fluid all have major influences on solute retention.

SFC offers speed, solvent savings and efficiency not available with HPLC and uses lower temperature than GC; thus can be used to analyze a much higher molecular weight range than is possible with GC. Both packed columns with well over 100,000 theoretical plates and open tubular columns can be used. Open-tubular columns, because of their permeability and length, usually have greater efficiency than packed columns and are often used with neat CO_2 and with pressure or density programmin'g. This allow easy, subnanogram universal detection of organic compounds.

The FIO is the most commonly used detecter for open-tubular SFC and UV is most the popular for packed columns SFC, but all chromatogrphic detectors including MS, FT-IR and NMR can be employed. Further improvement in design and reduction in cost will contribute to the development of SFE and SFC as powerful analytical tools for chemists.

Techniques Ancillary to Gas Chromatography

The analytical techniques discussed are of only qualitative (based on comparison only) and quantitative nature and give no information about the nature of the molecules separated by the chromatographic techniques. For identification purposes, one has to employ the spectroscopic techniques either in combination with gas chromatography or after separating the desired molecule by the liquid chromatographic techniques.

Retention Indices

A number of retention index systems have been introduced for the comparison of retention data obtained from the gas chromatogram. Most commonly used systems are that of Kovat's retention index and van den 0001 & Kratz system. These systems are based upon the correlation behaviour with a certain standard, mostly n-paraffin hydrocarbons under isothermal conditions (Kovat's system) and use of ethyl esters of n-aliphatic acids under temperature programming in the Kratz system. Kovat index system usually gives a linear interpolation between paraffin hydrocarbons under isothermal condition. To obtain a linear correlation between retention times under Kratz system, programmed rate should be kept low. In most cases, the algorithms of the adjusted retention times of n-paraffin hydrocarbons are a linear function of chain length over a range of atleast several members of the series. Kovat retention index for a single component is calculated using the following equation:

$$I^{a}_{b} = 100N + 100n \quad \frac{\log t' (R) A - \log t' R(N)}{\log t'_{R} (N-n) - \log t' R(N)}$$

1^{a}_{b} = Retention index of Liquid phase 'a' at temperature 'b'

t'R (N) and t'R(N+n)

are the adjusted retention times of hydrocarbons of carbon numbers N & (N-n), that are smaller and larger than the adjusted retention times of the unknown, t'R(A). Retention index under temperature programmed conditions is quite simple and is given by the equation:

$$IE = \frac{t(\text{unknown}) - t(n) + n}{t(n+i) - t(n)}$$

n = carbon number of fatty acids portion of reference ester used.

i = carbon number increment between subsequent reference esters.

t = retention time of respective peak.

Mass Spectrometry

The advent of fused quartz, bonded phase capillary columns has led to very reproducible columns from batch to batch, with the reproducible retention times identification of essential oil/flavour components is possible by retention time / mass spectrometry / computer searching algorithms.

With the modern GC-MS computer systems and resolution glass capillary columns now available, identification of constituents present at levels of 0.1% in a fragrance or essential oil can be accomplished with high accuracy.

Most GC-MS work has done using electron impact ionization (Ell. in which 70 eV electrons impact the compounds in the MS ion source, causing ionization and fragmentations. The introduction of the Ion Trap Detector (ITD) or ion trap mass spectroscopy has made available a relatively inexpensive mass spectrometer that has full computer searching capabilities. In addition, users can build their own library and search it with, TDS software. The Finnigan MAT ITD is a sophisticated GC detector, which uses a new mass technology for separation based on mass and retention time of the emergent peak. Positive indentification of the eluting peaks is done by supplementing GC retention data with the mass spectra obtained by ITD.

In the conventional mass spectrometers, ions are formed in the source region and then injected into the mass analyser. But in the ITD, ionization and mass analysis odour in the same place and as a result to tuning is required. The ANALYSIS programme then allows quick screening of the complex GC runs. The powerful INCaS-library search provides rapid searching of large spectral data bases. Versatile peak detection algorithms also provides rapid detection of co-eluating compounds. Latest developments in the field of gas chromatography allows efficient separation of co-eluting peaks through the use of multidimensio'nal gas chromatography.

Multidimensional GC-MS

In its simplest form, an MDGC experiment involves isolation of the components contained in a small segment or segments of a complex chromatogram Obtained by a first stage gas chromatographic columns (the precolumn) in an intermidiate cryogenic trap. The trapped chromatographic effluents are then separated by using a second or a third chromatographic column (The analytical columns) of different selectivity from the precolumn. For identification purposes analytical column (second or third column) is coupled with IR/MS.

HRGC-FTIR

Infrared absorption spectrophotometry is used extensively for its power as a structural confirmation tools (super imposable IR) and as an indicator of the presence or absence of functional group or other structural features. For many years chemist have been studying IR of pure substances isolated from adsorption column chromatography or by trappings from the GC outlets into appropriately sized glass capillary tubes.

Over the past few years, the use of an interferometer to scan the IR spectrum at a much faster rate has led to the development of a Fourier

Transform Infrared Spectrometry and with the help of required computer hardware and software technology has resulted in the combined GC-FTIR technique. The technique of high resolution gas chromatography coupled with FourierTransform Infrared Spectroscopy has become a powerful tools for the analysis of complex mixtures like the essential oils. The information content of GC-IR run often proves complementary to GC-MS.

During a HRGC- FTIR run, the IR data are acquired and stored continuously. From these raw data acquired by the FT-IR spectrometer, different chromatographic traces can be generated. Thus by using the FTIR, spectra are obtained for all the peak on the gas chromatogram. Since, FT-IR records the spectra in the vapour phase, these spectra are quite different from the corresponding condensed place. Further in vapour phase the molecule exhibit increased internal rotations which are hindered at normal temperatures. As expected, the most striking differences are observed in the FTIR spectra of linalool. The OH stretching bond (3400 cm) is absent vapour phase and other bands also exhibit slight shifts to higher wave numbers. In general vapour phase spectra exhibit less fine splitting as compared to condensed phase spectra. From the FID trace total IR chromatogram is generated by using the Gram Schmidt vactor orthogonalization algorithm or spectral window technique. The GS response is related to the IR characteristics of a compound and depends upon the selection of GS parameters. Like the starting point of GS vactor in the interferogram, vector dimensions and the number of reference vectors. The spectral window technique monitors the changes of the integrated IR absorbance in preselected wave number regions during the GC-FTIR run. Thus FTIR spectrometer is used as a multichannel detector. GC-FTIR has found application in many essential oils where GC-MS run provides little or no information. In the essential oil of Copaiba balsam, which containts mostly sesquiterpenes, GC-MS is of no help since Ei mass spectra of the sesquiterpenes is almost identical. Thus HRGC- FTIR has been found to give enough information about the sesquiterpenes by comparison of the vapour phase spectra of the sesquiterpenes with those of condensed phase spectra. FTIR is also helpful in the detection of two unresolved GC peaks either by direct comparison of the spectra or by a 3-D plot between wave number and retention time.

High Pressure Liquid Chromatography

HPLC is a useful techniques for those essential oils or flavouring components which are thermally unstable and do not survive at a high temperatures of gas chromatography. HPLC is fast, as compared to classical column chromatography and gives quantitative analysis of the material. Phototoxic coumarins have been detected in citrus oil by HPLCspectroscopic combined technique. By selecting the proper stationary phase and solvent composition, one may employ normal phase (polar stationary pha$e and less polar solvent) or reverse phase (non-polar stationary phase with polar solvents) chromatography for the separation of essential oil components.

In fragrance analysis, use of methanol-water system allows better evalution of effluent fraction odour without significant solvent interference.

Chemical Transformation

A number of precolumn chemical reactions and transformation like hydrogenation, epoxidation, ozonolysis, dehydration etc. are being conducted on essential oil constituents and the product submitted to GC -spectrometric identification procedures. Many complex reactions were conducted on the constituents of *Osmanthus* absolute for the identification purposes.

Techniques Ancillary to Liquid Chromatography

Essential oil components separated by any of the chromatographic techniques can be characterised separately by the spectroscopic methods like UV, IR, HNMR, C-NMR.

Ultra Voilet and Infra Red Spectroscopy

Absorption spectroscopy successfully supplements GC by. being primarily a qualitative method. The position of bands, which can be noted directly from the graphs, permits a conclusions as regards the constitutional characteristics of the molecule. Regarding total essential oils, ultra-voilet spectrophotometry has been used for a long time for the analysis of lemon oils of different origins. The lemon oils of Italian and Californian origin contain coumarins and thus can be differentiated on the basis of their coumarin contents with the help of UV spectrophotometry. Minutilli has applied this technique for the analysis of several other oils.

Infrared spectroscopy has also been used for controlling the purity of essential oils. Generally, this technique is used for the identification of unknown components of essential oils.

Nuclear Magnetic Resonance

NMR has become the choicest tool for the identification of pure organic compounds. The fragrance chemistry with its many complex structures of natural origin depends heavily on NMR, especially in the field of research.

Tremendous progress has been made in the field of NMR spectroscopy regarding the size of sample, resolution of complex or overlapping signals and to establish various atomic connectivities within the molecules. High resolution NMR and 2D NMR in combination with computer programming has given tremendous boost to establish the stereospecific structures of very complex molecules. Thus with the help of NMR techniques, It has become possible to elucidate the structures of very minor components of essential oils which could help in reconstituting the given essential oils in combination with synthesis and known chemical transformations.

HNMR gives information about the pattern of hydrogens attached to their respective carbons along with their spatial arrangements. For example, the two pinenes, (X- and ~- isomers, are easily detected with the help of HNMR spectra as the two gem dimethyl group have quite different chemical shifts in their spectra. Similarly, HNMR is constantly used for the elucidation of highly complex structure even in mixtures. C-NMR is an excellent technique for the elucidation of carbon skelton of organic molecules. Recently C-MN R spectroscopy has been used for the analysis of total essential oils. It offers particular advantages for the analysis of essential oils more easily and successfully than is possible by other techniques. Direct information about molecular structure and the functional groups of individual components is obtained from chemical shift values. This qualitative analysis of the essential oils investigated is based upon the comparison of the oil spectrum with the spectra of pure compounds under identical conditions. Since Cresonances are highly sensitive than proton resonances, it has become possible to analyse the essential oils containing stereoisomers like menthol, isomenthol, neomenthol, neoisomenthol, menthone, isomenthone, and other terpenes. The only limitation in this method is that we can't have accurate quantitative evalution of the constituents.

Detection of Synthetics in Natural Oils by Isotopes Analysis

Since natural essential oils are an important item of trade and hence likely to be adulterated with products of synthetic origin, so it has become necessary to check for these synthetics before they are put to use. Thus nuclear magnetic resonance and mass spectrometry has become powerful tools for the detection of a synthetic in natural essential oils by the use of stable isotope method. The basic principle is the evaluation of the abundance of stable isotopes such as C or H in molecules of different origin.

Isotope Analysis by MS

In this techniques the samples are burnt in oxygen in presence of catalyst and the carbon dioxide and water formed are collected and analysed. The water formed is then reduced to hydrogen and then both CO_2 and H_2 formed are analysed for their $^{13}C/C^{14}$ and $^{2}H/^{1}H$ ratio appears as a sensitive indicator of the biosynthetic formation for other aroma constituents like linalool, citral, menthol, trans-anethole and cinnamaldehyde. Similarly, difference in the $^{13}C/^{12}C$ ratios of decanolides of various natural origin indicated the addition of the synthetic racemic product.

Further, the combination of high resolution chromatography and isotope ratio analysis by coupling on line a gas chromatograph with an isotope mass spectrometer leads to highly improved quality control of natural essential oils and flavours.

Isotope Analysis by NMR

Since, mass spectrometry gives an over all isotope ratios of the material in comparison to NMR, which gives the direct site specific natural isotope fractionation of deuterium in organic molecules. Therefore, SNIF-NMR affords a clear picture of the origin of organic molecules. Several application of this technique have been developed in the field of aromas and flavours. In the ^{2}H NMR of anethole, six signals were obtained after proton decoupling. The statistical distribution of deuterium among the six molecular sites showed significant differences in anetholes prepared from different sources. Similar differences in deuterium content of natural and synthetic citral, camphor and vanillin indicated the presence of adulterants in the natural products. SNIF-NMR technique is also applicable to chiral molecules as the deuterium content in specific chemical site is quite distinct.

Intelligent Sensor Technology

It is a highly advanced technology for the measurement and analysis of aromas. The technology is unique in the sense that its performance emulates that of the human nose with levels of discrimination, sensitivity and reproducibility. It is commercialised under the name Aroma Scan technology.

Aroma scan technology is used to characterise, identify and discriminate between sample and aroma components at low ppb levels. The technology is based on the interaction of volatile chemicals with an array of semi-conducting polymer sensors under normal conditions, which enables the users to map aromas in a graphics and digital format. The sensor array contain 32 different polymers with different void geometries. It takes only a few seconds for each sensor to react to a volatiles the sample. Each polymer in the sensor array exhibits specific changes in electrical resistance measurable across each sensor element when exposed to different aromas and flavours. One constituent may interact with certain individual sensors but not with others. This selective interaction produces a pattern of resistance changes as bar chart output, called the odour map. Aroma scanning is the most powerful technique for the comparison of an unknown aromas against standard profiles by Aroma "Finger prints" into a two dimensional format. The final stage of data processing uses proprietary neural network pattern recognition algorithms in an Artificial Neural Network (ANN) to distinguish between similar or difficult to resolve aromas. The product of ANN processing is a recognition file comprising the factors that identify one aroma from another and the label which describes then. In future we may be able to make a library catalogue of the profiles of all the commercial samples and perfumery chemicals for rapid study of a particular essential oil or flavour.

32

Technology of Essential Oils

The preparation of essential oils does not fall directly within the scope of perfumes and cosmetics but their wide application in the manufacture of various perfumery and their valuable medicinal and other properties entitle them to greater attention than hitherto paid to them.

The production of essential oils in India is carried out, literally speaking, from north to south, with important centres of production in Punjab, United Provinces, Central Provinces, Orissa, the Nilgiris, Mysore and Travancore. The important oils apart from the Indian attars, are as follows:

(a) Eucalyptus oil.
(b) Gingergrass oil.
(c) Khus oil.
(d) Lemon Grass oil.
(e) Linaloe oil.
(f) Palmarosa oil.
(g) Rose oil.
(h) Sandalwood oil.
(i) Turpentine oil.

Small quantities of other oils are also produced in India but there is no proper organised effort and the production is thus spasmodic. A beginning has been made to produce citrus oils on a commercial scale in the Punjab and in the Bombay Presidency and of ajwan oil at Indore. Similarly at Kuppam in South India efforts are being made to distil patchouli oil from imported Singapore leaves whilst spasmodic production of geranium oil is reported at Yercaud on the Sheveroy Hills and of wormwood and camphor oil in the

Nilgiris. In Mangalore cinnamon oil and in Orissa salresin oil are being produced by crude methods. Any figures of production of these oils are not however available.

ODORIFEROUS ELEMENTS

There is a wide range of odoriferous materials available in India and elsewhere. Of course the flowers are the most noted illustration, but, besides these, there are substances like cinnamon, cloves, cardamom, lime, citrus, lemon, sandalwood, almond etc., etc., which possess peculiar odours of their own, primarily due to the presence of some essential principles in their structure. These may be extracted, and then sold as raw materials for perfumery and for medicine also.

PRELIMINARY TREATMENT

The general principle of manufacture is simple to understand, but great care should be exercised in handling the operations, if high quality of the final product is to be attained. All the materials used for extraction should be of the best type, fresh, undamaged and not perforated by worms and insects. The materials are first shelled and bruised carefully, crushed or cut into pieces and sometimes even pounded or made into paste by braying with a muller on a stone slab as preliminary steps to the manufacture of essential oils. In fact the raw materials should be in a state to be easily permeated by the perfume-bearing vehicle. The materials should also be freed from all dust or dirt. Perfect cleanliness should be observed during all operations. These factors decide the amount of essential oil that can be secured from the stuff.

PROCESS OF MANUFACTURE

The following general methods are adopted for the manufacture of essential oils:

(a) Maceration.
(b) Distillation.
(c) Expression.
(d) Enfleurage.
(e) Solvent extraction.

BY MACERATION

The general method adopted is to steep the raw materials in olive or sesamum oil· in an enamelled vessel or aluminium vessel. Employ no utensils that are liable to react on the oil. Glass, earthenware or porcelain utensils are generally used. The mouth of the vessel should then be covered up carefully to prevent the admission of dust and dirt. In case of substances that yield essential oils easily, without heat, the whole may be placed in the sun for a number of days. Heating in such cases would destroy the delicate essential oil. But when the articles are not of tender variety, but are hard and stiff by nature, simply placing in the sun would not be found sufficient. In such cases the extraction should be completed by the aid of moderate heat. It should be noted that the less an essential oil is heated, the better is its quality. The vessel, therefore, should not be heated, on a direct oven but on water bath so that the heating operation may continue slowly without causing the evaporation of the volatile essential oil or any deterioration in the final product. Generally, the heating need not be continued for more than half an hour. The vessel is allowed to remain undisturbed for a full day and finally the oil is pressed out or strained and the exhausted materials are thrown out.

Exhaustion of Oil-Bearing Sources

Particular notice should be taken that the raw materials after the sunning or boiling operations are fully washed out and no essential principle is allowed to run to waste. Upon this would materially depend the success of the manufacturers. The duration of sunning or of heating should always be so adjusted that the raw materials yield up the essential contents in full or in so far as possible without injuring the quality of the stuff produced.

Concentration of the Oil

The oil thus prepared will often be found to contain not as much essential oil as it can imbibe under ordinary conditions and it should be always the endeavour of the manufacturers that the essential oil prepared is surcharged with the maximum amount of the essential principle it is capable of containing. The quality of the oil is greatly dependent upon this factor and it is the ·concentrated preparations that command the market and fetch high prices as well.

To attain a high concentration the oil previously obtained is further treated with a fresh lot of the raw materials and the same operations are undergone in full, though the processes of extraction described here are sometimes followed alternately as will be evident from a study of the following recipes. This, however, does not finish the operation and the process is repeated over and over again to get the best results.

Collecting the Oil

A novel method of collecting the oil is adopted sometimes during the process of extraction. The raw materials after being finely bruised are put in a porous vessel and are covered over with sesamum or olive oil and put in strong sunlight. The vessel is put under the hole to collect the dripping oil which is fairly imbibed with the essential matters. The oil may again be poured over the raw materials for further extraction till these are fully exhausted.

The pressing out of the oil requires special care and unless this is done properly there are chances of great losses which should by no means be allowed to go undetected, if the industry is to be based on a sound footing. All measures should be adopted to get the maximum quantity of the oil. When the sunning or heating operations are finished, the oil should be strained out and the remainder should be squeezed forcibly to secure all the oil. The whole may also be allowed to drip through a fine clean cloth so that the oil may ooze out slowly, or a device as mentioned above may also be found profitable and practicable too.

BY DISTILLATION

Essential oils are also procured by distilling the odoriferous substances along with water. For this purpose the oil bearing substance is introduced into a still, water is poured upon it, and heat being applied, the oil is volatilised by the aid of watery vapour at the temperature of 212°F, though when alone it would probably not distil over unless the heat were 100°F more. The mixed vapours which pass over, condense and fall as a milky looking liquid into the receiver. This separates after a time into two portions, one of which is a solution of a part of the newly eliminated oil in water and the other is the oil itself which can then be collected. Roshagrass, lemon grass, camphor, eucalyptus, peppermint, rose, *ketaki,* sandal, orange, cloves, cinnamon, cardamom, citronella grass, and many oil bearing substances may be distilled in this way.

The Report of the Essential Oil Committee (Exploratory) by P.A. Narialwala and J.M. Rakshit writes that distillation process is the most widely used throughout the world. This system is found to be still prevalent in almost all the centres in India producing essential oils. This mehtod is however, a crude method as it affects both the quality and the yield of the oils. On the other hand, a better method would be distillation by steam since it is quicker in operation and gives a better yield and quality of oil and enables the operation to be controlled in a scientific manner. The difficulty of setting up steam distillation units in inaccessable places where aromatic plants grow has largely contributed to the Indian distillers still resorting to the old water distillation method because of its being the cheapest and most simple for conducting the operation. It is time that the essential oil manufacturers devote some thought on the problem of improving the distilling methods practised in India. A small distilling aparatus which may be used under open fire gives better results than the old water distillation method. The water distillation method is suitable for producing oil from roots, grasses, leaves and some varieties of flowers; it is, therefore, the most popular and universal method employed for the extraction of essential oils.

BY EXPRESSION

In a few instances the essential oils are obtained by direct expression of rinds and fruits, as in the case of lemons, oranges, etc., but in these cases the expressed oils are not equal to the products obtained by distillation. These are not so white, nor do they keep so well.

This method is utilised, and has been developed particularly like Italy, for the expression of delicate essential oils from the peels of citrus fruits like oranges, lemons, etc. The peels are pressed over sponges from which the absorbed oil is recovered by squeezing with hand. It is no doubt possible to extract the essential oil from citrus peels by steam distillation, but the oil has been found to lack the freshness of aroma which is usually associated with hand pressed oils which fetch a better price.

ENFLEURAGE

This method according to the Report referred to above is employed for extracting the oil from flowers like jasmine, tuberoses, etc., by mixing the flower with a pure fat on specially devised trays. The fat absorbs the odoriferous bodies present in the flowers and when it is saturated with the perfumes present in the flowers it is shaken with alcohol which dissolves the perfume but not the fat.

This method of extraction was known as practised in India many centuries ago and has been mentioned in "Ain-i-Akbari." It is practised in India even to-day for the production of scented oils whicft are generally made from sesamum seeds. Wetted sesamum seed are placed in alternate layers with the flowers, and are left over for 12 to 18 hours; the seeds are then crushed in a mill and the scented oil is obtained.

The Indian method of enfleurage is however different from the European method where the extract is obtained in a solid form known as "concrete" which consists of the flower oil in solution in natural waxes present in the flowers. From the 'concrete' the natural flowers oil, often called the 'absolute' is separated by suitable solvents. The "concretes" and the "absolutes" obtained by the enfleurage method are very expensive but are invaluable in the blending of high quality perfumes as well as synthetic flower oils.

SOLVENT EXTRACTION

This process* is generally used in recovering oils having a delicate flowery note, which may ordinarily be destroyed under steam distillation. The solvent commonly employed is petroleum ether of low boiling point. The solvent is boiled in a separate vessel, and the vapours are allowed to enter a rotary drum in which baskets containing the flowers to be extracted are fitted; these baskets are pierced so that the vapours pass freely through the flowers as well as from one basket to another; by keeping the drum in rotation, fresh solvent comes at regular intervals in contact with the flowers.

There is also another method in which the solvent is allowed to pass through a series of vessels, and extraction is carried out by the counter current system in which fresh solvent is allowed to pass over flowers which has already given up most of their perfume by previous extraction. The saturated solvent is evaporated and an "absolute" ot the flower perfume is obtained. Although the method has greatly improved lately and has partly replaced the enfleurage method, on account of its rapidity of execution, the quality of "absolute" obtained by the enfleurage method is still considered to be far superior. In fact both the methods are coupled in modem factories in the West and the flowers used in the enfleurage method are subsequently treated by volatile solvents for thorough extraction of odoriferous materials which had no time to dissolve in the fat. This method is not in use in India now.

ABSOLUTES

The manufacture of pure natural oils of flowers or "absolutes" of jasmine, moghra, bokul, etc., is practically unknown in India, but the attars of these and other flowers are produced at Kanauj and Ghazipur, where the method of manufacture consists of heating the flowers mixed with water under an open fire in a copper vessel which is connected to a pot containing sandalwood oil into which the vapours are allowed to condense. After the separation of water, the mixture of sandalwood oil and natural flower oil constitute the attar of India, and .the quality of an attar is determined by the concentration of natural flower oil in it.

PRESERVATION

Essential oils must be guarded from the action of light and air. Light turns the oils darker and sometimes blackens the oils. The oxygen from air acts on some essential oils, making them viscid. These oils should be bottled in clean and dry glass stoppered bottle and stored in a dark place. Addition of 1/2 to 1 per cent absolute alcohol to the essential oils preserves the same well.

PROPERTIES

Finally it should be known that some of the essential oils are colourless while others are green or dark brown in colour. As a general rule the essential oils are lighter than water though there are exceptions to the rule as in the case of cinnamon oil.

The oils are also liable to oxidation if exposed to air; hence they are to be carefully and tightly packed in phials filied to the top and sealed if necessary to prevent contact with air and consequent decomposition. Ground glass stoppers are mostly used to close the mouth air-tight. The phials should preferably be placed in the dark and in a cool, not damp place.

A few recipes are given below with notes culled from the Report of the Essential Oil Committee (Exploratory) by P.A. Narialwala and J.N. Rakshit:

AJWAN OIL

Ajwan oil is obtained from the Ajwan seeds and has use in the pharmaceutical and perfumery industry. This oil is produced at present on a commercial scale at Rao in Indore state; a little of it is also produced in the United Provinces. In Indore the oil is produced by steam distillation. It is said that one ton of seed yields about 56 lbs. of oil. From the oil is also recovered thymol crystals, after the extraction of which the residue is sold under a new trade name of *"Thymoil."*

AMLAOIL

I

Procedure: Take 2½ seers sesamum brayed to a paste, 5 seers emblic myrobalan' free from seeds and bruised, and 10 seers sesamum oil. Put the three ingredients together in an iron vessel and place in the sun for one month. Strain out only 5 seers of the soaking oil and put in a fresh lot of 5 seers sesamum oil. Leave aside for one month; strain out again 5 seers of oil and put in a third and fresh lot of 5 seers of oil. Repeat the operation for 6 months. Then strain the whole of the oil and mix together the former quantities. Put in a covered vessel.

Amla oil prepared in this way serves as a good hair dye. Smear the head with it every day half an hour before bath. The hair will be dyed black and no grey hair will be noticeable.

II

Procedure: Take 4 srs. of raw and good sesamum oil and 4 srs. cleaned and crushed emblic myrobalans. First steep the myrobalans in water for 24 hours; pound them thoroughly and dissolve in 16 srs. of water. Then put the oil in an iron pan and apply moderate heat. When the oil has bubbled for some time and the froth has subsided, remove the pan some distance away from the oven. Now take a Jadle with a long handle, fill it with the above decoction of myrobalan and sprinkle the same on the hot oil. This should be done from a distance, taking every precaution to prevent any accident. Just as the water will be poured on the oil there will be a deafening sound; but the operation should be carried through without any fear. After the whole quantity of the decoction is thus blended with the oil, put the pan on the fire and continue boiling. When the water has evaporated, remove the pan and set it aside with the oil for 7 days. Finally filter and bottle.

ANISEED OIL

Procedure: Take ~ sr. aniseed; pick and dust carefully. Pound and macerate them in ~ sr. good olive oil and put the pulp in a porous iron vessel. Hold a vessel under the hole and place the whole arrangement in bright sunlight. The oil will drip. When it is exhausted put the oil in a stoppered phial.

CAMPHOR OIL

Camphor oil is produced from camphor trees (Variety laurus Camphora) at Coonoor. On distillation of the leaves, solid camphor and camphor oil are obtained. About 500 lbs. of camphor and 100 lbs. of camphor oil are produced per annum at Coonoor. The percentage of camphor in the oil obtained from different portions of the tree by steam distillation is as follows:

Green leaves 40.6 per cent; leaves 43.0 per cent; dry leaves 30.5 per cent; twigs from 20 to 35.5 per cent; branches from 0 to 12 per cent; roots from 24.0 to 28.7 per cent; stumps from 17.5 to 25 per cent.

Camphor oil is now almost entirely produced in Japan. Camphor trees take several years to grow and to be of benefit for the production of camphor and camphor oil. Due to the commercial importance of these products attempts should be made to grow camphor trees on a large scale in various parts of India.

It may be mentioned here that camphor trees can be successfully cultivated in all parts of India with an annual rainfall of 40 inches and over and a satisfactory yield of oil, rich in camphor, can be obtained from the leaves.

CINNAMON OIL

Procedure: Take 2 ch. of pounded cinnamon and one seer good olive oil; put the two together in a vessel and close it up. Heat on the water bath for half an hour. Leave aside for 24 hours and then squeeze out the oil. Put the oil again into the same vessel and steep in it 2 ch. pounded cinnamon. Cover the mouth of the vessel and heat on the water bath for half an hour. Leave aside for 24 hours and then squeeze out the oil. For the third time put the oil into the same vessel and steep in it 2 ch. pounded cinnamon. Heat on the water bath for half and hour. Leave aside for 24 hours. Finally strain and bottle in a stoppered phial.

Mention may be made in this connection that cinnamon oil is distilled by a few firms in Mangalore by crude methods from the cinnamon bark as well as the leaves of the cinnamon trees which grow abundantly in Malabar and South Canara. The oils from the leaves and the bark differ in their chemical constituents, the oil from the bark being more valuable, though both the oils are of considerable importance in pharmaceutical industry, in the flavouring of the foods, and manufacture of aromatic chemicals. The oil from the bark, also known as Cassia Oil, yields the important aromatic Cinnamic Aldehyde whilst the leaf oil is a source of Eugenol. In view of the fact that cinnamon trees thrive well in India the development of the cinnamon oil industry from the bark as well as the leaf is an immediate possibility.

CITRUS OILS

Citrus oils find an immediate sale in India itself. The manufacture of the oils other than lime was undertaken after considerable research at the Chemical Laboratories of the Punjab University particularly. The manufacture of lime oils was also undertaken after a careful investigation of the problem by the Department of Industries, Bombay. The lime tree is indigenous to India and grows throughout the country. In Bombay Presidency the area under cultivation is estimated to be 1,200 acres.

The lime oil is used as a flavouring material for food and beverages and there is demand for it both in Europe as well as in the United States. The oil is distilled by steam from the rinds and juice of the fruits and it is reported that on an average about 2 per cent of oil is recovered.

In India, oranges, sweet limes, lemons, etc., grow in a number of places. The Central Provinces, the Punjab, the North Western Provinces, the Khasi Hills, in Assam, the Sheveroys and the Wynads on the Western Ghats, the Bamra State in Orissa and Coorg are important centres of cultivation of citrus trees. The following varieties of citrus plants are recorded as being grown in India.

1. Citrus Bigaradia Risso (Bitter Orange).
2. Citrus Aurantium Linn (Sweet Orange 'Narangi').
3. Citrus Nobilis Lour (Mandarin or Maltese Orange).
4. Citrus Decumana Linn (Paradise apple- 'Batabi' Limbu).
5. Citrus Medica Linn (The Citron).
6. Citrus Limonum (Limon-'Kaghzi').
7. Citrus Lemetta (Sweet Lime-'Mitha Limbu').
8. Citrus Acids (Sour Lime-'Limbu').

The varieties of essential oils that can be obtained from either the peels, the flowers or the leaves of each variety are given below in serial order:

1. Petit grain oil from the leaves of the bitter orange and bitter orange oil from fruits.
2. Oil of sweet orange from leaves, of the Narangi variety, oils of Neroli Portugal from flowers, and oil of sweet orange from fruits.
3. Oil of Mandarin leaves from leaves of Maltese Orange and oil of Mandarin from fruits.
4. Grape fruit oil from fruits of the Batabi limbu.
5. Oil of linnette leaves from leaves of the Citron and oil of citrus from fruits.
6. Oil of lemon from fruits of the Kaghzi limbu.
7. Oil of limmette flowers from flowers of sweet lime and oil of limmette from fruits.
8. Oil of lime from fruits of sour limes.

The citrus oils are indispensible in the manufacture of fine perfumery, but their largest use is as a flavouring material in foods, confectionery, aerated waters and tobacco. At present in all the citrus pantations in India a considerable quantity of fruits is allowed. to rot and go waste. If an attempt was made to recover the oil from the peels of those wasted fruits a considerable additional income would accrue to the plantations. The extraction of true oils from the peel is closely connected with the utilisation of the wasted fruit in the manufacture of marmalades, fruit juices, syrups, etc. Considerable scope, therefore, exists in the development of this industry.

Steps should, therefore, be taken to develop the manufacture of citrus oils, citric acid and pectin at the orange and lemon plantations in India so that not only new industries but new wealth may be created in the country.

CLOVES OIL

Procedure: Take one seer bruised cloves and macerate the same in one seer olive oil thoroughly. Put it in a porous iron pot and hold a vessel under the hole. Place the arrangement in hot sun and the oil will drip through the pores. When the oozing ceases, store the oil in a stoppered phial.

CARDAMOM OIL

Procedure: Take 2 ch. bruised seeds of cardamom major and 1 seer of good olive oil. Put the two together in a vessel, cover it up and heat on the water bath for half an hour. Set aside the vessel for 24 hours. Press out the oil and put it again in the vessel. Steep in it another lot of 2 ch. cardamom and heat on the water bath for half an hour. Set aside for 24 hours. Squeeze out the oil once more, steep in it a third lot of 2 ch. cardamom and heat on the water bath for half an hour. Set aside for 24 hours. Then press out the oil thoroughly and store in stoppered phials.

CASSIA OIL

Procedure: Take 4 ch. pounded white cassia leaves and 1 seer good olive oil. Put them in a stoppered phial and close up the mouth neatly. Place it in the strong sun for two months. After that press out the oil and store it in a stoppered phial.

EUCALYPTUS OIL

Eucalyptus oil is obtained from the leaves of the Eucalyptus trees which thrive well on the Nilgiris, the Annamalai and the Palni Hills. The area under cultivation on the Nilgiris is about 2,500 acres whilst the production of oil is nearly 22,000 gallons per annum, equivalent to about 85 tons. The entire production is consumed within the country. It may be interesting to mention here that U.P., Bihar as also certain tracts in Orissa are suitable for eucalyptus plantation. As eucalyptus oil has commercial importance, it would be of benefit to the country if its cultivation on a large scale is undertaken in these areas. Cultivation may be also undertaken of another variety of eucalyptus tree, known as eucalyptus citriodora; the leaves of this variety are reported to be rich in citrionella which is an important aldehyde in perfumery as well as in medicinal industry and is also a starting medium for the manufacture of menthol. The manufacture of eucalyptus oil is conducted by primitive methods as a result of which the purity of the oil varies from batch to batch. It is stated that Indian eucalyptus oil is deficient in the cineol content and, therefore, does not come up to the latest B.P. specifications. The oil contains 60 per cent cineol by volume, which is sufficient for all ordinary use. The Indian oil besides contains no aldehydes, such as valeric, butyric and caprioc aldehydes, the presence of which causes irritation to the throat resulting in coughing and other unpleasant symptoms, which is the case with the Australian oil. Moreover, the yield of oil obtained in the Nilgiris even by primitive methods is reported to be greater than the yield from Australian leaves of the same botanical name.

Procedure: The still used for eucalyptus oil is ordinarily 4 feet high and 2lh feet in diameter made with copper plates at the bottom and iron sheets at the sides. A foot above the bottom of the still is a perforated iron plate over which the leaves are placed so that they will not come in direct contact with the heat. Leaves of mature trees sixteen to seventeen years old are preferred to leaves of younger trees. They are dried for three days after picking before being distilled. Leaves dried in the shade give a greater yield of oil. Before the heating commences the still is filled with water and the required quantity of leaves is placed over the perforated plate. The cover of the still is tightly closed and the vapour is allowed to escape through a pipe into a tub, after first passing through a column of cold water. The condensed vapour contains a large percentage of water.

The oil, being lighter, rises to the surface and the water is allowed to pass through a tap at the bottom of the receptacle. Generally, boiling is continued for 8 hours, the water in the still being maintained at the same level by constant addition as it evaporates. The crude oil thus collected is refined by mixing it with one-sixth the quantity of water and adding a small amount of caustic soda. The mixture is again distilled in a similar but smaller still and the oil is passed through filter papers until it is got rid of all impurities. The material is not directly heated but it is worked up by stearn alone. By this means better quality and higher yield of the oil are both secured.

GERANIUM OIL

This oil is distilled from a variety of French geranium probably Pelargonium odoratissima. An acre of geranium rosat yields about 8 lbs. of oil. A wild geranium grows profusely in certain localities on the Nilgiris. The oil is obtained from the leaves and flowers. Geranium oil is an oil of great importance in the perfumery industry as, along with khus and patchouli oils, it forms the body of all good perfume compounds. It is also the basic medium for the manufacture of rhodinol and its esters. The Nilglris and the Sheveroy Hills are well suited for the cultivation of geranium plants. India can produce a geranium oil of first class quality, which will have not only a market in India but also a large market abroad. Care will have to be taken to see that the right variety of geranium is planted as there are 6 or 7 species of geranium, and certain varieties yield an oil which gives a peppermint note and which may not be acceptable to the perfume industry, which always prefers an oil having a predominant rose odour and without any subsidiary odours.

GINGER GRASS OIL

Ginger grass grows wild in some of the southern districts of Travancore where it is known as "Inchipul." There are two varieties of this grass, one white and the other red, but the oil from both the varieties is similar in respect of odour as well as other qualities. The oil is distilled by crude methods from leaves, grass and flowers on a very small scale. Ginger grass oil is a sweet smelling oil, is different in constituents from lemon grass and palmarosa oil, although it resembles palmarosa oil in odour. The ginger grass oil is, however, rich in Borneol which is of value to the perfumery industry, and it would be, therefore, worthwhile to develop the distillation of ginger grass oil on a larger scale.

KHUS OIL

Khus oil is distilled from the roots of the Khus grass which grows in abundance in widely different parts of India, viz., in Malabar, Orissa, the Punjab, Central Provinces, United Provinces and Bharatpur State. The grass grows wild and no systematic effort has been made to cultivate it or to find out its varieties or which of them will yield the best quality or the highest percentage of oil. The distillation of the roots is carried out by primitive methods on a fairly large scale in Bharatpur and in the United Provinces and to a small extent also in the Punjab and in Orissa. The season for the distillation of oil is from November to February. Khus oil has not only a large market in India itself but has possibilities of an export trade, if an oil of standard quality were to be produced.

LEMON GRASS OIL

Lemon grass grows mainly in the northern districts of Travancore and in a small area in Cochin on an elevation of about 500 feet. Formerly, the grass was also found in central and southern districts of Travancore but this has now ceased. The cutivation of grass is very haphazard and scattered over large areas, some of which are highly inaccessible. Lemon grass is a hardy plant and grows in almost any kind of soil, though it is reported that the more fertile the soil, the more the citral constant in the oil. The life of the grass varies from 6 to 15 years, but 8 to 10 years is the normal productive life. The sowing of the grass takes place towards the end of March or beginning of April and it is reported that the best yield of oil is obtained. when the grass is cut during the dry weather. Normally, there are four cuttings in the year at an interval of 6 to 7 weeks starting in May and ending with December. The distillation of the grass is carried out in old-fashioned stills. There is a small consumption of the oil in the country and the bulk of it is exported to Europe and America from Cochin. The solubility of the oil in 70 per cent alcohol is considered by the perfumery trade as a criterion of its purity. The causes of the insolubility are due to the presence of a different grass in the true lemon grass. This grass is like lemon grass in appearance but has a white stem and is usually called the white variety. As it is found to give a higher yield of oil, it is cultivated with true lemon grass, but its harmful effect to the purity of the lemon grass oil has not been realised.

Procedure: Use a steam bath. For heating by steam the most convenient apparatus is a cylindrical vessel 10" in diameter and 15" in height with a conical top. The outside jacket to enclose steam is 14" in diameter and 18" in height with a bottom of three inches height clear for water. The still can hold about 5 lbs. of grass or other similar material. The quantity of oil that can be obtained will depend upon the quality of the material and charges taken per day. It takes about an hour or so for complete distillation of one charge from the time the steam is allowed to pass through.

LEMON RIND OIL ETC.

Procedure: The distillation of substances, such as, roots, lemon-rinds, Pudina, Kevada, Rose flower, Betelvine leaves, etc., has been carried out by using the above apparatus quite successfully and efficiently and, therefore, it is recommended for the distillation of essential oils.

LINALOE OIL

Linaloe oil is produced from the carpels of Bursera Delpechiana and Bursera Aloexylon though the oil can also be distilled from the leaves as well as the wood. The distillation of the oil is carried out with modern stills under scientific control. Linaloe oil has great possibilities and the extension of linaloe plantation should be encouraged. The important aromatic constituent of linaloe oil is linalol from which it is possible to make linalyl acetate, an important aromatic chemicai for the perfumery industry.

Procedure: For this purpose citrus lemon of the *pati* variety will be required. Take half a seer of its fresh peels and 1 seer of olive oil. Put the two together in a vessel and heat on the water bath for half an hour. Remove and leave aside for 24 hours. Then press out the oil. Put the oil again in the vessel and steep in it another lot of 4 chhataks of dry peels of lemon grated finely. Close up the mouth of the vessel and place it daily in the sun for one month. Finally strain and bottle in a stoppered phial.

PALMA ROSA OR ROSHA GRASS OIL

This oil is produced from the rash a grass which grows abundantly in the Central Provinces, Bombay Presidency, in some parts of Nizam's Dominions and is also found in Baroda, Gwalior and Indore States. It is unfortunate that no attempt has been made in any of these States to distil the oil. The grass is said to be known in India from ancient times and until recently India was the only source of supply of this oil. Rosha grass is a perennial plant; it grows to a height of about 6 to 8 feet. It is grown from seeds which are generally sown in the month of June before the monsoon starts. In 4 to 5 months the grass is ready for its first cutting and distillation. The oil is distilled from the entire grass including the flower in stalk, the leaves and flowers yielding the most oil. There are eleven varieties of rosha grass of which the "Motia" variety is the best, from the point of view of yield of oil and fragrance; the other varieties yield poor quantity as well as quality of oil. An acre of grass yields 15 to 20 lbs. of oil, severe frost kills the grass and reduces its oil content to as much as 54 per cent. Only the best variety of grass should be grown which is the Motia variety. At present the grass grows in a wild state in the forests and is often inaccessible for exploitation. As India holds an important position in the supply of palma rosa oil, the cultivation of rosha grass should be carried out on most scientific lines.

ORANGE OIL

Procedure: Take one seer of fresh peels of orange and mince them. Take also one seer of olive oil. Put the two together in a vessel and heat on the water bath for 30 mins. Remove and place in the sun for a month. Finally strain.

PUMELO OIL

Procedure: Peel off the green skin of pumelos and mince them with a knife. Take half and put in a vessel. Pour into it one seer good olive oil. Then heat the vessel on the water bath for half an hour. Remove and cover up the mouth of the vessel closely. Place it in the sun every day for one month. Then strain and bottle. The oil will be nicely scented.

ROSE OIL

The rose oil of India or as it is more popularly known, the otto of rose, was known all over the world in olden days and had the reputation of being the finest quality. Even to-day the small quantity of rose oil that is produced in India is as good as, if not superior to the Bulgarian rose oil. It is of vital importance to the country that the manufacture of rose oil in India should be undertaken on a much larger scale than hitherto. Ghazipur, which was once known all the world over as 'the centre of Indian rose oil, now produces roses on a very small scale on account of degradation of the species and the impoverishment of the soil and the centre of gravity for the production of rose oil has shifted to Barwana in Aligarh District of U.P. The season for roses in Barwana lasts for only six weeks, from the middle of March. till the end of April, and it is reported that during this period as much as 200 maunds of rose petals are distilled per day and at the height of the season, which lasts for only about a week, the arrivals of flowers come to as much as 1,000 maunds per day. Most of the rose petals are, however, used up for the manufacture of rose attar and only about 5 to 7 lbs. of pure otto of rose is produced per annum. The distillation at Barwana is carried out by distillers from Kanauj by old methods and it is reported that about 13,000 lbs. of rose petals give about 1 lb. of rose oil, which means an yield of about .001 per cent; if a more modern method of distillation is adopted, it should be possible to obtain a higher yield. Systematic stud" of the manufacture of otto of rose by modern methods has been carried out by the Industries Department of the United Provinces and they have stated that the yield of oil can be raised to as much as 0.15 per cent by using an improved type of still, i.e., we can obtain from the existing crop of flowers at Barwana ten times more oil than what the crude method of distillation yields.

SANDALWOOD OIL

Sandalwood oil is obtained from the wood of the sandal trees which grow largely in the forests of Mysore, Coorg and Bombay Presidency. The· wood is commercially valued according to size, weight, physical appearance, etc., and has varied domestic uses. The wood is rich in oil and according to the research carried out at the Forest Research Institute, Dehra Dun, the oil is found in both billets and roots. The wood is generally disintegrated into small line powder before it is taken to the still for the extraction of the oil. The manufacture of sandalwood oil is conducted chiefly in Mysore and on a moderate scale at Kuppam, Mettur, Bombay, Kanauj and Karkal (S.K.) Most of the sandalwood oil factories operate modem stills with steam and the quality of the Indian oil is approved all over the world. There are, however, some factories in Mangalore which still extract the oil by crude methods of distillation, but their production is negligible and they are thus of no importance. With the development of the soap, toilet and perfumery industry and larger manufacture of pharmaceutical goods in India, there is every reason to believe that the manufacture of sandalwood oil will progress s.till further in the years to come.

Procedure: Take 5 srs. of sandalwood dust and 10 srs. of water. Put the two together in a suitable earthenware vessel for 48 hours. Then place on the water bath at steam heat for half an hour. Remove the vessel, cover it with a fine piece of cloth and place it in the hot sun. After a time a thin film will form on the surface of the decoction. Pick it out gently with a feather or cotton swab and put it gently in a clean phial. A similar layer will appear again and again on the freshly exposed surface. Pick out the films as soon, and as many times, as they are formed. Close the mouth of the phial air-tight, place in the sun for a month and store it away.

SALRESIN OR CHUA OIL

The oil is extracted by crude methods in Cuttack from Sal resion (Shorea Robusta) which is an exudation from sal trees which grow in Orissa. A systematic investigation of this oil would be desirable as it is reported that some years ago, as much as 1,000 lbs. of oil was extracted every day and was consumed by Kanauj distillers in the manufacture of incenses and attars.

TURPENTINE OIL

The oil of turpentine is obtained by stearn distillation of oleo resin which exude from various pine trees which are tapped at regular intervals by incision. Three factories, one at Jallo in the Punjab and another at Bareilly in D.P. and a third in Kashmir are carrying out the manufacture of turpentine oil. Though turpentine oil as such has no use in the perfumery industry it is an important oil of commerce for paint and varnish industries, as also in the manufacture of wax polish. Turpentine oil is also the starting material for the manufacture of terpineol (synthetic lilac), the economic manufacture of which, however, depends on the pinene contents, particularly the Alpha variety, of the oil. The turpentine oil produced in India is unfortunately poor in alpha pinene, the percentage of which is only about 30.

33

Essences and Ottos : Preparation of Essences

Perhaps the most democratic form of luxury indulged in by all lovers of perfumery is the essence, which is in principle an alcoholic solution dissolving essential oils either alone or in harmonious combination with others. The essence is also produced by distillation or by digestion. The pleasant aroma of the essences and their cheapness render them a most popular form of handkerchief and general perfumes.

The manufacture of essences is comparatively an easy task and does not involve complicated processes. Only what is required of the manufacturer is clean and careful manipulation. The object in view should be to arrive at a preparation the odour of which is pleasant and persists for a pretty long time and which does not leave any residue on evaporation.

MODE OF PREPARATION

To attain this end, most scrupulous attention should be attached to the selection of the constituents which enter into the composition of essences. The principal of these are alcohol and the essential oils. The alcohol used should be of the best quality available and rectified, if possible. Crude alcohol invariably contains a lot of impurities and its use as basis spoils the whole preparation.

The range of essential oils at the command of the essence manufacturers, thanks to the evolution of synthetic perfumes, is extensively large. The distinctly predominant odours. the manufacturers are capable of producing are thus no doubt numerous but this also renders the task' of selection of the perfumes and their combination all the more difficult. But in all cases fresh and the best quality oils should be employed, otherwise the preparation cannot be expected to be of a high order of excellence.

FLORAL EXTRACTS

The essential oils can often be replaced by the odoriferous bodies yielding the perfumes themselves. The raw odoriferous bodies are infused in rectified spirit. On prolonged maceration, the period depending upon the nature of the body and the easiness with which it yields up its perfumes, the essences are obtained. These essences generally go by the name of natural essences. But their manufacture is rather restricted and the majority of essences met with in the market is derived from artificial sources and are made from the essential oils. Of course the concentrated forms of natural essences can be preserved and may be diluted with spirit either alone or in combination with ohters to give the most delicate preparations.

CLASSES OF ESSENCES

It will be thus noticed that the essences may be broadly divided into two groups, natural and artificial. The latter allows of further division, viz., *Simple* and *Compound.* The simple essences which are generally of the cheapest type and of inferior quality are prepared by dissolving a single essential oil, or generally a cheap synthetic preparation, ina not too pure form of alcohol. The compound essences on the other hand-and the same remark holds good in the case of the handkerchief essence~tai1 the use of more than one essential oil; besides, these preparations are designed to conform strictly to the ideal . types of essences, and hence require the use of the best quality alcohol and perfumes.

BLENDING

In preparing artificial essences too much- attention cannot be devoted to blending of the perfumes which should be made in a judicious manner so that the combination gives out a most pleasant smell and appeals to the general taste. Harmony of blending is the biggest thing to be attained in the preparation of essences and when this is achieved, success is more than.

Blending of the perfumes should be universally followed by keeping the whole for a certain time undisturbed for maturing. This allows the odour of the alcohol and the foreign odours in essential oils employed to disappear and conserve the resulting scent.

FILTERING AND PACKING

The preparation should always be filtered before final packing. Turbid and unclean preparations do not command respect. The solutions should be perfectly clear and transparent. Ordinarily it will be found that the filtered solutions often cause deposits to form at the bottom of the container on long standing. Hence the essences as a general rule are allowed to stand for a few weeks and then filtered so that no residue can form later on.

The packing of the essential oils in phials also demands expert knowledge. The vessels should be carefully washed and dried before the essence is poured into them. By no means the essence should be packed in wet or even moist phials; for the least trace of moisture is sufficient to upset the equilibrium of the product, to precipitate a part of the perfume essence and to modify the odour. The vessels should also be filled completely and no space should be left above the liquid; for, in such cases alcohol and essential oils being volatile substances may volatilise partially and thus cause deterioration of the preparation. The vessels should then be stored in cool and dark places. It has been found that under these conditions the essence gains in quality and sweetness and improves.

While putting in the market the essences should be packed in decent glass containers fitted with glass stoppers. By no means ordinary cork should be used as this is liable to be injured by the spirit contained within. Finally the phial is capsuled, finely labelled and packed in cardboard boxes either sirigly or three or six at a time.

34

Natural Essences

The chief application of floral extracts lies in the manufacture of handkerchief perfumes, scents, essences, etc. The process of preparation is essentially the same in every case. Freshly blooming scented flowers are selected, freed from green stalks and cleaned from dirt and dust. The picked flowers are then digested in spirit. When flowers are not available, essential oils of the flowers or substitutes may be employed. Where the spirit has not been defined, rectified spirit is to be understood. By proof spirit is meant a mixture of equal bulks of alcohol and water while spirit of wine stands for the alcohol of commerce. After a time the liquid is filtered and the scent carefully bottled.

BAKUL

Procedure: Take *Bakul* flowers 8 oz., clean and free from dust; put them in a stoppered phial and pour in 20 oz. Cologne spirit. Close the mouth. Leave aside for 3 days and filter. Again soak 12 oz. fresh flowers in the filtered spirit and leave aside undisturbed for 48 hours. Finally filter and put in a stoppered phial.

HENNA

Procedure: Mehndi flowers 8 oz., proof spirit 16 oz. Put these two ingredients together in a stoppered phial ror 15 days. Wring out the flowers and throw them away. Put 12 oz. fresh flowers in this spirit and filter after 7 days. Store in a stoppered bottle.

MUSK HENNA

Procedure: Take 1/16 tollah pure musk; 10 oz. *Mehndi* flowers; 20 oz.

spirit. First macerate the musk in the spirit and put it in a stoppered phial. Throw in the flowers; shake well; close up the mouth and set aside for 10 days. Filter and store in a stoppered phial.

KETAKI

Procedure: Procure 6 oz. pollens of *Ketaki* flowers and 6 oz. tender leaves of the same plant, also 24 oz. proof spirit. Finally chop the leaves. Put all these ingredients into a wide-mouthed stoppered phial for 20 days. Filter through filter paper.

BELA

Procedure: Take 16 oz. *Bela* flowers free from stalks and 20 oz. Cologne spirit. Put these two ingredients in a wide-mouthed stoppered phial for 48 hours. Wring out the flowers and put in 8 oz. fresh flowers. Set aside for 24 hours and then filter through filter paper. Store carefully in a stoppered phial.

MALLIKA

Procedure: Put together 8 oz. *Mallika* flowers free from stalks and 12 oz. proof spirit into a wide-mouthed stoppered phial. Wring out the flowers after 3 days and throw in 8 oz. fresh flowers. Leave aside for 48 hours and then filter through filter paper and store in a stoppered phial.

GANDHARAJ

Procedure: Take 200 *Gandharaj* flowers free from stalks and 32 oz. spirit of wine. Put the two together into a stoppered phial for 3 days and then wring out the flowers. Put in 200 fresh flowers and leave for 48 hours. Wring out the flowers; put in a third lot of 100 flowers and set aside for 24 hours. Finally filter through filter paper.

HASU-NO-HENNA

Procedure: Put together 16 oz. *Hasu-no-henna* flowers and 16 oz. spirit in a wide-mouthed stoppered phial for 24 hours. Filter through filter paper; throwaway the exhausted flowers. Put in 16 oz. fresh flowers in the same spirit and leave aside for 24 hours. Repeat' this process for 6 times; filter through a filter paper and finally put in a stoppered phial.

CHAMPAKA

Procedure: Procure 100 *Champaka* flowers and then put in a stoppered phial. Pour 24 oz. spirit of wine into it and leave for 48 hours. Strain the liquid and throwaway the exhausted flowers.

Put in 200 fresh flowers and leave for 24 hours. Finally filter through filter paper and bottle.

JAHURI CHAMPAKA

Procedure: Take 100 *Jahuri Champalal* flowers and 20 oz. proof spirit. Put the two together into a wide-mouthed stoppered phial for 24 hours. Wring out the flowers, then throw in 100 fresh flowers and set aside for 24 hours. Repeat this for seven times. Finally filter through filter paper and store in a stoppered phial.

KANTALI CHAMPAKA

Procedure: Procure 250 *Kantali Champalal* flowers and spirit 20 oz. Put the two together into a wide-mouthed stoppered phial, and close the mouth tightly. Strain after 15 days and throw away the exhausted flowers. Soak a fresh batch of 250 flowers into the spirit and filter after 48 hours. Store in a stoppered phial.

ROSE

Procedure: Procure 16 oz. dried buds of Rose (any scented variety) and 20 oz. spirit of wine. Put the two together into a wide-mouthed stoppered phial for 20 days. Filter through filter paper and store in a stoppered phial.

TUBEROSE

Procedure: Put 8 oz. *Tuberose* and 12 oz. proof spirit together into a wide-mouthed phial for 7 days. Strain and throwaway the exhausted flowers. Put 8 oz. fresh flowers into the spirit; close up the mouth and set aside for 15 days. Put in a stoppered phial.

CHAMELI

Procedure: Take 12 oz. *Chameli* flowers free from stalks, put in a wide-mouthed stoppered phial and pour in 16 oz. Cologne spirit. Leave for 48 hours, strain and throwaway the flowers. Put in 8 oz. fresh flowers, leave for 24 hours, then filter and store in a stoppered phial.

JASMINE

Procedure: Procure 16 oz. single *Jasmine* free from stalks and 12 oz. spirit. Put these twoo together into a wide-mouthed stoppered phial for 24 hours. Strain and throwaway the exhausted flowers. Put in 8 oz. fresh flowers, close up the mouth tightly and leave for 24 hours. Finally filter through filter paper and store in a stoppered phial.

KHUS

Procedure: Procure 12 oz. *Khus* root; pick them and free them from dirt. Pound them finely. Soak the roots in 16 oz. spirits of wine and put the two together into a wide-mouthed stoppered phial. After a month filter through filter paper and put in a stoppered phial.

FANTI

Procedure: - Procure 8 oz. *fanti* flowers free from stalks; put in wide-mouthed stoppered phial and pur in 12 oz. spirit. Strain after 48 hours and throwaway the exhausted flowers. Put in a fresh lot of 12 oz. flowers and filter through filter paper after 24 hours. Finally store in a stoppered phial.

ORANGE

Procedure: Procure 8 oz. dried peels of Orange and mince them fine. Soak them in 12 oz. spirit in a wide-mouthed stoppered phial. Close up its mouth and set aside for 1 month. Finally filter through filter paper and store in a stoppered phial.

AMBERGRIS

Procedure: Put 12 dr. Ambergris in a stoppered bottle and pour into it 3 pints of Cologne spirit. Close the mouth tightly and set aside for a month. Finally filter and store in a stoppered phial.

MUSK

Procedure: Macerate thoroughly 24 grs. of pure Musk in a stone mortar. Dissolve the same in 16 oz. spirit of wine and put the solution in a stoppered phial for 20 days. Shake once a day for 10 minutes every time. Finally filter and store in a stoppered phial.

PATCHOULI

Procedure: Procure 12 oz. clean and dry leaves of *Patchouli* and 12 oz. proof spirit. Put these two together into wide-mouthed stoppered phial; close the mouth tightly and set aside for one month. Then filter through filter paper and store in a stoppered phial.

CLOVES

Procedure: Take 1 ch. picked and cleaned Cloves and 20 oz. spirit of wine. Put the two together into wide-mouthed stoppered phial for a month. Then filter and store in a stoppered phial.

LAVENDER

Procedure: Take fresh Lavender flowers 20 oz. and spirit 32 oz. Put the two together into a stoppered phial. Close the mouth and leave for 1 month. Filter through filter paper and store in a stoppered phial.

PUMELO

Procedure: Procure Pumelo flowers, free from stalks, 8 oz. and spirit of wine 16 oz. Put them in a wide-mouthed stoppered phial for 48 hours. Strain and wring out the flowers and put in 8 oz. of fresh flowers. Set aside for 48 hours and strain as before. Again add 8 oz. of fresh flowers and filter after 48 hours. Pack in stoppered phials.

CASSIA

Procedure: Take oil of Cassia 4 dr. and Cologne spirit 12 oz. Keep in a stoppered bottle for 15 days and shake the bottle daily for 5 minutes. Finally strain and pack.

WHITE ROSE

Procedure: 16 oz. petals of white rose are put in a widemouthed bottle; 16 oz. of spirit is poured over them and the mouth is then closed. After 3 days, strain and reject the exhausted flowers. Again introduce 8 oz. of fresh flowers and close the mouth. After 48 hours filter and pack.

ORANGE

Procedure: 2 drs. of oil Neroli are taken in a bottle. 20 oz. of spirit is poured over it and the mouth of the bottle is closed. After 15 days filter and add 1 dr. of oil Neroli. Keep in stoppered phials.

BERGAMOT

Procedure: Oil of Bergamot 4 oz. and spirit of wine 30 oz. are taken in a stoppered bottle and kept for 7 days. Finally filter and then pack.

VIOLET

Procedure: 8 oz. of finely powdered orris root is digested in 24 oz. of spirit of wine in a stoppered bottle. Set aside for 1 month. Finally filter and phial.

ROSE GERANIUM

Procedure: Put 4 dr. of oil of Rose Geranium and 16 oz. of spirit in a stoppered bottle and keep for 20 days. Then filter and phial.

LEMON

Procedure: 8 oz. of fresh lemon peels are minced and digested in 20 oz. of spirit of wine in a stoppered bottle. Mix well and set aside for three days in a warm place. Finally filter and phial.

SANDALWOOD

Procedure: Mix together 4 oz. of Sandalwood dust and 8 oz. of white chalk and digest in 12 oz. of spirit and set aside in a stoppered bottle for a week. Then strain through filter paper and to the filtrate add 1 oz. of sandal oil. Store in a bottle for 2 weeks before phialing.

Procedure: Finely powdered Sandalwood dust weighing 16 oz. is digested in 12 oz. of Cologne spirit in a wide-mouthed stoppered vessel. Set aside for a month, then filter and pack.

35

Manufacturing of Artificial Essences

The preparation of simple essences consists primarily in mixing some Heico perfume, such as heiko bela, heiko rose, heiko patchouli, heiko jasmine, heiko musk, heiko chameli, etc. in rectified spirit 60 over-proof.

The method of preparation is as easy as it is simple. The whole is allowed to mature for a fortnight or more, during which period the containing bottle is shaken three times daily for 15 minutes every times. The usual proportion recommended by perfumers is 1 oz. of the heiko scent in 45 oz. of the spirit. Sometimes a small quantity of musk, essence of musk or essence of ambergris is added to render the perfume more persistent and also to improve the odour. The perfumes may be packed in tubes.

SIMPLE ESSENCES

The few recipes given below offer the clue to the manufacture of manyothers of similar types :

1. Heiko Lily, 1 oz.; Essence Amber, 2 oz., Spirit, 45 oz.
2. Heiko Tuberose, 1 oz; Essence Ambergris, 1 oz.; Spirit, 45 oz.
3. Heiko Lily of the Valley, 4 dr.; Essence Musk, 1 oz.; spirit, 24 oz.
4. Heiko White rose, 4 dr.; Musk 2 dr.; spirit, 24 oz.

Essnece from Country Ottos

simple essences are also prepared by dissolving country made ottos in spirit with the addition of benzoic acid. The mode of preparation is exactly the same, only the time of maturing is lengthened to one month. A few typical recipes follow :

1. Otto of Jasmine of Santal, 1½ tollah; Spirit, 24 oz.; Benzoic Acid, 15 gr.

2. Otto of Henna or Bakul, 2 tollah; spirit oz., Benzoic Acid, 15 gr.

3. Oil of Chameli flowers, 1 tollah, Benzoic Acid , 8 gr.; Musk 2 gr.; Spirit, 16 oz.

Handkerchief Essences.

The essences prepared according to the process described above may be mixed in suitale proportions to give cheap handkerchief essences as follows:

I

Essence	Rose	16	oz.
"	Keora	2	oz.
"	Jasmine	2	oz.
"	Lily of the Valley	3	oz.
"	Amber	1	oz.

Procedure : Mix together, Shake for 15 minutes, three times a day for three days. Then use.

II

Essence	Chameli	16	oz.
"	Rose	4	oz.
"	Jasmine	2	oz.
"	Neroli	1	oz.
"	Amber	½	oz.
"	Musk	½	oz.

Procedure : The same

Compound Essences

The preparation of compound essences taex the best skill of the perfumers. As already remarked much would depend upon perfect manipulations. For marketing, pack them a decent phials with glass stoppers. A few recipes follows :

Forget-Me-Not

Essence	Amber	2	dr.
"	Orange	1	dr.
"	Vanilla Bean	4	dr.
"	Ylang Ylang	4	dr.

"	Jasmine	3	dr.
"	Rose	8	dr.
"	Sandal	2	dr.
Otto	Neroli	1	dr.
	Bergamot	2	dr.
	Musk	30	Minutes
Rectified Spirit		2	Bottles

Procedure : Add the ingredients one by one in a big vessel and have them thoroughly mixed together with shaking. Put the whole air-tight in a stoppered vessel for a fortnight during which period shake it thrice daily for 15 minutes at a time. Finally filter through filter paper and phial. The aroma of this preparation is very delightful and lasting.

Remember-Me

Otto	Jasmine	1	dr.
Flora	Jasmine	2	dr.
Otto	Orange Flower	1	dr.
"	Rose (Turkish)	30	minims.
Oil	Cloves	15	minims.
"	Geranium Rose	4	dr.
"	Citron	3	dr.
"	Bergamot	2	dr.
Oil Lavender (English0		1	dr.
Essence Amber		2	oz.
"	Musk	1	oz.
Rectified Spirit		2	Bottles

Procedure : As in Forget-me-not.

Sir Walter Scott

Exact Rose or Istambal		1	dr.
Otto	Orange Flower	30	minims.
"	Bergamot	30	minims.
"	Lavender	15	minims.
Essence Jasmine		1	oz.
"	Musk	1	oz.
Alcohol		1	bottle

Procedure : As in Forget-me-not.

Essence Jasmine

Otto of Jasmine		1	dr.
Flora Jasmine		2	dr.
Heiko Jasmine		1	dr.
Otto de Rose		30	minims.
Essence	Neroli	2	dr.
"	Musk	2	oz.
Alcohol		1	bottle

Procedure : As in Forget-me-not.

Glori Daucher

Essence Victoria		12	oz.
Exact Rose or Istambal		1	dr.
Otto	Sandal	30	minims.
"	Jasmine	1	dr.
"	dr Rose (Virgin)	1	dr
Heiko Amber		2	dr.
"	Pitunia	1	dr.
"	Tuberose	30	minims.
Rectified spirit		2	bottles

Procedure : Mix the ingredients one by one with shaking. Put the whole air-tight into a stopered vessel and shake it thrice daily for 15 minutes at a ttime for not less than a month. Finally filter and pack in phials.

Kiss-me-quick

Essence	Jasmine	2	oz.
"	Orange Flower	2	oz.
Spirit	Tonka Bean	½	oz.
"	Ambergris	1	dr.
Cologne Spirit		12	oz.

Procedure : As in Glori Daucher.

Jockey club

Essence of Rose		4	oz.
"	Cassia	2	oz.
"	Jasmine	4	oz.
"	Ambergris	4	dr.
Tincture Orris		4	dr.

Procedure : As in Glori Daucher.

Musk Rose

Otto de Rose		1	dr.
Sandal Oil		1	dr.
Musk		2	dr.
Essence	Vanilla	1	oz.
"	Jasmine	1	oz.
Benzoic Acid		15	gr.
Spirit		1	bottle

Procedure : As in Glori Daucher

Essence Victoria

Otto de Rose (Virgin)		1	dr.
Oil	Neroli	2	dr.
Otto de Coriander		16	minims.
Oil of	Bergamot	4	dr.
"	Pimento	24	minims.
"	Lavender	16	minims.
Musk		4	gr.
Benzoic Acid		2	dr.
Spirit		4	bottles.

Procedure : As in Glori Daucher.

American Beauty

Otto de Rose (Virgin)		4	dr.
Essence	Neroli	1	oz.
Heiko	Rose	2	dr.
Essence	Jasmine	1	oz.
Otto Cedar Wood		12	minims.
Musk		8	gr.
Benzoic Acid		1	dr.
Alcohol		4	bottles

Procedure : As in Glori Daucher.

Essence Tuberose Lily

Heiko	Lily	4	dr.
"	Jasmine	1	dr.
"	Tuberose	2	dr.
Otto de Rose		30	minims.

Oil	Bergamot	1	dr.
Essence Amber		1	dr.
Alcohol		1	bottle

Procedure : The constituents are mixed together thoroughly one by one and the whole is then allowed to stand undisturbed for 7 days. Then filter, a shake the whole for 15 minutes at a time, thrice daily for 7 days. Finally pack in phials.

Essence Rose

Extract Rose or Istambal	2	dr.
Magnesium Carbonate	4	dr.
Alcohol	1	bottle

Procedure : First incorporate well the extract rose with the magnesium carbonate in a stone mortar and then add to it then alcohol. Shake the whole trhice daily, 15 minutes at a time, for a fortnight and then filter and phial. The residue left after filtering in the blotting paper when dissolved in one bottle of distilled water will give rise to a very good quality of rose water.

Nizam Monte Cristo

Rectified Spirit		24	oz.
Extrat	Rose or Istambal	30	minims.
Otto de Rose (Virgin)		30	minims.
Heiko	White Rose	1	dr.
Otto	Keora	15	minims.
"	Orange Flower	10	minims.
Essence	Chameli	1	oz.
"	Jasmine	1	oz.
"	Tuberose	1	oz.
"	Ambergris	1	oz.

Procedure : Into the rectified spirit add the ingredients one by one and shake well for 5 minutes after each such addition. Finally keep the whole in stoppered bottle and shake thrice daily, 10 minutes at a time, for seven days together. Finally filter and phial. The preparation is quite a novel invention.

Sultana

Spirit		2	bottles
Otto de	Rose (Turkish)	1	dr.
Tincture	Orriis Root	4	oz.
"	Musk	2	oz.

Essence	Sandal	1	oz.
"	Bergamot	2	oz.
"	Lilac	4	oz.
"	Lavender	4	oz.
Flora	Jasmine	1	dr.
Otto	Keora	4	dr.

Procedure : As in Nizam Monte Cristo.

Lavenia

Spirit		24	oz.
Oil of	Lavender (Mitchams)	50	minims.
"	Orange	30	minims.
"	Neroli	30	minims.
"	Rosemary	1	dr.
"	Bergamot	1	dr.
Otto de	Rose	15	minims.
"	Keora	1	dr.
Essence	Amber	2	oz.
"	Cedrat	4	dr.
"	Narcissus	4	dr.
"	Jasmine	4	dr.

Procedure : As in Nizam Monta Cristo.

Jung Bahadur

Spirit		2	bottles
Heiko	Jasmine	4	dr.
Flora	Jasmine	4	dr.
Otto	Chameli	2	dr.
"	Keora	1	dr.
"	Sandal	1	dr.
"	Orange Flowers	1	dr.
"	Rose (Turkish)	1	dr.
Essence	Civet	2	oz.
"	Amber	1	oz.
"	Heliotrope	4	oz.
"	Rose Geranium	4	oz.

Procedure : As in Nizam Monte Cristo.

Jubilee Rajanigandha

Spirit		100	oz.
Heiko	Tuberose	2	oz.
Heiko	Pitunia	2	oz.
"	Hycynth	1	dr.
"	Oppoponex	1	dr.
Flora	Jasmine	1	oz.
"	Narcissus	30	minims.
Oil	Neroli	1	dr.
"	Bergamot	1	dr.
"	Lavender (English)	2	dr.
"	Sandal	1	dr.
Otto de Rose (Virgin)		1	dr.

Procedure : As a Nizem Monte Cristo. The Preparation is most pleasing.

Madhumati

Essence	Lilac	6	oz.
"	Canaga	6	oz.
"	Rose Geranium	8	oz.
"	Vanilla	2	oz.
"	Ambergris	2	oz.
"	Bergamot	4	oz.
"	Lavender	6	oz.
"	Sandal	3	oz.
Oil	Neroli	1	dr.
Otto de Rose		1	dr.

Procedure : The ingredients are put one by one in a bottle, themouth of which is then closed. Shake a bottle thrice daily, 10 minutes at a time, for fiteen days when the preparation will be ready for use.

Canaga Kusum

Spirit		1	bottle
Otto	Orange Flower	1	dr.
"	de Rose	30	minims.
"	Keora	1	dr.
Oil de	Rose Geranium	2	dr.
"	Lavender (English)	1	dr.
Essence	Sandal	1	oz.

"	Citron	1	oz.
"	Cassia	½	oz.
"	Amber	2	oz.

Procedure : Into the spirit contained in the bottle add the essential oils one by one, shake the bottle for 3 minutes each time. The bottle is then closed airtight and kept in a kool place for 15 days. Shake the bottle twice daily for 10 minutes every day for a fortnight. Finally filter the whole and phial in a stoppered vessel.

Marsenil

Alcohol		24	oz.
Extract	Rose or Istambal	1	dr.
Heiko	Rose	30	minims.
Otto	de Rose	30	minims.
"	Jasmine (or Heiko)	1	dr.
Flora	Jasmine	30	minims.
Heiko	Amber	1	dr.
"	Lily	1	dr.
Oil	Rose Geranium	1	dr.
Essence	Musk	1	oz.
"	Keora	1	oz.

Procedure : Take the alcohol in a big bottle and add the other ingredients one by one. The bottle should be shaken for 5 minutes after the addition of each of the ingredients. When all the ingredients are added into the alcohol, the bottle is stoppered air-tight and kept in that position for a fortnight. The bottle should, however, be shaken thrice daily, 10 minutes at a time. Finally the whole is filtered and phialed. The preparation is exquisite and the scent lasts for 7 days.

Lily Blossom

Spirit		48	oz.
Heiko	Lily of the Valley (New)	4	dr.
Heiko	Lily	2	dr.
"	Lime Blossom	2	dr.
Flora	Jasmine (or Heiko)	1	dr.
Otto	de Rose	30	mimims.
"	Khus	1	dr.
Oil	Neroli	1	dr.
"	Sandal	1	dr.

Essence	Amber	1	oz.
"	Civet	1	oz.
"	Musk	½	oz.

Procedure : As in Marsenil

Chandra Mallika

Alcohol		1	bottle
Heiko	Hyacynth	1	bottle
Heiko	Lily	1	dr.
"	Amber	1	dr.
"	Oppoponax	1	dr.
Otto	Keora	1	dr.
Heiko	Reseda	1	dr.
"	Pitunia	1	dr.

Procedure : As in Marsenil.

Cherry Laurel

Spirit		24	oz.
Oil	Cherry Laurel	4	dr.
Heiko	Amber	1	dr.
Otto	de Rose	15	minims.
"	Keora	1	dr.
Essence	Jasmine	1	oz.
"	Musk	1	oz.
"	Neroli	1	oz.
"	Bergamo	1	oz.

Procedure : Add into the spirit the other ingredients one by one, shaking the whole for 5 minutes after each such addition. Then keep the whole in a stoppered bottle for 10 days and shake in thrice daily for 4 minutes at a time during the period. Finally filter and phial.

Emperor

Spirit		48	oz.
Essence	Neroli	2	dr.
"	Amber	2	oz.
"	Musk	1	oz.
"	Violet	4	oz.
Oil	Lavender (English)	1	dr.
"	Primento	30	minims.

Oil	Coriander	30	minims.
Essence	Bergamot	4	oz.
"	Neroli	4	oz.
"	Jasmine	8	oz.
"	White Rsoe	6	oz.
Otto de Rose		1	dr.

Procedure : As in Cherry Laurel

Cashmere Bakul

Spirit		48	Oz.
Otto	Bakul (Country)	3	dr.
Flora	Narcissus	4	dr.
Heiko	Narcissus	2	dr.
"	Pitunia	2	dr.
"	Amber	1	dr.
Essence	Mimosa	1	oz.
"	White Rose	1	oz.
"	Jasmine	4	oz.
"	Sandal	1	oz.
"	Neroli	1	oz.

Procedure : As a Cherry Laurel.

Coronation

Alcohol		48	oz.
Otto	Nageswar	4	dr.
"	Chameli	1	dr.
"	Bela	1	dr.
"	Henna	1	dr.
"	Keora	2	dr.
Flora	Jasmine	1	dr.
Oil	Neroli	30	minims.
"	Bergamot	30	minims.
"	Sandal	40	minims.
"	Lavender	1	dr.
Otto de Rose		30	minims
Heiko	Lily of the Valley (New)	1	dr.
"	Amber	2	dr.

Procedure : As in Cherry Laurel.

Cherry Vanilla

Spirit		24	oz.
Heiko	Mellifluers	2	oz.
Tincture Vanilla		4	oz.
Oil	Cherry Laurel	1	dr.
Otto	Orange Flower	30	minims.
"	Rose Geranium (French)	4	dr.
Essence	Ambergris	1	oz.
"	Bergamot	2	oz.
Otto de Rose		30	minims.

Procedure : As in Cherry Laurel.

Prince Rose

Spirit		36	oz.
Pure	Musk	12	gr.
Extract	Rose or Istambal	90	gr.
Otto de	Rose	1	dr.
"	Jasmine	1	dr.
"	Orange Flower	30	minims
Essence Violet		4	oz.
"	Amber	4	oz.
Essence	Vanilla	1	oz.

Procedure : As in Cherry Laurel.

Bouqet Empress

Spirit		48	oz.
Oil of	Rose Geranium	4	dr.
"	Geranium	2	dr.
"	Neroli	1	dr.
"	Lemon	30	minims.
Oil of	Bergamot	30	minims
"	Sassafras	4	dr.
"	Lavender (Mitchams)	1	dr.
Heiko	Jasmine	30	minims.
"	Lily	2	dr.
"	Amber	2	dr.
"	Musk	1	dr.
Essence Vanilla		3	dr.
Oil	Hasu-no-Hena	4	dr.

Procedure : As in Cherry Laurel.

Durbar

Spirit	Cassia	4	oz.
"	Violet	8	oz.
Oil	Bergamot	4	dr.
"	Citron	1	oz.
Flora	Jasmine	4	dr.
Otto	Orange Flower	1	dr.
" de Rose		30	minims.
Essence	Amber	4	oz.
"	Rose Geranium	6	oz.
"	Lily of the Valley	8	oz.
"	Sandal	1	oz.
Oil	Lavender	30	minims.
Tincture Grass			to Colour

Procedure : The ingredients are mixed with shaking one by one. Keep Aside in a stoppered vessel for three days and during that period shake the vessel thrice daily for 5 minutes at a time. Finally filter and pack.

Viceroy Verbena

Spirit		72	oz.
Heiko	Verbena	1	oz.
Essence	Amber	3	oz.
"	Musk	1	oz.
Tincture Orris		2	oz.
Oil	Neroli	30	minims.
Otto de	Rose	1	dr.
"	Sandal	1	dr.
Flora	Jasmine	2	dr.
Oil	Lavender (Mitchams)	1	dr.

Procedure : As in Durbar.

Napoleon Lily

Spirit		24	oz.
Heiko	Lily	4	oz.
Essence	Amber	1	oz.
"	Tuberose	½	oz.
"	New-mown hay	½	oz.
Otto de	Rose	30	minims.

Heiko	Jasmine	1	dr.
"	Khus (or Otto)	30	minims
Otto	Sandal	30	minims.
"	Keora	30	minims.
Chypre			
Oil of	Rosemary	100	minims
"	Bitter Orange	½	oz.
"	Petit Grain	2	dr.
"	Bergamot	2½	dr.
"	Neroli	45	minims.
"	Alcohol	80	oz.

Procedure : Mix and after 4 days add 10 oz. of distilled water. Allow to stand for a fortnight and filter.

Heliotrope

Heliotropin		160	grains
Vanillin		24	grains
Coumarin		16	grains
Essence of Musk		160	minims.
Ylang Ylang Oil (Syn.)		60	minims.
Geraniol		32	minims.
Benzldehyde		8	minims.
Rectified Spirit		1	gallon
Essence Bouquet			
Oil of	Neroli	15	minims.
"	Lemon	1	dr.
"	Bergamot	½	dr.
Cassie	Extract	1	oz.
Essence of Ambergris		1	oz.
Tincture of Orris		1	oz.
Spirit of Rose		8	oz.
Alcohol		5	oz.
Lilac			
Terpineol		2	fl.oz.
Vanillin		40	grains
Jasmine Otto (Syn.)		2	fl.dr.
Geraniol		32	minims.
Palmarosa Oil		32	minims.
Rectified Spirit		1	gallon

Hyacinth

Hyacinthin	1	dr.
Oil of Neroli	10	drops
Essence of Musk	50	drops
Tincture of Benzoin	10	drops
Jasmine Extract	10	dr.
Orange Flower Water	5	dr.
Alcohol to make	10	oz.
Bridal Bouquet		
Oil of Sandal	½	dr.
Rose Extract	4	oz.
Jasmine Extract	4	oz.
Orange Flower Extract	16	oz.
Essence of Vanilla	1	oz.
Essence of Musk	2	oz.
Tincture of Storax	2	oz.
Oriental Bouquet		

I

Oil of Lavender	100	drops
Otto of Rose	1	dr.
Jasmine Extract	2½	oz.
Essence of Vanilla	2½	oz.
Alcohol of Produce	40	oz.

II

Heliotropin	15	grains
Coumarin	8	grains
Oil of Neroli	2	dr.
" Geranium	2½	dr.
Essential Oil of Almond	5	drops
Jasmine Extract	10	oz.
Alcohol	30	oz.
III		
Heliotrpin	60	grams
Terpineol	50	grams
Bergamot oil	30	grams
Phenyl acetaldehyde	24	grams
Syn. Musk	5	grams

Cananga Oil	5	grams
Alcohol	10	litres

IV

Terpineol	15	parts
Vanillin	1	parts
Musk Ambrette	1	part
Ylang Oil	1	part
Benzyl Acetate	2	parts
Linalol	1	part
Ionone	1	part
Cananga Oil	1	part
Infusion Ambrette Seeds, 20 per cent.	25	parts
Alcohol	1000	parts.

36

Preparation of Ottos

There is an air of freshness associated with the natural floral ottos rarely discernible even in the best of artificial. essences. Moreover, the scent of the former is of more permanent nature and not at all evanescent, like the latter. It is, therefore, quite natural that floral ottos find wide application in the indigenous art of perfumery in preference to others.

The reputation of Indian attars once spread beyond the boundaries of India. Place like Ghazipur, Jaunpur and Kanauj, the important centres of production, were well-known throughout the world. Unfortunately the attar industry to-day is in a deplorable condition. The decline may be attributed to development of wide range of synthetic perfumes in the West which are now being used in the production of toilet goods, soap, confectionery, etc., etc.

Ottos may be described as blends of flower oils' with sandalwood oil in varying proportions. The quality of the otto is in fact determined by the proportion of floral oil used in its preparation.

FLORAL OTTOS

The fundamental principle underlying the preparation of floral ottos is similar in every case while the basis of all of them is the same. Freshly bloomed flowers before their full expansion are selected as they are the most fragrant. They are stalked, removing the green calyxes and gently freed from dirt and dust without injuring the petals. Care should be exercised in this respect, otherwise the otto will be contaminated. They are steeped in water or sandal oil, heated on the water bath or warmed by the sun and finally filtered through a funnel. The filtered otto is collected in a stoppered phial and placed in the sun for a number of days to clarify. A sediment is allowed to form at the bottom so that the supernatant liquid gradually gets thin, limpid and clear.

ROSE

I. Procedure: Procure 4 oz. fresh rose petals all of one colour (say, crimson) and free them from dust, etc. Next take 16 oz. sandal oil in another vessel and heat on the water bath for half an hour. Take away, throw the petals into the oil, cover tip and set aside for one hour. Then squeeze out the oil from from the soaked petals and heat the oil again on the water bath for half an hour. Take away and soak in it 4 oz. fresh petals for an hour. Squeeze out the oil, and repeat the above process once again. Finally squeeze out the oil and store in a stoppered phial. Put in the sun for one month and it will be clear.

II. *Procedure:* Procure rose petals of one colour and layout 1h i inch thick in a vessel. Cover them with a clean piece of rag I moistened with sandal oil and folded 4 times. The cloth should J be thoroughly wetted by rasping. Layout over the rag another f lot of rose petals. Make up in this way sixteen layers. Then close I up the mouth of the vessel and place in the sun for 15 days. Finally press out the otto. Store in a stoppered phial and place in the sun for a month to clarify.

III. *Procedure:* The cleaned petals are placed in a clean vessel of glass, porcelain or earthenware, and covered up with pure water (rain or spring). Now place this vessel in some op~ space for a I week or so to be warmed by the sun. After 3 or 4 days an oily substance will float on the surface which will appear like a scum the next day. This is rose otto. These oily spots must be removed by sponging with a cotton swab and squeezed into a phial.

About two lakhs of roses are required to prepare 2 1h tolas of pure rose otto. But the ottos sold in the market are generally adulterated with sandal oil. The roses must be all of the same variety, otherwise the q\1ality of the product will suffer.

IV. *Procedure:* Take 8 ch. of petals of red roses of the same variety. After freeing them of dirt and dust put them into a wide-mouthed glass bottle. Put in 30 grains of benzoic acid and pour in 8 ch. of pure sandal oil. Stopper the bottle closely and place in the sun for three days. Then squeeze out the digested petals and throw in 8 ch. fresh rose petals. Stopper the bottle and place in the sun. Repeat the process six or seven times. A concentrated otto of excellent quality will thus be obtained.

BELA

Procedure: Take 8 ch. freshly bloomed double or single *Bela* flowers (Arabian jasmine); white chalk, 2 ch.; sandal oil, 1 seer. First powder the chalk and boil it in water on an earthenware vessel. Remove after one hour, strain away the water and dry the chalk powder thoroughly. Now place the flowers on a widemouthed porcelain jar; throw in the chalk powder and cover up the jar. After 3 days throw out the withered flowers. The powder should be gently sifted and put in a glass vessel. Now pour in the sandal oil and put in the sun daily for a fortnight. Finally filter through a piece of flannel and the filtrate will be a good otto.

The bela otto is produced from jasmine flowers of Moghra variety which are grown at Kanauj, Jaunpur, Ghazipur and Sikandarpur. The Moghra flower is a variety of jasmine but is quite different to the pure jasmine. It may be stated that the crop of the former variety is 10 times as large as that of true jasmine. The bela otto has aroma quite different from that of jasmine. An "absolute" may be obtained from the flowers by the enfleurage process.

CHAMELI

Procedure: Take 21h srs. stalked *Chameli* flowers Jasminum Grandiflorum. (Put into clean jar and strew) over them 15 grs. benzoic acid. Close up the mouth and set aside for 24 hours. Next day pour into it ,24 oz. sandal oil, close up the mouth and place in the sun for 20 days. Then filter through filter paper on a funnel, store in a stoppered phial and place it in the dew for one month.

JASMINE

The jasmine. otto is obtained from Jasminum Auricu1atum Vahl known as *juhi,* which flowers in April and again in July to October.

Procedure: Petals of Jasmine, 2 ch.; sandal oil 8 ch. The stalks of the flowers must be gently removed with the help of a piece of broken glass avoiding contamination by hand. Then place 1f.z ch. of petals on a glass vessel, cover up with a piece of fine linen (muslin); pour on it 2 ch. of sandal oil. Then place another layer of 1f.z ch. of petals arranged in 4 similar layers. Close up the vessel and set aside for 24 hours. Then strain out the spent flowers, reject them and repeat the above process with fresh flowers, but with the same oil for half a dozen times. Press out the oil and store in a stoppered phial. Place in the sun for one month to clarify. A good otto will be obtained.

It may be further pointed out that in preparing the cheaper varieties of the otto, 6 to 8 maunds of flowers is added to about 10 lbs. of sandalwood oil whilst the superior quality is produced by storing the otto of one season for 3 or 4 years during which period fresh jasmine extract is added to it every year.

MALLIKA

Procedure: Procure a quantity of freshly bloomed flowers Jasminwn Angustifolium) and layout a portion of it one inch thick in a spacious vessel. Spread over it some cleaned and beaten cotton, 1f.z inch thick, covering all sides. Layout on it another layer of flowers and form in this way 10 layers. Pour on the top 1 sr. sandal oil, cover up the mouth of the vessel and place in the sun for 20 days. After that pour out its contents on to a piece of flannel and squeeze out the oil. Store it in a stoppered phial and place in the sun to clarify.

MADHUMALATI

Procedure: Take 1f.z sr. *Madhumalati* flowers. Gently free them from dust. Put them in an aluminium vessel. Pour 1 sr. sandal oil into them and heat on the water bath for 15 minutes. After 24 hours wring out the flowers. Steep in the oil another lot of 1f.z sr. flowers and heat on the water bath for 15 minutes.

Repeat the process 12 times. Finally strain through a piece of flannel. Put in a stoppered phial and place in the sun to clarify. Finally filter.

HENNA

Procedure: Put 4 oz. *Henna* flowers into a wide-mouthed bottle; throw in 15 grs. benzoic add and pour in 20 oz. clear sandal oil. Place in the sun for 16 days. Then filter through filter paper fitted in a funnel. Put the filtered oil again in the bottle and soak a fresh lot of 6 oz. flowers. Close the mouth and set aside for one month. Finally filter through filter paper and store in a stoppered phial.

MUSK HENNA

Procedure: Take 8 oz. *Mehndi* flowers; 6 grs. musk; and 12 oz. sandal oil. First macerate the musk with a little sandal oil in a stone mortar. Dilute it with the remainder of the oil and put in wide-mouthed bottle. Throw in the flowers, shake well, close up the mouth and set aside for one month. Finally filter through a funnel and store in a stoppered phial.

CHAMPAKA

Procedure: Put 500 freshly bloomed *Champaka* flowers in a jar and strew over them 15 grs. benzoic add. Pour 24 oz. sandal oil into it, close up the mouth and place the phial in the sun and in the dew at night for one month. Finally filter through filter paper. Put in a stoppered phial and place in the sun for a fortnight to clarify.

KANTALI CHAMPAKA

Procedure: Procure 100 fresh and clean flowers and 1 sr. sandal oil. Put the two ingredients together in a vessel; close up the I mouth and heat on the water bath for half an hour. Take away and leave aside for 24 hours. Strain through a funnel and separate the flowers. Put the oil in the above vessel and soak in it a fresh lot of 100 flowers. Heat on the water bath for half an hour and set aside for 24 hours. Separate the flowers as before and put the oil in the vessel. Soak in it a fresh lot of 100 flowers, cover the mouth and place in the sun for 16 days and in dew at night. After that filter through filter paper and store up in a stoppered phial. Place in the sun for one month to clarify and finally store in a stoppered phial.

JAHURI CHAMPAKA

Procedure: Procure 400 freshly bloomed *Jahuri Champaka* flowers, reject the green stalks and put in a porcelain jar. Strew over them 15 grs. benzoic acid and pour in 24 oz. sandal oil.

Place in the sun for 15 days, and squeeze out the otto. Put in a stoppered phial and place in the sun and in dew at night for one month.

DOLAN CHAMPAKA

Procedure: Procure 2,000 stalked *Dolan Champaka* flowers. Take 10 srs. of clear water in a large earthen bowl. Dissolve in it 2 dr. saltpetre and stir briskly. Now throw the flowers into it, mix gently and place in an open space. After seven days a thin film will appear on the surface. Remove this carefully with a feather without disturbing. Put in a stoppered phial. When all the films are collected, close the mouth and place in the sun for a month and in the dew at night.

NAGESWAR CHAMPAKA

Procedure: Procure 1 sr. selected and clean *Nageswar* flowers and 1 sr. sandal oil. Put the two ingredients together in a vessel, close up the mouth and heat on the water bath for half an hour. Take away, leave aside for 24 hours and press out the oil. Put the oil again into the vessel and soak in it 1 sr. picked flowers. Heat on the water bath for half an hour and then leave aside for 15 days in a cool place. Then press out the oil and store in a stoppered phial. Place in the sun and in dew at night for a mon6 to clarify.

BAKUL

Procedure: Procure 5 srs. of picked *Bakul* flowers. Dirt and dust should be gently removed, otherwise the final product will be spoilt. Put the flowers in a glass, stone or earthenware vessel and fill up with 16 srs. of clean water. Dissolve 4 dr. salt in the water previously. Place the vessel in the sun continuously for 8 or 10 days in a place open to the sky. On the 4th. or 5th day a thin oily film will appear on the surface; it will form into scum in a day or two. Carefully take this away with a feather or a cotton swab and put in a glass phial. Remove it as often as it forms. When all the scum is thus cleared, place the phial in the sun to clarify. Add 8 oz. sandal oil to 4 dr. extract.

GANDHARAJ

Prl'cedure: Procure 5 srs. fresh *Gandharaj* flowers free from dirt and reject the stalks and green parts. Lay out ½ sr. of flowers at the bottom of a porcelain jar, strew over it 1 oz. magnesium carbonate. Spread out on it another layer of 1h sr. flowers at the bottom of a porcelain jar, strew over it 1 oz. magnesium c~rbonate. Spread out on it another layer of 1h sr. flowers and strew over it 1 oz. magnesium carbonate. In this way make up 10 layers. Close up the mouth of the vessel and place in the sun and in dew at night for a fortnight. Now separate the flowers after dripping and pour into the residue of the jar 1h sr. sandal oil. Place the vessel in the sun for 15 days and finally filter through filter paper. Place in the sun for a month to clarify.

HASU-NO-HENNA

Procedure: Pick bunches of *Hasu-no-henna* flowers just at dusk weighing 5 srs. Layout 1 sr. at the bottom of a vessel and spread over it a piece of clean rag covering all sides. Layout on it another layer of 1 sr. flowers and form in this way 5 layers with rags intervening. Finally cover up with rag and pour 20 oz. pure sandal oil. Cover up the mouth and place in the sun for 20 days. Press out the oil and store in a stoppered phial. Place in the sun for a month to clarify.

PATCHOULI

Procedure: Take 21h srs. of *Patchouli* leaves; pick, dust and clean, and pound them into fine powder. Then layout 1h sr. of the powder at the bottom of a vessel and spread on it a piece of cotton cloth. Layout on it another layer of 1h sr. powder. In this way form 5 layers covering the last one with cotton cloth. Pour on the top 1 sr. sandal oil, close up the mouth of the vessel and place in the sun for a month and in dew at night. After that press out the oil and store in a stoppered phial. Finally place in the sun for 1 month to clarify.

TUBEROSE

Procedure: Take 1 sr. fresh *Tuberose,* put them in a vessel together with 1 sr. sandal oil, close up the mouth and heat on the water bath for 20 minutes. Leave aside for 12 hours. Then squeeze out the oil and put the oil again into the vessel. Soak a fresh lot of 1 sr. flowers and repeat the process for seven times. Finally press out the oil and store up in a stoppered phial. Place in the sun for a month and in dew at night to clarify.

KEORA

Procedure: Take half seer pollen of *Keora,* one seer tender leaves of the plant finely minced and 1 sr. good sandal oil. Put these three ingredients mixed together in a porcelain jar and close up the mouth tightly. Place in the sun for a month and then press out the oil. Store in a stoppered phial and place in the sun for a month to clarify.

KAMINI

Procedure: Take 1 sr. *Kamini* flowers free from stalk, put in an aluminium vessel, pour into it 1 sr. sandal oil, close up the mouth and heat on the water bath for half an hour. Set aside for 24 hours and then sequeeze out the otto. Put it again into the vessel and soak in it a fresh lot of Vz sr. flowers, and repeat the process twice. Finally press out the oil and store in a stoppered phial.

KHUS

Procedure: Procure 10 srs. of *Khus* root; free them from dirt and cleanly wash in water. Dry them in the sun and pound into fine powder. Put the powder in a retort, pour 30 srs. clear water, close up the mouth and apply heat. When half the water has boiled over, remove it from fire. Now collect otto from the distillate.

According to a more convenient method boil down 30 srs. of water until 10 srs. have evaporated. Put the pounded *Khus* roots in an,earthen vessel and pour the boiled water over them. Leave it in an open space. After 7 or 8 days a scum will arise on the surface. Soak the froth with cotton and put in a stoppered phial. Place it for a month in the sun and in dew at night to clarify. Finally pack in stoppered phials.

JANTI

Procedure: Take half seer of stalked *Janti* flowers and put in a wide-mouthed bottle. Pour into it 2 srs. good sandal oil. Close the mouth and place in the sun and in dew for 24 hours. Then squeeze the soaked flowers and immerse in the oil a fresh lot of half seer flowers. Close the mouth and place in the sun and in dew for 24 hours. Repeat the process for 16 times replacing the soaked flowers by fresh ones. Finally press.

PUMELO

Procedure: Take 3 srs. of *Pumelo* flowers free from stalks, put them in a wide-mouthed bottle. Pour into it 1h sr. sandal oil, close up the mouth and place for a month in the sun and in dew at night. Press out the oil, store in a stoppered phial and place in the sun for a month to clarify. The flowers must be freshly blown and not in bud.

SHEPHALICA

Procedure: Take 4 ch. stalked *Shephalica* flowers, put in a vessel and pour over them half seer sandal oil. Cover up and set aside for 24 hours. Filter through a funnel. Put the otto again into the vessel and soak into it a fresh lot of 2 ch. flowers. Repeat the process 10 times. Thereby a concentrated otto will be obtained. Finally clarify by placing for one month in the sun and in dew at night.

SANDALWOOD

Procedure: A large globular clay pot, with a circular mouth, about 21h feet deep by about 6 feet circumference at the bulge is taken. The mouth of the pot is closed with a clay lid having a small hole in its centre, through which a bent copper tube about 51h feet long is passed for the escape of the vapour. The lower end of the tube is conveyed inside a copper receiver, placed in a large porous vessel containing cold water; For preparation of the sandalwood oil, the white or sapwood is rejected, and the heart-wood is cut into small chips, of which about 25 seers-or 50 lbs. are put into the pot. As much water is then added as will just cover the chips, and the distillation is carried on slowly for 10 days and nights, by which time the whole of the oil is extracted. As the water from time to time gets low in the still, fresh supplies are added from the heated contents of the refrigerator. The yield of the oil by the above process is said to average 2.5 per cent.

II. *Procedure:* Reduce the sandalwood to fine powder by filing, and soak the powder in water for 48 hours, before placing it in a copper still tinned inside. Change the receivers directly they are full, return the watery layer of the distillate at certain intervals to the still, and continue the distillation for about a week day and -night, maintaining a uniform heat and observing the utmost cleanliness. The above method of distillation requires a high consumption of fuel.

The modern method of distillation would not only reduce the cost of production but also increase the percentage of yield of the oil. The plant required has to be of special design consisting of the following:

1. A rasping machine, with which to comminute the sandal wood into fine filing.
2. An efficient form of steam still complete with tubular condenser, Florentine flasks, etc.
3. A small copper still for re-distillation of the oil. 4. A boiler capable of generating super-heated steam.

ARTIFICIAL OTTOS

Ottos are being gradually replaced by cheap foreign synthetic perfumes. Some otto manufacturers have resorted to the practice of adding aromatic chemicals to their blends with a view to cheapen the cost to enable them to compete with the perfume compounds from Europe. It is evident that the taste in India is being more and more influenced by Western blends.

Artificial ottos are prepared from artificial sources, mainly from heiko scents. A typical recipe follows:

To prepare Otto *Bela* take Heiko *Bela* 2 oz. and Sandal Oil 8 oz. Mix together and keep aside for 15 days.

MARKETING

The otto preparations should be perfectly clear and free from turbidity. The phials should be perfectly dried before the ottos are poured into them as the presence of moisture tends to separate the aromatics.

The glass phials must have ground glass stoppers in place of cork stoppers which due to the presence of cork impart a peculiar odour. To exclude air the stoppers are covered down to the bottle necks with capsules of animal membrane.

37

Rose and Keora Water

ROSE WATER AND OTTO

The rose principally cultivated in this country for the manufacture of rose water is the Damask Rose (Rose Damascena), otherwise known as Bashra or Persian Rose.

The flowers are plucked early in the morning and conveyed in large bags to the distillers. The apparatus for distilling is of the simplest description; it consists of a large copper or iron boiler, well tinned, capable of holding from 8 to 12 gallons with a large body, a rather narrow neck, and a mouth about 8 inches in diameter, on the top of which is fixed the head of the still. This is merely a *dekchi* with a hole in the bottom to receive the tube of water which is well luted with flour and water. This tube is composed of two pieces of bamboo fastened together at an acute angle and covered in their whole length with a coating of string, over which mud is luted to prevent the vapour from escaping. The lower end of the tube is carried down into a longnecked vessel or receiver, called a *bhubka.* This is kept in a *handi* of water, which as it gets hot is changed. The end of the tube in the *bhubka* is padded with cloth to keep in the vapour. The boiler is let into an earthen furnace, and after being charged with the roses and a sufficient quantity of water, distillation is slowly proceeded with. A boiler of the size described will hold about 10,000 roses; about 10 seers of water will be poured on these flowers, and 8 seers of rose water will be obtained. After distillation, the rose water is placed in ,a glass carboy and exposed to the sun for several days to become ripe, after which the mouth is stoppered with cotton over which a covering of moist clay is put to prevent the scent from escaping.

To procure the attar, after the rose-water has been distilled, it is placed in a large metal basin which is covered with wetted muslin to prevent dust and insects from getting in; this vessel is then let into the ground which has been previously wetted with water and allowed to remain there during the whole night. While it cools a little film of *attar* forms on the surface of the rose water which is removed in the morning by means of a feather and placed in a small phial, and day after day, as the collection is made, it is placed for a short time in the sun, and after a sufficient quantity has been procured, it is poured off clear into small phials. The first few days' distillation does not produce such fine *attar* as is obtained afterwards, since it is mixed with dust and particles of dirt from the still. It has been calculated that one tola of *attar* is produced from one lakh of roses approximately. More, however, may be obtained if the roses are full-sized and the nights cool enough to allow of the coagulation.

The rose water should always be distilled twice, the water procured from the first distillation being used to pour over the roses for the second one.

Distillation may however be dispensed with in preparing rose water as the following recipes will show:

I

Rose	5	seers
Clear Water	10	seers

Procedure: First put the cleaned rose petals in an earthen vessel. Next heat the water in another earthenware vessel. Then pour the boiling water on to the petals and close up the containing vessel so that air is excluded. Strain after one hour and the filtrate will be good rose water to serve all purposes.

II

Rose Petals	5	seers
Water	10	seers

Procedure: Put in an earthenware vessel; close the mouth with a plate luted with mud. Apply gentle heat for 3 hours and allow to cool. Strain when cold and the filtrate will be good rose water.

III

Rose Oil	2.5	grams
Clove Oil	0.25	gram

Alcohol to make	100	C.c.
Distilled Water	10,000	C.c.

Procedure: Mix the first two ingredients and add alcohol to make 100 C.c. Now mix the spirituous liquid with 10,000 C.c. of boiling distilled water and allow to stand until it has undergone the viscous fermentation. and blend producing a stuff superior to most of the commercial rose water.

The above recipe obviates the necessity of distilling rose petals and yields rose water of satisfactory quality on simply mixing the ingredients mentioned in the recipe.

KEORA WATER

I

Keora flower	100	seers
Water	1	maund

Procedure: Select only the white petals rejecting the green leaves and the pollen. Proceed to distillation as in the case of rose water (page 101). The distiller is a tinned copper or iron boiler having a capacity of 8 to 12 gallons. The boiler is let into an earthen furnace, and charged with Keora flowers and a sufficient quantity of water. Temperature is not allowed to go high and distillation is carried on slowly. After distillation the Keora water is kept for 7 days in sunlight to mature.

II

Keora flower	50	seers
Water	10	seers

Procedure: Select only the white petals, over which pour 10 seers of boiling water and close up the containing vessel so that air is excluded. Set aside for 24 hours. Strain and phial.

III

Keora flower	50	seers
Water	10	seers

Procedure: Put the water in an earthenware vessel and throw in the white petals of Keora. Place the whole in the sun for a week and strain. The filtrate will be good Keora water.

38

Toilet Waters

Lavender Water

I

Essential Oil of English Lavender (Burgoyne)	4	oz.
Otto de Rose (Virgin)	2	dr.
Rectified Spirit	4	bottles

Prodcedure : Mix together and use after three months

II

Oil Lavender (Herrings)	3	oz.
Rectified Spirit	3	bottles
Tincture Orris	4	oz.
Otto de Rose	1	dr.

Procedure : Mix together and use after one month.

III

Oil Lavender (Grease, France)	1	oz
Essence Ambergris	4	oz.
Eau de Cologne	80	oz.
Rectified spirit	4	oz.

Procedure : Mix together and use after one month.

IV.

Oil of Lavende (English)	4	dr.
Essence of Bergamot	20	minims.

Essence Lemon (or Civet)	20	minims.
Otto de Rose	20	minims.
Essence Ambergris	1	dr.
Rectified Spirit	3	pints
Orange Flower Water	4	oz.
Rose Water	12.	oz.
Burnt Alum	20	gr.

Procedure : Shake several times and store away in a cool place. Finally strain through filter paper and phial.

V

Oil Lavender (Burgoyne)	3	dr.
Oil Bergamot	3	dr.
Otto de Rose	5	minims.
Oil Cloves	6	minims
Musk	2	gr.
Oil of Rosemary (true)	1	dr.
Honey	1	oz.
Benzoic Acid	2	scruples
Rectified spirit	1	pint
Distilled water	3	oz.

Procedure : Mix togetehr and allow to mature for 6 months

VI

Oil of Lavender (Mitchams)	3	dr.
Oil Bergamot	20	minims.
Oil Neroli	6	minims.
Otto de Rose	6 or 12	minims.
Essence of Civet	8 or 10	minms.
Essence Muskc	20	minims.
Rectified Spirit	20	oz.
Orange Flower water	4	oz.

Procedure : Mix together and shake for several times. Store away in a cool place for 3 months. Strain and use.

Amber Lavender

Oil of Lavender (Eng.)	1	oz.
Essence Amber	6	oz.
Rectified spirit	1	bottle

Procedure : Mix and use afer 1 month.

Lily Lavender

Lily lavender, petunia lavender etc., maybe prepared in the same manner by replacing essence amber by essence lily, petunia, etc.

Enlish Lavender Water

Oil of Lavender (Mitchams)	4	oz.
Rose Water	1	bottle
Magnesium Carbonate		q.s.
Alcohol	3	bottles

Procedure : First macerate the oil of lavender with such a quantity of magnesium carbonate in a stone mortar that the whole mixture is converted into a powdery mass. Now pour the rose water and incorporate the powder well into it. Then strain into a glass jar and add alcohol. Store aside for six months.

Ambergis Lavender Water

Oil Lavender(Mitchams)	8	oz.
Essence Musk	4	oz.
" Ambergris	1½	oz.
Oil Bergamot	1½	oz.
Rectified Spirit	2	gallons

Procedure : This will yield an excellent Lavender water. To be kept for 3 months to mature.

Eau De Lavender Millefleurs

Oil Lavender (English)	2	oz.
Essence of Bergamot	1	dr.
" Lemon	1	dr.
Otto de Rose	1	dr.
Essence of Millefleurs	1½	oz.
" Ambergris	4	dr.
Rectified Spirit	6	pints

Procedure : Mix and use after 6 months when the water fully matues.

Odoriferous Lavender Water

I

Oil Lavender (Mitchams)	20	oz.
Oil Bergamot (Burgoyne)	5	oz.

Essence Ambergris	4	dr.
Orris Root Poweder	4	oz.
Rectified Spirit	5	gallons

Procedure : Mix together and strain after one month.

II

Alcohol	3750	c.c.
Oil of Lavender	100	grams
Oil of Thyme	10	grams
Tincture of Musk	10	grams
Distilled Water	500	c.c.

Procedure : Dissolve the essential oils in the alcohol and then the musk. Lastly, pour the distilled water. Seal the mouth of the jar or bottle and allow to mature for a month before use.

Florica Water

Oil of Lavender	½	oz.
" Bergamot	1	oz.
" Cassia	1	dr.
" Clove	½	dr.
" Neroli	½	dr.
Essence of Musk	½	oz.
Alcohol	64	oz.
Cinnamon water to make	80	oz.

Mix in the above order.

Violet Water

Oil of Sandal	4	dr.
" Bergamot	4	dr.
" Rose Geranium	1	dr.
" Neroli	1	dr.
" Bitter Almonds	15	drops
Musk	1	gr.
Tincture of Benzoin	4	dr.
Powdered Orris Root	2	dr.
Water	60	oz.
Alcohol	100	oz.

Macerate 30 days and filter. The produce is coloured with just a trace of green dye.

Eau De Cologne

I

Oil	Bergamot	1	oz.
"	Lemon	½	oz.
"	Rosemary	2	dr.
"	Neroli	30	minims.
"	Lavender	4	dr.
"	Orange	2	dr.
Rectified Spirit		2	lbs.

Procedure : The ingredients are mixed with brisk shaking one by one. Set the whole aside in a stoppered vessel for a fortnight and during that period shake the vessel thrice daily at a time. Finally filter and pack.

II

Cardamom minor (seeds)		1	tola
Oil	Neroli	14	minims.
"	Citron	14	minims.
"	Bergamot	14	minims.
"	Rosemary	14	minims.
Spirit		1	bottle

Procedure : Proceed as in I.

III

Otto of Orange Flower		1	dr.
Oil	Orange	1	oz.
"	Lemon	1	oz.
Essence Cedrat		4	dr.
Oil	Rosemary	4	dr.
"	Lavender	2	dr.
Spirit		1	bottle

Procedure : Proceed as in I.

IV

Oil	Neroli	30	minims.
"	Orange	1	dr.
Oil	Lemon	1	dr.
Oil	Rosemary	30	minims
Essence Bergamot		4	dr.
Spirit		20	oz.

Procedure : Proceed as in I.

V

Oil	Neroli	2½	dr.
"	Lavender	30	minims
"	Orange	50	minims
"	Rosemary	40	minims
"	Lemon	4	dr.
"	Bergamot	1	dr.
Spirit		1	bottle

Procedure : Proceed as in I.

39

Technology of Flavours

Inroduction

The appreciation of flavour is a universal everyday experience and is the integrated response to a complex mixture of stimuli primarily on the senses of smell and taste but also on those associated with sight (color and appearance), tactile sensations (texture and mouth-feel) and pain (pungency). As a consequence, flavour chemistry in its broadest context is a specialized branch of organic chemistry that impinges on many other disciplines, including botany, zoology anatomy, physiology, cytology, etc., for its complete understanding.

Flavour chemistry is here taken to mean the identification and chemical nature of components responsible for the odor and flavour of natural products of plant and animal origin, and the objective study of their biogenesis, biosynthesis and deterioration. It is obviously not feasible in this context to discuss the whole scope of organic chemical reaction involved in the synthesis of odorants and flavourants in this laboratory or commercially. Every year, there are literally hundreds of aromatic chemicals synthesized, either as end products or as intermediates (nearly 6,000 compounds have been identified to date). While most of these are identical to those found in nature, others have no such counterparts. The majority of such synthetics never achieve any commercial importance, but a few do reach full manufacturing scale; they find application in flavourings and fragrances once their safety in use is established. The chemistry of synthetic aromatic chemicals in well described in the literature.

For the flavourist and anyone associated with flavour applications, knowledge of the sensory mechanisms by which these substances are perceived and recognized is very desirable. This too, a very specialized field of physiology, and structural chemistry. However, this subject is beyond the scope of this book and the reader should consult the review by Thompson or one of the more detailed references contained therein. The problems associated with sensory assessment, agreement on test methods and the means of communicating sensory responses and data will be discussed in a later chapter.

Whether naturally occurring, induced by processing or cooking or intentionally added, flavour in food and related consumables is due to chemicals embracing some inorganic of alphatic and aromatic organic chemicals. Taste (e.g., sweetness bitterness etc.) and certain other attributes (e. g., punegency astringency, etc.) are due to nonvolatile components. The odor of foodstuffs is the predominant contributor to their distinctive and often diagnostic flavour profile. Hence a study of the volatile components is of relatively greater importance to the flavour chemist and to the flavourist aiming to match or reconstruct a given natural profile than is taste. In the case of fruits flavours, however, the acid/sugar ratio can significantly alter the appreciation of the aromatic impact.

The technical literature contains an ever increasing number of articles and research papers on the biochemistry of natural products. Most of these studies are qualitative and contain long lists of components that have been isolated and identified. After having ignored the sensory properties of these compounds for years, we are seeing more emphasis put upon determining the sensory contribution of the flavour compounds identified.

Flavour Classification

Flavours may be classified in many ways, but from the point of view of their chemistry, the most realistic classification is that based on their mode of formation, either naturally by biosynthetic pathways from known precursors, or by processing in which biological, chemical or physical conditions are imposed on natural flavours are mostly metabolites so that their formation in living tissues is complex and dependent on genetic factors and is influenced by by environmental conditions during the natural growth cycle. Flavours products depending on the starting materials and the processing conditions imposed.

In this section, the chemistry of odor and taste- stimulating components will be dicussed in the following group:

a. The biochemistry of volatile and nonvolatile constituents that are formed during normal plan metabolism and remain in situ when the plant is harvested (e. g., essential oils, fruit and vegetable flavours).

b. Flavouring components resulting from enzyme-catalyzed reactions (e.g., enzyme-modified dairy products).

c. Flavouring constituents produced as a result of microbiological action and fermentation (e. g., wines, dairy products tea).

d. Flavours resulting from heat processing or cooking (e.g., cooked meat flavours, roasted coffee).

A basic knowledge of organic chemistry is assumed, and the aim here is to present an outline of the more important aspects of current knowledge and indication of present progress, rather than an in-depth review of the literature on the subject, leaving the reader to pursue specific topics by reference to the bibliography.

Flavour Formation in Plants

Knowledge of precursors and pathways leading to the formation of flavour in fruits and lacking in many areas. Emphasis has been placed on determining what constitutes flavour rather than on the mechanisms of flavour formation, and the task of elucidating metabolic pathways in very complex biological systems is difficult at best. Other than academic interest, there is little incentive to determine metabolic pathways leading to flavour formation. However, there is a strong interest in determining what chemicals make up a flavour since this knowledge could be used to study the appearance of an off-flavour, produce an artificial substitute, estabished nature identical status or determine species flavour differences. The result is rather long lists of flavour chemist found in each plant, but little understanding of how or why they are there.

In this chapter we examine some of the known mechanisms of flavour formation in fruit and vegetables. This discussion is generally limited to the formation of volatile flavours or aroma and excludes the taste sensations.

Biogenesis of Fruits Aroma

The typical flavour of fruit such as bananas peaches, pears, and cherries is not present during early fruit formation, but develops entirely during a rather brief ripening period. This flavour development period, or ripening, occurs during the climacteric rise in respiration. During this period, metabolism of the fruit changes to catabolism and flavour formation begins, Munute quantities of lipids, carbohydrate, protein, and amino acides are enzymatically converted to volatile flavours. The rate of flavour formation reaches a maximum during the postclimacteric ripening phase.

An overall view of flavour formation during ripening of fruit is show in Fig 39.1. Flavours are formed from major plant consituents (e.g.,

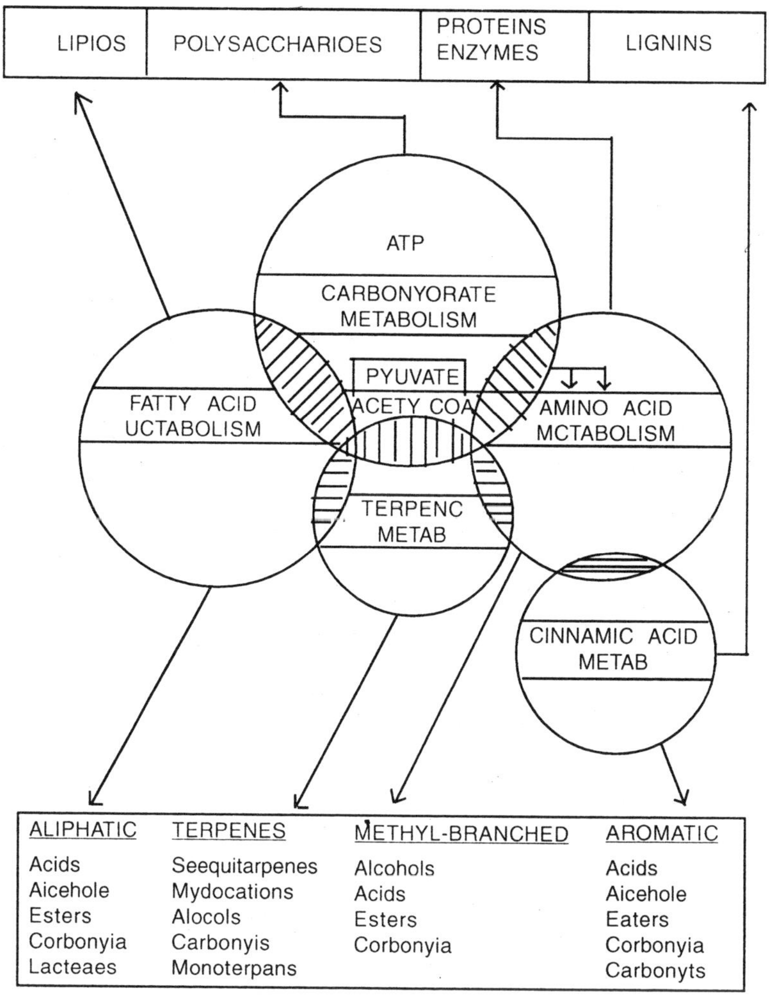

Fig. 39.1 : Biosynthesis of fruit volatiles.

Table - 39.1

Predominant Human Nutrients in Production of Aroma Components in Foods

Nutrient	*Aroma Component*
Carbohydrates	
Glucose	Organic acids:
Fructose	Pyruvic acid, acetic acid, propionic acid, acetoacetic acid,
Sucrose	Esters:
	Pyruvates, acetates, propionates, butyrates, acetonacetates, hexanoates, octanoates
	Alcohols:
	Ethanol, propanol, butanol, hexanol, octanol
	Aldegydes:
	Acetadehyde, propanal, butanal, hexanal, octanal
	Terpenes:
	Monoterpene, linalool, limonene, α-pinene, citronellal, citral, geranial
Amino acids	
Alanine	Pyruvic acid, acetaldehyde, ethanol
Valine	Isopropanal, isopropanol, α-keto-isobutyric acid
Leucine	3-Methylbutanal, 3-methylbutanol, α-keto-isocapproic acid
Isoleucine	2-Methylbutanal, 2-methylbutanol
Phenylalanine	Benzaldehyde, phenylacetaldehyde, cinnamaldehyde
	Hydrocinnamaldehyde, *p*-hydroxy cinnamaldehyde,
	p-Hydroxy phenylacetaldehyde,
	p-hydroxy cinnamaldehyde
Serine	
Threonine	Pyruvic acid
Glycine	Thiazoles
Cystine/cysteine	Glyoxal
Serine	
Fatty acids	
Linoleic acid	trans-2trans-4-Decadienal, hexanal, trans-2-octenal
	trans-2-Pentanal, trans 2-hexenol, hexanal
	cis-3-Hexenal, cis-3-hexenol
	trans-2trans-4-Heptadienal, propanal
Organic acids	
Citric acid	
Oxaloacetic acid	Glyoxylic acid, glyoxal, pyruvic acid, acetaldehyde
Malic acid	Ethanol
Lactic acid	
Vitamins	
Carotenoids	
β-Carotene	β-Ionone

[a] From Salunkhe and Do.

cabohydrates, lipids and protein) under genetic control. Each metabolic pathways is connected to other metabolic pathway. As direct products of a metabolic pathway or as result of interaction between pathways or end products, a host of volatile flavours are produced that contribute to the flavour of a ripe fruit. Table 39.1 present typical flavour compounds which are formed from each major food constituent.

Flavours from Fatty Acid Metabolism

Volatile flavour compounds may be formed from lipids via several different pathways. They involve hydroxyacid and lipoxygenase catalyzed oxidation. While the primary products of these pathways are aldehydes and ketons, additional oxidatation also yield substantial quantities of acid, alcohols, lactones and esters.

In growing fruit, metabolic pathways exist to synthesize a variety of fatty acids, which are then incorporated into triglycerides and other lipids. However, once ripening commences, these metabolic pathways function as deterioration mechanisms and break these lipids down to flavourful compounds. The formation of flavours via this mechanism is exemplified by considering flavour formation in pears. The decadienoate esters are generally considered carries of the flavour of pear. These esters are believed to be formed via β-oxidation of linoleic acid (see Fig. 39.2). Linoleic acid is metabolized, two carbons at a time, to shorter chain CoA derivatives which may react with alcohols to yield esters. During this process isomerization may occur to yield the trans-cis isomers. It is interesting that the β-oxidation pathway can account for all the of the volatile that have been identified in pear.

Further enzyme-catalyzed reactions will occur, such as additional oxidation or esterification. Tressi and Drawert have demonstrated the conversion of labeled acetate to acetate esters and labeled butanoate to butanoate esters by postclimacteric banana slices. They have further shown the conversion of hexanotic acid to hexnol by these tissues.

The production of lacones presents a second means of obtaining flavour from lipid sources. Lectones are very important to the flavour of peaches, apricots and coconuts. Numerous investigators have proposed oxidative pathways that would result in lactone formation. A major pathway involves lipoxygenase action on linolenic accid. There is little information on the formation of lactones by mechanisms other than oxidative degradation. Tang and Jennings did propose that lactones could be formed during fatty acid synthesis. Their proposal involved hydration of ϒ–δ double bond to yeild the corresponding lactone. They conceded that there is no known mechanism

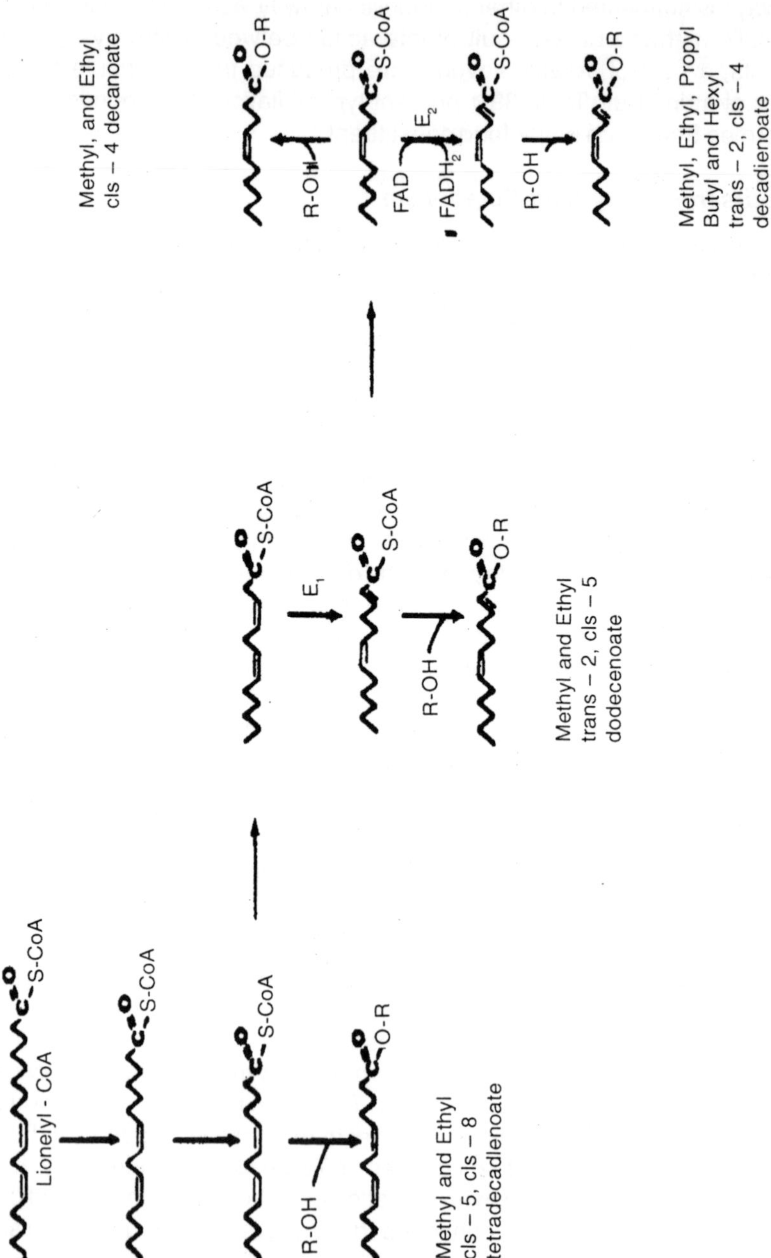

Fig. 39.2 : Proposed pathway for the production of unsaturated esters in pears.

to place a double bond in the $\gamma-\delta$ position, but suggested a double bond shift (from $\beta-\gamma$ position) followed by hydration.

The widest variety of flavour compounds formed from lipids arises via lipoxygenase activity. Many of the aliphatic esters, alcohols, acids and carbonyls found and fruit are deprived from the oxidative degradation of linolenic acids as well as subsequent interaction and degradation. While an overview of this process will be presented here, the reader is encouraged to consult the more detailed review by Gardner and Schreier.

The initial step in flavour formation is lipase action to liberate free fatty acids. Lipoxygenase enzymes can then attack the free fatty acids (linoleic and linolenic acids) to yield various hydroperoxides. Enzyme systems (hydroperoxides lyases) act on these hydroperoxides to produce flavour compounds. All of these enzyme systems act in a stereospecific manner, thus yielding flavour compounds with definite chiral form . This defined chirality differentiates flavour compounds of natural origin from those sysnthesized chemically (This is a significant both in terms of sensory properties and the determination of natural/artificial status). Further oxidation and interaction yield a large number of flavour compounds.

Flavours from Amino Acid Metabolism

Amino acid metabolism generates aliphatic and branched chain alcohols, acids, carbonyls and esters, which are important to the flavour of fruit. Yu Olson and Salunkhe demonstrated that valine, leucine, alanine and aspartic acid could be converted to short chain carbonyls by tomato extracts. The enzymes involved in these transformations were found to be located in different sites in tomato. The soluble tomato fraction isolated via centrifugation acted on leucine while the mitochondrial fraction metabolized both alanine and aspartic acid. The activities of these enzymes were substantially higher in field-grown vs. hothouse tomatoes. This undoubtedly accounts for some of the flavour differences between hothouse and field-grown tomatoes.

Studies on banana tissue slices have shown that lecine and valine concentration increase about threefold following the climacteric rise in respiration. Radioactive labeling studies have shown that these two amino acids are transformed into branched chain flavour compounds, which are essential to banana flavour. As can be seen in Fig. 39.3 the initial step is deamination of the amino acid followed by decarboxylation. Various reductions and estedrification then lead to a number of volatiles which are significant to fruit flavour.

Aromatic amino acids also may serve as important precursors to fruits flavour. Some of the aromatic flavour compounds have been shown to come from fyrosine and phenylalanine (Fig. 39.4). Odors characterized as "phenolic" or "spicy" could arise via this pathways.

Flavours Formed from Carbohydrate Metabolism

Returning briefly to Table 39.1, one can see that a large variety of volatile flavours can be traced to carbohydrate metabolism. If one considers plant metabolism, it is clearly established that plants obtain all of their energy directly from photosynthesis. The photosynthetic pathways involve turning CO_2 into sugars that are metabolized into other plant needs, e.g., lipids and amino acids. Therefore, one may state that nearly all plant flavours come since of the other flavour precursors come from carbohydrate metabolism. However, there are few flavour constituents that directly from carbohydrate metabolism.

An exception are the terpenes, which may arise from either carbohyrate or lipid metabolism. Citrus products obtain their characterstics flavour from terpenes. Limonene, a monoterpene hydrocarbon possessing little odor is the major terpene in most citrus oils. The oxygenated terpenes, often comprising less than 5 per cent of the oil, generally provide the characteristic flavour of different citrus species. For example, citrus is considered the flavour impact component of lemon oil, yet it is unusual to find more than 2 per cent citrus in a single fold oil.

Terpene formation (Fig. 39.5) is known to involve the condensation of two molecules of isoprene (isoprene being synthesized from acetate via mevalonic acid) to form the beckbone of the monoterpenes. The following step is cyclization to close the ring and then rearrangement to create the host of terpense found in nature.

The interconversion of terpenes can occur via several pathways. The conversion of neryl pyrophosphate and linaloyl pyrophosphate to terpinolene, α-terpineol and limonene is shown in Fig. 39.5. Additional terpene conversions have been traced to oxidoreductase systems in citrus fruits.Figure 39.5 also shows the interconversions of geraniol, geranial, citronellol and citronellal. Enzyme systems capable of oxidation/reduction reactions could account for a host of terpenes in citrus products.

The peel of citrus fruits contains a large number of flavone glycosides, some of which are bitter. Bitter compounds in citrus, particularly grapefruit,

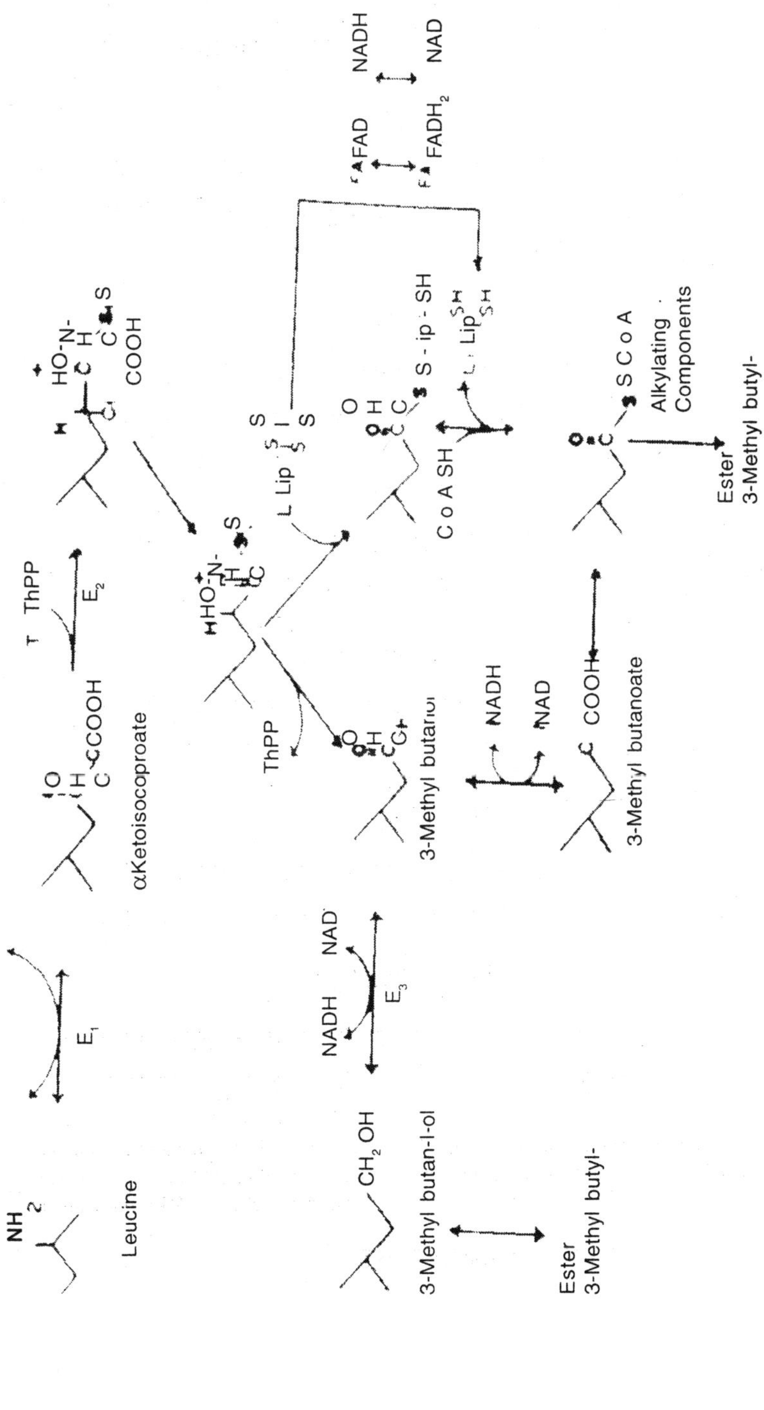

Fig. 39.3 : Conversion of amino acids into aroma components of banana

have been the subject of considerable study since these components limit consumer acceptance. There has been an additional interest in glycosides of flavour compounds for a long time, since some flavour compounds such as benzaldehyde (in bitter almond) and methyl salicylate (sweet birch) are unavilable for recovery via distillation until the starting plant material has been fermented to free the flavouring compounds from their respective glycosides.

Recently, there has been an expanded interest in glycosides, since researchers are finding that a significant amount of flavour compounds in other plant materials may be bound to glycosides and be unavailable for flavouring. Fruits, such as pineapple (Ho et al.), mango (Salles et al.), passion fruit (Engel and Tressl), (Winterhalter), papaya, graps, apricot, and vanilla beans have been shown to contain significant quantities of glycosidically bound flavour constituents. These constituents are generally phenolic or terpene in nature. It is of interest that some of the flavour changes that have been credited to chemical reaction during cooking, aging (e.g., winer) or other processing steps are now being linked to the simple release of glycosidically bound flavour constituents. An example is the development of a cooked pineapple note in canned pineapple (the release of 2,5-dimethyl-4-hydroxy-3 (2H)-furanone). This note was originally believed to arise in the heated pineapple due to thermally induced degradations in the pineapple sugars.

Flavour Formation in Vegetables

Flavour formation in vegetables is quite different than in fruits since vegetables do not have a ripening period as fruits do, while some vegetables will develop partial flavour during growth and the remaining flavour during cellular disruption, most vegetables develop all characteristic flavour constituents during cellular disruption. Cellular disruption may be due to cutting a vegetable prior to use, to cooking, or to the chewing process. Cellular disruption permits the mixing of enzymes and substrates which had been separated within the cell, thereby resulting in the generation of volatile flavour substances. A few examples of vegetables that contain flavour prior to cellular disruption are celery (phthalides and selines), asparagus (1, 2-dithiolane-4-carboxylic acid), and bell pepper (2-methyl-3-isobutyl pyrazine).

An overview of vegetable flavour formation is presented in Fig. 39.6. Similiar to flavour development in fruit acid, carbohydrate, and amino acid metabolism serve to provide the precursors of vegetable flavour. Also, the

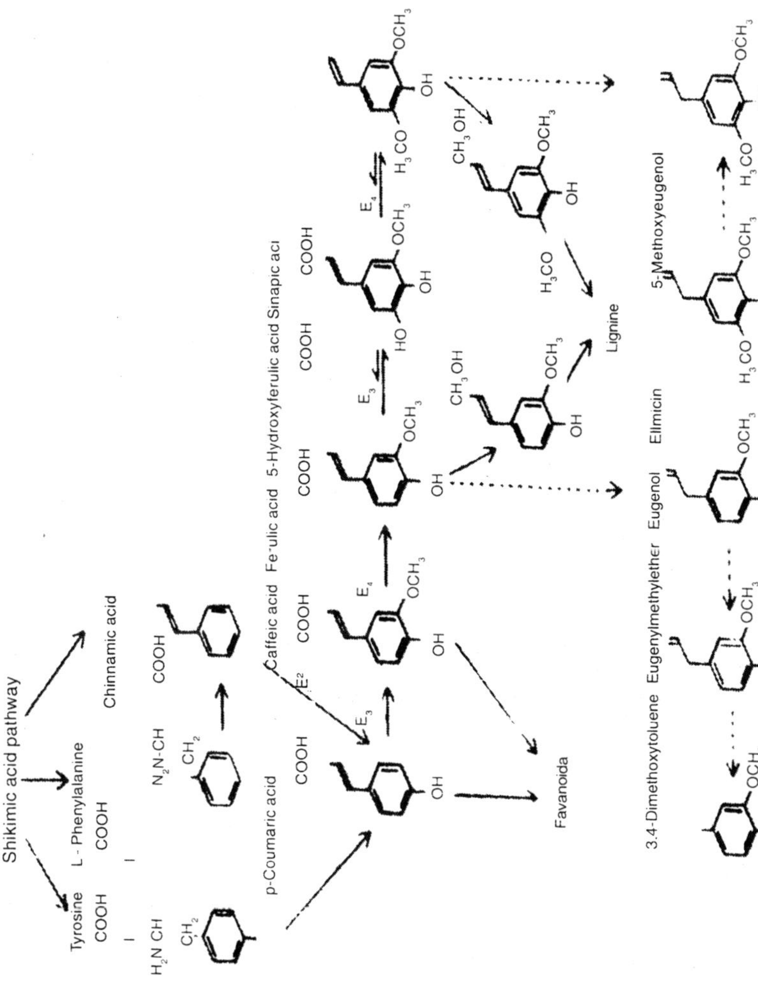

Fig. 39.4 : Pathways for the formation of phenolic acids and phenol esters in banana.

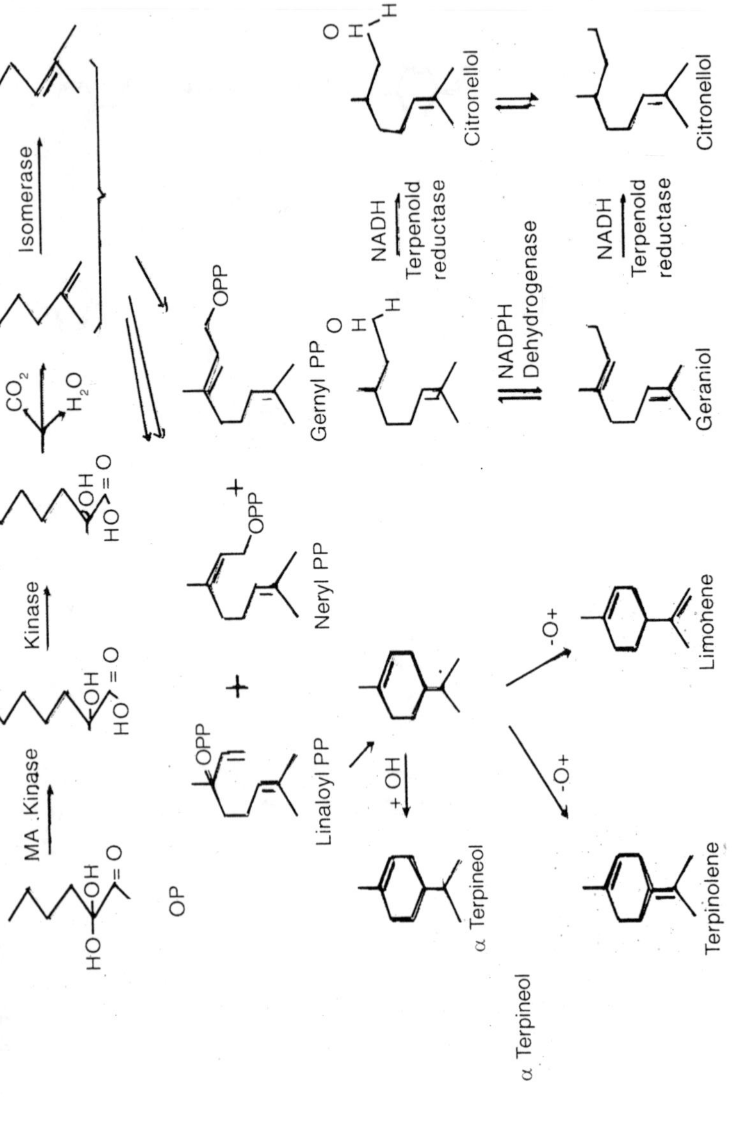

Fig. 39.5 : Metabolic pathways leading to the formation of terpenes in citrus fruits.

action of lipoxygenase on linoleic and linleinic acids to produce volatile carbonyls and alcohols is similar in vegetable flavour formation to that in fruit flavour formation. The major difference in flavour development lies in the importance of sulfur-containing flavour precursors to vegetable flavour. The thioglucosinolates and cysteine sulfoxides serve as precurspsrs to numerors volatile sulfur compounds. An excellent review on the role of sulfur compounds in food flavour has been written by Shankaranarayana et al.

Flavour Formation from Cysteine Sulfoxide Derivatives

Undoubtedly the best illustration of flavour formation from cystein sulfoxide precursors comes from studies on onion flavour. Intact onion cells have virtually no characteristic flavour untill cellular disruption (cutting, blending, chewing, etc.). Only seconds after cell damage, the union develops

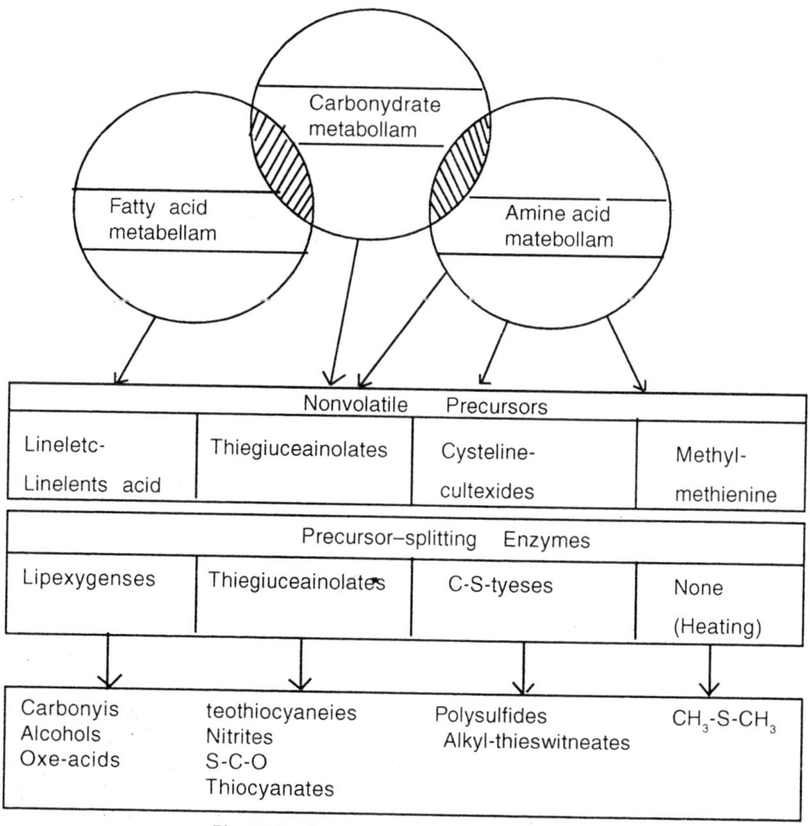

Fig. 39.6 : Formation of flavour in vegetables.

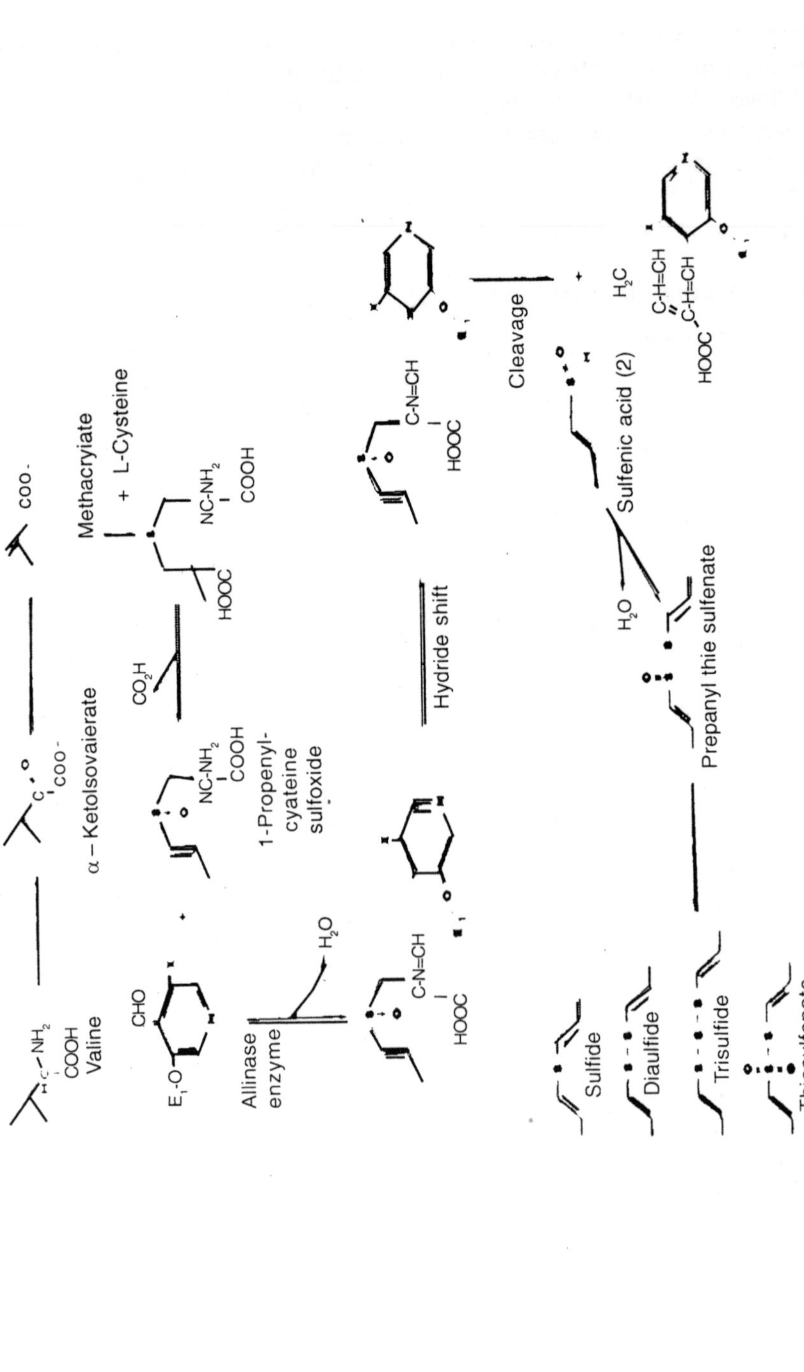

Fig. 39.7 : Biosynthesis of S-L-cystene sulfoxide, and subsequent flavour formation in onions.

full flavour. This rapid formation of flavour is characteristic of the genus *Allium* as a whole. This genus includes onions garlic and chives. S-Alk(en)yl-L-cysteine sulfoxides serve as precursors of flavour in the genus. An investigation of 27 Allium species found that they could be placed into three groups based on the predominance of certain amito acid precursors (Freeman and Whenham). The predominant precursors were S-1-S- propyl (onion), S-2 propenyl (garlic), and S-methyl (A. aflaturense B. Fedtschenko) cystein sulfoxides. A pathways for the formation of S-1 propenyl cystein sufoxide has been proposed by Granroth (1970) and is presented in Fi. 39-7. The mechanism of flavour formation from alkyl cysteine sulfoxide (alliin) is also outlined in Fig. 39.7. While the initial steps of this pathways are enzymatic reactions beyond sulfenic acid are purely chemical in nature sulfenic acid is extremely reactive, readily forming the unstable thiosulfinate intermediate by reaction with a second sulfanic acid molecule. This thosulfinate decomposes to form a relatively stable thiosulfonate and mono, di- and trisulfieses. Considering that severa; different alkyl precursors are available in each *Allium* species , a host of different mono-, di-, and trisulfides can be formed via different sulfenic acid combination. It is these mono-, di., and trisulfides which are most important in determining typical *Allium* flavour.

Matikkala and Virtanen found that nearly half of the cysteine sulfoxide precursors of onion are bound up as a ϒ– glutamyl pertides. The alliinase enzyme cannot act upon these cysteine sulfoxide flavour precursors until they freed from the glutamyl peptide. This can be accomplished only via the action of a ϒ-L-glutamyl transpepudase enzyme. This enzyme transferrs the glutamyl moiety to another amino acid. The glatamyl transpeptidases are present only in sprouted onions, not mature onions. Therefore nearly one-half of the flavour potenial of the onion cannot be utilized for the flavour formation.

The Cruciferate family also obtains a flavour contribution from alkyl cysteine sulfoxide precursors. The Brassica plants, part of the Cruciferae family include: broccoil brussels sprouts, cabbage, cauliflower and rutabagas. S-Methyl -L -cysteine sulfoxide is the primary cysteine sulfoxide derivative found in this family. An investigation of fresh cabbage flavour found that 6 per cent of the volatiles was dimethyl disulfied, 6 per cent dimethyl trisulfide, 3 per cent dimethyl terasulfide, and 1.5 per cent methyl ethyl trisulfide.

Flavour Formation from Gluconsinolates

Most of the vegetables containing glucosinolates belong to the Cruciferae family. More than 50 different glucosinolates have been identified to date (Tressi et al.). Glucosinolates are nonvolatile flavour precursors that are enzymatically hydrolyzed to volatile flavours when cellular structure is disrupted. The volatile products initially are isothiocyanates and nitriles. Secondary reactions lead to the formation of several other of flavour compounds. Fig. 39.8 outlines the pathways proposed to explain the formation of flavour compounds in the radish. The glucose moiety is initially hydrolyzed from the glucosinolate. This results in an unstable molecule that readily splits out HSO_4^-. Depending upon molecule rearrangements,either an isothocyante or a nitrile result. Further reactions result in the formation of thiols, sulfides, disulfides and trisulfides

Additional Pathways for Vegetable Flavour Formation

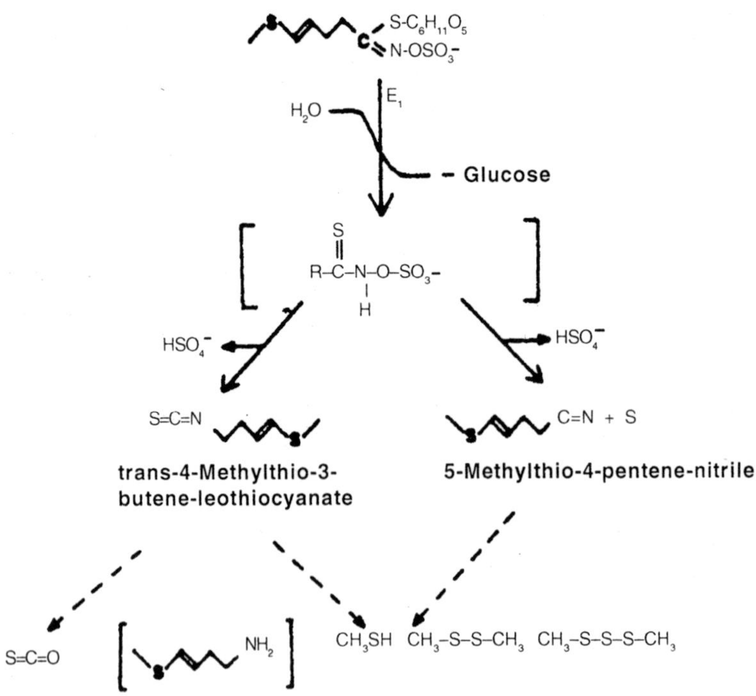

Fig. 39.8 : The formation of volatile flavours in radish root.

Carbonyls and alcohols may be present in significant concentrations in vegetables. These carbonyls and alcohols typically arise via fatty acid degradation by lipoxygenase. The mechanism of formation is similar to that discussed previously for carbonyl formation in fruit. However, each plant has a unique fatty acid composition and ancillary enzyme system. Therefore although the overall mechanism of flavour formation from fatty acids is similar between plants, each plant does develop its own unique carbonyl profile .

A similar analogy could be made for the formation of terpenes in vegetables. Terpenes are rather common to vegetables and arise from mevalonic acid similar to the mechanism of formation in fruit. Yet each vegetables containing terpenes has a unique terpene profile.

Location of Flavour in Plant

As one might expect,flavour is typically distributed nonuniformly in the plant. MacLeod and MacLoed have shown that allyl isothiocyanate more abundant in the outer leaves than in the inner tissues the bulb into individual leaves and the stem. They examined each section for lachrymator and pyruvate, but leaves moving towards the plants center and stem. Total terpenes are more concentrated in the crown of carrots than in the midsection or tip. Not only is there a difference in total flavour depending upon the plant part being examined, but there may also be a difference in flavour profile. Therefore, if one dissected a plant and ate different individual parts, it would not be unusual to find a slightly different flavour character for each part.

Influence of Genetics, Nutrition Environment, Maturity and Storage on Flavour

There is tittle question that not all apples, oranges or coffee taste the same. We often select a particular variety of apple (e.g., Delicious) because we prefer the flavour Genetics determines the enzyme systems and precursors involved in flavour formation. Plant environment also influences flavour. Soil nutrition provides some of the essentials for flavour devlopment. For example,a radish will not develop characteristic flavour if there is little sulfer in the soil. Growing conditions (e.g., temperature) influence activity of different enzyme system and can significantly alter flavour development. Certainly the stage of maturity and storage conditions can further influence flavour. We known that each piece of fruit or vegetable is an individual in appearance and flavour.

There is much literature reporting on differences in flavour due to genetics, environment, harvesting time and postharvest treatment. Further information in this subject area can be found in the following references: Paillard, Eskin, Salukhe and Do, Freeman, and Heath and Reineccius.

Conclusions

While flavour development in fruits and vegetables proceeds along many common paths, there are also several contrasts. Fruit flavour develops during a short ripening period, while vegetable flavour develops primarily during cellular disruption. Fruits depend heavily upon esters for their characteristic flavour, while sulfur compounds are typically more important to vegetable flavour.

Similarities exist in the formation of alcohol, aldehydes, ketones and acids by enzymatic pathways. The enzymatically catalyzed oxidation of lipids is a particularly important pathway for flavour formation in both fruits and vegetables

While the pathways leading to flavour formation are known for many compounds, in other cases many pieces of the synthesis puzzle are missing. It is unfortunate that most of the research on biosynthesis pathways of flavour formation was done in the early 1979s and that, of late, this area of study has received minimal attention.

As noted earlier, many factors influence the flavour of a fresh fruits or vegetable. These factors include plant growing environment, stage of maturity and conditions of storage from harvesting to consumption.

Chemistry of Essential Oils

Essential oils are obtained by steam or water distillation expression of solvent extraction from many odorous plant sources and are of prime importance to the flavour chemist. These products, which give the plant its distinctive aroma, are complex mixtures of organic chemicals whose nature and relative proportions are also determined by the plant species and agricultural factors, such as environment, climate, soil conditions, time of harvesting and postharvesting handling prior to distillation.

The chemicals present in general formula may be classified as follows:

a. Hydrocarbons of the general formula $(C_5H_8)_n$–the terpenes.

b. Oxygenated derivatives of these hydrocarbons.

c. Aromatic compounds having a benzenod strucure.

d. Compounds containing nitrogen or sulfur.

These constituents are synthesized by the plant during its normal development and the chemical composition of the oils is generally characteristics of any given plant species. The proportion of the chemicals present in any given essential oil remains within predictable limits so that the quality of an oil may often be expressed in terms of one or more specific component (e. g., citral in oil of lemon, the menthol/ menthone ratio in oils of peppermint, etc.). The constituents range over the whole field of organic chemistry and clear relationships have long been recognized in their biogenesis, chemical character and sensory attributes. However, research is still required to established the precursors and the precise biochemical pathways involved in their formation in the growing plant. The biogenesis of the terpene hydrocarbons and their oxygenated derivatives, which form such a diverse and significant fraction of many essential oils, has already been the subject of much research and conjecture over the post three to four decades; but in spite of modern instrumental techniques now available to the classical analysts, is still not fully understood. As research progresses, many aspects of this branch of organic chemistry are published in the chemical literature and reference should be made to *Chemical Abstracts* for updated information. One should also follow the proceedings of the International Congress of the Essential Oils, Fragrances and flavours and journals such as the journals such as the journal of Essential Oil Research.

Terpenes

The chemical structure of the terpenes was established by Wallach in 1887. He proposed the co-called "isoprene rule" by which terpenes were considered to be fusion products of two or more isoprene (C_5H_8) moieties. The general formula of the terpenes is, therefore, $(C_5H_8)_n$; where n = 2 the hydrocarbons are known as monoterpenes or simply as terpenes; where n = 3 they are called sesquiterpenes (C_{30}) and tetraterpenes (C_{40}) are also known.

The typical terpenoid hydrocation structures are shown in Fig. 39.9. A comprehensive chart, which provides a graphic picture of the configurative relations in the monoterpene series, was published in 1963 by Dragoco Co., Holzminden, Germany.

Although the terpene hydrocabons are quantitatively significant in the composition of many essential oils (Table 39.2), they possess little flavour

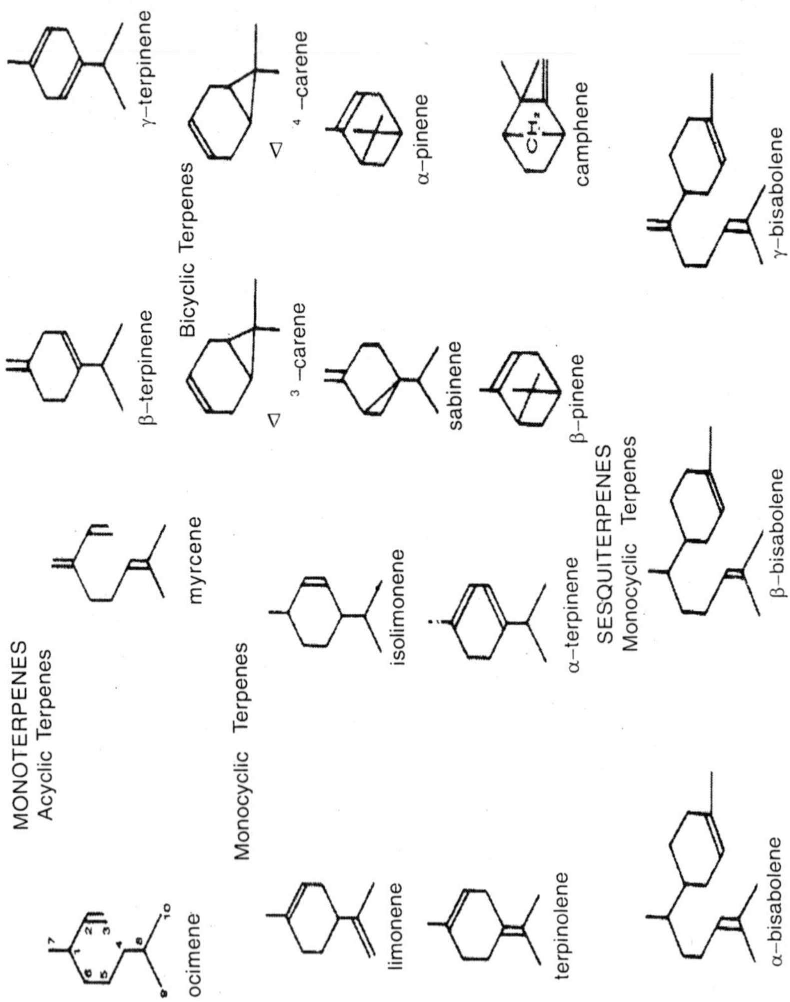

Fig. 39.9 : Pathways in the biosynthesis of terpenes.

value. It is probably inaccurate to say they have no odor or flavour oxygenated derivatives, their contribution is small other than to convey a definite "freshness" to the odor profiles.

The principal terpene hydrocarbons and the essential oils in which they occur are listed in Table 39.2.

Oxygenated Terpenoid Compounds

Oxygenated derivatives of the terpene hydrocarbons include alcohols, aldehydes, ketones and esters. These occur widely throughout the essential oils and major contributors to their distinctive and flavours.

The principal oxygenated terpenoid derivatives are listed in Table 39.2. Reference should be made to one of the standard texts for details of their physical and sensory characteristics for specific details of their manufacture and chemical reaction.

Benzenoid Compounds

The aromatic compounds based on benzene form another important group of flavouring and fragrance components. As with the terpenes, these constituents of an essential oil are the result of biochemical reactions directly associated with the plant's metabolism. They include the whole range of organic functional groups (i.e., alcohols acids, esters, aldehydes, ketones, phenols, phenol ethers, lactones, etc.) In many cases, their biogenesis and biosynthetic pathways have not yet been fully established, but it would seem that stem most n-propyl benzene (C_6H_5 $(CH_2)_2CH_3$) as a precursor that is enzymatically activated. The resulting products are found in various stages of oxidation with many diverse functional groups attached to the benezene nucleus. The biogenesis of naturally occurring aromatic compounds has been developed by many workers during the best 40 years. The chemistry involved is far outside the scope of this brief review, some of the intermediate and final molecules display considerable structural complexity in which spatial and stereoisomerism are common.

After many years of research, the chemistry of the major constituents of essential oils is particularly well documented, and their synthesis and reactions have been researched. Some of these are of considerable economic importance to the flavour industry, and the following three examples illustrate just some of the simpler synthetic conversions that exist :

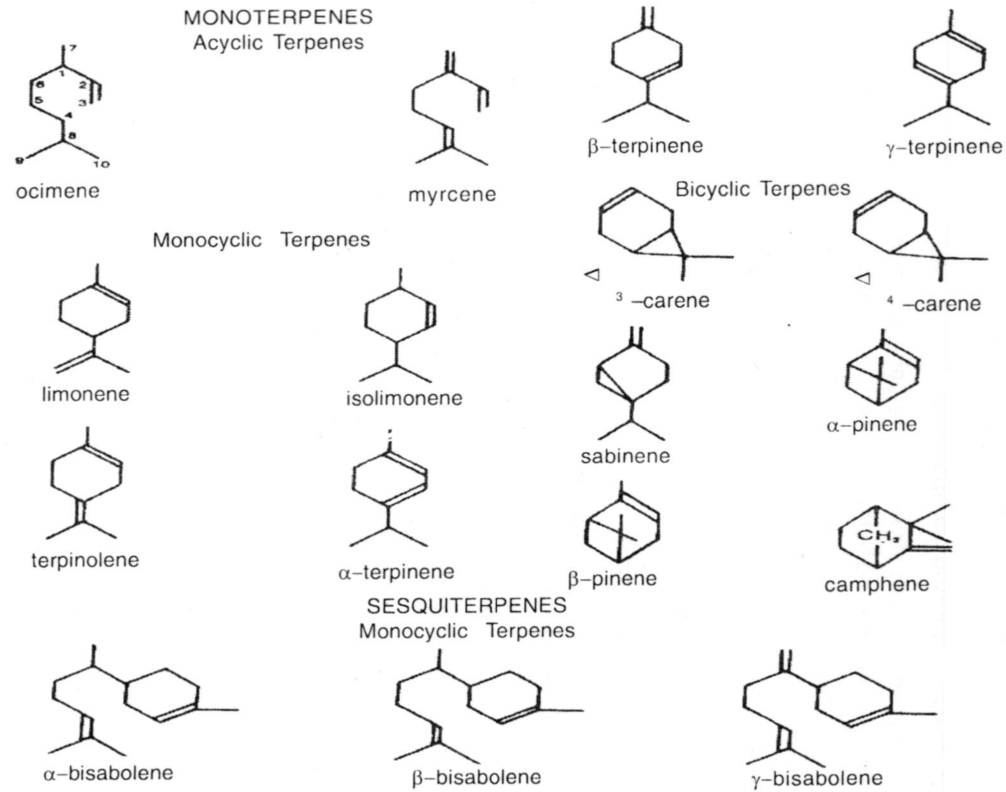

Fig. 39.9 : Pathways in the biosynthesis of terpenes.

Bicyclic Terpenes

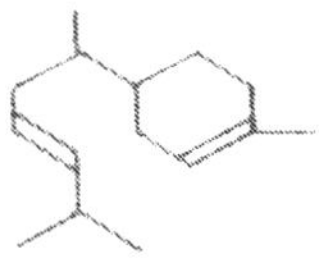

α -cadinene

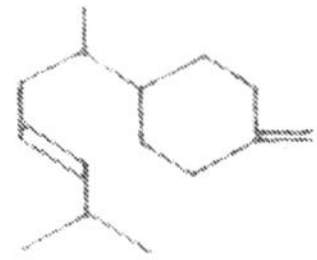

β -cadinene

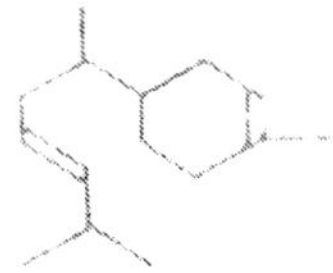

γ -cadinene

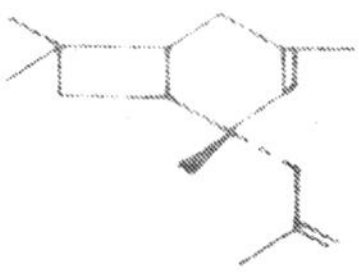

β -caryophyllene

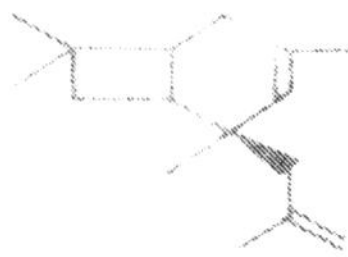

γ -caryophyllene

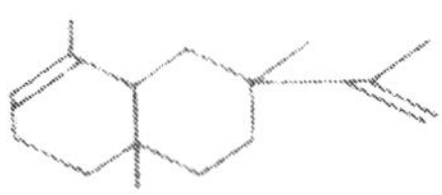

α -selinene

β -selinene

DITERPENES

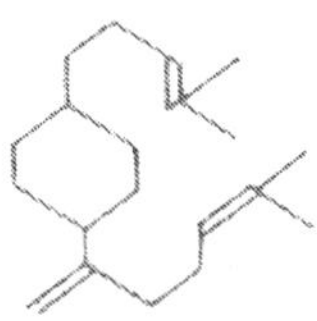

Camphorene

Fig. 39.9 : Continued

a. The conversion of eugenol to vanillin.
b. The conversion of safrole to heliotropin
c. The preparation of anisaldehyde from anethole.

In this context there is little value in reiterating the basic chemistry of these aromatic constituents and reference should be made to the many standard texts for a fuller treatment of this subject principal.

Compounds Containing Nitrogen and Sulfur

Organics containing either nitrogen or sulfur are not very widely distributed in the essential oils themselves, but plant materials containing much albuminous matter do yield compounds on distillation such as ammonia, trimethylamine: hydrocyanic acid and hydrogen sulfied.

Nitrogen Compounds

The following naturally occurring nitrogen containing compounds are of interest to both the flavourist and perfumer.

Indole–Found in oils of Jasmine and neroli bigaride as well as many citrus oils.

Skatole–Found in glandular excretion of the civet cat.

Several essential oils contain esters of anthranilic acid (o-amino benzoic acid), the most important being:

Methyl Anthranilate–Found in oils of neroli bigrade and in many floral oils, in orange and lemon oil in trace quantities and also in some varieties of grape juice.

Dimethyl Anthranilate–An important constituent of tangerine (Mandarin) oils.

Sulfur Comounds

Sulfur occur frequently in plants probably arising from the degradation of glucosides. Hydrogen sulfide is present in the distillation waters of certain umbelliferous fruits; and dimethyl sulfide $(CH_3)2S$ is present in the prime distillation of American peppermint oil from which it is removed by rectification. Several other sulfur-containing compounds characterize the so-called "essential oils" of onion garlic, mustard etc.

Sulfur-Containing Oils

Onion Freshly minced onion are allowed to stand are then distilled.A dark brown oils may be recovered in a yield of 0.002 to 0.005 per cent depending on the type of onions used and their ripeness. The composition of this so-called "onion oil" was studied ealier by Brodnitz and Pollack and more recently by Sass-Kiss et al.. Twenty volatile sulfur-containing compouds were identified in this latter stud.

The following compounds are among the most abundant:

methyl-1propyl disculfide

23,4-dimethyl thiophene

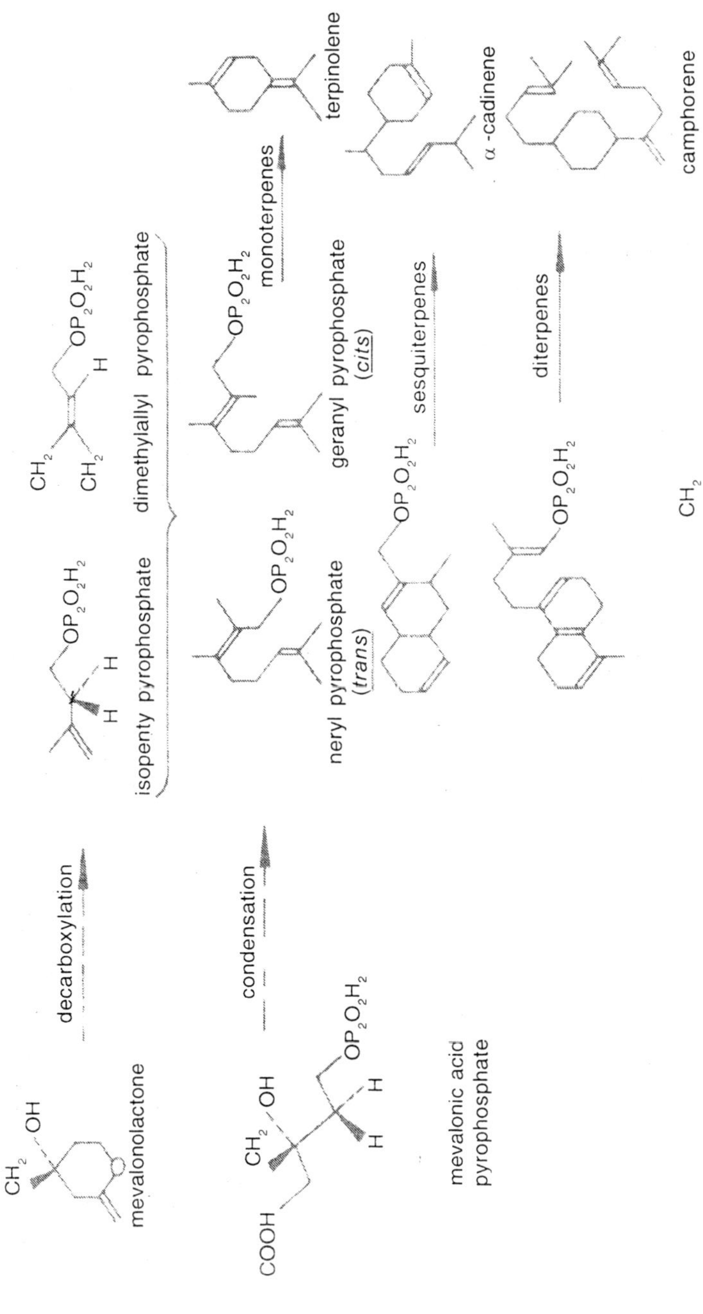

Source: After Croteau and Loomis (1975)

Fig. 39.9 : Continued

cis methyl-1-propenyl disulfide
trans methyl-1-1-propenyl disulfide
di-1-propyl trisulfide
cis-1-propyl propenyl disulfide
methyl-1-propyltrisulfide
methyl-1-propyl trisulfide
di-1-propyl trisulfide

Table - 39.2

Terpenoid Content of Essential Oils

Essential Oil	*Total Terpenes %*	*Principal Terpenes (Guenther 1948-1952; Lawrence 1976-1978)*
A'lspice (pimento berry)	25-35	α-phellandrene, caryophyllene
Anise, China star	10-20	α-pinene, α-and β-phellandrene, *p*-cyemene, dipentene, limonene
Caraway	40-50	limonene, α-pinene
Cardamom	50-55	limonene, sabinene
Cassia/cinnamon	20-30	caryophyllene, α-phellandrene, p-cymene, α-pinene
Celery seed	80-85	α-limonene, selinene
Clove bud	10-20	β-caryophyllene
Coreander	30-35	α- and α-pinene, ϒ-terpinene
Dill	35-45	limonene, phellandrene
Fennel	20-30	α-pinene, α-phellandrene, dipentene
Ginger	90	zingiberene, β-pinene, α-and β phellandrene, α-camphene, myrcene, *p*-cymene, 2-selinene, β-elemene
Lemon peel	96	α-and β-pinene, camphene, α-limonene, α-phellandrene, ϒ-terpinene
Lime	90	α-and β-pinene, limonene, dipentene, bisabolene
Marjoram	40	α-terpinene
Nutmeg/mace	60	α-pinene, camphene, diprnyrnr, *p*-cymeme, limonene
Orange, sweet peel	95-98	α-limonene
Parsley seed	50	α-pinene
Pepper, black	70-80 Monoterpenes	α-thujene, α-pinene, camphene, sabinene, β-pinene, myrcene
	20-30 Sequiterpenes	α-phellandrene, -3-carene, α-terpinene, terpinolene, α-cubebene, α.·. β-copaene, α-elemene, β-caryophyllene, β-farnescene, umulene, β-selinene, α-selinene, β-bisaboiene
Pepermint	30	α-pinene, limonene, phellandrene, cadinene
Rosemary	85-90	α- and β-pinene, camphene
Sage	65	α-pinene
Thyme	60-80	β-pinene, *p*-cymene, ϒ-terpinene, caryophyllene, camphene

Table - 39.3

Principal oxygenated terpenoids and their sources

Compound	*Form*	*Opt. Form*	*Present in the essential oil of.*
		MONOTERPENE ALCOHOLS	
Aliphatie			
Citronellol		d	Java citronella, geranium, Eucalyptus citriodora, savin, Spanish verbena
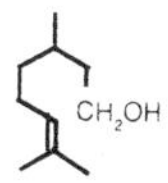		l	Reunion geranium, Bulgarian rose
Geraniol 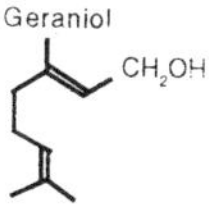			Palmarosa, rose, geranium, citronella, lemongrass, linaloe, lavender, eoriander, ylang-ylang, neroli, petitgrain
Linalool 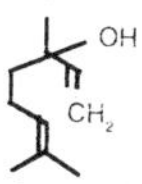			Mexican linaloe, rosewood, nutmeg, orange, coriander, orthodon supp.
Nerol 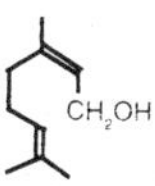			Neroli bigarade, petitgrain, rose, Mexican linaloe, lavender, bergamot, citronella
Monoeyelie			
Carveol 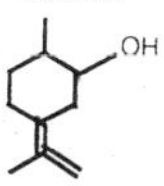			Caraway, spearmint
Dihydro carveol 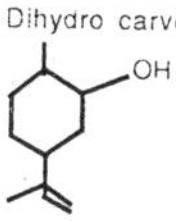			Caraway, *Mentha* spp.
Dihydro-α-terpineol 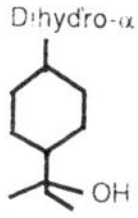			American turpentine, pine
Menthol 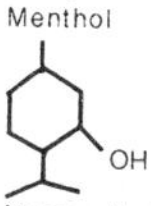		l	Peppermint, *Mentha arvensis*
Neomenthol Stereo isomer of menthol		d	*Mentha arvensis*

Table - 39.3

Principal Oxygenated Terpenoids and their Sources

Compound	From	Opt. Form	Present in the Esential Oil
of:			
		MONOTERPENE ALCOHOLS	
Monoeyelie			
Perilly alcohol 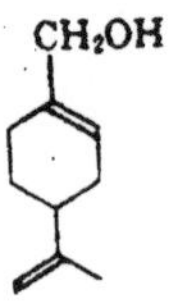			Gingergrass, bergamot, savin, monarda, lavandin, spearmint
Pulegol 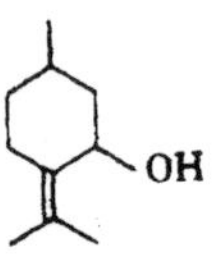			Not found free in nature but is. intermediate in the formation of menthol
Isopulegol 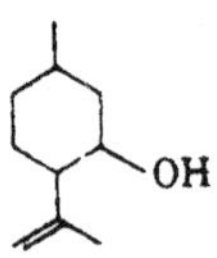			L emongrass, in other oils in association with eitronellal
Terpineol 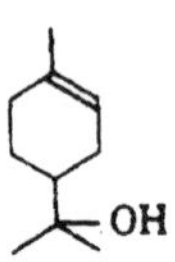		d	Cupressus spp., cardamom, star anise, marjoram, clary sage, neroli
		l	Savory, lavandin, lemon, lime, einnamon leaf
		dl	Mexican linaloe, Eucalyptus globulus, petitgrain
Bicyclic			
Borneol 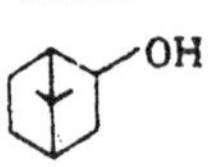		d	Nutmeg, olibanum, rosemary, lavender, spike lavender, ginger
		l	Pine, citronella, coriander, valerian
Myrtenol 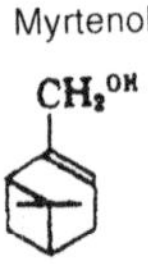			Myrtle
		d	Spanish eucalyptus
Pinocampheol 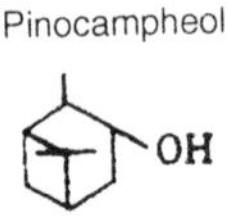			Hyssop

Table - 39.3

Principal Oxygenated Terpenoids and their Sources

Compound	From	Opt. Form	Present in the Esential Oil of:
MONOTERPENE ALCOHOLS			
Bicyclic			
Pinocarveol 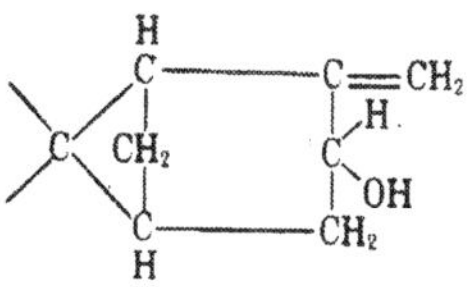			Eucalyptus
Sabinol 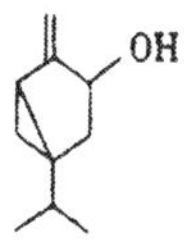			Savin, *Cupressus* spp.
Thujyl alcohol 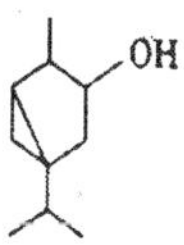			Wormwood
SESQUITERPENE ALCOHOLS			
Aliphatic			
Farnesol 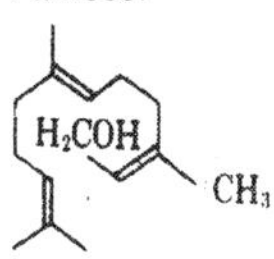			Ambrette seed, neroli bigarade, rose, cananga, citronella, lemongrass, palmarosa, and many floral oils
Nerolidol 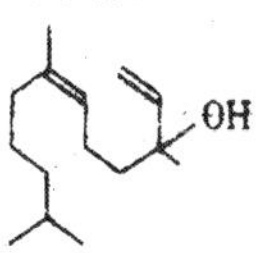			Neroli bigarade, balsam Peru, balsam Tolu, ylang-ylang
Monocyclic			
Elemol 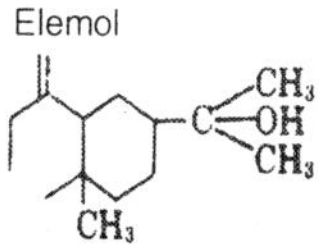			Elemi, Java citronella

Table - 39.3

Principal Oxygenated Terpenoids and their Sources

Compound	*From*	*Opt. Form*	*Present in the Esential Oil of:*
SESQUITERPENE ALCOHOLS			
Monocyclic			
Zingiberol 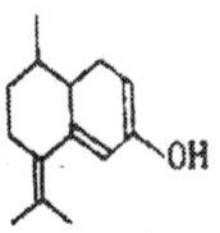			Ginger
Bicyclic			East Indian sandalwood
Santalol 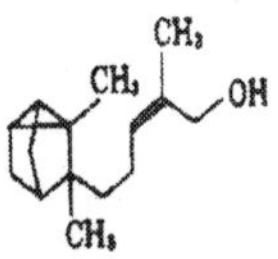	α		
Cadinol 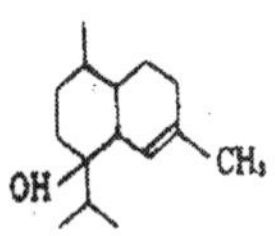	α	d	Galbanum, amyris (West Indian sandalwood)
		l	Cubed, cade, Java citronella
Guaiol 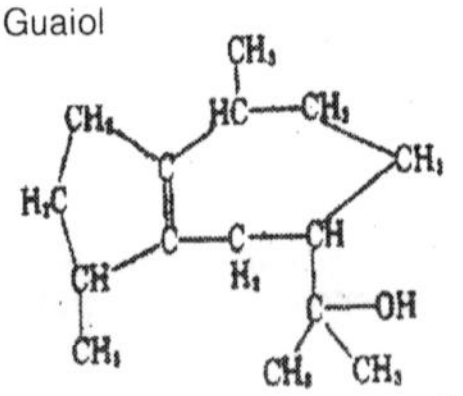			Guaiac wood
MONOTERPENE ALDEHYDES			
Citral *(geranial)* 2-*trans*-3,7 -dimethyl-2,6-octandien-1-al 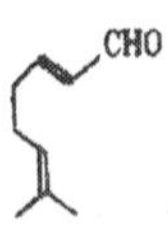			Lemongrass, monarda, *Eucalyptus* spp. Leptospermum citrata, Backhousia *citriodora,* Java citronella, lemon, lime, ginger (Commercially, citral is a mixture of the two isomers)
Citral *(neral)* 2-*cis*-3,7 -dimethyl-2,6-octandien-1-al 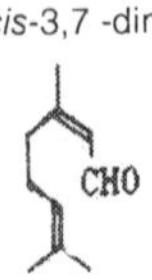			

Table - 39.3

Principal Oxygenated Terpenoids and their Sources

Compound	*From*	*Opt. Form*	*Present in the Esential Oil of:*
	MONOTERPENE ALDEHYDES		
Citronellal (rhodinal) 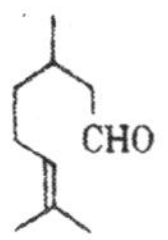		d	Citronella, *Eucalyptus citriodora* and other spp., lemon, rose
		:	*Backhousia citriodora, Litsea cubeba,* lemon, tangerine, Ocimum spp.
	MONOTERPENE KETONES		
Carvone 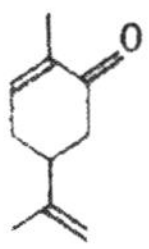		d	Caraway, dill seed and dill weed
		l	*Spearmint*
		dl	Gingergrass
Dihydrocarvone 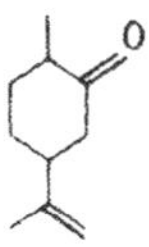			Caraway
Menthone 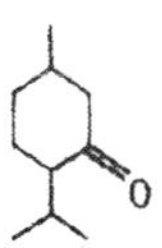		d	*Nepeta Japonica*
		l	Pennyroyal, pepermint, buchu leaf, calamintha nepeta
Isomenthone Isomer of menthol		d	Pennyroyal
		l	Geranium
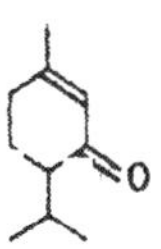		d	*Mentha arvensis, Andropogon* spp., Cymbopogon spp.
		l	*Eucalyptus* spp.
Piperitone 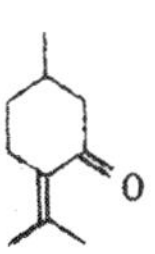		d	Pinnyroyal, *Mentha arvensis*, Calamintha *nepeta*
Pulegone 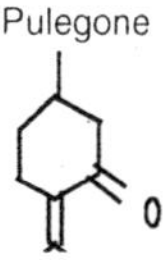			

Table - 39.3

Principal Oxygenated Terpenoids and their Sources

Compound	From	Opt. Form	Present in the Esential Oil of:
Bicyclic	**MONOTERPENE KETONES**		
Camphor		d	Camphor tree, sassafras, spike lavender
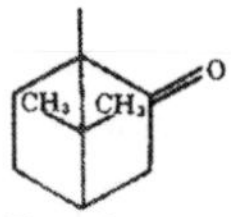		l	Basil, Dalmatian sage
Fenchone 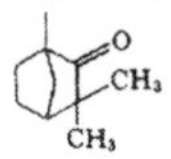		d	Fennel
Santenone 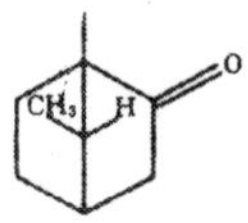			East Indian sandalwood
Thujone 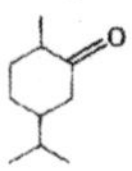			Thuja, Dalmatian sage, and other spp.
			Tansy, wormwood
Verbenone 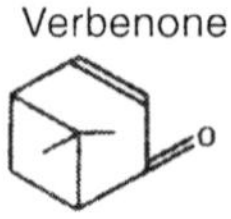		d	Spanish verbena, *Eucalyptus* spp.
	SEQUITERPENE KETONES		
Turmerone 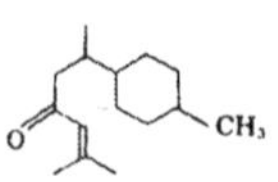			Turmeric
Ionone 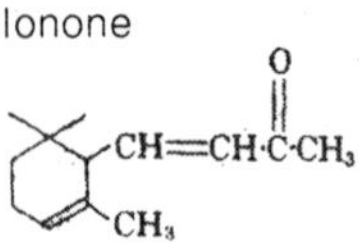	α	d l dl	In many oils
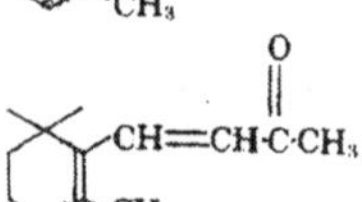			Raspberry distillate
Irone	β		
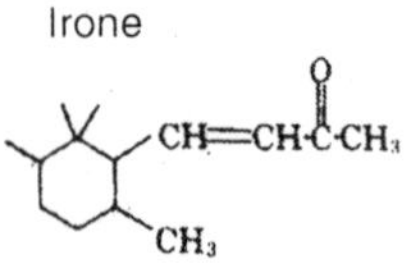			Orrisroot, raspberry distillate
	α		

Garlic (*Allium sativum* L.) The primary precursor present in garlic is S-(2-propenyl)-L-cysteine sulfoxide, which leads to the formation of allyl thiosulfinate (or allicin) that characterizes the freshly crushed garlic. On standing, this compound forms allyl disulfide, the thiosulfonate, and trace quantities of allyl trisulfide.

The organoleptic differences between onion, garlic, and the other alliaceous species are explained in terms of the quantitative and qualitative differences in the occurrence of the four precursors-1-propenyl-, 2-propenyl-, 1-propyl- and methyl-L-eysteine sulfoxide (Freeman and Whenham 1975), Garlic has recently been the subject of considerable study in many fields due to positive health claims.

Mustard The characteristic flavour and pungency of this widely used condiment is also dependent upon enzymic reaction involving odorless precursors. Mustard exists in several varieties of which two are of commercial importance:

White mustard–the seeds of *Brassica alba* Boissier

Black (brown) mustard–the seeds of *Brassic nigra* (L). Koch or *B. juncea* (L). Cosson

When freshly ground, the seeds exude only a very slight but distinctive odor. When mixed with water, the aroma is rapidly and sharply intensified, becoming strongly pungent. This is due to enzymatic action on thioglucoside precursors. The so-called "mustard oil" is a distillate of the aromatic compounds produced by this reaction, the chemistry of which differs somewhat between species.

White Mustard

The principal constituents of the seeds are : fixed oil (about 25 per cent), a crystalline thioglucoside, sinalbin, and an enzyme, myrosinase. In the presence of water, the sinalbin breaks down to yield D-glucose, sinapine hydrogen sulfate, and isothiocyanate or sinalbing mustard oil). This latter product has little odor, but is intensely pungent and is a vesicant.

Black (Brown) Mustard

The seeds contain: fixed oil (about 35-40 per cent), protein (about 20 percent), the thioglucoside, sinigrin, and the enzyme, myrosinase. Under conditions similar to those described above the sinigrin breaks down to yield allyl isothiocyanate, which is a very volatile compound having the characteristic pungency associated with this condiment. The chemistry of the reaction was presented briefly earlier in this chapter.

FRUIT FLAVOURS

Whereas certain aromatic plant materials, including some spicy fruits (e.g., pimento berry, black pepper, coriander, etc.), have a high content of odiferous constituents that can be recovered readily in the form of essential oils, the flavour components of table fruits are present in relatively low concentrations. Although this enables the fruits to be eaten and enjoyed per se, the recovery of concentrates that would be of vlaue to the flavourist or food processor is limited. In most cases,the expression of fruit juices does not yield a product having a significant level of flavour, and their concentration without degradation of the thermolabile aromatic constituents poses considerable technological problems. The volatile aromatic chemicals responsible for the characteristic odor profiles of specific fruits belong to all classes of organic compounds, and for most fruits long lists of components have already been identified (Maarse and Visscher 1989). Unfortunately, the degree of contribution that such chemicals make to the flavour profile is poorly documented and, generally, the flavour chemist is only able to use lists of constituents as a guide, relying on sensory assessment to establish the proportion necessary in a mixture to create the correct nuances in the final profile.

Aromatic Components

The aromatic chemicals responsible for the distinctive odor and flavour profiles of fruits comprise:

a. Aclohols in the homologous series C_1 to C_{12} with a preponderance of even-numbered carbon atoms.

b. Carbonyls form a significant fraction of the odor pattern of many fruits (e.g., benzaldehyde in stoned fruits, 5-hydroxy-2-methylfurfural inpineapple, furfural in strawberries, etc.).

c. Acids present in the volatile fractions of fruits are limited to two, namely: formic and acetic. The acids most usually associated with fruit flavour are nonvolatile and will be discussed later.

d. Esters are without doubt the most important and numerous aromatic components of fruit flavours, their nature and proportion often being characteristic of a given fruit.

e. Lactones are responsible for the characteristic aromatic notes of many fruits and give peaches and apricots their quite distinctive profiles. A whole series of lactones has been isolated from both unripe and ripened fruits and it has been found that the ratio of the various lactones changes during the ripening process. The ratio of δ- and γ- lactones present is of importance in establishing the flavour quality of the fruit.

f. Phenols in the form of tannins, are present in many fruits and are responsible for the characteristic astringency. Their presence is more marked in unripe fruit and diminished as the fruit ripens, probably due to polymerization.

Fruit Sugars and Acids

Sugars

The carbohydrates present in fruits are of considerable importance in the assessment of their quality and edibility. Those of interest to the food and flavour chemist may be classified as:

Sugars

Monosaccharides

Pentoss	Arabinose, ribose xylose
Hexoses	Fructose, galactose, glucose
Disaccharides	Lactose, maltose, sucrose
Trisaccharides	Raffinose

Nonsugars (Polysaccharides)

Pentonsans	Araban, xylan
Hexosans	Celluose, dextrin, glycogen, inulin stach

The principal sugars found in fruits are fructose and glucose, which are reducing sugars and sucrose, which is a nonreducing sugar. The amount of sugar present depends on the fruit and the normal retabolic factors associate with its development.The speed of change in composition is gereatest at maturation as the fruit ripens. The relative proportions of these sugars, which differ significantly in their sweetness levels, varies considerably between fruits as well as with the stage of ripeness. It is the balance that determines the ultimate level of sweetness of the fruit, although the palatability is more directly related to the balance of the sugars and fruit acids present, with many fruits being characterized by this aspect of the flavour profile.

Acids

Without the organic acids (e.g., citric, malic tartaric etc.), the flavour of fruits would be either sickeningly sweet or unpleasntly insipid. Some fruits are particularly rich in organic acids either in the free state or combined as esters; these may be classified as follows:

Aliphatic

a. Monocarboxylic acids (e.g., acetic acid in grapes)

b. Monocarboxylic acids with alcoholic or carbonyl groups (e.g., glyoxylic acid in unripe apples)

c. Di- and tricarboxylic acids (e.t., L-malic acid in apples, citric acid in many fruits)

d. Suger acids (e.g., gluconic acid in plums)

Cyclic

a. Monocarboxylic acids (e.g., p-coumarylquinic acid in apples)

The principal organic acids of importance in flavourings are listed below, although not all of these are found in fruit flavours. Their use in foodstuffs is described by Dziezak (1990).

Principal Carboxylic Acids

Aliphatic	**Monobasic Acids**
Formic	$H \cdot COOH$
Acetic	$CH_3 \cdot COOH$
Butyric	$CH_3(CH_2)_2 \cdot COOH$
Glyceric	$OH \cdot CH_3 \cdot COOH$
Lactic	$CH_3CH(OH) \cdot COOH$
Glyceric	CH_2OH $CHOH$ $COOH$
Pyruvic	$CH_3 \cdot CO \cdot COOH$

Glyoxylic	$CHO \cdot COOH$
	Dibasic Acids
Malonic	$HOOC \cdot CH_2 \cdot COOH$
Adipic	$HOOC(CH_2)_4 \cdot COOH$
Fumaric	$HOOC \cdot CH{:}CH \cdot COOH$
L-Malic	$HOOC \cdot CH2 \cdot CH(OH) \cdot COOH$
Tartaric	$HOOC \cdot CH(OH) \cdot CH(OH) \cdot COOH$
	Tribasic Acids
Citric	$CH_2 \cdot COOH$
	$HO \cdot \; C \cdot COOH$
	$CH_2 \cdot COOH$
Cylic	
Benzoic	COOH

FLAVOUR OF DAIRY PRODUCTS

When considering the flavour of dairy products, one can readily divide the topic into the fresh vs.fermented products. Fresh products would include milk, ice cream and butter, while fermented products include cheese, buttermilk,yogurt and a host of lesser product (in terms of markct volume). While the flavour of fermented dairy products will be discussed later in this chapter, when flavours from fermention in general are discussed, this section will provide some coverage of this area (Cheddar and blue cheeses) as well as the flavour of milk.

Milk

Fresh milk has a bland but characteristic flavour. One might describe it as being slightly sweet/salty in taste with a delicate but weak aroma (Badings). The sweetness comes from lactose (ca. 4.7 per cent). while the saltiness comes from the milk salts. The aroma is made up of nearly two hundred components most of which are present in very low concentrations (total aroma concentration less than 1-100mg/kg milk–Badings) and thus milk has a subtle aroma rather than anything characteristic. If one were to characterize milk aroma, it might be to describe it as "cooked," which is an artifact of pasteurization rather than inherent to the milk itself.

The volatiles present in commercial milk are derived from several sources, including the metabolic activity of the cow, volatiles in the air the cow breathes, components in the diet of the cow and thermally induced compounds arise primally from protein (various sulfur compounds) or nonenzymatic browing (Streecker aldehydes and heterocyclic compounds). Milk is seldom used as a flavouring material itself, but rather serves as a precursor for flavour development, either by providing sugar and amino acids for browing or the precursors of fermented flavours. As is noted later in this chapter, the fatty acids of milk are unique flavouring character to heated and fermented dairy products.

Cheese

Cheddar Cheese

The manufacture of Cheddar cheese consists essentially of allowing milk to become acid by the growth of Lactic streptococci adding rennet to form a soft coagulum, cutting this coagulum and allowing the small cubes of clotted milk to lose whey and mat together. The curd is finally milled, salted and packed into a hoop or mold where it is subjected to considerable pressure. The formed cheese is then allowed to ripen for 3 to 9 months. Most factories have now instituted control ripening rooms in which temperatures and humidity are automatically regulated.

During this ripening period the texture is changed and the characteristic flavour is formed. Those two events are closely related. The aroma of cheese arises mainly from volatile components formed in the curd as ripening proceeds. These components include esters, fatty acid, aldehydes, ketones alcohols amines and sulfur compounds. The chief chemical changes in ripening of Cheddar type considered chronologically are (1) fermentation of lactic acid and small amount of acetic and propionic acid and CO_2, (2) Proteolysis and (3) lipolysis. The most obvious chemical change is the break down of the proteins. About 25 per cent of the total protein becomes soluble in ripe Chedder cheese. The gradual change from the rubbey curd of green cheese to the mellow waxy ripe product appears to be due chiefly to the action of the proteolytic enzymes. However, it appears that flavour is chiefly due to the fermentation reaction and to lipolysis. Breakdown of the fat has not received much attention, but it is possible that lipolysis influences not only the flavour but also the texture.

Flavour Development

The flavour of cheese is the result of a vast number of chemical and biochemical reaction that take place sequentially or simultaneously in the protein-water-fat miniral system that constitutes green cheese. These reactions are due to the action of:

1. Starter bacteria and their enzymes.
2. Secondary microflora and their enzymes. These microflora arise from the indigenous microflora of milk that survive pasteurization or from post pasteurization contamination.
3. Coagulant.
4. Indigenous milk enzymes (particularly important in cheese made from raw milk).

Role of microorganisms The role of microorganisms in the development of characteristic flavour of Chedder cheese is well recognized. It is well established that bacteria free cheese are flavoursless, while those containing only starter organisms are flavourful.

The primary role of the starter streptococci is to convert lactose into lactic acid. The acid reduces the pH of the system . The starter also participates via glycolysis, proteolysis and lipolysis in the development of Chaddar flavour. This has been demonstrated by the absence of Chaddar flavour development in cheese acidified by purely chemicals means via-d-gluconic acid lactone.

Other bacteria like Lactobacillus *plantarum, Lactobacillus pediociccus* and Micrococcus lactic also may contribute to flavour (Mabbit,). Keen et al. even concluded that 2-butanone,a flavour compound of Chedder cheese, is formed only when nonstarter organisms are present. Those bacteria come from indigenous microflora in the milk of from post pasteurization contamination. Becteria are normally present in the under milk cisterns. Bacterial counts of first drawn milk vary from about 100 to many thousand per ml. There is however, little information about types of organism responsible or the stage in the ripening process at which their influence is exerted.

Enzymes Most starter organisms die out papidly in cheese; there is only a 0.5 to 5 per cent survival rate four weeks of ripening. At this time, the flavour development is not achieved. Therefore, if appears that the contribution of the starter to Cheddar flavour development is due to its enzymes rather than the metabolism of viable cells. Becterial enzyme systems are capable of numerous reactions:,reduction,oxidation, dehydration, hydrolysis deamination decarboxylation, phosphorylation. These enzymes systems are released into the medium when the bacteria die and lysis of the cell walls occure.

Enzymes other than those of the starter also contribute to Cheddar flavour development. Rennet is used to induce milk coagulation. About 90 per cent of milk coagulating enzymes in rennet are discarded in the whey. The remaining 10 per cent play a part in maturing Cheddar cheese.

In addition, therefore, of course, enzyme naturally present in milk. Many enzymes in milk are produced by the mammary gland cells, but of these enzymes may be derived from the blood or lympathic system around the gland. Milk enzymes include: lipase, peroxidase, proteases, esterase, xanthine, oxidase, catalase, lactase, amalyase and aldolase. Some of them play an important role in Cheddar flavour development. Enzyme activity is responsible for some of the differences in flavour observed between pasteurized and raw milk cheese. Enzymes will not be inactivated by pasteurization and will participate in flavour development of Cheddar.

Microorganisms and enzymes are responsible for the production of flavour compounds and precursors of flavour compounds. By their activity they also set the physico chemical conditions (pH, oxido-reduction potential), which will regular secondary reaction. However, it is not clear what part of flavour development is due to each of these agents (microorganisms and enzymes) when the contribution is exerted during the maturation process and how important they are to Cheddar flavour

Flavour chemicals Maarse and Visscher have listed 213 volatile constituents as being identified in Cheddar cheese. In terms of contribution to the flavour of Cheddar cheese fatty acids, carbonyls, sulfur compounds and amino acides-peptides are the grouping which have received the most attention.

Fatty Acids

Free fatty acids in cheese are drived from either the breakdown of the fat by lipolysis or the metabolism of carbohydrates and amino acids by bacteria Lipolysis or the metabolism of carbohydrates and amino acids by bacteria Lipolysis is the principal contributor of free fatty acids of chain length C4 or greater. Although most researchers agree that rancidity develops (i.e., an objection able odor) when free fatty acid levels reach excessive levels, there is no consensus on the contribution of fatty acids to Cheddar cheese flavour development. Kristoffersen and Gould, Kristoffersen, Orhan and Tuckey, Singh and Kristoffersen, Harper, Walker, Patton, Foda et al. , and Harper et al. concluded in flavour of the participation of fatty acids in the flavour of Chadder. But others, Reiter et. al. Singh and Kristoffersen.

Law and Sharp, Dacre, and Manning and Price concluded that fatty acids do not have a direct contribution to Cheddar flavour.

Carbonyls

A large number of carbonyl compounds (30) have been detected in Cheddar cheese Walker and Keen suggested that methyl ketones derived from esterfied C_6 to C_{14} β-Ketoacids and not by β-oxidation of the higher fatty acids.

The exact role of the carbonyls Cheddar flavour is uncertain. Acetaldehyde is a precusor of ethol and thus has been implicated in the formation of esters (Vedamuthu et al.). The methyl ketones have been extensively examined for their role in Cheddar flavour. Walker and Keen studied the formation of methyl ketones and concluded that they did not impart a typical mature Cheddar flavour to cheese. However, they conceded that a minor but direct contribution may be made by 2-pentanone, 2-heptanone and 2-nonanone. More recent work by Manning indicated that 2-pentanone could be directly implicated in Cheddar flavour.

Sulfur Compounds

Volatile sulfur compounds have long considered important to Cheddar flavour, although Aston and Douglas concluded that none of the volatile sulfur compounds could be considered to be useful as a reliable indicator of flavour development. Hydrogen sulfur was the first volatile sulfur compound implicated in Chadder cheese flavour. Kristoffersen and Gould and Kristofferson proposed that certain ratios of H_2S to short chain fatty acids were necessary for proper flavour development. Lawrence, Manning and Manning and Price could not establish a relationship between H_2S concentration and characterstic flavour. They concluded that although H_2S may contribute to Cheddar flavour, its presence was not essential.

Keeney and Day identified methional in Cheddar cheese headspace. Methonal is a product of the Strecker degradation; i.e., a reaction between an amino acid and a diketone resulting in the formation of an aldehyde of one carbon atom less than the original amino acid. When methionine undergoes Strecker degradation the main product is methional. Walker, in contrast, could not confirm the presence of methional in cheddar distillate methional is capable of the further breakdown to methanethiol. Law and Sharpe studied the formation of methanethiol in Cheddar cheese and concluded that it was unlikely to be the product of bacteria or their enzymes.

Methanethiol has been indentified in cheese by Labbey and Day, Libbey et al., Manning and Robinson, Manning, and Manning and Moore. Manning showed a strong relationship between the contribution of methanethiol in the headspace and the flavour intensity of Cheddar cheese. The formation of methantiol in cheese was studied by Manning.

Dimethyl sulfide has been detected in Cheddar cheese by Patton et al., Krogger and Patton, Morris et al, Bills et al., Mc Gugan et al., Manning and Robinson, Manning, and Manning et al.. Patton et al. claimed that dimethyl sulfeid was responsible for a "top note" in all good-quality Chedder. On the otherhands, Manning concluded that its presence was essential to Cheddar flavour because it occurred inconsistently.

Carbonylsulfied has also been found in Cheddar cheese (Aston) and Douglas 1981 and 1983; however, they conculuded that this compound was unlikely to make direct contribution to Cheddar cheese flavour.

Amino Acids and Peptides

Mulder, Happer, Kosikowski, and Kristoffersen and Gould found that the flavour of cheese increased with total free amino acid concentration. In contrast, Dacre and Law et al., did not find any correlation between flavour development and amino acid concentration.

On the basis of findings prior to 1979, most researchers concurred that the free amino acids made little or no direct contribution to cheddar cheese flavour, but these amino acids provide an important background, usually chracterized as brothely, upon which characteristic flavour was superimposted. Work by McGugan et al. has thrown some doubt onto the simplicity of this view. These authors concluded that the volatiles may contribute mainly to the quality of the flavour, while the water soluble fraction provides the intensity of the flavour.

The contribution of peptides in this particular small peptides are probably similar to those of free amino acids. However, peptides are better known for their role in the production of bitterness in Cheddar cheese. Bitter peptides were isolated from Cheddar cheese by Harwalkar, However, and Elliot, Richardson and Cremer, Hamilton et al., Schalinatus and Behnke, and Edwards and Kosikowski.The production of peptides and amino acids in the cheese is mainly due to the protecolytic action of the rennet and the starter.

Flavour Balance

From the preceding discussion two main conclusions arise:

1. No compounds have been isolated that can be singly associated with Cheddar flavour.
2. There is no general consensus about the identity of the compounds of even groups of compounds responsible for Cheddar flavour.

The most widely accepted theory on Cheddar cheese flavour is the component balance theory, whereby, Cheddar flavour is supposedly composed of a number of different compounds that must be present in the correct proportion. This hypothesis, however, does not unite the widely divergent views concerning the individual components to cheese flavour: fatty acids carbonyl compounds, amines peptides, amino acids, sulfur compounds and others.

Furthermore, even though this hypothesis was proposed more than 35 years ago, very few workers have tried to determine the ratios that lead to good Cheddar flavour . Most of the work published dealt with the study of one particular class of compounds independent of the other chemicals present in Cheddar. This fact may explain why the literature is full of so many opposite conclusions.

Kristoffersen started that desirable flavour occurs only when free fatty acids and hydrogen sulfide are presented in definite interdependent concentrations. At twelve months, when the ratio of micromoles of free fatty acids to the micromoles of hydrogen sulphide per 100g of cheese is 14.2, the flavour was described as balanced . When the value of this ratio was 7.2, the cheese was described as sulfide-like, and fatty acid-like with a ratio of 27.9.

Ohren and Tuckey suggested that part of the components balance of the Cheddar flavour was due to a balance of free fatty acids and acetate. Their results suggest that at 6 months a good-flavoured cheese should contain between 60 and 140 micromoles of free fatty acid + acetate per 5 grams of cheese and that the ratio of micromoles-free fatty acid to micromoles of acetate should be between 0.55 and 1.0.

Roquefort (Blue) Cheese flavour

Roquefort and other blue-veined cheese are traditionally made from pasteurized milk containing 3.5 per cent fat and about 9 per cent nonfat solids. Streptococcus lactis culture is added the milk coagulated with rennet and curd separated. Cultures of the mold *penicillium roqueforti* may be added either to the milk before coagulation or sprinkled onto the surface of the separated curds. The cheese is then formed with a relatively loose texture and 2.5-3 per cent salt added.

Flavour Development

The freshly made cheese has little flavour and the strong characteristic flavour and appearance are only produced during the 60- to 90-day ripening period. A good quality Roquefort cheese has a sharp peppery note, but is still smooth to the palate. Lawrence found a continuous lipolysis of triglycerides and the simulta neous conversion of liberated fatty acids to methyl ketones by the spores and mycelia of the proqueforti during ripening 2-Pentanone and 2- heptanone, probably derived from caprylic acid, and 2-nonanone are of prime importatance in the flavour profile.

The chemicals identified in blue-veined cheese are broadly silimar to those reported as present in Cheddar and other cheeses. The formation of these compounds and their relative importance to the characteristic flavour profile of blue cheese have been reviewed by Day. Maarse and Visscher have provide a tabulation of flavour compounds found in blue cheese.

Fermentation

Although the commecial development of a submerged fermentation process for the production of blue cheese flavour was patented as early as 1963 by Watts and Nolson, the production of a blue cheese flavour under controlled conditions is the subject of continued research.

FUNGI

It has long been recognized that fungi have distinctive odors and hence may be a potential source of flavouring materials. Mushroom aroma (1-octene-3-ol) is procuced by *Aspergillus oryzae* and blue cheese aroma by *penicullum* species. Ceratocystis species have been studied in some detail for their ability to produce fruit aromas. The character of the aroma was found to be dependent upon the organism being studied time of growth, nitrogen source and carbon source (Hanssen) and Sprecher. While aroma production by various fungi have been studied, the quantity of aroma compounds produced are typicalluy too low to be of commercial significance. The aroma constituents are typically in the low parts per million range, which is adequate for providing an aroma to the culture but too low to recover cost effectively for flavouring purposes. The most likely role of fungi in producing flavour will be as biological catalysts to accomplish desired chemical transformations or for the production of individual chemicals (e.g., geraniol by *C. variospora, Schindler*).

BLACKTEA AROMA

The freshly packed green leaves of the tea plant *Thae (Camellia) sinesis* require processing in order to include the formation of the characteristic odor and flavour of black tea. The harvested leaves are first allowed to wither, during which time the carotenoid, amino acids and flavonol precursers of the odor and colour are formed. The leaves are then to broken to release the oxidase enzymes present in the cell sap and ensure their close contact with the precursors. They are then spread out in the layers and allowed to ferment for several hours during which a primary oxidation occurs and the leaves assume an agreeable odor and colour. The fermented leaves are then "fired" at about 85°C; this induces a secondary oxidation, a reduction in moisture content and the full development of the characteristic odor and colour of black tea.

The enzymatic formation of black tea aroma has reviewed by Sanderson and Graham and Bokuchava and Skobeleva. It is established that the biosynthesis takes place in line with the processing conditions and Sanderson, Co, and Gonzales have outlined the likely stages in the biochemical reactions involved.

The main precursors of the odor components are amino acids and carotenoids including β-carotene, lutein neoxanthin and violaxanthin. Quantitative studied by these researchers have shown that the carotenoid content of the leaves is significantly reduced during fermentation and that the products of the primary oxidation of β-carotent are β-ionone plus terpenoid carbonyls. A secondary epoxidation takes place during the "firing" and results in the formation of dihydroactinidiole, an epoxyionnes. Other carotennoids present similarly oxidize, yielding α-ionone, linalool and substituted hydroxy and epoxyionones. Sanderson and Yamanishi listed 145 identified components of black tea aroma. As of 1989 this number increased to 541.The most important of these are limonene phenylethyl alcohol, linalool, gerniol, trans-2 hexenal, phenylethyl acetaidehyde, α-and β-ionones isovaleric acid, benzoic acid, o-cresol, dimentyl sulfied and nethylformyl pyrrole together with some 18 esters and lactones.

The colour of black tea is due to the oxidation of tea flavanols by a catechol oxidase enzyme system.

FLAVOUR FORMATION DURING THERMAL PROCESSING

The predominate flavour of some food products develops during thermal processing, either during food manufacture or home preparation. Some examples of these foods are meals, chocolate, coffee, french fries and baked goods. These primary routes of flavour formation in these foods are the Maillard reaction, caramelization and thermal oxidations in fats. This section of the chapter will present an overview of these means of flavour production.

Nonenzymatic Browning

Nonenzymatic browning (NEB) encompasses browning reaction, including Maillard browning, caramelization and ascorbic acid browning. This reaction is responsible for some of the most pleasent flavours enjoyed by man. There is no question that freshly baked bread, steak, freshly brewed coffee or chocolate is appreciated by the consumer. Yet none of these flavours existed in the product until the food processor (or cook) heated the product to develop the flavour. Hurrell has presented an excellent review of the Maillard reaction in food flavour formation. While the following will present an overview of this reaction,details may be found in several other publications, including Vernin; Parliment McGorrin, and Ho; Finot et al.; and Maarse.

General Overview of Maillard Browning

Hodge was the first to present an outline of the overall reactions involved in Maillard browning. Generally speaking. Maillard browning is a reaction between carbonyls and amines. The carbonyls in foods most often are reducing sugars,while the amines come from either amino acids or proteins. The major end products of the Maillard reaction are melanoidins and other nonvolatile (and insignificant to flavour) compounds. However, number of intermediates and minor products of the reaction are formed that are significant to flavour. Reineccius et al. have shown that while 1.3 g (per 100g beans) of reducing sugars and amino acids (total) were reacted during the roasting of cocoa beans, only 0.9 mg of pyrazines were formed. Thus about 0.07 per cent of the reactants were transformed into pyrazines, while the remainder of the reactants went into other products. Yet these pyrazines are exceptionally important to the flavour of chocolate. It is typically these minor products that make the largest contribution to flavour.

Factors Influencing Browning Rate

It should be noted that many factors influence the rate of browning and the particular flavour pathway predominating in reaction. The influence of system composition is obvious if one roasts coffee, cocoa or soy beans. The influence of system processing conditions on browning flavour development is equally obvious if one considers the sensory quality of roasted vs. stewed meats. Both products have the same precursor systems for reaction. However, there are considerable flavour difference between the two foods.

The vast majority of research on the factors that influence browning has related to either the disappearance of starting materials (e.g.,lysine/ glucose reactions) or the production of brown pigments. The limited amount of work studying factors that influence flavour formation has focused largely on the flavour compounds formed via the heating of model systems. While system composition (e.g., sugar and amino acid type) and thermal processing parameters have been varied in some of these studies, there have been very few methodical studies conducted in this area. Most studies have related overall sensory properties to variations in reaction mixture composition or process (Table 39.4).

Temperature

The influence of temperature on flavour formation may be understood better by recalling that each particular pathway of flavour formation has its own activation energy. To illustrate this influence, consider the plot shown in Fig. 2.10 (please note that this plot does not contain valid data, but is only for illustrating an idea). In this plot 2,3-dimethylpyrazine has the highest activation energy, followed by cyclopentenolone and hydroxymethylfurfural. Activation energy is equal to the slope of the line divided by R (natural gas constant). This plot shows that 2,3-dimethylpyrazine would have the largest rate constant (or highest rate of production) at high temperatures followed

Table - 39.4

Aromas Generated by Amino Acids with Sugars[a]

	Glycine	*Glutamic Acid*	*Lysine*	*Methionine*	*Phenylalanine*
Glucose	Burnt candy	Chicken tray	Burnt fried potatoes	Cabbage	Caramel
Frutose	Beef broth	Chicken	Fried potato	Bean soup	Dirty dog
Maltose	Beef broth	Baked ham	State potato	Harsh, horseradish	Sweet
Sucrose	Beef broth	Charred meat	Boiled meat	Overcooked cabbage	Chocolate

* From El'Ode *et al.* (1966).

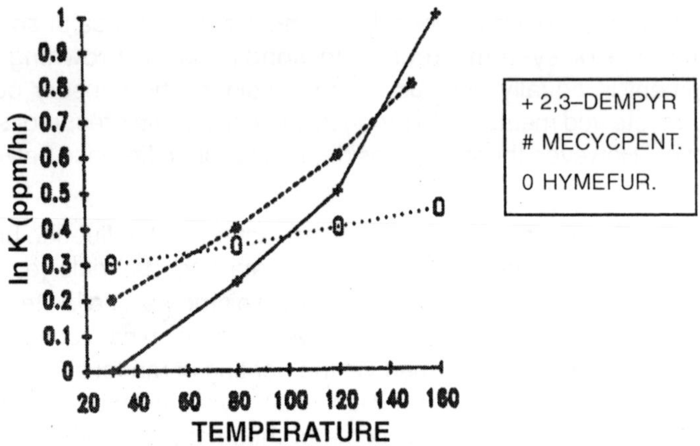

Fig. 39.10 : Hypothetical data for 2,3-dimethylpyrazine (+), methyl cyclopentenolone (*), and hydroxymethyl furfural (O).

by cyclopentenolone and then hydroxymethylfurfural. As temperature is decreased to typical storage temperatures, the furfural would be produced at the highest rate and now the pyrazine would have the lowest rate. Since each pyrazine, furan, furfural, etc., would have its own activation energy, one could put several hundred lines on this figure and realize how important temperature is in influencing the formation of flavour compounds via NEB.

A kinetic study by Leahy reported an activation energy of approximately 35 keal/mole for pyrazine and 2-methyl pyrazine and about 43kcal/mole for the dimethyl pyrazines. These high activation energies indicate a very strong temperature dependence of pyrazine formation and explain why pyrazines (roasted, nutty, toasted notes) do not occur during storage, but only during high-temperature treatment.

There are other implications of the point made by presenting Fig. 39.10. It is clear that one will not get the same flavour balance by using one temperature vs, another. This becomes relevent when a flavour company develops a reaction flavour at one temperature (e.g., 160°C in a lab scale reactor) and then goes into the production area and expects to achieve the same flavour profile using an atmospheric kettle limited to ca. 100°C. Longer process time at a lower temperature will not necessarily give the same flavour as a shorter time at a higher temperature–in fact, we would be rather surprised if we did obtain the same flavour character! Our knowledge of classical browning does not prepare us for this occurrence, since we can readily develop more color by adjusting time and temperature of heating.

pH

Our classical knowledge of nonezymatic browning tells us that as we go up in pH, we develop more browning. Can we depend on this truth for flavour formation? Unfortunately not. pH influences many (but not all) of the reaction rates in the browning reaction and this in fluence is not uniform. Thus, we need to use a particular pH to force the browning reaction as we wish. For example, meat-like reaction flavours must be heated at pHs around 5 to 5.5. Meat-like flavour cannot be obtained at other pHs. Chocolate flavours are typically run at pHs about neůtrality.

Water Activity

Water activity has been found to have a pronounced infience on the rate on nonflavour browning reaction. A maximum reaction rate is generally observed at a water activity of 0.6-0.7. For flavour, several researchers have noted that water activity has an influence both on the rate of flavour formation as well as flavour character. The work by Shu and Ho demonstrates how water activity (or proportion of propylene glycol) can influence flavour production (Fig.39.11). Another example is for the formation of chocolate reaction flavours. A very nice chocolate flavour can be produced by heating selected amino acids in propylene glycol as the solvent (zero water activity). The same flavour can not be produced in an aqueous system.

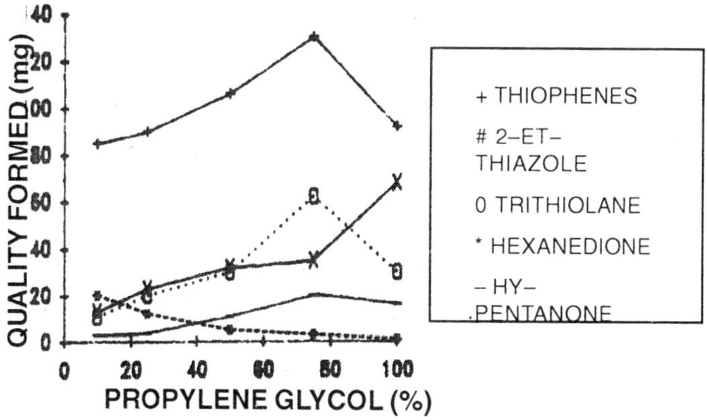

Fig. 39.11 : The formation of selected volatiles as a function of water content in a model system.

Influence of Fat

For typically does not participate directly in the browning reaction, yet may be quite important in influencing flavour formation via browning. Fat is required to give the " species" notes to meat-like reaction flavour (except for beef, which may become "beefy without beef tallow in the reaction). While fat will make a flavour contribution due to primary degradation products (e.g., unsaturated aldehydes formed from chicken fat during heating), fat will also make a flavour contribution by participating in the browning reaction. Fat makes its contribution to browning flavours by yielding long chain aldehydes for participation in browning. There is no source of long chain aldehydes in foods except for the facty acids. As the fat degrades due to heat treatment, the various long chain carbonyls formed will radily participation in browning, producing uniquely flavoured saturated and unsaturated compounds.

Summary

Overall, the condition that influence the Maillard reaction as measured by either loss in nutritional value or the generation of pigments may or may not have a similar effect on flavour. To develop flavours based on the Maillard reaction, one cannot depend upon the classical information presented ingeneral textbooks or general college courses. The knowledge is generally not available, and thus a great deal of art and trial and error are involved in producing flavours via Millard browning. This creates untold amounts of frustration on the part of both customer and creative chemists serving these customers. The frustration comes in terms of creating the exact profile desired and reproducing this profile. While flavour production can most often be accurately controlled by monitoring system pressure or temperature (in distillations) or solvent choice or temperature (extractions), the Maillard reaction is so poorly understood and so complices that there really aren't any good means of process control or quality control.

Formation of flavour Compounds

The most abundant flavour compounds formed via the Millard reaction are aliphatic aldehydes, ketones, diketones and lower chain length fatty acids. However, heterocyclic compounds containing oxygen, nitrogen, sulfur or combination of these atoms are much more numerous and significant to the flavour of browned foods (Vernine and Vernin 1982) Sobstantial work has been devoted to the identification of flavour compounds, elucidatiopn of pathways for formation, and evaluation of sensory properties of these compounds. Thus, the reader is directed to Maarse and Visscher for compounds identified, the browning literature in general for pathways, and Fors for sensory properties. Information on the formation of flavour in bread, meat, seafood, beer, coffee, cacao and tea,and nuts has been reviewed recently.

Flavours from Lipids

Lipids undergo changes during the processing of food that make a flavour contribution. These changes may include the indirect effects noted earlier in this chapter or more direct effects to be discussed at this point.

Deep Fat Fried Flavour

Chang et al. have pointed out the market significance of deep fat frying in their review of deep fat fried flavour by noting that over 1.1 billion lb of fat is used in the United States annually to process franch fried potatoes, doughnuts and potato chips. They also noted that the major part of the 10 billion lb. of fat consumed by Americans yearly is used for fried foods. While part of the desirability of deep fat fried foods lies in the physical properties imparted to the food by this process (crisping effects as well as increased palatability due to fat absorption), the characteristic " french fried" flavour is quite popular and unique to this process.

The characteristic deep fat fried aroma is considered to arise three mechanisms: (1) the hydrolysis of triglyerides; (2) oxidation of unsaturated fatty acids; and (3) pyrolytic reactions. The relative imporatnce of these reactions depends upon the frying oil, fried material and frying conditions.

Hydrolytic Reactions

Hydrolytic reactions require the contact of the triglyceride with water. Additives (e.g.,) emulsifiers) or the buildup of oil degradation products will increase these reactions. The presence of anions or cations will also catalyze these reactions.

Oxidation

The primary source of flavour development in heated oils is lipid oxidation. Dissolved oxygen is consumed rapidly during frying and thus becomes the rate limiting factor. The process of lipid oxidation at elevated temperature is similar to that which occurs at room temperature with a few exceptions. First, the oxidation process takes place with limited oxygen. This changes the relative proportions of end products, primarily a lower level of di-and trisubstituted oxidation products.

Second, the hydroperoxides formed are very unstable at elevated temperatures and thus do not build up during the frying process, but all tend to be readily decomposed during frying. The effect of this is a more random generation of flavour compounds since the reaction is no longer limited to the degradation of the least stable hydroperoxides.

Pyrolysis Reactions

Pyrolysis reactions do not take place until temperatures exceed 200°C. This is higher than normal frying temperatures and thus pyrolysis reaction do not occur unless the oil is overheated or comes in contact with hot metal surfaces. Acrolein, a major products of pyrolysis, is a pungent, irritating volatile compounds originating from the dehydration of free glycerol. Pyrolysis is considered to have a negative effect upon the flavour of deep fat frying oils.

Effect of Frying Condition on Flavour

The flavour of frying oils is not optimum at the start of frying with fresh oils. The fresh oil has few degradtion products responsible for the desirable flavour of deep fat fried foods.Therefore, the flavour quality of fried foods increases as the oil is used until off-flavours start to dominate the flavour profile.

Frying temperature has an effect on the formation of desirable flavour,but little effect on the rate of oil deterioration (oxygenlimiting) until pyrolysis occurs. Pyrolysis reactions yield bitter. pungent and irritating end products. Normal frying temperatures range from 120-195°C.

Traces of metals have a significant influences on flavour since they catalyze oxidation. Similar to room temperature oxidation, inon is the most catalytic followed by copper, cobalt and nickel.

Antioxidants are effective in increasing oil stability. Tochopherol is the most abundant natural antioxidant. Synthetic antioxidants (TBHQ and BHT) are commonly used. One must recall that BHT is volatile and would be lost from the frying oil. Anthfoaming agents (e.g., methyl polysiloxance also lend stability to the frying oil by preventing foaming and thus limiting oxygan contact.

Mechanisms of Flavour Formation

The mechanism of flavour formation is quite detailed and beyond the scope of this book. Excellent reviews are available in this subject area and the reader may go to Pokorny or an earlier review for more detail.

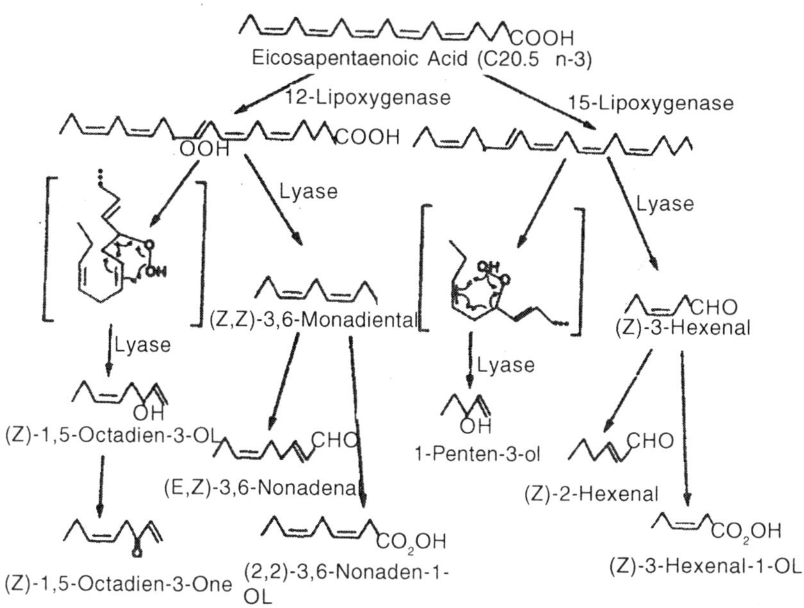

Fig. 39.12 : Proposed mechanism for the enzymatic biosynthesis of some fresh volatile seafood flavour compounds for eicosapentaenoic acid.

Lactones

Lactones may be formed in foods via microbial action. extensive lipid oxidation or biosynthetic routes. It appears that due to inborn errors in metaboilsm, hydroxy acids may be synthesized and incorporated into the triglycerides of certain living organisms. These hydroxy acids are relatively unstable and are readily hydrolyzes from the triglyeride in the presence of water with heat. Hydrolysis of the hydroxy acid result in its cyclization to a lactone. Since the hydroxy acid has no flavour as long as it is bound to the triglyceride, thermal processing frees the acid and a flavourful lactone is produces. This process is one of the simpler ways in which flavour may be formed during the processing of foods.

Seafood Flavours

Lipid-derived aroma compounds play a key role in the flavour of fresh seafood. When the seafood is harvested, enzymatic reactions (lipoxygence) initiate oxidation of the higly polyunsaturated fatty acids (e.g., arachidonic acid, eiocosa-5,8,11,17-pentaenoic acid, and docosa-4,7,10,13,16,19-hexaenoic acid), thereby yielding fatty acid hydroperoxides. These hydorperoxides are further broken down by lyase enzymes to alcohols, which then are attacked by oxidase enzymes to form volatile flavour compounds (ketones and aldehydes) that produce the characterstic seafood flavour (see Fig.39.12) The majority of these compounds are common to normal lipid oxidation of fish, but the exzyme-mediated nature of flavour formation results in a flavour quite different from that associated with lipid oxidation.

White lipids play a major role in the formation of seafood flavour. other precursors and types of flavour compounds are also of significance. Josephson has reviewed the role of sulfur compounds, isoprenoid-related compounds, amines and hydrocarbons in fresh seafood flavour (or off-flavour) He has also included a discussion of the role of thermal processing on flavour development in seafood.

Caramelization

Caramelization is the process whereby sugars are thermally decomposed to yield a host of nonvolatile products as well as characteristic flavour compounds. Unite Maillard browning, this process is not amine catalyzed so the reaction proceeds only at high temperatures. Tempertaure of 150°C or greater are generally required for the reaction to proceed. The reaction proceeds more rapidly at high in the manufacturing of caramel flavourings.

FLAVOURS FORMED VIA FERMENTATION

Fermentation is a process that provides us with a variety of new flavours to enjoy. We come in contact daily with a veriety of food products produced via fermentation. Some example include soy sauce, cheese, yogurt, bread, beer, wine, fermented fish products and sausages.

Flavour may be developed from the primary metabolism of the microorganism or from residual enzamatic activity once the microbial cell has lysed. For example,primary metabolism is responsible for much of the flavour of alcoholic beverages, while residual enzymatic activity is essential for the development of aged cheese flavour.

A large number of different classes of flavour compounds can be produced by microorganisms. Tressl et al. have microorganisms may accomplish (Table 39.5). This section will present some metaboilc pathways leading to the development of flavour in fermented food products. The book by Margalith is recommended for greater detail.

Esters

Esters are quite imporatnt to the flavour of both natural foods (e.g., fresh fruit) and fermented foods. Of the fermented foods, esters are probably the most imporatnt class of flavour compounds in alcoholic beverages. Maarse and Visscher have listed 94 different esters as being identified in beer. Most of the esters found in beer are formed via primary fermentation. They have been linked to the metabolsm of lipids by yeast. Lipid metabolism provides a large number of acids and alcohols that may undergo esterification to yield a variety of esters. While pure chemical reaction can lead to ester formation, this reaction is too slow to account for the esters in most foods. Nordstron has demonstrated that esterification is controlled by intracellular enzymes.

Acids

Acid production via microorganisms is important to the flavour of many fermented foods.Certainly, the importance of acids to both fermented dairy products and pickled produces cannot be overemphasized.

The acid of greatest importance to the flavour of fermented dairy products is lactic acid. Lactic acid is an optically active acid existing as the D, L or optically inactive mixture depending upon the microorganism involved in its synthesis. There appears to be no difference in flavour between the optical isomers. Lactic acid is characterized as being odorless and having a sour milk taste.

Table - 39.5

Reactions catalyzed by microbes[a]

Oxidation	*Acylation*
Oxygenation of CH or C═C	Transglycosidation
Dehydrogenation of CHOH	Methylation
Dehydrogenation of CH–CH	Condensation
	Cleavage of C–C
Reduction	
Hydrogenation of C═O	Decarboxylation
Hydrogenation of C═C	Dehydration
	Amination/Deamination
Isomerization	Halogenation
Esterification/Hydrolysis	Phosphorylation

[a] From Tressl et al. (1978).

The organisms most commonly associated with lactic acid formation are classified as being either homofermentative (e.g., *Lactobacillus bulguricus,* which produces primary lactic acid,>85 per cent of metabolic end products) or heterofermentative (e.g., *Leuconostoc* sp., which produces lactic acid, acetic acid, ethanol, carbon dioxide, and other metabolites). The homofermentative organisms employ the Embden-Meyerhof pathway for lactose fermentation, while the heterofermentation organisms metabolze lactose via the hexose-monophosphate pathway. Lactic acid will reach concentrations of up 2 per cent or greater in cultures of *L.bulgaricus* or *L. acidophillus.*

Lactic acid is also formed in wines during fermentation from L-malic acid. Malic acid is a very tart acid present in grapes that needs to be converted to lactic acid to "smooth out" the harsh acidity. This "malolactic" fermentation is the result of bacterial (most commonly Leuconostoe sp.) action during the läst stages of fermentation.

Numerous other acids are produced during fermentation. Most microorganisms have active lipase systems that attack trigly-cerides to yield glycerol, monoglycerides, diglycerides and free fatty acids. These free fatty acids can make a substantial contribution to the flavour of various cheeses and sausages. Secondary reactions of the free fatty acids (e.g., oxidation) can again yield a host of new flavour compounds.

Acids may also come from the deamination of amino acids. The products are various aliphatic (linear and branched chain) and aromatic acids.

Carbonyls

Carbonyl flavour compounds make a particularly significant contribution to the flavour of fermented dairy products. Diacetyl is one of the most important carbonyls to the flavour of these products. It has a buttery, nut-like flavour Diacetyl is produced via the fermentation of citrate in dairy products. The most important citric acid fermenters are *Leuconostoc citrovorum, L. creamoris, L. dextranicum, Streptococcus lactis* subspecies *diacetylactis, S. thermophilus* and certain strains of *Proprionibacterium shermani.* The metabolic pathway leading to the synthesis of diacetyl is somewhat controversial. Kempler and McKay have presented a summary of the two best accepted pathways (Fig. 39.13). Both pathways involve the degradation of citrate to acetate and oxaloacetate, which is then decarboxylated to form pyruvate. Apparently, diacetyl is relatively nontoxic Apparently, diacetyl is relatively nontoxic to the bacteria cell so excess pyruvate is channeled into diacetyl.

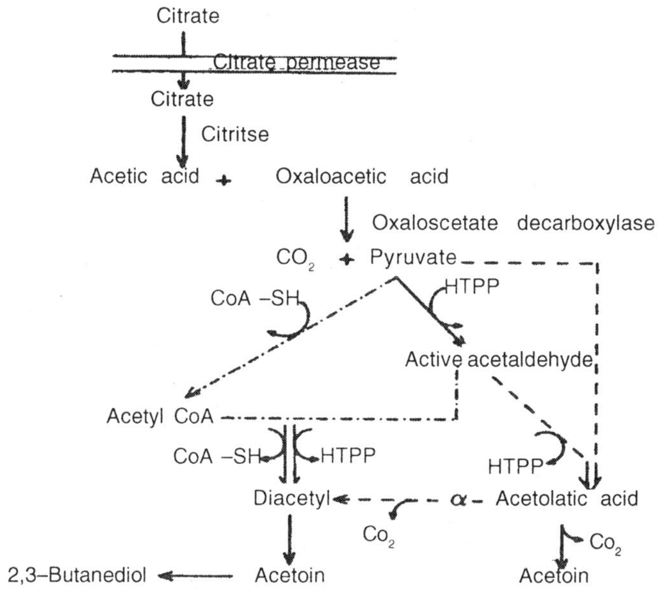

Fig. 39.13 : Formation of diacetyl during fermentation in dairy cultures.

Unfortunately, diacetyl is not stable in most cultured food products. The micro-organisms that synthesized the diacetyl also contain diacetyl reductase, which reduces diacetyl to flavourless acetoln and 2,3-butanedlol. Thus fermented products such as buttermilk, which depend on diacetyl for flavour, have an optimum or peak flavour. As the product is stored, the diacetyl is reduced, and flavour strength and quality decrease.

A second dairy product where carbonyls are considered as flavour impact compounds is yogurt. Here, acetaldehyde is credited with providing the characteristic pungent green character. Acetaldehyde is a metabolic end product of *L. bulgaricus* and/or *S. thermophilus* during the fermentation of milk to yogurt.

Carbonyls are quite important to the flavour of cheeses. Maarse and Visscher have noted that a total of 30 aldehydes and methyl ketones have been identified in the volatile fraction of Cheddar cheese. Carbonyls (methyl ketones) may arise in fermented products initially via lipase activity of the microorganism. Dairy products contain a significant quantity of β-keto acids, which are readily hydrolyzed from the triglyceride by microbial lipases and then decarboxylated to form the odd carbon number methyl ketones.

Methyl ketones and aldehydes may also be formed via microbially induced lipid oxidations. The oxidation may be initiated by microbial lipases, hydrogen peroxide produced by microorganisms and/or lipoxidase-like activity.

A final mechanism for the formation of carbonyls via microorganisms involves the transamination and decarboxylation of free amino acids. Morgan has demonstrated the production of 3-methyl butanal by *S. lactis var. maltigenes*. MacLeod and Morgan have documented the production of 2-methyl butanal, methional and phenylacetaldehyde from leucine, methionine, and phenylalanine, respectively, by the same microorganism.

Carbonyl compounds typically are significant to the flavour of most fermented food products. As has been shown, these carbonyls may arise due to carbohydrate or citrate metabolism, lipid oxidation or amino acid degradation.

Alcohols

Alcohols typically make a minor contribution to flavour unless present in relatively high concentrations (ppm) or they are unsaturated (e.g., 1-octen-3-o1). Alcohols may arise via primary metabolic activity of a microorganism (e.g., ethanol) or by reduction of a carbonyl to the corresponding alcohol.

Reazin et al. have outlined metabolic pathways leading to the major congeners during grain fermentation (Fig. 39.14). This figure illustrates that the fusel alcohols (alcohols larger in size than ethanol) can be formed from either carbohydrate or amino acid metabolism. Alcohol production from amino acids may occur by transamination, decarboxylation and reduction or by oxidative deamination followed by decarboxylation and reduction. In either pathway, the product is always the amino acid minus the amine group and one carbon atom.

The alternate metabolic pathway yielding alcohols involves the reduction of the corponding carbonyl (Fig. 39.15). Lamparsky and Klimes (1981) demonstrated this mechanism by finding the equivalent alcohols (as aldehydes) in Cheddar cheese. Secondary alcohols corresponding to the methyl ketones found in blue cheeses have also been reported.

Terpenes

Currently the production of terpenes by microorganisms is primarily of academic interest. There are no fermented food products commercially available that derive their characteristic flavour from terpenes. The interest in terpene synthesis by microorganisms is due to the potential for the commercial production of specific terpenes via fermentation.

Collins and Halim identified geraniol, citronellol, linalool, neral, citral, geranyl acetate and citronellyl acetate as metabolic products of *Ceratocystis variospora*. Later, nerol, citronellol and geraniol were found to be produced by *Trametes odorata*.

The biosynthetic pathways leading to terpene formation in microorganisms is not well characterized. It is assumed that a pathway similar to that found in plants also operates in microbial syntheses. This basically involves the conversion of mevalonate (MVA) into isopentyl pyrophosphate and 3,3-dimethyl allyl pyrophosphate, which condense to form geranyl pyrophosphate . Lanza and Palmer have provided evidence via radio-active labeling that this pathway occurs in the synthesis of geraniol in *Ceratocystis moniliformis*.

Lactones

Lactones make a significant contribution to the flavour of several fermented food products, particularly dairy products and alcoholic beverages. Tressl et al. have summarized some of the previous literature on lactone synthesis by microorganisms in fermented alcoholic beverages. As can be seen in Fig. 39.16, lactones may be formed from amino acids. Pathway A shows the oxidative deamination of glutamic acid to yield 2-oxoglutrate. The 2-oxoglutrate is decarboxylated to produce 4-oxobutyrate, which is then reduced to the 4-hydroxy butyrate. The cyclization of 4-hydroxy butyrate yields γ-butyrolactone.

Pyrazines

Pyrazines are generally associated with non-enzymatic browning. However, pyrazines have also been found as a result of microbial action. *Bacillus subtilis* was the first organism found to produce a pyrazine. Since that time, several pyrazines (2-acetyl, dimethyl, 2-methoxy-3-ethyl, 2,5 or 2,6-diethyl-3-methyl, trimethyl, tetramethyl and trimethylpyrazine) have been identified in aged cheese. The mechanism of their formation is not clearly settled. While it has been assumed that pyrazines were formed as the result of enzyme catalyzed reactions, recent work by Reps, Hammond, and Glatz, Rizzi, and Rizzi has shown that pyrazines can be formed via nonenzymatic pathways at ambient conditions. This raises the possibility that microorganisms are providing low molecular weight precursors of the pyrazines as molecular end products, but pyrazine formation proceeds by

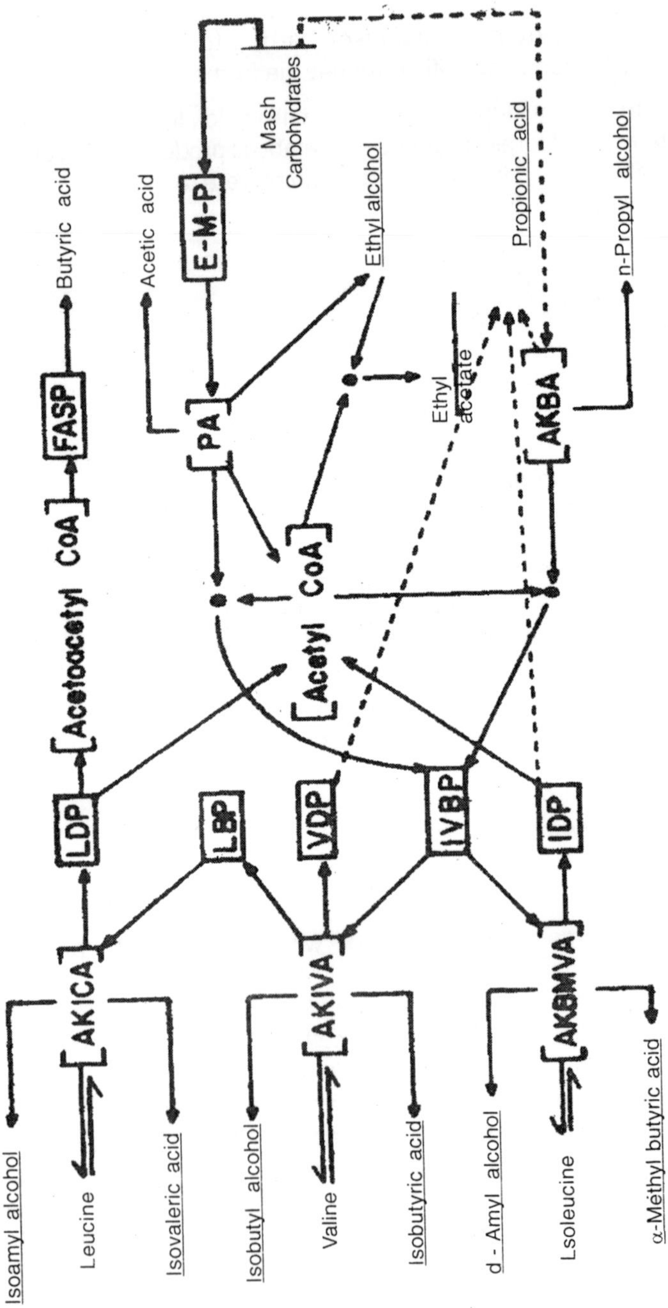

Fig. 39.14 Proposed metabolic pathways for the synthesis of whiskey congenets.

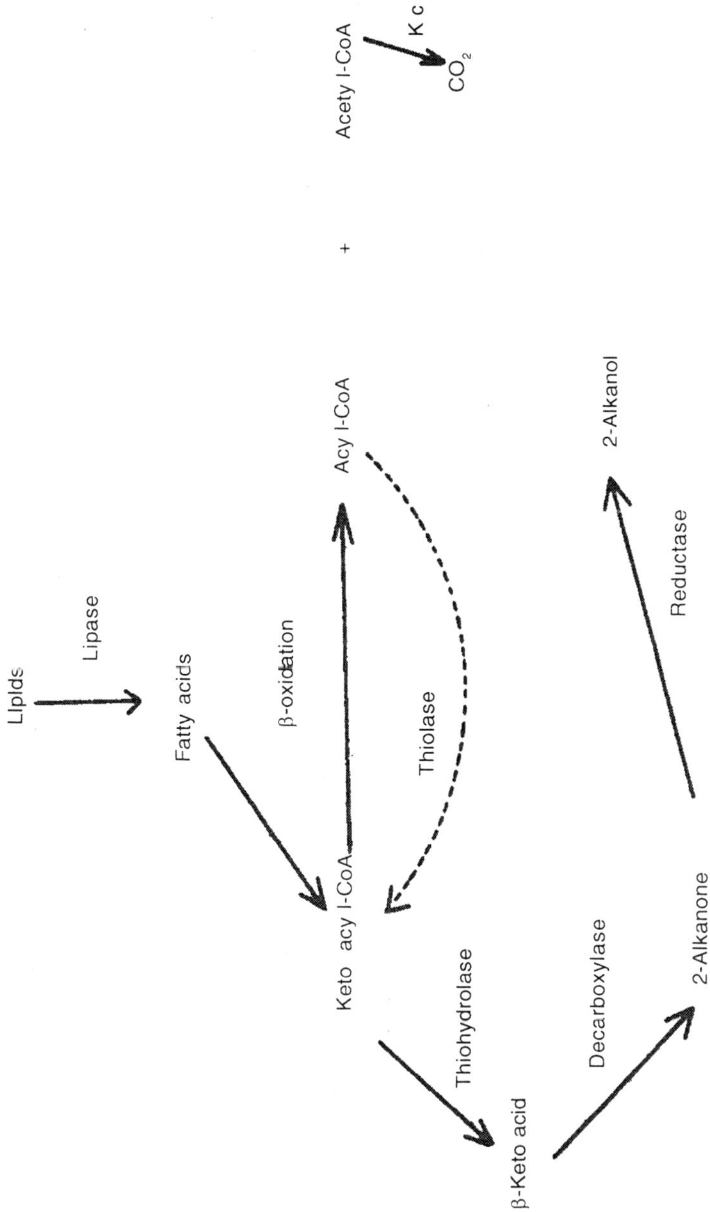

Fig. 39.15 Metabolic pathways leading to the formation of methyl ketones and the corresponding 2-alkanols.

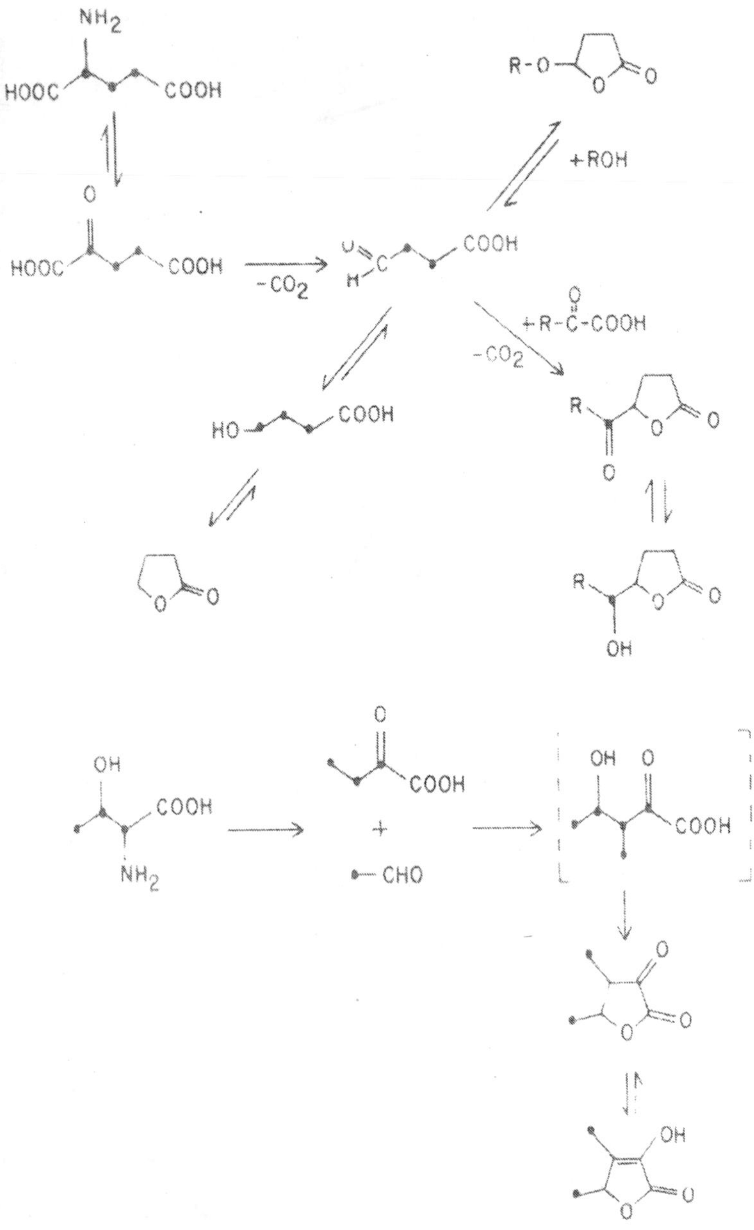

Fig. 39.16 : Formation of lactones by microorganism.

purely chemical pathways.

Pyrazines have also been linked to the generation of off-flavours in foods due to microbial action. *Pseudomonas taetrolens* has been shown to produce a musty-potato aroma (2,5-dimethyl pyrazine and 2-methoxy-3-isopropyl pyrazine) in milk and other refrigerated foods. A similar flavour defect has been found in cheese containing *Ps. mucidolens*. A mutant of *Ps. taetrolens* has recently been isolated, which is of interest for the commercial production of 2-methoxy-3-isopropyl pyrazine. The parent culture was found to produce about 40 ppb of this pyrazine, while a mutant produced by chemical treatment produced about 15,000 ppb. Since the sensory threshold of this compound is about 0,001 ppb, 15,000 is a sufficient concentration to be of commercial significance.

Conclusions

Some of the mechanisms leading to the formation of several classes of flavour compounds via microorganisms are outlined in this chapter. At this point, two additional ideas should be mentioned. First, we have only considered the formation of flavour via metabolic activity of the living microorganism. Microorganisms can contribute to flavour by leaving active enzymes in the product following death and cell lysis. A good example of the significance of bacterial enzymes to flavour is in aged cheeses. This aspect of flavour has been discussed in the section of this chapter that dealt with cheese flavour.

The second idea that should be brought out in closing this section of this text is that the flavour system in a fermenting product is very dynamic. One microorganism may produce a metabolite, which initially accumulates in the product and may make a significant contribution to flavour. A second organism may then reach significant metabolizing this first metabolite. Therefore, the flavour of the product will change. Microorganisms may also alter flavour compounds produced in the product via other mechanisms, e.g., lipid oxidation or non-enzymatic browning. Thus, lipid oxidation of NEB may result in a different flavour in a fermented product than in a nonfermented product.

40

Role of Perfumer

As we all know that perfumery all along has been a less known subject, still less talked about and hence a layman has the impression that a mysterious veil is surrounding the whole subject. I shall try to tear off this veil by elaborating and discussing various aspects of perfumery.

We appreciate and enjoy our life through five senses, namely, sense of sight, sense of hearing, sense of smell; sense of taste and sense of feel. These five senses are not present in all the animals and as go down the ladder we find that some of the lower creatures possess only few of these senses. Those animals who possess few senses and if sense of smell happens to be one of them, the same plays the most important role in their life. Hence sense of smell in lower animals is highly developed. As we go up ladder we find that so-called developed animals have got comparatively less developed sense of smell. However, this sense of smell is still superior to that of human beings. I shall now cite a couple of examples of animal kingdom to show how the sense of smell is used by them. The sense of smell has two functions to fulfil the first being Self Preservation and the second is, Procreation. In the case of self preservation, the sense of smell helps to locate the food for the animal and also detect the hidden enemies or the dangers. That is how the animal could preserve itself. The second function of procreation helps animal to continue its progeny. Taking these two as the important criteria of sense of smell, it is amply clear that in the lower animals it helps to locate and identify food, hidden dangers, enemies as well as their mates. Some insects which are currently being studied have been found to possess a highly developed sense of smell. In the case of gypsymcth, female gives out some secretion which contains sex attractants. The males of the species even if our to five miles away from the female locate it through the smell of secretion for the purpose of mating to help continue the progeny. It will not be out of place to mention that this very behaviour of gypsymoth has provided a new approach to the population control of the undesirable insects and rodents. Synthetically made sex attractants are being tried to attract males of the species to trap and thus destroy the male population.

The second example which can be cited is that of canine species. To help detection of crime, trained dogs are extensively used. Highly developed sense of smell together with the imparted training helps a dog to memorize the left over body odour of the criminal at the crime spot. With the help of this odour memory dog is able to follow the trial and ultimately identify the criminal.

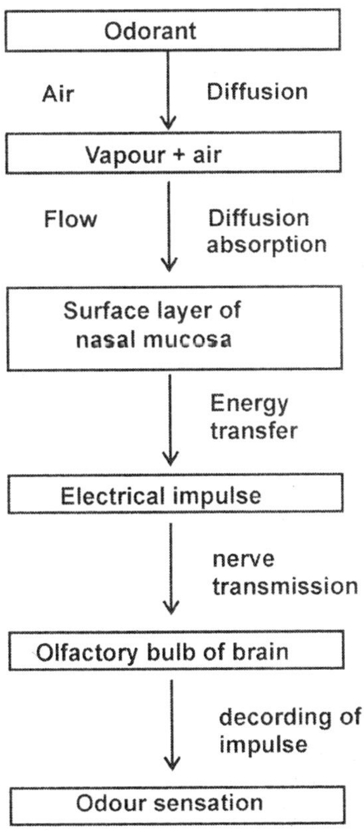

Fig. 40.1 - Mechanism of Olfaction

These two examples clearly indicate that the sense of smell in animals is highly developed. On the contrary, in the case of a human being the truth is far from that. Even though sense of smell does not help a human being in self preservation and procreation but it certainly helps him in what may be called to 'enjoy life'. Sense of smell is the most important criterion so far as the perfumery field is concerned.

After identifying the relevance of sense of smell in human being, it would be of interest to known some thing about the mechanism of olfaction.

When an odorant vaporizes, its vapour diffuses with air to form a mixture of vapour + air. This mixture enters through nose and reaches the base of the nose where 'surface layer of nasal mucosa' is located. When the diffused molecules of odorant come in contact with sensory buds of nasal mucosa, energy transfer takes place which in turn gives rise to electrical impulses are transmitted through nerves to reach the region of brain known as 'olfactory bulb'. It is here that decoding of the electrical impulses takes place to give odour sensation.

Although much is known about the general outline of the mechanism of olfaction, we still have limited knowledge about what exactly happens at the surface layer of nasal mucosa so as to give rise to electrical impulses and also at the stage of decoding of these impulses in olfactory bulb region of the brain. The sense of smell is considerably influenced by the environment under which the observer receives odour sensation. This also depends on the physical and psychological conditions as well as the frame of mind of an individual. It is further conditioned by the association of the odorant with certain recollections. Thus the sense of smell is highly subjective. Although the limitations and the shortcomings of the subjective behaviour of the sense of smell is well established, yet a perfumer has to depend on it for the evaluation of odour characteristic of a given odorant. It goes to the credit of the perfumer to have evolved a technique of converting the subjective nature of sense of smell to a more rationalized objective study. As an illustration of this technique the following example can be cited. Say, if six individuals were to describe the colour of a spectacle's frame independently, the varied description given by these six persons will give an impression of the existence of six different frames. However, if the same individuals were asked to describe the difference in colour of the two arms of same frame, the reaction will be uniform to indicate that it relates to one spectacle's frame. Thus a purely subjective analysis has been converted into objective observation by bringing an element of comparison.

The same applied to the olfactory study of perfumery materials. On comparison of the test sample against a predetermined standard, a perfumer arrives at a conclusion regarding the quality of the material under study. In the event of difference in odour of the test sample against the standard, an experienced perfumer can pinpoint the possible reason of the observed variation.

Furthermore, it is this technique which enables the perfumer to be more accurate in determining the odour characteristic of a perfumery in comparison with the most sophisticated instrumental techniques of quality determination. The comments of a perfumer are very often not appreciated if the same are of adverse nature. Such comments are generally misunderstood and labelled as biased. The fact that this is not true is illustrated by the following example.

One of the leading perfumery company in the UK settled a dispute between the quality control and manufacturing departments on one hand and a perfumery department on the other by referring six geraniol samples to a dozen leading perfumers of different countries. The above six geraniol samples were of different origin, yet comparable spectroscopically among themselves. Perfumers were requested to ascertain whether they could detect the Odour difference in six samples and could name the source of origin. All the examining perfumers could independently identify five out of six samples. The sixth sample was branded as unconventional in its origin. This sample in fact was produced from 'Nindi oil' which was then unknown to perfumery industry. This set at rest all the controversy in this particular firm under reference and thus established the supremacy of human nose over modern sophisticated instruments. That this subtle assessment was possible goes to prove that perfumer's nose can detect minute traces of impurities which otherwise cannot be detected by physico-chemical and instrumental analysis. Well, this does not take away the element of subjective nature of odour but nevertheless the need to adopt a standard practice of olfactory assessment of perfumery materials was strongly felt due to the fact that after all a perfumery material has ultimately to subscribe to the odour requirement alone. This desire led Indian Standard Institution to go into the formulation of a standard method of olfactory analysis through its Chemical Division Council CDC 11 for the first time in 1963. Author had the privilege to be associated with this effort which ultimately culminated in laying of an Indian Standard, "Method for olfactory assessment of natural and synthetic perfumery materials" (IS: 2284-1963). This pioneering effort was considered as a very valuable contribution at the International Standards Organization level also.

Standard method of olfactory assessment presupposes that standard practice of manufacture of natural and synthetic perfumery materials is adopted. Age old practice of using natural perfumery materials in their crude form was replaced by methods of winning odoriferous components evolved by the alchemists. It was later accredited to the knowledge of botany that modern practices of expression, hydro and steam distillation, extraction processes by fats, oils and solvents with recourse to milder working conditions of pressure and temperature so as to prevent the loss of subtle odour on bad handling, were evolved. Of late, low temperature extraction of thermolabile delicate flowers of lily of the valley, tuberose, jasmine, etc. has been developed with the use of low boiling solvents like isobutane. It is suggested that the ultrasonic wave diffusion methods which are being tried for the isolation of fixed oils may find an application in the field as well. On the natural theme it is thus the products like essential oils, oleoresins, resinoids, concretes, pomades and absolutes which are made available to perfumers. The total number of such items is of the order of 450 to 500. Though a dismal picture of Indian total is hardly about 30 items despite the country being blessed with a varied climatic and ecological conditions. Nevertheless a beginning has been made in indigenously growing mentha and citronella with a view to make the country self-sufficient.

Human inquisitiveness to probe deep into the composition of naturally occurring odoriferous materials led him to analyse, identify and ultimately synthesize these materials. The tempo of this advancement in the field of synthetic was faster after World War II, though the beginning was already made in the first decade of this century. Cumbersome and lengthy methods of analysis and identification gave way to latest instrumental techniques such as GLC, IR, UV, NMR and Mass spectra. Highly sensitive, accurate and quick methods afforded volume of information about the chemistry of molecules. These methods require minute quantity of product under study. Organic chemists equipped with such and other implements could over a period of time establish their relationship with odour and as a result of this effort newer organic chemicals were evolved to create varied shades of odours, some of which have riot been hitherto found in Nature itself. The total number of perfumery chemicals now available to perfumers exceed five thousand. Once again the Indian picture in this regard is quite disappointing in that the total number of chemicals available are hardly one hundred and fifty. Outcome of the efforts put in by the national laboratories as well as commercial research institutions are yet to bear noticeable results.

In order that a sense of concord is brought into the five thousand and odd odorous materials available to perfumers it has led to classifying these into groups of similarities based on their odour and motivated effect. This has thus resulted in four main groups and equal number of intermediate groups as visualized by Paul Jellinek (Figure)

The four main odour groups are as follows:

(i) *Alkaline, blunt:* All animal odours which can be called fatty, (waxy), sweaty (rancid), cheesy, putrid, urinal faecal, ammoniacal.

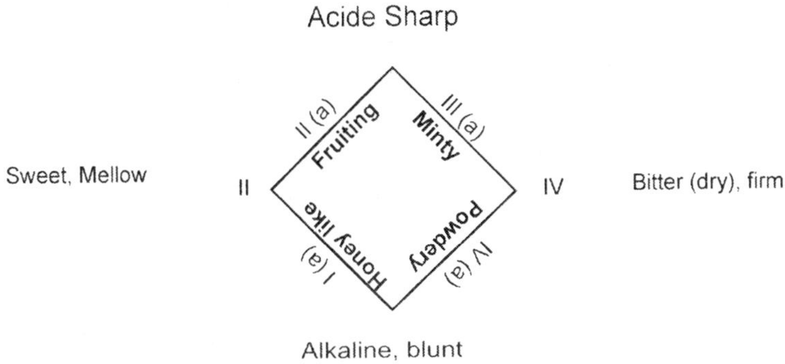

(ii) *Sweet, mellow:* Odours of flowers and balsams which can be characterized as floral and balsamic as well as those called rose like, violet-like, lilac-like, etc.

(iii) *Acidic, sharp:* The odours of various terpenes and camphors usually characterized as camphoric, resinous, green, acidic.

(iv) *Bitter (dry), firm:The* odours of all vegetable materials except flowers, i.e. seeds, roots, leaves and green or woody stalks, which can be called spicy, (piquant), woody, green mossy, burnt (phenolic).

There are odours which cannot be classified in any of the main four groups but which take either an intermediate position or belong to two consecutive groups at the same time. The four intermediate odour groups are as follows:

(i) a *Honey-like:* An intermediate type of odour between groups (i) and (ii), could be described as honey-like or as combining a sweet-floral with an animal (waxy and faecal) note.

(ii) a *Fruity:* An intermediate type between (ii) and (iii) is fruity odour which usually has sweet-acidic character.

(iii) a *Minty:* An intermediate odour type between groups (iii) and (iv) can be described as minty and as combining a green with a camphoric note.

(iv) a Powdery: An intermediate odour between woody and mossy odours (group iv) and alkaline odours (group I) has powdery . note. Aromatics which have powdery, dusty or choking note are quite popular in modern perfumery.

These odour groups create a definite effect on .human beings. The effects created by different odour groups can be likewise classified into four main effects and equal number of intermediate effects as outline.

The effects created by four main odour groups are as follows:

(i) *Erogenic (Sex-stimulating):* Aromatics in odour group " namely animal and similar odour create erogenic effect.

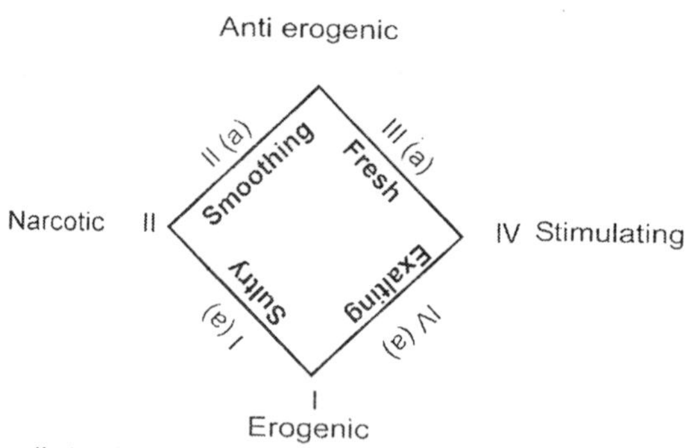

(ii) *Narcotic (intoxicating):* The odurs of flowers and balsams have intoxicating effect.

(iii) *Anti-erogenic (refreshing):* Aromatics in this odour group has a neutralizing or deodorizing action on animal odours and hence anti erogenic.

(iv) *Stimulating (activating):* Spicy, bitter or firm odours, peculiar to vegetable kingdom except the blossom exert a purely stimulating effect.

The intermediate odour types have the following corresponding effects:

(i) a *Sultry: The* combination of erogenic and narcotic produces a sultry effect, i.e. balsamic and animal odour combination gives sultry effect.

(ii) a *Soothing:The* narcotic effect of sweet floral odourtogether with anti-erogenic effect of camphoric odour gives a soothing effect.

(iii) a *Fresh:* There is no doubt that minty odours have a refreshing effect. This combined effect resulting from an interaction of two components 'stimulating' and 'anti-erogenic' can be di:!scribed as 'fresh'.

(iv) a *Exalting:The* combination of stimulating and erogenic effect gives rise to exalting effect.

The classification of odorants into various odour groups and the recognition of the effects that are created by different odour groups hae considerable importance in the art of perfume creation.

As in the case of music it is the composition of,different notes in a given scale which gives rise to musical composition, similarly by the harmonious and skilful blending of individual odours and their effects, a perfumer is evolved. In any art, the personality of an artist is projected in his creation, in the same way perfumer's personality is reflected in his perfume composition. Thus a combination of various perfumery materials, based on their rate of evaporation, creates a harmonious composition which takes into account the continuity of odour effect achieved by skilful blending of top note, middle note and dry out note.

Initially perfumes were consumed for personal use by the affuent of the society where cost was of no consideration. With the advent of synthetic perfumery chemicals, together with the advancement in technology the cost of perfumes generally came down to a level where their use in consumer products such as cosmetics, soaps, etc. has become feasible. Before evolving a perfume for a given consumer product it becomes necessary for the perfumer to take into consideration various factors such as the cost of perfume, its compatibility in the product, its capacity to project a brand image and nature of packaging. Thus basically an artistic subject, perfumery becomes highly technologically involved. Application of perfumes is not only limited to products like cosmetics, soaps, detergents and agarbattis but with every passing day the list of consumer products wherein perfumes are used, is fast mounting up. Such diverse products like inks, paper, plastics, leather, textile, paints and industrial odour masking agents are few of the newer products where perfumed find their direct application. Use of perfumes has thus come to stay in almost every walk of life and scope seems to be unlimited. With the use of perfumes in newer areas the perfumers' involvement becomes critical, say for instance dispensing innovation like aerosol packaging itself presents problems of highly complex nature. As in everything else, the instant preparations, the dispensing of perfumes and flavours as and when required at will has been made possible by a new and novel technique of what is known as encapsulation of perfumes and flavour in suitable plastic micro-cells. Among other products, this technique has also been applied in the manufacture of toilet paper. Apart from offering the perfume or flavour in fresh condition at the point of use, encapsulation prevents loss due to evaporation and ill-effects of auto-oxidation.

41

Quality Control in Aromatic Plants

Introduction

Aromatic or essential oil bearing plants release pleasant fragrance on mascreation or distillation of different parts, namely leaves (e.g. mints, geranium, grasses), flowers/inflorences (rose, lavender, plamarosa), roots (vetiver), bark (cinnamon), wood (cedarwood, sandalwood) and seeds (muskdana, coriander) etc. This property is essentially conferred by the essential oil with specific chemical constituents (s) that is present in those plant-parts. Both the oils and their active constituents (aroma products) are of great commercial value both in international as well as indigenous market. Indeed, during the last three decades, essential oil industry has grown leaps and bound across the world, the size of the industry now exceeding $ 6 billion per annum. As such, the demand for essential oils has increased tremendously in global trades. The current surge of interest for green (herbal) products, in preference over the synthetic (aroma) products in favour of natural essential oils and aroma chemicals in plant origin.

India holds an unique advantage of beign capable of producing variety of natural essential oils. Hence, it has to rise from the present status of the "sleeping giant" to a vibrant producer and supplier of essential oils to the world market. The current economic liberalization and globalization policy of the Government has captulated the prospects of sizeable export of these oils. However, in the world market, quality of oil is the benchmark. A superior quality of oils and aroma products axiomatically fetches higher price and tends to establish a place of pride in international market. This is all the more important due to intense competition with other countries, on slought of synthetic products notwithstanding. The factors that influence the quality parameters of essential oils and consequences of genetic manipulation of quality composition in different essential oil bearing plants are dealt in the following sections with particular emphasis on genetic control of the essential oil quality.

I would first like to eleborte the biosynthetic pathway of essential oil so that the quality control can be exercised more intelligently.

II. Biosynthetic pathway of essential oil

Essential oils are mainly a complex mixture of acrylic and /or cyclic minoterpenoids. These terpenoids are commonly referred to as secondary metabolities that are linked to primary metabolism by the rates with which the substrate can" branch off" from the primary pathways and funnel into the secondary biosynthetic routes. Thus, there is tight intergration of secondary metabolism with the primary metabolism pathways and with the general ontogenic development of the plant. Myriads of monoterpenes encounterd in plants are generated through a variety of secondary transformations, viz., dehydrogenation, isomerization, hydroxylation, acetylation,etc. of their corresponding progenitors. These tranformations are catalyzed by enzymes exhibiting both "group specifity" " absolute specifity"). For instance, conversion of geraniol into citral trans in the leaves of lemongrass is catalyzed an NADP+ dependent dehydrogenase (i.e. geraniol dehydrogenase enzyme) as reported by Singh et. al.

Thus, the biosynthetic pathway of essential oils and bioconversion and/ or interconvertion of various chemicals chemical constituents of the oil are regulated by specific enzymes operative at particular sites in the whole chain reaction of metabolism. I furnish herebelow two example to explain in involvement of enzymes at every step of the biosynthetic pathway of essential oil and its constituents; one in cymbopogon species (*aromatic grasses*) and the other, in *Mentha* species (mints).

1. Metabolic interconversion of monoterpenes of Cymbopogon

Following the mevalonate cycle, the biosynthesis of monoterpenes commences from sucrose to geranyl pyrophosphate through mevalonate pyrophosphate and geranyl pyrophosate converted to monoterpenes.

In all the three commercially exploited aromatic grasses, the biosynthetic pathway follows the same route where geraniol perform in anaploretic function as illustrated below :

(a) **Palmarosa** : Gernaiol and geranyl acetate (ester) are the two main constituents of palmarosa oil. Geraniol is synthesized by conversion of geranyl prophosphate and later, the geraniol is converted through acetylation into geranyl acetate.

(b) **Lemongrass** : Citral is the main constituent of lemongrass oil. Using radiolabelled precursors in *C. flexuosus*, Akhila relveased that geraniol is convered through dehydroxylation into citral trans (geranial) which is turn undergoes a further change to become nerol and nerol is finally converted into citral-*cis* (neral).

(c) **Citronella** : Similarly in C. winterrinus, Akhila found that geraniol is first converted into citronellol which in turn is converted into citronellal. By a little chemical modification, part of citronellol is also converted into citronellyl acetate. All the three constituents are important components of citronella oil.

2. Biosynthetic of monoterpenes in Mentha

In Mentha species tha major quality constituents of oil are menthone, menthol of menthyl acetate in M. arvensis, piperitone in M. piperita, carvone in M. spicata and linalool in M. citrala. I would not explore all, but biosyntheitc interconversion of monoterpenes in M. arvensis and M. piperita will serve our purpose for the present. In general, the transformation commence from terpinyl carbinium ion to menthyl acetate through a sequence of step involved.

(a) **M. piperita** : Pipertone is the main constituents of the oil. It is synthesized by conversion of terpinyl carbonium (isopiperitenol) into terpinolene (isopiperitone) which in turn in transformed into piperitone.

(b) **M. arvensis** : Menthol and menthyl acetate are the major quality constituents of Japanese mint oil. Menthone present in dementholated oil (DMO) has been found to be very useful perfumery. The biosynthesis of these components follow the sequencial steps piperitone → pulgone → menthone → menthol→ menthyl acetate. However, menthol often reverts bak *in vivo* to menthone, thus affecting the quality of oil adversely.

Thus, the chemical conversion of the common precursor-geranyl pyrophosphate into different compount viz., geraniol and geranyl acetate in palmarosa; citronellol, citronellal and citronellyl acetate in citronella and citral-a and citral-b lemongrass are essentially catalysed/regulated by corresponding enzymes operating the different steps of conversion. For instance, while studying the activity and level of some important power generating enzymes in young leaves of *Cymbopogon flexuosus* singh et. al. established that transformation of geraniol into citral trans is catalysed by the enzyme geraniol dehydrogenase. Similarly, in Mentha piperita , the isopiperitenol dehydiogenase enzyme was found to be responsible for transformation of isopiperitenl to isopiperitone and subsequently isopiperitone to piperitone. Likewise, carvone biosynthesis is conditioned by carveiol dehydrogenase in M. Spicata (cf. Singh et. al.). Biosynthetic pathways, in several more species have been reported by Thakur and Akhilla. In brief, all the secondary metabolic processes, such as dehdydrogenation, acetylation, hydroxylation, isomerization etc. are controlled by respective enzymes at each step of transformation. And it is here that the genetic has a great role to play in regulating the activities of these enzymes so as to maintain/improve the aroma quality. Genetic manipulation of concerned enzymes under human condition is all the more imparative for ensuring sustainable supply of quality products at the cheapest cost.

Several factors, such as enviornmental regime, processing techniques, chemical analysis, condition of the raw material and so on influence the oil quality. However, the genetic factors controlling the quality parameters are of paramount consequence. Appropriate technological imputs can modify the genetic nature of oil components on permanent basis.

III. Genetic manipulation of enzyme activity

As stated earlier, quality of aroma products especially the essential oils depends much upon quantum of the major constituent, and delicately balanced profile/proportion of minor constituents. The natural chemical component are biosynthesized under the influence of certain enzymes. The formation of these very enzymes is under genetic control. We can follow two approaches of genetic manipulation of enzymes activity.

(a) Changing the kinetic property of enzymes(s)

(b) Blocking the formation of enzymes(s)

(a) **Enzyme-linked kinetic changes** : Creative agencies (genetical techniques) which can modify the genetic background thus influencing the formation and expression of enzymatic activities, are diverse selection schemes, judicious hybridization and mutuation techniques including polyploidization among, Mendelian approaches. Somaclonal (cellular) selection and somatic hybridization could be very useful techniques among modern biotechnological approaches. These convertional and modern techniques can very effectively modify the kinetic property through changes in dose effect of enzymes concerned. Such enzyme-linked changes might exert diversifying effect in two ways.

(i) Accretion of decretion of the quantum of major compound(s) a chracteristic changes.

(ii) Modification of the chemical profile, i.e. proportion of minor constituents which really confer the requisite " aroma value" to the oil-a diversifying change.

(b) **Blocking of enzyme synthesis** : The recent innovation in genetic engineering has opened up the possibility of even blocking the synthesis of a particular enzyme at a particular step of biosynthetic pathway. Antis-sense RNA is one such technique. Such an exercise will axiomatically cause inactivation of enzyme. The added advantage of ths proportio may be stopping further conversion of a desired compound, thereby enhancing its quantum yield.

2. Genetic manipulation of marker traits

Market traits : In many aromatic plants, some visible characters have been found to manifest strong/weak coupling (positive) or repulsion (negative) phase of linkage (genetic correlation) with quality paratmeters /constituents of essential oil. For instance, the essential oil content itself is correlatted with oil composition in *Mentha piperita* and *Cymbopogon martinii* at anthesis. In *C. winterianus*, the relative number of glandular microchairs on the abaxial surface of leaf-epidermis is reported to be associated with chemical composition of the oil. Similarly, the number of epidermal glands during expansion has been shown to be proportionate to camphor has content in the oil of Salvia officinalis. Massino et. al. have found number of trichomes to be corrleated with quality of Mentha virdis oil. Thus secretary structures like glandular trichomes, and glandular hairs, often serve as genetic markers for oil quality in many essential oil bearing plants.

Genetic manipulation : The genetic correlation (r_8) of marker traits with specific quality constituent can be appropriately strengthened or weakened, as the case may be, through strainght selection after mutagenesis. Undesirable linkages can be broken by mutuations causing chromosomal inversion or translocation. Further, should be breeding system permit, disruptive selection can also bring but sustantial modifications of genetic correlation.

3. Genetic manipulation for tolerance to seasonal variation

Both the content and quality of essential oil are considerably influenced by climate/season. Even diurnal effects on oil quality are also on record. In fact, Banthrope et. al. have proposed the existence of two metabolically distinct pools of terpenes one being sensitive to external regime while another being relatively neutral. The relative size of these two pools may depend on species as well as on environmental conditions.

However, sensitivity of oil quality and content to external factors is, to a large extent under genetic control as observe by Sharma et. al. in *Cymbopogon* species and *Mentha* arvensis. Deployment of suitable/appropriate models of adaptive breeding as eleborated by Sharma (1994) would cut the Gordian's knot clean. Selection favouring individual buffering (genetic homeostasis) is a technique of choice.

Thus, there are several stratagies or technical inputs that a geneticist/ plant breeder can deploy for quality breeding in aromatic plants. No doubt, applications of these techniques have been made and success achieved as illustrated in the next selection.

4. Genetic manipulation of quality : Application and scientific outputs

The scientific inputs (plant breeding techniques based on genetical principles) abumberated in the preceding section have hither to contributed significantly to improve/modify not only the quality but also the content and quantity (yield of the essential oils in aromatic plants. They have effected changes in oil quality in three ways :

1. Improved (increased proportion of major active constituents(s) of the oil.
2. Modified chemical profile-relative proportion of minor constituents which confers distinct " aroma value" to the oil.
3. Genetically rectified oil composition by removing undesirable constituent (s) or reducing unwanted component.

In the following sub-sections, I would furnish some successful example from different crops genetically manipulated for oil quality at different institutions/laboratories.

1. Improved major constituents(s) of oil

Judicious applications of cloline breeding repeated clonal selection, mutuation breeding and inter specific hybridization has resulted into several superior varieties in a number of essential oil bearing plants. As many as 20 much genetically improved varieties (V) with higher content of the main constituents of the oil than the already prevailing commercial checks (ch) have been chronicled in different species of aromatic flora. The percentile gain for major component in terms of checks (% ▲ V/ch) ranges from 7% to

100%, thus indicated the profound role of genetic manipulation on quality control of aromatic oils in various crops.

2. Modified chemical profile of oil

Alteration of the delicately balanced proportion of chemical compounds of the essential oil might changes its " aroma/odour value". Genetic manipulation of some of the aromatic crops has helped develop superior varieties with major active constituent other than that obtained in the natural species. For instance, cloline breeding in *Cymbopogon flexuosus* which contains citral as the main component (75-85%) of its oil, gave birth to GRL-1. The oil of GRL-1 contains 85% geraniol rather than citral. Since it is vegetatively propogated vis-a-vis palmarosa which is seed propogated, advantage of maintaining genetic uniformity of oil quality in clonal progenies of GRL-1 over palmarosa (with segregating progeneis) is distinct. Similar are the varieties RRL-57 and 59 developed by mutuation breeding and RRL-38 by repeated clonal selection in *c. flexuosus*. Another variety RRL-86 also developed by clonal selection possesses geranyl acelate (50%) rather than citral as the major acetate (50%) rather than citral as the major component of its oil. The changes of *C. nardus* var. *confertiflorus* anc *c. khasianus*, both having geraniol as the major component of their oils, into the corresponding mutant varieties RL-1000 and mutuant-A with geranly acetate as major constituent are also among the same fashion.

In Mentha arvensis (with menthol as the major constituent of oil) also two mutants were evolved by mutuation of breeding with altered chemical component : RL-85/4 had 55% pulegone, and the other mutant B 45% menthone instead of high menthol in their oils.

Thus, genetically plant breeding techniques are very effective in altogether changing the chemical profile of oils in different aromatic crops.

3. Genetically rectified defects in oil composition

More often than hot, oils of some varieties strains have one or two minor constituents which are undesirable or unwanted because they denigrade the oil quality, causing considerable problem in fractionation of pure compounds notwithstanding. They need to be promptly minised, if not completely removed. This could be successfully achieved by adopting appropriate techniques. I can enlist three example here.

(i) In palmarosa, high percentage of the ester-geranyl acetate (GA) is not desirable hence need to be lowered down so as to increae the proportion of geraniol (G). Half-sib family selection in var. *Trishna* (with 75% G and 16% GA) resulted into development of a new var. *Tripta* with only 10% GA and 81% G.

(ii) Similarly in Citronella oil, high elemol content (EC) deteriorates oil quality. Following somaclonal selection (cellular breeding) the vr. Bio-13 was developed which has reduced (5%) EC as compared to 12% EC in the parental variety.

(iii) Likewise, a var RRL-59 C. Flexuosus which is a good source of geraniol citronellal/citronellol, suffered from the presence of a small percentage of methyl eugenol (ME) in its oil, causing difficulty in separation of the main constituents. A massive screening for a desirable mutant among irradiated progenies led to isolation to a ME-deficient mutant.

Thus, it is obvious that quality control of the essential oils through genetic manipulation/plant breeding is a reality; earlier exploited, the greater is the gain.

V. Conclusion

Application of genetics through appropriate plant breeding techniques, has brought out tremendous changes in essential oil composition/quantity of a number of aromatic plants; it has improved the proporation of major constituent of the oil; it has changes the chemical profile relative proportion of minor components and it has also rectified the defects, i.e. eliminated the undesirable component in the oil. Thus, plant breeding (i.e. applied genetics) is a powerful scientific technique to improve or modify the quality constituents of essential oils. Besides as pointed out by Sharma and Kumar, the genetic changes brought out by plant breeding are :

(i) Permanent, i.e. stable/heritable over generation

(ii) The cheapest, i.e. requiring no external inputs.

(iii) Environmentally clean and biofriendly

Thus, plant breeding commands a strong control of the oil quality over time, cost and environs.

This is just the beginning of genetic manipulation of oil quality in essential oil bearing plants. Efforts on selection for genetic markers, and for minizing the genotype x environment interaction, i.e. for genotypes stable for oil quality over seasons/climate has not been commensurate with genetic information of biotechnological tools which have amzaing potential for genetic modification of quality is yet to commence in right earnest. Once all these techniques are successfully applied in full swing in all the essential oil bearing plants, genetic assurance of oil quality and aroma products can be guratned with confidence. Moreover, the application of the genetical principles under the expert hands of geneticists/plant breeders can conqurrenty impart impressive uniformity of the crop as well as its end-products, help sustained supply of quality oil and also ensure effective conservtion of aromatic plant genetic resources for posterity.

42

Palmarosa Oil

Introduction

The essential oil obtained from palmarosa (*Cymbopogan martinii var. motia*) forms an important raw material in perfumes and cosmetics industry. Since this oil is an important foreign exchange earner, attempts were made to increase its production. Studies were already conducted to asses the requirements of major nutrients for the crop. But the micronutrient requirements of the crop is not clearly understood. It is imperative to know the effect of various micronutrients on the grass and oil yield and quality of theoil of the crop. Micronutrients increase the chlorophyll content in leaves, improve photosynthetic efficiency and intensify the respiratory activities of the plant. Many micronutrients are constituents parts of the active centres of enzymes and vitamins. Hence, investigations were carried out at Aromatic and Medicinal Plants Research Station. Odakalli to study the response of Palmarosa to micronutrient application.

Materials and Methods

The treatment consisted of foliar applications of 0.5 and 1% each of borax, zinc sulphate, copper sulphate, manganese sulphate and Agromin,soil applications of 25 kg/ha of Chelamin and each of the above nutrients except Agromin and an absolute control. The experiment was laid out in Randmised block design replicated thrice.Foliar application was given when the crop was at the peak vegetative phase after each harvest. The experiment was conducted for two years, the data of which is presented below.

Results and Discussion

Oil Yield

The data revealed that there was significant difference in oil yield between treatments. soil application of Chelamin (Chealated zinc) produced the highest oil yield which is significantly superior to the control. This may be attributed to the role of zinc which helps slow release of the nutrient avoiding wateful reactions in the soil. Soil applications of copper sulphate 25 kg/ha also was significantly superior to control. Similar observations were recorded by Nair et. al. in lemongrass. This may be due to the role of copper as a catalyst in enzymes reactions in the oxidation of diphenls and hydroxilation of monophenols. Increase in oil yield over control by chelamin was 36.36% whereas it is 32.55% in the case of copper sulphate (Table 42.1).

Eventhrough foliar applications in general did not increase the oil yield significantly, application of $MnSo_4$ (0.5%) produced higher oil yields than control.

Herbage Yield

The data showed that there was no significant difference between treatments in the case of herbage yeild (Table 1). But application of 25 kg/ha each of Chelamin and Copper sulphate and foliar application of 0.5% Manganese sulphate produced higher herbage yield than the control.

Oil Recovery Percentage and Geraniol Control

Application of Chelamin 25 kg/ha or Copper Sulphate 25 kg/ha produced very high oil recovery percentages on fresh weight and dry weight basis. The increase in oil recovery by Chelamin and Copper sulphate was 0.06 and 0.07% (0.52 and 0.54%) respectively over control (0.47%) on a fresh weight basis. Soil application of zinc sulphate also increased the oil recovery percentage over control so also foliar appliction of $MnSo_4$. Similar results were obtained by Chatterjee et. al. in Java citronella.

Geraniol content was high when foliar application of Manganese sulphate and zinc sulphate was done on the crop. Soil application of copper sulphate also produced higher geraniol content. Experiments at Central Institute of Medicinal and Aromatic Plants on Java citronella also produced the same results.

So far Palmarosa application of 25 kg/ha either of Chelamin or Copper sulphate of foliar application of (0.5%) Manganese sulphate was found to be good for oil yield and geraniol content.

Table 42.1. Effect of Micronutries on Palmarosa

Treatment		*Oil yield liy/ha*	*Herbage yield t/ha*	*Oil recovery percentage FW*	*DW*	*Geraniol Content (percentage)*
1. Foliar application of Agromin	1%	119.4	52.06	0.47	1.72	84.77
2. Foliar application of Agromin	0.5%	105.3	50.62	0.48	1.76	84.40
3. Foliar application of Boron	0.5%	131.3	56.18	0.44	1.61	85.90
4. Foliar application of Boron	1%	129.2	60.92	0.44	1.61	86.34
5. Foliar application of Copper sulphate	0.5%	102.2	55.28	0.48	1.76	84.75
6. Foliar application of Copper sulphate	1%	116.78	57.40	0.47	1.72	83.20
7. Foliar application of Zinc sulphate	0.5%	106.84	62.37	0.46	1.68	87.46
8. Foliar application of Zinc sulphate	1%	104.53	54.62	0.47	1.72	86.06
9. Foliar application of Manganese sulphate	0.5%	145.87	70.53	0.49	1.79	88.03
10. Foliar application of Manganese sulphate	1%	124.48	52.25	0.53	1.94	85.47
11. Foliar application of Boron	25 kg/ha	99.17	55.74	0.42	1.54	86.86
12. Soil application of Copper sulphate	25 kg/ha	164.08	71.18	0.54	1.98	87.52
13. Soil application of Chelamin	25 kg/ha	168.79	71.53	0.53	1.94	84.97
14. Soil application of Zinc sulphate	25 kg/ha	121.12	59.15	0.55	2.01	84.32
15.Soil application of Manganese sulphate	25 kg/ha	99.13	79.69	0.53	1.94	84.93.
16. Control		123.70	59.55	0.47	1.72	87.73
C D (O.05%)		35.39	N S	—	—	—

43

Chemical Composition of Lemongrass Varieties

Materials and Methods

Sixteen accessions of Lemongrass present at the Medicinaland Aromatic Plants garden in Colelge of Horticulture, Trichur were evaluated. The accessions were Perinthalmanna, Attapaddi and Vadakkekhadu collected from the respective places in Kerala.OD-9, OD-414, OD-330, D-440, OD-393, OD-301, OD-399, OD-325, D-19 and OD-442 received frm Aromatic and Medicinal Plants Research Station, Odakkali, NLG-84 and NLG-85 received from Narendra Dev Agricultural University, Faizabad and RRLB-1 received from Regional Research Laboratory, Bhuvaneshware. These accessions were eplanted at M&AP garden, Vellanikkara and leaf samples were taken after 60 days. The samples were distilled for 2 hours in a Clavenger's apparatus. The oil thus otained was dehydrated with anhydrous sodium sulphate and analysed using GC with SE-30 glass column (2M), N_2 as carrier gas and flame ionisation detector. Ovn temperature was 120-180°C programmed at 6°C/min. The percentage of each compound was determined with a PC-AT computer attached to the GC using the area normalisation method (Table-1). The compounds were characterised using a standard oil and the retention times were considered for the comparative study (Table-2). Two samples for each entry were analysed and the man value was taken for comparision.

Results and Discussion

The first major obtained is that of mycrene (Table-1). Comparison of its percentage shows that it is lowest in OD-19 (0.01%) and highest in OD-393 (12.8%). In all the high quality oils its percentage is below 0.5%. Amounts of methyl heptenone varies from 0 to 2.46. The percentage of depentene varies from 0.19 to 0.82. The fifth major terpene varies from 0.12 to 1.68. Methyl heptenal varies from 0.20 to 2.76. The next major compound linalool varies from 0.32 to 1.94. Citronellal is found to vary from 0.65 to 5.03. The percentage of n-decanal varies from 0.52 to 2.57. The next compound an aldehyde is found to vary from 0.32 to 1.77. It was found to be below 1 in the best quality oil. The second major compound of all the lemongrass sample analysed is citral b (except NLG-85). It has a variation of 13.76 to 35.17. In almost all the good quality oil its oil percentage is above 30, whereas in poor quality oil it is below. However, there is 28.15% citral-b in OD-9 (total citral percentage is 70.75) and 39.13 in NLG-84 (total citral content 82.56%). Maximum citral b is in OD-399 (35.17%) and the lowest in NLG-85 (13.76%).

The citral 'a' content varies from 22.63 to 56.03. In the case of this compound all the good quality oils are found to have above 50 and in the poor ones are very low, i.e. below 35. Only OD-9 is having 42.6% which has a total content of 70.75. There also NLG-85 has the lowest content while Peninthalmana has the highest. In the case of NLG-85 alone there is another major peek between citral 'a' and 'b' and the percentage is 20.10. After citral 'a' the peak is that the ester of Nerol which varies from 0.62 to 8.10. The content of geraniol ester is found to be higher than Nerol ester in all the accession. Nerol varies from 0 to 15.41 and was found to be almost nil in 3 accessions OD-9, OD-330 and OD-19. Geraniol content varies from 0.41 to 10.92. In case of Perinthalmanna the geraniol content is found to be very less compared to that of Nerol. It varies of different accessions differently. The last major peak is that of farnesol which varies from 0.12 to 11.73.

Hence each accession is different from the other for its percentage composition of components. There are differences in the unidentified components also. In the case of NLG-85 alone a major peak was obtained in the chromatograph, probably a meso from the citral.

Table 2

S. No.	Ret. Time	Sl. No.	Ret. Time
1. Mycene	1.00	10. Citral b	8.85
2. Methylpheptenone	2.37	11. Citral a	9.45
3. Dipentene	3.84	12. Nerol acetate	10.97
4. Terpene	5.32	13. Geranyleacetate	11.97
5. Methyltheptenol	5.97	14. Nerol	12.13
6. Linalool	7.19	15. Geraniol	13.03
7. Citronellal	7.51	16. Farnesol	14.37
8. n-decanal	7.83	17. Total idenfified	
9. C10 aldehyde	8.10	18. Total unidentified	

Table 43.1 : Percentage of various components present in the lemongrass oli of different accessions

Sl. No. L.G. variety	Compound Nos. 1	2	3	4	5	6	7	8	9	10	11	12	13	14	15	16	Iden tified 17	Uniden tified 18
1. Perinthamanna	0.41	0.20	0.69	0.26	0.64	0.91	1.24	0.54		33.98	56.03	0.26	0.92	2.13	0.47	0.12	99.2	0.8
2. Attapadi	3.90	0.82	1.26	0.58	1.1	0.85	0.71	1.41		18.5	34.2	0.64	4.93	3.34	9.30	0.25	82.71	17.29
3. Vadakkekkadu	0.15	2.18	0.47	1.68	2.33	1.94	1.03	2.57		31.80	50.21	0.11	1.44	0.41	0.41	0.50	98.68	1.32
4. OD-9	2.28	0.53	1.54	1.58	1.32	0.83	1.11	0.92		28.15	42.60	0.32	3.97	-	10.10	1.43	97.28	2.72
5. OD-414	1.19	0.12	0.51	0.90	0.71	0.87	0.75	0.63		19.61	29.77	0.20	3.47	15.41	10.92	11.73	97.38	2.62
6. OD-330	1.58	-	1.04	0.12	0.93	0.85	0.82	1.28		31.90	50.94	0.19	1.68	-	5.24	0.31	97.35	2.55
7. OD-440	0.23	0.25	2.82	0.51	0.34	1.22	1.79	1.72		32.78	52.62	0.13	0.67	0.17	1.40	0.80	97.34	2.66
8. OD-393	12.8	1.96	2.43	1.09	2.76	1.29	1.24	1.31		1932	34.76	0.26	1.60	1.27	3.45	0.29	87.6	12.4
9. OD-301	0.85	0.12	0.50	0.30	0.72	0.43	0.92	1.4		33.42	53.53	0.15	0.62	2.01	1.32	0.75	97.42	2.58
10.OD-399	0.33	0.11	0.42	0.34	0.71	0.42	0.92	1.62		35.17	53.76	0.32	1.17	0.59	0.42	0.78	97.75	2.25
11.OD-325	1.77	0.12	0.93	0.18	0.56	0.69	1.11	0.76		31.22	49.55	0.37	1.79	0.86	0.66	0.46	91.62	8.38
12.OD-19	0.01	2.32	0.17	0.13	0.92	1.35	1.81	1.96		34.37	52.85	0.13	0.82	0.17	1.48	0.78	99.7	0.3
13.OD-442	0.60	0.13	1.50	0.46	0.39	0.32	2.40	0.83		31.49	54.12	0.17	0.68	-	2.39	0.26	96.62	3.38
14.NLG-84	0.23	2.46	0.52	0.31	0.63	1.46	2.22	0.81		29.13	53.43	0.33	2.30	0.17	1.20	0.86	96.65	3.35
15.NLG-85	0.14	0.32	1.86	0.53		1.50	5.03	2.28		13.76	22.63	1.60	8.10	1.34	2.27	2.52	66.9	33.1
16.RRL8-1	0.46	0.19	1.23	0.18	0.20	0.48	0.65	1.04		34.33	54.68	0.48	2.18	0.51	0.78	0.67	98.38	1.63

44

Kewda Essential Oil and Attar

Introduction

Pandanus odoratissimus Linn syn. ***Pandanus Fascicularis*** Lam popularly known as kewda belongs to the faimly ***Pandanacea***. It grows wild in several parts of India but luxuriant and gregarious growth is concentrated along the coastal belt in the Ganjam district Orissa. Flowers from male trees are valued for their aroma and are processed to produce three commercially important products viz. essential oil or Rooh. otto or attar and kewda water which find use in perfume and flavour compositions. It is estimated that the annual trade of these products is valued at 300-350 million rupees which provides a good economic activity in about 50 villages in Ganjam district.

From gas chromatographic and GC-MS analysis of the essential oil two major compounds methyl either of ß-phenyl alcohol (PEME) and Terpinene-4-ol have been identified. In the case of attar, the major components are α- and ß santaols derived from sandalwood oil (ISI, 1993) and PEME. Attars are also produced using either liquid paraffin or dioctyl phthalate as base material in which case they appear as the major component. In order to estimate methoxyl and hydroxyl values of rooh or attar by conventional method of functional group analysis, a relatively large quantity of sample is needed. Since the rooh costs about Rs. 200 per gram and attar Rs. 20-30 per gram, it is desirable to devand/or standardise micro/semi procedures for analysis of kewda products.

In the producers standardised by us and described in this paper about 5 mg of sample for methoxyl group determination and 40-50 mg for hydroxyl group determination are required. In the case of rooh the methoxyl group estimated may be expressed directly or as PEME while hydroxyl group may be expressed as Terpinene-4-ol. In case of attar (sandal wood oil base), hydroxyl group may be expressed as α/β santalol.

Materials and Methods

The rooh or attar samples received are first dried over sodium sulfate and filtered before use. All the reagents and chemicals are of analytical grade of purified before use.

Reagents required for methoxyl value determination.

1. Phenol : Freshly distilled value determination
2. Acetic Acid : This is purified by adding some acetic anhydride to react with water if any, and then heated for one hour to just below the boiling in the presence of CrO_2 [2 g for 100 ml] and then fractionally distilled using vireus column (Perrin et. al. 1980)
3. Acetic acid -Potassium acetate -Bromine solution : 10 g of potassium acetate is dissolved in 50 ml glacial acetic acid and diluted with the acide to 100 ml. To this 3 ml of bromine is added. This is always freshly prepared.
4. Sodium acetate solution : 25 g of sodium acetate dissolved in 100 ml distilled water.
5. Formic acid : Analytical grade forming acid is dried by refluxing with phthalic anhydride for 6 hours and then fractionally distilled (Perrin et. al. 1980).
6. Standard $Na_2S_2O_3$ solution (Steyemark, 1961), 0.01 N: 2.48 g of $Na_2S_2O_3.5H_2O$ dissolved is distilled water and made upto one litre. To this 0.5 ml of chloroform is added.
7. Potassium iodide : Analytical grade.
8. Dilute sulfuric acid : 10%
9. Hydro acid : 250 ml of analytical grade acid is purified by heating it gently for 2 hours, while an air condenser is fitted to the reaction flask and nitrogen gas is bubbled into the flask. When heating is stopped, the gas flow is also stopped as passing the gas at room temperature would produce fuming acid. A blank methoxyl group determination is carried out to confirm the purity of the acid, otherwise the reflushing with nitrogen is repeated.

Reagents required for hydroxyl value determination.

1. Acetic anahydrice : This is made acetate free by fractionally distilling the analytical grade reagent. (Perrin et. al. 1980)
2. Pyridine : It is made water free by heating it under reflux over KOH pellets, then distilled and stored over solid KOH pellets. (Perrin et. al. 1980)
3. Standard NaOH solution : 0.04N : : 0.IN carbonate free Titrisol (E merk(ampule was diluted to 500 ml. From this, 100 ml was again diluted to 250 ml to get 0.04 N. This 0.04 N alkali was standardised with 0.04N oxalic acid solution.
4. Phenolphthalein indicator : 1% solution of phenolphthalein in 95% ethanol.

Determination of Methoxyl Group

Methoxyl values of samples are determined using a modified Clark alkoxyl apparatus. The arrangement for carrying out the experiment and the dimensions of different components are given in Fig. 44.1. First the scrubber is filled upto half and sodium acetate solution and the volumeric receiver with freshly prepared acetic -potassium acetate-bromine solution upto two third capacity. The sample is introduced into a capillary by means of a microlitre syringe. About 2-4 mg of sample accurately weighed in the apillary is added to the reaction flask is immediately connected to the condenser with scrubber. The source of carbon dioxide is connected through the side arm of the reaction flaks is immediately connected to the condenser with scrubber. The source of carbon dioxide is connected through the side arm of the reaction flask and the reaction mixture is then heated under reflux for two hours while circulating ice-cold water in the condenser. At this stage water is drained from the condenser and the boiling is continued for an additional two hours. The receiver and inlet tube are disconnected, the stopper removed from the end of the siphon, the unit titled and the contents siphoned into a 250 ml conical flask containing 5 ml of sodium acetate solution. The receiver and inlet tube are washed with enough distilled water (about 30 ml). Formic acid is then added dropwise until excess of bromine is destroyed. To this solution 0.5 g of KI and 5 ml of 10% sulfuric acid are added, the flask is stoppered and set side for 5 minuts. The liberated iodine is titrated in usual way with 0.01 N standard sodium tiosulphate using starch as the indicator. It is to be noted here that the time of distillation described in the literatue procedure for driving out Mel formed is found to adequate and variable results were obtained. However, increasing the total distillation time to 4 hours, instead of 3 hours is sufficient.

The overall reactions are shown below :

1. $Ch_3I + Br_2 \longrightarrow Ch_3Br + IBr$
2. $IBr + 3H_2O + 2Br_2 \longrightarrow HIO_3 + 5Hbr$
3. $HIO_3 + 5HI \longrightarrow 3I_2 + 3H_2O$
4. $3I_2 + 6Na_2S_2O_3 \longrightarrow 6NaI + 3Na_2S_4O_6$

From the volume of the sodium thiosulfate consumed, the methoxyl group is calculated as follows :

1 ml of 0.01 N sodium thiosulfate solution is equivalent to 0.05173 mg of methoxyl.

$$\frac{\text{ml.of 0.01 N } Na_2S_2O3 \times \text{o.5173} \times 100}{\text{weight of sample}}$$

Percentage of PEME =

$$\frac{\text{ml.of 0.01 N } Na_2S_2O3 \times \text{o.5173} \times 100}{\text{weight of sample}} \times \frac{136}{31}$$

Where, the moleculare weight of PEME = 136
and the methoxyl group weight = 31

Determination of Hydroxyl Group

About 40-50 mg of sample of introduced by means of a syringe into a previously weighed sample tube, 50 mm long and 5 mm O.d., closed at one end and drawn into capillary at the other. It is then centrifuged to push the sample to the bottom and weighed accurately upto 0.01 mg. To this about 90-100 mg of acetic anhydride is added and reweighed. About 4-6 drops pyridine and a very small glass plunger are pushed through the capillary. After centrifuging again the tube is sealed, shaken and set aside. A blank is run simultaneously. After 24 hours the tube is placed in a 100 ml conical flask containing about 5 ml of distilled water. It is then broken by means of a heavy glass rod and the released acetic acid is titiated against standard alkali using phenolphthalein as indicator. The overall reactions are shown as follows :

1. $R\text{-}OH + AC20 \longrightarrow R\text{-}OAC + AC\text{-}OH$
2. $AC_2O + H_2O \longrightarrow 2ACOH$

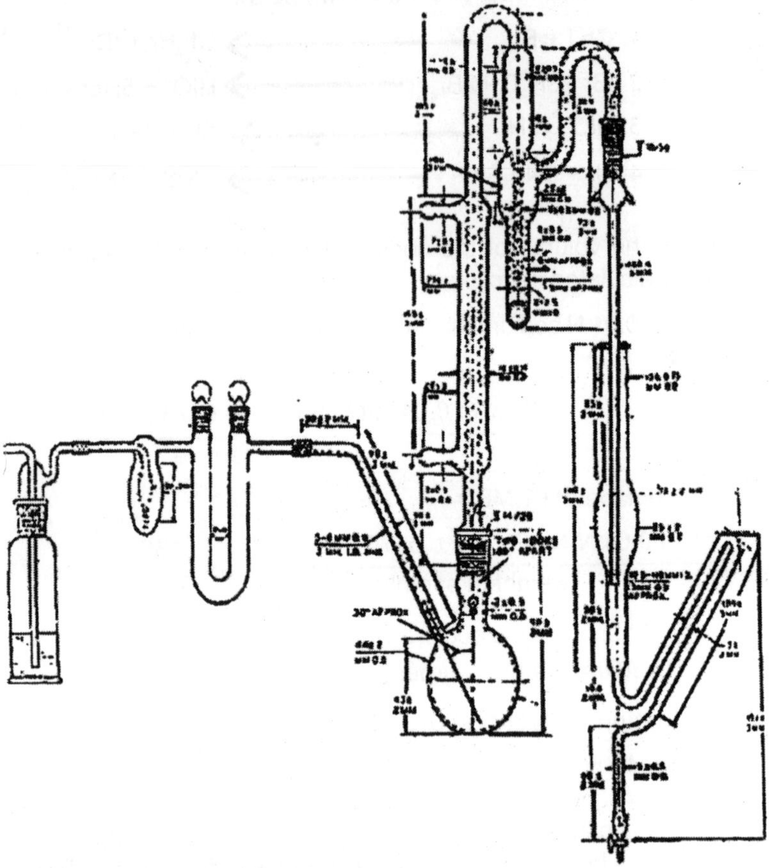

Fig. 44.1 Set up for Methoxyl value determination

Methoxyl Value Determination

Sl. No.	Sample Code	Amoungs of Oil in mgs	% Methoxyl value	% PEME calculated from methoxyl value	PEME Determined from GLC
1.	KA-1	2.965	16.225	71.1	70.221
2.	KA-2	2.750	15.424	67.6	66.719
3.	KA-3	3.305	16.021	70.2	68.719
4.	KA-9	2.975	18.083	79.3	78.384
5.	KA-10	3.220	15.583	68.3	66.313

Hydroxyl Value Determination

Sl.No.	Sample code	Amounts of oil in mgs	% Hydroxyl value	Terpinene-4-ol calculated from hydroxyl value	Terpene-4-ol determined from GLC
1.	KA-1	46.2	1.425	12.91	9.622
2.	KA-2	48.2	2.276	22.00	19.390
3.	KA-8	54.9	0.977	8.80	6.724
4.	KA-9	50.2	1.472	13.336	7.330
5.	KA-10	47.1	2.148	19.40	17.134

alkali using phenolphthalein as indicator. The overall reactions are shown as follows :

In fig-44.2 are plotted the percentage PEME in the rooh sample against methxyl value obtained by the micro determination. A linear curve shows that no other compound in the rooh contributes to the methoxyl value. The graph may also be used to directly determine the PEME content the methoxyl values.

Unlike the methoxyl value, the hydroxyl value obtained and percentage to Terpinene-4-ol analysed by GLC did not show a linear relationship indicating

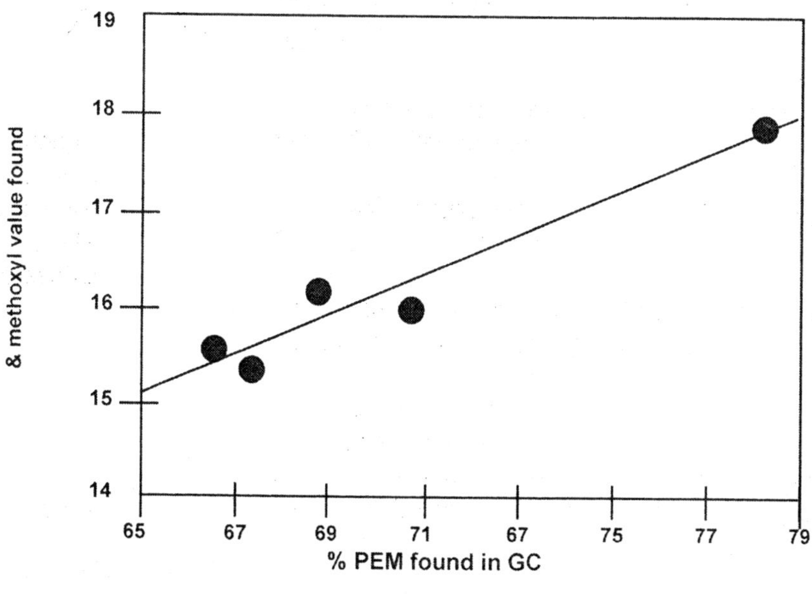

Fig. 44.2 : Relationship of methoxyl value with PEME content in Kewda Oil

In the case of attars also, five samples of all collected from market have been alalysed. It can be seen that sandalwood oil also has alkoxyl containing compounds and has an average methoxyl value of 2.305. In order to determine the methoxyl value of attars the base value of 2.305 has been substracted from the determined values and the amount of PEME in attars is calculated. Similarly, the hydroxyl value may be espressed as α or ß santalol using a following equation.

$$\text{Percentage of } \alpha/\beta \text{ santalol} = \%\text{ Hydroxyl value } \frac{244}{17}$$

Where molecular weight of α/ß sanalol=244
Group weight of hydroxyl=17 .

Methoxyl Value Determination

Sl.No.	Sample code	Amount of sample in mgs	% Methoyxl value found	% Methoxyl value after substrating from blank	% PEME present in attar calculated from Methoyxl value
1.	Sandal wood oil	3.306	2.305	-	-
2.	ATPC-A	2.825	4.02	1.723	7.561
3.	ATPC-4	3.935	3.812	1.507	6.612
4.	ATPC-5	3.485	4.019	1.714	7.520
5.	ATC-6	3.290	3.773	1.468	6.442
6.	ATPC-7	3.015	3.774	1.469	6.447

Hydroxyl Value Determination

Sl.No.	Sample code	Amounts of Sample of mg	% Hydroxyl Value	% of α/ß santalol calculated from hydroxyl value
1.	ATPC-A	51515	7.179	103.04
2.	ATPC-4	50.57	7.151	102.65
3.	ATPC-5	48.355	7.855	112.74

Conclusion

A few sample of rooh and attar have been analysed chemically for methoxyl and hydroxyl values. These determinations give a fairly good idea of a quality of these high value products.

Kewda Flower

RT	Area	Area %
0.42	8000	0.023
0.51	67740	0.196
0.63	9950	0.029
0.71	1433000	4.155
0.91	119000	0.345
1.33	2704	0.008
1.59	2313	0.007
2.49	306600	0.889
2.83	201400	0.584
3.25	527500	1.530
3.63	62030	0.180
4.31	427200	1.239
4.39	1069000	3.100
5.14	22870000	66.113
6.60	367200	1.065
6.95	296700	0.860
8.49	5909000	17.134
9.76	294000	0.852
10.18	91940	0.267
10.73	96640	0.280
11.18	53050	0.154
12.39	81360	0.236
13.37	25090	0.073
14.60	29250	0.085
15.68	9620	0.028
16.98	12240	0.035

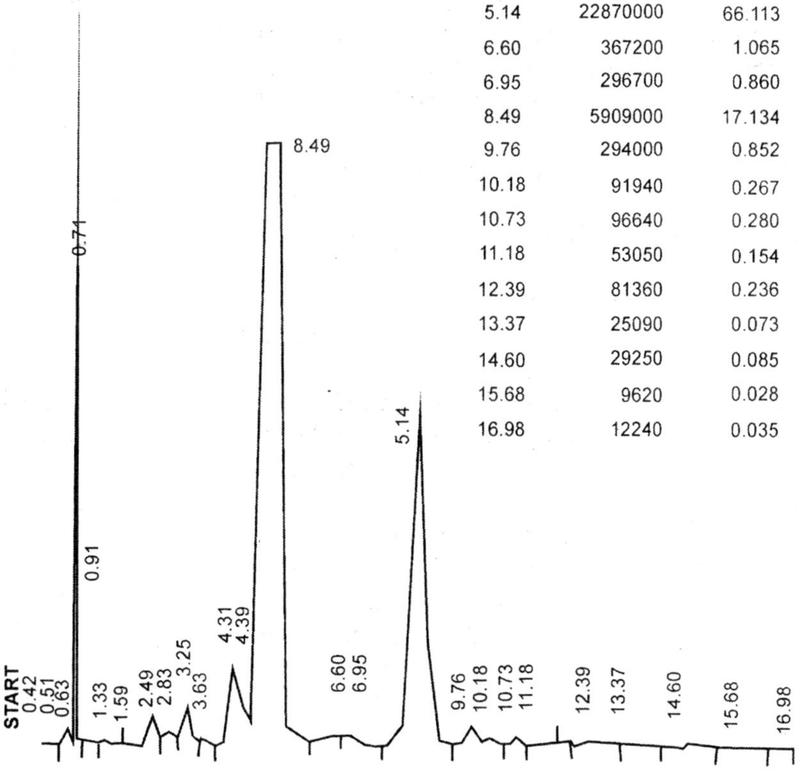

45

Palmarosa Oil

Introduction

The chemical composition of Indian palmarosa oil distilled from flowering plants has been studied in detail. The volatile oil composition varies greatly depending on season of harvest, stage of crop growth and plant part distilled. Recent, studies on composition of oil plamarosa seeds, showed that it is a good source of oil of and geraniol. Palmarosa crop is cultivated by transplanting 4 weeks old seedlings as well as direct sowing of seeds in field. As the seedlings are highly aromatic, therefore, the composition of the volatile oil of the seedlings was examined and results are presented.

Materials and Methods

The experiment was conducted in the Experimental Farm of Central Institute of Medicinal and Aromatic Plants, Field Station, Hyderabad. Palmarosa nursery was raised in june 1994 using seeds of cv. *Trishna* and following recommended agricultural practices. Four weeks old seedlings were harvested on 27 July 1994 and samples of 500 g each were distilled in Clevenger's apparatus for 3 hours. The essential oil samples, thus obtained, were pooled, dried over anhydrous sodium sulphate and analysed gas chromatographically. GC anlysis was carried out using a Perkin Elmer Gas Chromatograph (model 8500) equipped with FID and a glass capillary column BP-1 (25 m x 0.5 mm) coated with dimethyl siloxane. Temperature programming was done from 60°C-200°C at a rising rate of 5°C/min. with a final hold time of 10 min. Nitrogen was used as carrier gas at a flow rate of 40 mLI min. and with 10 p.s.i. inlet pressure. Samples were injected with a split ratio of 1 :80. Volatile constituents were identified by comparing retention times of the peaks with those of authentic compounds run under the same conditions, Kovat's indices with that of literature data and by peak enrichment on conjection of standard compounds, wherever possible.

Results and Discussion

The 4 weeks old seedlings were 19 em -39 em tall with an average height of 23 em, had 4-9 leaves with an average of 5 leaves per seedling, with fresh weight of 0.45 -1.35 g having a mean weight of 0.82 g per seedlingand yielded 0.75%-0.85% volatile oil (on fresh weight basis) with an average oil content of 0.79% indicating that the transplant ready seedlings were rich in essential oil. The GC analysis data are presented in components accounting for 98.15% of the oil (monoterpene hydrocarbons: 5.65% oxygenated monoterpenes: 68.63%, sesquiterpene hydrocarbons: 0.61 %. terpene esters: 23.22% and others; 0.04%) were identified, out of which 5 major constituents accounted for 94.08% of the oil. These were: myrcene (2.61 %), (E)-~-ocimene (1.56%),linalool(1.69%), geraniol (66.625) and geranyl acetate (21.60%). Compared to the oil, generally extracted from palmarosa plants at full bloom or early seedling stages, the seedlings oil contained lesser percentages of linalool and geraniol, but higher levels of geranyl acetate. The geranyl acetate content of whole herb at vegetative stages(20.46%) \'.*Jas* comparable to that of seedlings (21.60%). Akhila et al., further analysed different plant parts at different stages. The geraniol and geranyl acetate percentages of seedlings oil were comparable to those of stem (64.27% &27.14%), leaf (65.93%, & 24.92%) oils at flowering before start of anthesis and stem (63.63% & 26.43%), inflorescence (66.85% & 25.03%) oils at full bloom stages (Akhila et al., 1984). In the same study, the geraniol and gernyl acetate concentrations of whole plant (55.65% & 35.29%), stem (43.935 &41.905) and leaf (56.82% & 31.69%) at onset of flowering were, found to be much lower and higher respectively, compared to the contents of these compounds in the present study. However, at the end of blooming all the plants had higher contents of geraniol, linalool and lower concentration of geranyl acetate than reported in this ivestigation.

As the seedlings were found to be rich in essential oil, it is worthwhile to examine the chemical composition of seedlings oil under different agroclimatic conditions with a view to search for specific locations which can yield good quality oil. This study also brings out that under conditions of severe moisture stress, harvesting the seedlings of direct sown or transplanted crop and extracting oil from them may provide insurance against total crop loss.

46

Sandalwood

Introduction

Sandalwood oil obtained from the heart of ***santalam album*** tree, is one of the precious essential oil used in perfumery and cosmetics. India is among the major producers of this oil. The wood is also used for incence making and carving. Sandal trees are found in the southern states of India namely Tamil Nadu and Karnataka. The major constituents of sandalwood oil are (+) -α and (-)-β santalols which are responsible for good quality. The higher the percentage of santalol content, the better is the quality of oil. Due to ever increasing demands of sandalwood, trees were introduced in the other parts of country on experimental basis.

The present communication reports the quality evaluation of the oil produced from sandalwood trees grwon at Lalkuan District (UP) and that of the oil from Karnataka in Southern India.

MATERIAL AND METHODS

Mateials

Heartwood of about fifteen years old tree grown in Munshi Paudhshala, Lalkuan was made into fine chips and hydrodistilled for 18 hours in Clevenger's apparatus. The oil was made moisture free. The oil from Karnataka origin was collected from a distiller.

Apparatus

The gas chromatographic analysis was carried out on Varian CX-3400 using a 30 m x 0.25 mm Supeolowax capillary column (Supelco, USA). Oven temprature was programmed from 100°C to 220°C @ 5°C/min with initial and final hold of 2 min and 4 min. Injector and detector temperatures were maintained at 220°C and 240°C respectively. Hydrogen was used for calculation of percentage of components.

The GC/MS analysis was carried out using Shimadzu QP-2000 instrument: GC column HP-1 fused silica capillary 50 m x 0.25 mm; temperature program 100°C to 250°C @ 10°C /min with initial hold of 5 min. E1 at 70 ev. 250°C.

Results and Discussion

The results of GC analysis are given in table 46.1. The components were identified based on GC/MC data and the standard published literature. The physico-chemicl data fr the oils are given in table 46.2. It is evident from this table that the sandalwood oil from the Nainital is as good as that from Karnataka. Moreover, the content ß-santalol (22.2%) is slightly higher in the former which makes it a better oil, since the ß-santalol is responsible for the characteristics odour of the sandalwood oil.

Table 46.1-Chemical Composition of sandalwood oils.

Components	Percentage	
	Sandalwood oil from Lalkuan	sandalwood oil from Karnataka
α-santene	0.130	0.031
α-santalene	0.401	1.014
α-bergamotene	0.076	0.206
(E)-epl-ß-santalene	0.541	1.220
ß-santalene	0.682	1.890
ß-famesene	0.236	0.384
α-santalal	3.075	2.609
ß-santalal	1.621	0.449
cis-a-santalol	45.613	47.904
trans-a-santalol	0.255	5.966
epl-ß-santalol	3.991	3.810
ß-santalol	22.208	20.317
trans-ß-santalool	0.635	0.398

Table 46.2-Chemical Composition of sandalwood oils.

Properties	Is Specification	Northern India	Southern India
Colour and apperance	Nearly colorless to golden yellow sometimes viscid oily liquid	Yellowish tinge.	Golden yellowish tinge
Odour	Pleasant, sweet woody and persistent	characteristics sandalwood wood odour	Characteristic sandalwood wood odour
specific gravity	0.962-0.976	0.968	0.972
α_D	-15° to -20°	-18.38º	-17.28°
n^{20}_D	1.499-1.506	1.500	1.502

47

Technology of Palmarosa Oil

Introduction

Palmarosa (Cymbopogon martinii var. motia) is one of the important perennial aromatic grasses, cultivated in India for its valued essential oil which finds wide application in perfumery and cosmetics industries. India ranks first among the countries producing palmarosa oil and is the major supplier of its oil to the world market.

Palmarosa can be propagated using different methods viz.; spliting of clumps, direct seeding and use of nursery raised seedlings; however last one is most common method used for commercial production of crop. Once planted, palmarosa crop remains economically viable for 4-5 years. However for sustained crop yield, maintaining optimum crop stand is essential. A poor crop stand may lead to recurring loss to the growers, which is not very uncommon due to poor establishment of seedlings. Nutrient status of seedlings at the time of planting is vital for their establishment and initial growth, as the seedlings remain autotrophic for some time after their transfer from seed bed and depend upon the food material reserved in them. Age of seedlings is another important factor which affects the establishment and growth of plant. Ready et. al. observed that under late planting condition the yield of transplanted rice was significantly higher with 45 days old seedlings than 30 and 60 days old seedlings.

In the present communication we report the result of experiment conducted to study the effect of age of seedlings and nursery bed nutrient management on plant establishment, growth and herb and oil yield of palmarosa.

Materials and Methods

An experimental was laid out using four ages of seedlings (30,40,50 and 60 days), grown with four fertility levels (0:0:0, 25:12.5;50:25:25 and 75:37, 5.37, 5 N, P_2O_5 and K2O kg/ha) in nursery beds in factorial R.B.D., replicated thrice, at the research farm of Central Institute of Medicinal & Aromatic plants, Lucknow (26.5° Niatitude, 80.5°E longitude and 12°M altitude and an average rainfall 1000mm). The soil of experimental plot was sandyloam in texture, low in organic carbon (0.28%) and available N (100 kg/ha) and medium in available phosphorous (11.0 kg/ha) and potassium (112 kg k/ha). Seeds were sown in raised nursery beds on different dates (10,20, 30 May and 10th June) so as to have seedlings of desired age on 10th July, 1987, the date on which the seedlings were planted in the field. The whole amount of P_2O_5 and K_2O and half of N, as per treatment, were mixed in soils in nursery beds before sowing of seeds. Rest of N was todressed 20 days after sowing.

The crop was planted at the spacing of 45 x 30 cm in plots of 4.5 x 3.0 M in size. The crop received 80 kg N, 60 kg P_2O_5 and 60 kg K_2O/ha during two harvest period whole of phosphorous and potassium and one third of N was applied at the time of planting as basal dressing and rest of N was topdressed in equal splits; 45 days after planting and 20 days after first harvest.

Two harvests, first 80 days after planting on Oct, 1, and second 67 days after first harvest on Dec.7, 1987 were taken. Plant establishment (%) and number of tillers per plant were recorded at 60 days after planting (DAP). The herb and oil yield of first and second harvests were recorded. The oil content in fresh herb was determined by hydrodistilation in Clevenger's apparatus and oil yield estimated. Herb and oil yield of first and second harvest were added to get the total herb and oil yield.

RESULT AND DISCUSSION

Plant Establishment and Growth

Plant establishment and tiller production per plant recorded 60 DAP indicated a maximum 89% establishment with 40 days old seddlings. Both younger (30 days) and older aged (50 and 60 days) seedlings recorded significantly lower plant establishment, the lowest being with 60 days old seedlings (Table 47.1). The number of tillers per plant were less affected due to age of seedlings. While the better estabilshment of 40 days old seedlings is through to be due to optimum dry weight (0.4 g/seedlings) and root development, the poor establishment of 60 days old seedlings was possibly due to injury to the root system at the time of uprooting from the nursery beds. Thirty days old seedlings could be withstand a changed environmental conditions n the field due to less dry weight (0.20 g seedlings) and carbohydrates content. Rice seedlings with better dry matter and carbohydrates content have been fond to tolerate submergence stress better than those had less dry matter. Fertilization of nursery beds results into significantly higher tiller production per plant. However, the effect of different nutrient levels on tiller prodution was same. Seedling after their transfer from nursry to field remain autotrophic till the development of root system. Hence, nursery fertilised seedlings owing to their better nutrient status did not face nutritional stress and could continue with optimum metabolic process and produced more tillers.

Herb and Oil Yield

Total herb and oil yield with 40 days seedlings was 8.0 to 22.0 higher than both younger and older aged seedlings. The different was more apparent in the first harvest only, the second harvest it was at par to 30 and 60 days old seedlings (Table 47.2).

Fertilization of seedlings had a significant effect on herb and oil yield. Seedlings fertilized in nursery bed gave 12.0 higher herb and oil yield over unfertilized seedlings. However, like age of seedlings, the increase in yield was limited to first harvest only. Seedlings fertilized with different levels of N, P2O5 and K2O and similar effects. The increase in yield with nursery fertilized seedlings maybe a result of higher number of tillers of the seedlings and also their better nutrient status, which helped in better growth and development. Costgan was also of the opinion that difference in fianl yield of crop is caused by differences in nutrient uptake and growth during earlystae of plant establishment. Rice seedlings grown after dia-ammonium than those grown without dia-ammonium phosphate application. Since, the seed bed was adequately supplied with different nutrient, all the the seedlings having either higher or lower nutrient status could overcome the differences in the later stages of the crop growth (second harvest).

Seedlings Growth and Development

Age of seedlings and fertilization both had positive effect on growth and development of seedlings. Older the seedlings, the higher the height, no, of tilelrs, no. of leaves and fresh and dry weight of seedlings. Fertilization of seedlings with either of the level brought about 100% increase in growth and development of the seedlings over those received no fertilizer applicatin (Table 47.3)

Conclusion

On the basis of results obtained in present studies, it may be concluded that for achieving an optimum plant population, use of 40 days old seedlings, raised under optimum supply of nutrients through fertilization of nursery beds of essential. The study further reveals that in palmarosa crop, planted at 45 x 30 cm spacing, poor plant establisment upto 20% maylead to corresponding loss in the first harvest only. Thereafter, there is no loss in yield in subsequent harvests.

Table 47.1. Effect of seedlings and nursery bed nutrient management onplant establishment and tillering of palmarosa.

Treatment (60 DAP)	% plant establishment (60 DAP)	No. of tillers/plants
Age of seedlings (days)		
30	82	24.4
40	59	26.3
50	80	27.4
60	69	23.7
SEm±	1.7	1.5
ISD (P=0.05)	5.0	NS
Fertility levels ($N:P_2O_5:K_2O$, Kg/ha)		
$F_0$0:0: 81.0	23.2	
$F_1$25:12.5:12.5	82.0	25.1
$F_2$50:25:25	78.0	25.6
$F_3$75:37.5:37.5	80.0	27.8
SEm± 1.7	1.5	
ISD (P=0.05)	NS	4.0

Table 47.2-Effect of age seedlings and nursery bed nutrient management on fresh herb oil yield of palmarosa.

Treatment	Fresh herb yield (q/ha)			Oil yield (kg/ha)		
	I harvest	II harvest	Total	I harvest	II harvest	Total
Age of seedlings (days)						
30	197.0	89.0	286.0	78.8	35.6	114.4

40	253.0	81.0	334.0	101.2	32.4	133.6
50	207.0	102.0	309.0	82.8	40.8	123.6
60	184.0	89.0	273.0	73.6	35.6	109.2
SEm±	6.9	4.9	10.0	2.8	2.0	4.0
LSD (P=0.05	19.8	14.0	28.7	7.9	5.6	11.5
Fertility levels ($N:P_2O_5:K_2O$ kg/ha)						
$F_0$0:0:	190.0	85.5	275.5	76.0	34.0	110.2
$F_1$25:12.5:12.5	215.0	93.0	308.0	86.0	37.2	123.2
$F_2$50:25:25	218.0	91.0	309.0	87.2	36.4	123.6
$F_3$75:37.5:37.5	218.0	91.5	309.5	87.2	36.6	123.8
SEm±6.9	4.9	10.0	2.8	2.0	4.0	
LSD (P=0.05)	19.8	NS	28.7	7.9	NS	11.5

Table 47.3. Effect of age of seedlings and fertility levels on growth of palmarosa seedlings.

Treatment	Height of seedlings (cm)	No. of tillers/ seedlings	No. of leaves seedlings	Fresh wt. of each seedlings (g)	Dry wet. of eash seed ing (g)
Age of seedlings (days)					
30	13.1	1.0	6.5	2.1	0.2
40	2.4	1.4	7.5	2.7	0.4
50	36.8	1.4	7.8	2.9	0.4
6058.8	1.7	10.0	4.9	1.0	
SEm±	0.35	0.04	0.04	0.18	0.07
LSD (P=0.05)	1.0	0.1	0.1	0.5	0.2
Fertility levels ($N:P_2O_5:K_2O$, Kg/ha)					
$F_0$0:0:	15.9	1.0	6.1	2.0	0.2
$F_1$25:12.5:12.5	32.4	1.2	7.0	2.8	0.3
$F_2$50:25:25	37.7	1.7	8.7	3.5	0.6
$F_3$75:37.5:37.5	47.0	1.	9.9	4.3	0.9
SEm±	0.35	0.04	0.04	0.18	0.07
ISD (P=0.05)	1.0	0.1	0.1	0.5	0.2

48

Lemongrass Oil

Introduction

Lemongrass oil is a richsource of citral. The oil is mainly used in perfumery and pharmaceutical industry. The yield potential of this grass is low and the main reasons of this is the non-availability of high oil yielding varieties and non-adoption of proper agro-techniques for cultivation. CKP25 a new high oil yielding variety of lemongrass has been developed by Rao and Sobti and released for commercial cultivation. Its improved agrotechnology has been developed covering major agronomic parameters like time of planting, harvest management nitrogen requirement and effect of triacontanol. The information on optimum plant density has not been worked out so far.

The yield is significantly influenced by the plant population per unit area. Generally spacing exerts its effects in two ways: Under wider spacing, individual plant may yield more with low yield per hectare whereas under narrow spacing individual plant may yield low with more yield per hectare due to increase In plant population. Thus optimum plant population must be ensured. The present investigation was, therefore, undertaken to determine the optimum plant density on newly developed CKP-25 lemongrass variety to achieve higher yield.

Materials and Methods

The fielcj trial on CKP-25variety of lemongrass was conducted at the Experimental Farm of Regional Research Laboratory, Jammu for three consecutive years in 1 st, 2nd and 3rd year crops respectively. Five different inter and intra row spacings consisting of 30 cm x 30 cm, 30 cm x 40 cm, 40 cm x 40 cm, 40 cm x 50 cm, 50 cm x 50 cm were compared in a randomized block design replicated seven times in a net plot size of 36 cm^2. The soil of the experimental plot was sandy loam with 7.6 ph and poor in organic matter. Two-three slips per hill were planted on 6 February, 1989 and irrigated immediately. A uniform dose of poultry manure @ 10 tonnes per hectare was applied two months before planting the crop. Phosphorous and potash were applied at 80 kg and 120 kg/ha as basal dose before planting. Nitrogen was applied at 100 kg/ha in first year and equally divided into four cuttings. Half dose of 1 st cutting was applied after 30 days of planting and rest half at an interval of 20 days. In three subsequent cuttings nitrogen was applied within 7 and 20 days in equal quantity after taking each harvest. Crop was kept weed free by weeding and hoeing as per need. After taking harvest, crop was irrigated within 3 days everytime and thereafter as and when required.

In second and consecutive years the nitrogen dose was increased to 340 kg/ha to meet the nutrient requirement of crop in view of more number of harvests taken. The dose was distributed into 80 kg, 80 kg, 60 kg, 75 kg and 45 kg for 1 st, 2nd, 3rd, 4th and 5th harvests. Each dose was equally splitted twice and half was applied within seven days after the harvest and second dose after 20 days of first application in each harvest. Due to dormant period of growth in winter season in 2nd year, 1st dose of nitrogen was applied in the month of March and rest as per the schedule. The crop was harvested as and when the plants attain the height of one metre. Pooled data of all the harvest observations of agro-morphological characters. including fresh herbage and oil yield were recorded for each harvest and analysed statistically separately and are presented in table 48.1. The essential oil was obtained by steam distillation at pilot scale. The citral content was determined following the method described by Guenther.

RESULTS AND DISCUSSION

Effect on Plant Height and Number of Tillers

A perusal of data (Table 48.1) on plant height revealed non-significant increase in 30 cm x 30 cm spacing treatment in comparison to other treatments. Number of tillers per plant in first, second and third year crops demonstrated significant increase in 50 cm x 50 cm spacing over rest of the spacings. Minimum number of tillers (70, 76 and 73) were recorded in narrow spacing treatment (30 cm x 30 cm) and maximum was recorded (138, 142 and 135) in wider spacing treatment (50 cm x 50 cm) in 1 st, 2nd and 3rd year crops, respectively. This may be due to more availability of nutrients and less competition between the plants resulting more number of tillers at wider spacing and also allow more availability of light to the plants resulting into enhancement in growth and over all synthesis and metabolic activities.

Effect on Herbage and Oil Yield

The fresh herbage yield (56.73 t/ha) at 30 cm x 30 cm spacing treatment showed significant increase over 50 cm x 50 cm being maximum number of plants (1, 11,111 /ha) in 1 st year crop. Rest of the treatments were at par. During 2nd and 3rd year crops all the treatments revealed non-significant differences and were at par in respect of herbage yield. Maximum herbage (85.83 and 76.0 t/ha) was obtained in 30 cm x 30 cm and 40 cm x 50 cm spacing combinations during 2nd and 3rd year crops, respectively. Higher herbage yield in 30 cm x 30 cm spacing treatment might be due to the higher population besides better establishment of crop upto 2nd year. A wider spacing reduced the number of plants per unit area which could not be compensated by increase in number of tillers per plant. These findings are in agreement with the earlier findings of singh et al. and singh. However, in 3rd year 40 cm x50 cm spacing treatment produced highest herbage that might be compensated with plant in this spacing as compared to narrow plant spacing treatments.

Oil yield revealed significant increase upto 40 cm x 50 cm spacing over 50 cm x 50 cm spacing. A spacing of 40 cm x 50 cm also demonstrated significant difference in oil yield over 30 cm x 30 cm spacing combination in 1 st year crop. Maximum reduction (11.34 per cent) was noticed in oil yield with wider (50 em x 50 cm) spacing as compared to 30 x 30 cm spacing treatment in 1 st year crop. However, the oil yield reduction came closer in 40 cm x 50 cm and 50 cm x 50 cm spacing treatment being 3.68 per cent in 2nd year crop. During 3rd year crop 40 cm x 50 em spacing treatment demonstrated 3.4 per cent increase over 30 cm x 30 cm spacing treatment, oil yield in 2nd and 3rd year crops showed non-significant difference among all the spacing treatments. Maximum oil yield 445.1 and 355.2 kg/ha was obtained in five harvests and followed four harvests in 30 em x 30 cm and 40 em x 50 cm spacing treatment in 2nd and 3rd year crops respectively. The oil yield was mainly affected by higher herbage produced with the spacing combitions.

Oil and Citral content:

The oil and citral content of the crop did not differ significantly in response to various spacing treatments. Third year crop showed a decline tr:end in oil per cent. However no difference was obtained among the various spacing treatments, Citral content remained same in three consecutive years.

It is concluded from this study that spacing of 40 em x 40 cm may kept to suit the requirements of both the prograssive and average farmers as narrow spacing 30 cm x 30 em, 30 em x 40 em offer little scope for machnical operations and requires a higher initial expenditure for planting material.

Table 48.1. Effect of plant densit on plant height, number of tillers/plant, fresh herbage and oil yield, oil and citral content of CKP-25 hybrid varietyof lamongrass.

Spacing (plants/ha)	Plant height (cm)	Tillers per plant	Fresh herb (t/ha)	Oil yield (kg/ha)	Oil content (%)	citral content (%)
			1st year Crop			
30 cm x 30 cm (1,11,111)	100.2	70.2	56.7	296.3	.522	81.5
30 cm x 30 cm (83,333)	100.0	89.4	55.4	285.8	0.515	81.9
40 cm x 40 cm (62,500)	99.5	93.7	56.3	287.1	0.511	82.4
40 cm x 50 cm (50,000)	99.0	115.0	55.2	273.8	0.496	82.0
50 cm x 50 cm (40,000)	98.2	138.2	52.2	262.7	.502	81.5
C.D. 5%	N.S.	16.60	3.23	20.88	-	-
			2nd Year Crop			
30 cm x 30 cm	106.2	76.0	85.8	445.2	0.518	81.8
30 cm x 40 cm	105.7	93.2	83.3	435.4	0.522	81.5
40 cm x 40 cm	104.2	101.0	83.8	440.2	0.525	81.9
40 cm x 50 cm	102.6	119.82.5	428.8	0.519	82.0	
50 cm x 50 cm	101.0	142.3	82.8	432.1	.528	82.8
C.D. 5%	N.S.	3.122	N.S.	N.S.	-	-
			3rd Year Crop			
30 cm x 30 cm	102.0	73.0	72.5	343.5	0.473	80.7
30 cm x 40 cm	101.4	92.4	73.47	341.9	0.465	82.4
40 cm x 40 cm	100.5	100.0	72.3	340.5	0.471	81.8
40 cm x 50 cm	100.2	103.0	76.0	355.2	0.467	82.6
50 cm x 50 cm	99.0	135.2	71.6	335.2	0.468	81.5
C.D 5%	N.S.	.59	N.S.	N.S.	-	

49

Patchouli Oil

Introduction

Patchouli oil is one of the most important and valuable raw materials used in the perfumery industry and is obtained by the steam distillation of shade dried leaves. India requires about 50 tonnes of patchouli oil annually and all of it is being imported as the production is mearge in our country. Since patchouli is a tropical plant several attempts have been made since forties to introduce this crop in India and to evaluate the oil produced. Vasanthakumar *et al.* assessed the suitability of five exotic cultivars for production of quality oil and reported that the growth and yield of crop were maximum at Banglore. Varshney opined that the formation and accumulation of essential oil are predominant during the active growth period and nitrogen has a positive effect upto certain level on the growth of leaf material (herbage) and yield of essential oil in crops where oil is synthesized and accumulated in leaves as in case of patchouli. Saha *et al* obtained significantly higher herb yield with 160 Kg N per hectare and found that N had no effect on oil.

Materials and Methods

The field trial was conducted at the experimental plots of Indian Institute of Horticultural Research, Hessaraghatta, Banglore. The soil was red sandy loam, low in available nitrogen (175Kg/ha), low in phosphorous (8.0Kg) and medium available potash (150 Kg) with pH 6.00. The treatments consisted of three cultivatars namely IIHR 1, IIHR 2 and IIHR 5 and four nitrogen levels viz. 50,100 and 200 Kg N per hectare and these 12 treatments with three replication were laid out in Randamised Complete Block Design. The sapling were raised from shoot tip cuttings in the month of June. Two month old rooted cuttings were planted as per the treatments in main field at a spacing of 60 cm x 60 cm in the last week of August. Recommended dose of phosphorous and potash and 1 16th nitrogen of each treatment were appljed at planting and 1/6th nitrogen was applied at 75 DAP. During the growth of second harvest N was given twice. First and second harvest, were done in middle of February and June, 1993 respectively. Observations on various growth characters were made during active growth period and at harvests. The fresh herbage yields were recorded and oils were distilled using Clevenger's apparatus at each harvest. The oil content was calculated on air dried weight basis.

A. Growth Attributes of Patchouli :

1. Differences due to Cultivars

The data presented in Table-49.1 indicate that the growth in terms of plant height and leaf area index (LAL = Leaf Area per plant divided by land area occupied by individual plant) was maximum with variety IIHR 5 followed by IIHR 1 and IIHR 2 at 75 DAp, first and second harvests. The cultivars differed significantly. The cultivar IIHR 5 recorded 51.06, 90.45 and 69.24 cm height and 0.77,1.76 and 1.49LAI, respectively at 3 sampling periods. With regards to number of branches IIHR 5(9.5, 15.0 and 16.1 per plant) and IIHR-1 (8.5, 15.6, and 16.2 per plant) had significantly higher branches than IIHR 2(7.8, 12.6 and 15.8 per plant) at 75 DAP and first harvest. The growth in terms of number of leaves, cultivar IIHR-1 (132.8 per plant) had maximum number of leaves at 75 DAP, thus showing no correlation between the leaf number in each plant and LAI. Because of poor regeneration capacity though good in quality cultivar IIHR 1 did not survive after first cutting. Hence the observations on number of leaves per plant, LAI and yield parameters could not be made.

2. Growth as influenced by Nitrogen:

The results indicated that N at 200 Kg per hectare recorded maximum height (77 .39 cm) over other nitrogen doses but was on par with N at 150 Kg per hectare (72.41 cm) at first harvest. Whereas during 2nd harvest N at 150 Kg per hectare had maximum height of 63.09 cm. Similar trend was also observed with regard to number of branches per plant at first and second harvests. The number of branches per plant at all the stages and LAI at 75 DAP and at harvest did not differ significantly though these parameters increased with increasing level of N fertilization. Similar observations were reported in their study by Saha *et.al.* The cultivars into nitrogen interaction effects was not found significant with any of the growth attributes studied in

B. Oil Content, Fresh Herbage Yield and Oil Yield

1. Variation Due to Cultivars :

Fresh herbage yield of cultivar IIHR-5 at both the harvests (8.43 and 6.12t1ha) was significantly superior over IIHR-1 and UHR-2 at first harvest (5.83 and 3.42 t/ha, respectively) and IIHR-2 (5.05 t/ha) at second harvest.Significa~tly higher essential oil was found in cultivar IIHR 1 (2.73%) over IIHR-2 (2.34%) and IIHR-5(2.1 0%) during first harvest. Both the cultivars IIHR-1 (33.4 Kg/ha) and IIHR-2(15.74 Kg/ha) at first harvest and in the second rarvest IIHR-5(32.61 Kg/ha) over IIHR 2 (25.76Kg/ha). On an average, the cultivars, IIHR-1 and IIHR-5 yield about 60-70 Kg of oil per hectare from two cuttings in duration of 7-8 months.

2. Influence of Nitrogen on Yields:

The fresh herbage yield in both the harvest was maximum with N application 200 Kg/ha (6.93 and 7.11 t/ha) but was on par with N at 150 Kg t/ha (6.44 and 5.99 t/ha respectively). The oil content showed the similar trend in f(rst harvest with N at 200 Kg per hectare recording 2.70 per cent which was significantly superior over all the other N treatments. However, in the second harvest N at 100 Kg per hectare had higher oil content of 3.44% and later on it declined. The interaction between cultivars into nitrogen was found significant. In the first harvest, in all the varieties, the oil content increased with increase in N application. However, during 2nd harvest N at 100 Kg per hectare provided maximum oil in IIHR 2 and decreased further. The oil yield in the first harvest followed the similar trends as that of oil content and N at 100 Kg per hectare provided higher oil content compared t050 Kg but was at par with 150 and 200 Kg N. Similar trend was observed in herbage yield, oil content and oil yield of patchouli with N fertilization in Arunachal Pradesh conditions. The interaction effect on oil yield due to cultivars and nitrogen showed similar trends as that of oil content. Considering the cost of nitrogen, the N dose at 150 Kg per hectare could be adopted for getting optimum yields in patchouli in Bangalore conditions.

Table 49.1. Growth attributes of patchouli at 75 dats after planing (75 DAP), first harvest (H1) and second harvest(H2).

Treatments	*Plant height (cm)*			*Number of branches/plant*			*Number of leaves/plant*			*Leaf area index*		
	75DAP	*H1*	*H2*	*75DAP*	*H1*	*H2*	*75DAP*	*H1*	*H2*	*75DAP*	*H1*	*H2*
Cultivers												
IIHR-1	48.18	71.05	46.92	8.5	15.6	16.2	132.8	363.1	-	0.41	1.06	-
IIHR-2	38.08	55.38	57.88	7.8	12.6	15.8	89.4	260.9	227.9	0.31	0.86	0.78
IIHR-5	5106	90.45	69.24	9.5	15.0	16.1	94.8	444.5	183.7	0.77	1.76	1.49
CD at 5%	2.84	4.98	3.49	0.72	0.82	NS	22.5	76.8	55.5	0.08	0.31	0.19
Nitrogen (KG/ha)												
50	44.54	68.76	53.17	8.4	13.7	14.3	108.4	304.1	179.5	0.47	1.04	0.78
100	45.63	70.63	57.51	8.6	14.5	16.7	100.4	359.1	225.1	0.48	1.24	1.08
150	46.72	72.41	63.09	8.9	14.4	17.8	101.7	374.6	309.5	0.48	1.31	1.47
200	46.92	77.39	58.28	8.6	15.1	15.5	112.0	381.1	323.4	0.55	1.25	1.22
CD at 5%	NS	5.75	4.04	NS	0.96	1.02	NS	NS	NS	NS	NS	0.27

Table 49.2: Fresh herbage yield, oil content and oil yield of patchoull as influenced cultivars and nitrogen fertilization.

Treatments	*Fresh herbage yeild (t/ha)*		*Oil content(%)*		*Oil yield(Kg/ha)*	
	I harvest	*Indl harvest*	*I harvest*	*Indl harvest*	*I harvest*	*Indl harvest*
Cultivers						
IIHR-1	5.85	-	2.73	-	33.46	-
IIHR-2	3.42	5.05	234	2.61	15.74	25.76
IIHR-5	8.43	6.12	2.10	2.64	35.79	32.61
CD at 5%	0.69	0.92	0.17	NS	4.76	5.81
Nitrogen (KG/ha)						
50	4.40	4.35	1.99	2.06	17.37	17.50
100	5.87	4.89	2.43	3.44	28.17	33.75
150	6.40	5.99	2.46	2.63	30.45	31.83
200	6.93	7.11	2.70	2.35	37.33	33.66
CD at 5%	0.79	1.29	0.20	0.41	5.50	8.22
Interaction	NS	NS				

50

Rose-Scented Geranium

Introduction

Scented-geraniums belonging to the genus *Pelargonium* are different from ornamental geraniums. The *Pelargoniums* are native to South Africa. A number of species, theircultivars and hybrids of *Pelargoniumwere* introduced in the Shevory Hills of Tamil Nadu by some enterprising French people from where systematic cultivation of the crop spread to other regions, firstly to the high altitude areas and then to plains. The cultivation and production of scented geraniums in different countries are detailed in Table 50.1.

Table 50.1. World Production of geranium oil.

Country	*Production (tonnes year^{1})*
China	80
Egypt	40
Russia	20
Algeria	15
Morocco	10
Reunion	10
India	2
Israel	Emerging country

Work Done at CIMAP Field Station, Hyderabad (1) Botanical identification of species:

There exists an ambiguity regarding the correctness of the botanical nomenclature adopted for the varieties grown in India. Rajendra Gupta opined that the cultivars available in India could be probable hybrids between P. *graveo/ens* x *P.radens.* However, our research based on morphology, oil glands/plant hairs and chemical composition of the essential oil indicated that these cultivars could be putative hybrids with P. *graveolens* x *P.capitatum* as their putative parents. The hypothesis, however, was put forward tentatively and until the correct botanical identity of all the cultivars grown in India should be referred as *Pelargonium* species. It should be noted that many authors still use the botanical nomenclature *P. graveolens* (=Pelargonium species) forthe geranium cultivars grown in India. In the world literature, all the varieties yielding commercial geranium oils are regarded as hybrids and are referred as *Pelargonium* species and not as *P. graveolens.*

(2) Genotypes / Varieties :

In India, there are three genotypes/cultivars which vary in their boimass/ essential oil yields and chemical composition of their essential oils.They are cvs. Bourbon / Reunion (recently christened as *Bipuli),* Algerian /Tunisian (recently christened as *Hemanti)* and Egyptian / Kelkar (introduced by the courtesy of Sri G.D. Kelkar of M/s S.H Kelkar & CO.Pvt. Ltd., Mumbai and recently christened as *Kuntf).* Keltar is not commercially cultivated and has high content of geraniol(>35%), while the Bourbon is commercially cultivated both in high altitude and plains conditions and is rich in both citronellol and geraniol (20-30% and 18-25%, respectively). The Algerian oil resembles that of Chinese oil, while the Bourbon oil is classified as African type due to the presence of high amount of 10-epi-y-eudesmol and trace amount of guaia-6, 9-diene. Among the three varieties, Kelkar gives highest recovery of oil. Recently 2 genotypes obtained from leaf cuttings of "Bourbon" and containing high amounts of isomenthone (.60%) have been reported. Work needs to be done on evolving high yielding varieties of all these genotypes.

Cultivation Practices

(1) Planting:

The geranium crop is propagated vegetatively by terminal cuttings as seedlings have been observed only in some places (Bang lore, Kodaikanal and Lucknow) with low amount of seed production and poor seed viability. Treating the terminal stem cuttings with 2000 ppm IBA by quick-dip method hastens the rooting process as well as the growth of the cuttings. However, as only a limited number of terminal stem cuttings can be obtained from then mother plants, technology has been generated for the development of leaf / single node stem cuttings. By this technology sufficient number of planting material can be obtained from a limited number of mother plants at reasonable cost. However, some studies indicated that the chemical composition of some of the leaf cuttings could be different from that of mother plants. Therefore, detailed investigations are needed before commercialising propagation by leaf cuttings.

(2) Spacing:

Geranium is generally planted in winter season with a spacing of 60 cm between rows and 45 cm between plants within the row. Paired-row spacing can also be adopted in this crop.

(3) Intercropping :

Due to its initial slow growth legumes can be intercropped in geranium itself. It can also be grown as an intercrop in agreforestry system in the alleys of *Eucalyptus citriodora*

(4) Fertilizers:

The crop respnds to application of 120-150 kg N ha year. 15-17% increase in oil yield can be obtained through application of neem-cake coated urea over prilled urea. P and K fertilizers did not increase the yields of geranium. N needs to be applied to each harvest as no residual effect of N applied to the previous harvest was observed. The quality of geranium oil was not affected by fertilizer application.

(5) Plant Growth Regulators:

Plant growth regulators{PGR) such as 1M, ISA, GGG, Triacotanol, Ethephon, Gytozyme, crop+, Siozyme crop + and Ghamatkar increased geranium yields by more than 100% and influenced the quality of the oil in pot-culture studies. The results need to be confirmed through field studies.

(6) Weeds:

Geranium is susceptible to weed competition during the first 90 days after planting or 90 days before harvesting. Uncontrolled weed growth reduced boimass yield by 40.6 - 58.3 % and oil yield by 46.9 - 65.0% and adversely affected the quality of oil. It is, therefore, advised that the crop should be kept weed-free during these periods.

(7) Partial Shade:

Yields of herb and oil were affected adversely by partial shade (when the crop was grown under trees) in comparison to plants grown in the open. The quality of oil, however, was not significantly affected by partial shade of the trees, except for some minor changes in some of the oil components.

(8) Season:

The crop gives lowest biomasss and essential oil yields and essential oil concentration during summer months. Rainy and autumn season months recorded highest biomass <;1nd essential oil yields and maximum essential oil concentration.

(9) Pests and Diseases:

There are no major insect pests on this crop in Andhra Pradesh. Wilt and leaf blight caused by fungi, are the main diseases threatening the cultivation of this crop in the plains in A.P. Wilt diseases occurs during summer season, while leaf blight occurs during rainy season. In severe cases of infestation plant moralities and yield reductions range from 70 % to 80 % or more. Spraying Captafol (0.1-0.3 %) at 15 days intervals controls the leaf blight disease, whereas, spraying the crop and drenching the soil with Carbendazim (0.1 ~O. 3%) checks the spread of wilt disease. These two diseases are posing a form dable challenge to the scientists. Developing a resistant variety to these diseases will go a long way in establishing geranium cultivation in A.P. plains.

(10) Harvesting, Distillation and Economics:

Leaves are the main plant parts containing geranium oil and contributing most to the biomass, through petiole and tender stem also contain traces of oil. Among the leaves, young leaves contain more oil than bigger and older leaves. Therefore, harvesting of 15-17 cm of growth which contain tender stems with young and expanding leaves the entire herb. The herb after harvesting as drying of biomass reduced the oil recovery under semi-arid tropical climatic conditions. In commercial distillations low oil recovery (0.06 -0.16%) is a problem and efforts are being made to improve the recovery oil. Wherever possible, the crop should be hydro-distilled with cohobaton facility for obtaining higher yield of good quality oil. With an average oil yield of 20-30 kg ha-1 yr1 and with an oil price of Rs. 3500-4000 kg-1, a farmer can

earn a gross profit of Rs.70,000/- to 1,20,000/- ha1 yr1 which is much higher compared to many other agricultural/aromatic crops. Higher yields (30-40 kg ha-1 yr1) and profit (Rs. 1 ,05,000-1 ,60,000) can be obtained by following the technologies described above.

(11) Quality of Oil

The quality of the essential oil of cV.Bourbon is of international standard. Quality of the oil is influenced by a number of factors such as weeds, drying of biomass prior to distillation, distillation method, season conditions of storage of oil etc. Recent evidence indicates that oil quality is affected by comminution of plant material prior to distillation and diseases. The crop harvested during summer season yields an oil with high amount of citronellol and low—amount of geraniol. Therefore, summer harvesting is not recommended. Similarly, citronellol content increases and geraniol content decreases in improperly stored oils (containing a small amount of water, half-filled in aluminium container and stored under ambient conditions), whereas, the quality changes are minimal in properly stored oil (oil that has been dried over anhydrous sodium sulphate, filled upto the brim in an aluminium container or amber coloured bottle, tightly stoppered and stored under ambient conditions). Therefore, the oil should be carefully stored retain its quality.

51

Basil Oil

Introduction

Ocimum basilicum L. (Fam. Labiatae), popularly known as Basil is a native of Central Asia but also widely cultivated throughout the world particularly in India, Bulgaria, Romania, Egypt, Israel, Camoros, Yugoslavia, U.S.A, Madagaskar and Pakistan. The plant is reported to be of medicinal value and finds use in Indian system of medicine. It is reported to have stomachic, anthelmintic, antipyretic and expectorant properties. It's oil is used to food, flavour and pharmaceutical industries.

Several chemotypes of basil are reported by sobti and Pushpangadan like methylcinnamate/methyl chavicol/eugenol/geraniol and linalool types. Khanna et al. examined the composition of the oil from plant cultivated on normal soil and reported constituents containing mainly methyl chavicol and linalool. Indian basil (methyl chavicol) is cultivated as a commercial crop for its essential oil. Its production in India is estimated of multiple applications particularly in food, flavour and pharmaecutical industries. It is also used as a starting material for the synthesis of anethole. Considering the economic importance of oil, the plant was raised under usurland utilizatio plan on alkaline soil which is not suitable for cultivation of food crops.

Materials and Methods

The material for study was obtained from Western U.P. where is in commercial cultivation and planted at Benthra Reserach Station of the Institute. The soil is Banthra is clayey, saline having pH 9-10 and exchanable sodium more than 20%. The crop came up at Banthra quite successfully under the prevailing agro-climatic condition.

On hydro distillation, it gave 0.4% of a volatile oil on fresh weight basis possessing a sweet odour resembling that of Funnel. Taste of the oil was lightly sweet. Chemical composition of the oil was determined by GC/MS on Hewitt Packard GC/MS Model H.P. 5996 coupled with computer library of 80,000 compounds and fitted with a WACOT SE30 (Methyl silicon gum) capillary column of 12 mx 0.32 mm. Other conditions of the experiment were maintained as given below :

Carrier gas	Helium
Flow rate	40 ml/Sec
Injector temp.	230°C
Chromatographic temp.	35°C to 290° with rising rate 10°C/min
Mass range	40-800

The constituents were identified by comparing GC/MS spectra of the peaks with those of the given in the library and reported literature. The major constituents were further confirmed by thei CO GCL and CO TLC. Results of the investigations are given in Table 51.1.

Results and Discussion

Studies have revealed that the alkalinity of the soil practically had no effect on the yield and quality of the oil. The oil contains phenolic ethers in major concentration, as is clear from the Table1. In addition, it contains fairly good amount of linalool (17.56) 1.8 cineole (3.67%0 and generyl acetate. Their presence contributes to the sweet and fine odour of theoil. Anethole, methyl-eugenol and methyl -iso-eugenol add to its delicacy. The terpene and sesquiterpene contents are fairly low. High concentration of methyl chavicol (61.50%) contributes to sweet raste and fennel like odour of the oil. Methyl chavicol is a starting material for the synthetic prepartion of anethle which is largely required chemical in the pharmaecutical and flavour industry. The oil under investigation can form a potential raw material for anethole. Besides, it can directly be used as a flavouring material andin perfumer blending.

Table 51.1

S. No.	Compound identified	Percentage
	Hydrocarbons	
1.	Ocimine	0.55
2.	Camphene	0.75
3.	α-pinene	0.31
4.	Caryophyilene	0.32
5.	Zingeberence	0.68
6.	Humelene	2.45
7.	ß-bisabelene	0.10
Oxide		
8.	1:8 Cineole	3.6
9.	Carophyliene	0.3
10.	Linalool Oxide	0.2
Alcohol		
11.	Iso methol	0.24
12.	Linalool	17.56
13.	Nerol	0.15
14.	Iso-neo-menthol	0.24
15.	Trans geraniol	0.10
Aldehyde		
16.	Citral	1.56
Ketones		
17.	Camphor	1.22
18.	Methyl heptenone	0.11
Esters		
19.	Geranyl Acetate	0.14
Phenols		
20.	Eugenol	1.2
Phenolic ethers		
21.	Methyl eugenol	3.1
22.	Methyl iso eugenol	1.5
23.	Anethole	0.12
24.	Methyl chavicol	61.50

52

Turpentine Oil

Introduction

Resins often occur mixed with some essential oils known as oleoresin. Oleoresins obtained from Pinus species of the Himalayan forest are important non-wood forest products. The total world annual resin production is about 600,000 metric tonnes, North America is the largest producer of resin and India occupies 7th position.

The oleoresins on distillation yields turpentine oil and rosin. Turpentine oil from chir pine is a mixture of alpha-pinene (25-30%), beta-pinene (5-10%), delta-3-carene (50-60%), longifolene (2-5%) and other terpenes (-5%). Alpha -pinene is one of the most important terpenes and has been utilized for the manufacture of synthetic camphor, terpineol, isoburnyl acetate, isoburneol and other products, which are used in perfumery, pharmaceutical and pesticide industries. Beta-pinene on pyrolysis gives mycrene which on hydrochlorination and subsequent treatments gives gernyl acetate, neryl and linalyl acetate under different conditions of further leading to the formation of a number of compounds including citral, alpha and beta-ionones, Longifolene is a rare constituent of Indian turpentine and on acid isomerization gives isomer, isolongifolene, which has shown a greater industrial potential as raw material for a production of perfumery material for the production of perfumery derivatives. Pine tar is used in rubber industries as an emulsifier.

Materials and Methods

The study was carried out in 1993 in the campus area of Dr. Y.s. Parmar University of Horticulture and Forestry, Solan, near oachghat at an elevation of 1200 of 1225 meter. The tapping season was March to October. The Climate of the area is sub-temperate, with the average rain fall ranging from 100-130 cm. The temperature ranges from 2°C to 33°C in winter and 20°C to

33°C in summer. The trees in the forest were measured at breast height for diameter (d.b.h.) The trees falling in the diameter range 20-30 cm only, were cosnidered for the present experiment and four diameter classes viz. 27.50-30.0 cm (D1), 25.0-27.5 cm (D2), 22.5-25.0 cm (D3), 20.0-22.5 cm (D4) were differentiated. Forty trees were selected randomly in each diameter class, which comes out to 160 trees in total. The "Rill Method" of resin tapping as described by Failla (1949) was used. The composite resins samples were collected from different diameter classes in every month. The turpentine oil samples were analyzed using "Blue-Star Gas Chromatograph".

Results and Discussion

Results indicated significant differences in the effect of month, diameter class and interaction between month and diameter class on alpha-pinene, beta-pinene, longfifolene and other constituents. The maximum (mean value) alpha-pinene (38.43%) was recorded in the month of October. Among the diameter class, the maximum (mean value) alpha-pinene (35.28%) was recorded in diameter class D4, which was at par with maximum alpha-pinene content (44.51%) was obtained on October month from D4 (lowest diameter) and minimum (27.43%) in the month of June from D1 diameter (Table 52.1).

Beta-pinene content varied between 9.97% to 7.62. The maximum beta-pinene content (mean value) was found in the month of October followed by June and July, where the minimum content was obtained during September preceeded by August. Among the diameter classes D3 recorded the maximum (mean value) content of 9.44% and minimum (mean value) 8.90% in D4. The highest content was recorded in the month of September from D3 and lowest in the same month from diameter class D4.

The data (Table-2) showed maximum content (55.17%) of delta-3 carene in month of June and minimum (46.69%) and month of October (mean value). Among the diameter classes maximum content (53.57%) and minimum (50.98%) was noticed in D2 and D1 (mean values). The highest content (56.94%) recorded in month of June from D2 and minimum (42.13%) in the month of October from D4 (lowest diameter). Longifolene content (mean values) varied between 1.59% to 4.25%. Maximum content was observed in the month of August followed by July and minimum was observed in October. among diameter classes, maximum content (3.41%) was recorded n D1 and minimum (2.19%) in D4 (mean values).

The maximum content (4.39%) of other constituents was recorded in the month of September followed by October and August (mean values). The mainimum content (2.58%) was recorded in July. the diameter class D1

Tabel 52.1. Effect of deameter class and month on per cent alpha and beta-pinene.

Diameter Class	Month					
	June	July	August	September	October	Mean
D1 (27.5-30.0 cm)	27.43 (09.77)	28.65 (09.87)	28.96 (08.20)	39.53 (07.80)	32.36 (09.01)	31.38 (08.93)
D2 (25.0-27.5 cm)	27.73 (09.29)	31.33 (08.17)	29.81 (09.12)	35.53 (06.38)	32.87 (11.84)	31.45 (08.96)
D3 (25.5-25.0 cm)	33.93 (09.18)	28.63 (09.64)	33.34 (06.18)	29.55 (11.90)	43.72 (10.30)	34.03 (09.44)
D4 (20.0-22.5 cm)	31.80 (09.85)	32.99 (09.72)	30.50 (10.98)	38.10 (05.22)	44.51 (08.73)	35.28 (08.90)
Mean	30.22 (09.52)	30.40 (09.49)	30.91 (08.62)	35.30 (07.62)	38.43 (09.97)	
Treatment			**C.D.0.05**			
Diameter class (D)			0.036 (0.018)			
Month (M)			0.040 (0.019)			
Diameter class x Month (M x D)			0.081 (0.039)			

Note : The values within the paranthesis are beta-pinene content.

Table 52.2. Effect of diameter class and month on per cent delta-3-carene, longifolece and other constituents.

Diameter Class	Month					
	June	July	August	September	October	Mean
D1 (27.5-30.0 cm)	50.80 (03.33) 04.56*	54.66 (03.37) 03.43*	52.03 (05.49) 05.25*	44.27 (01.20) 07.18*	49.12 (03.63) 05.61*	50.98 (03.41) 05.21*
D2 (25.0-27.5 cm)	56.94 (03.14) 02.88*	55.59 (03.13) 02.22*	52.93 (03.86) 01.73*	52.87 (02.39) 02.82*	49.52 (02.70) 03.06*	53.57 (03.04) 02.54*
D3 (25.5-25.0 cm)	53.94 (01.30) 02.62*	55.66 (03.37) 02.75*	52.52 (03.74) 03.21*	49.48 (03.11) 05.95*	45.98 (00.01) 00.01*	51.52 (02.30) 02.71*
D4 (20.0-22.5 cm)	54.99 (01.22) 02.13*	52.41 (02.94) 01.92*	52.57 (03.32) 02.00*	53.69 (02.88) 01.61*	42.13 (00.01) 04.62*	51.60 (02.19) 02.46*
Mean	55.17 (02.22) 02.80*	54.58 (03.20) 02.58*	52.51 (04.25) 03.05*	50.08 (02.40) 04.39*	46.69 (01.59) 03 32*	
Treatment						
Diameter class (D)			0.030 (00.21) 00.01*			
Month (M)			0.034 (00.23) 00.67*			
Diameter class x Month (M x D)			(00.46) 00.03*			

Note : The values within the paranthesis are per cent longifolene. The values with star are per cent other constituents.

recorded (mean values) maximum content (5.21%) and D4 recorded the minimum content (2.46%). The maximum content (7.18%) was obtained in the month of september from D1 (highest diameter) and minimum (0.01%) from D3 in the month of October (Table 2).

In the chemical composition of turpentine oil, alpha-pinene increased from June to October and also with decrease in diameter classes, beta-pinene did not show any definite trend both month and diameter class wise; delta-3-carene decreased from June to October but no definite trend was observed in diameter classes; longifolene and other constituents also did not show the definite trend both diameter class was well as month wise.

53

Essential Oil Constituents : Hydrodistillation Vs CO_2 extraction

Introduction

Out of large number of Aromatic and Medicinal plants, only few have been exploited for the production of essential oil, perfumery and insecticidal properteis. For present study selection of plant material was made because the essential oil of these plants is valued for various purposes.

Collistemone lanceolatus

It belongs to the family Myrtaceae, which is cultivated in India as an ornamental plant. Commonly it is known as " Bottle brush". The oil from leaves extract is valued for both perfumery as well as medicinal properties.

Murrya koenigii

It belongs to the family rutaceae and is commonly known as "Curry patta" tree. The oil from the leaves are widely used for flavouring curries. Green leaves eaten raw as cure for dysentery, bruises and applied externally to cure eruptions. The oil is valued for both flavouring as well as medicinal purposes.

Lantana camara

Belongs the family Verbinaceae, which is an aromatic shrub, grown in india as an ornamental plant. The whole plant shown anti malarial (Weenen et. al. 1990) and pesticidal properties. Essential oil from leaves extracts shows diaphoratic, carminative, antiseptic and fungitoxic activities. Essential oil from seed has antimicrobial and anthelmintic activities.

Tagetes erecta

Belongs to the family Compsiteae and is commonly known as "Marigold". The plant is valued for ornamental, medicinal as well as perfumery properties. Infusion of the herb is valued as a cure against rheumatism, cold and bronchitis. Root extract as laxative and leaves are used in renal troubles, muscular pains and is applied to boils and curbuncles. Infusion of leaves shows carminative, diuretic and vermifuge properties.

Ocimum sanctum

Belongs to the family Labiatae, commonly known as "Holy basil". The plant is valued for its perfumery, flavour as well as its health giving properties and hence grown in many homes, it also keeps mosquito away. Juice of its leaves is applied in bronchitis and throat problems. Decoction of leaves is useful in malaria and other fevers. It is also useful in ring worm, rashes, ear infections and other skin diseases.

Materials and Methods

The plant materials were collected from institutional area of purchases from Khari Baoli market, New Delhi.

Air dried leaves of these plants were distilled in Cleavenger's apparatus and oil samples collected were dried using anhydrous sodium sulphate.

For supercritical extraction process, air dried leaves of these plants were crushed to powder using mixer which were then seived and particle size of 0.5 mm was packed in extractor thimble using glass wool on both the ends. The extractor was then connected to the rest of assembly and carbon dioxide was passed through the sample present in extractor thimble, desired sub/ super critical temperature was maintained with the help of water thermostate and air driven pump was used to push carbon dioxide to maintain pressures (e.g. 60, 80, 100, 150 and 200 bar). The oil from sample was collected, weighted before and after experiment and the yield was obtained by substracting the two weights.

Results and discussion

Percentage yields of various plants is shown in Table 1., for both hydrodistillation and supercritical extraction process. It shows higher yield of extracts with supercritical extraction process. For each sample at a particular set of temperature and pressure, the percentage yield was maximum as shown in table 1. Previous work done in our laboratory shows that aroma qualityof extracts improved with carbon dioxide extraction as compared to hydrodistillation process. The physical constants shown in table 2., also indicate improved aroma quality of carbon dioxide extracted essential oil.s The major constituents of essential oils, identified by GC analysis are shown in table 3. GC conditions are; column; Chromosorb W, H.P.; Column temperature : 80°C-230°C, Flow rate of N2 (carrier gas): 30 ml/min., Injection temperature: 240°C; Detector : F.I.D.

Conclusion

The above study shows that extraction using liquid carbon dioxide is conveninet and superior in terms of both quanity as well as qualitative properties of the extracts as compared to traditional hydrodistillation process. Qualitatively terpenes components of essential oil gets oxygenated resulting in constant deterioration with time in the quality of compounds in hydrodistillation process, while less percentage of terpene and hydrocarbon compounds were obtained with liquid carbon dioxide extraction and hence the quality of the essential oil remain uncharged with liquid carbon dioxide extraction process.

Acknowledgement

One of the auther is thankful to CSIR for financial support and Indian Institute of Technology for providing necessary laboratory facilities.

Table 53.1. Yield and time fot separation of essential oils: Hydrodistillation Vs CO_2 extraction

S. No.	Materials	Hydrodistillation		Carbon dioxide extraction	
		time (min.)	% yield	time (min.)	% yield
1.	*Callistemone lanceolatus*	360	0.8	30	2.0
2.	*Murrya koenigii*	360	0.2	30	0.89
3.	*Lantana camera*	360	0.4	30	1.0
4.	*Tardetes erecta*	360	0.3	30	1.2
5.	*Ocimum sanctum*	360	0.3	30	2.0

Table 53.2. Physical properties of the essential oils : Hydrosistillation Vs CO_2 extraction

S. No.	Materials	Physical Properties	Hysrodistilled	CO_2 dextracted
1.	*Callistemone lanceolatus*	Refractive Index (at 30° C)	1.4603	1.4922
		Optical Rotation	+14.7	+15.0°
		Specific Gravity (at 30° C)	0.9081	0.9224
2.	*Murraya koenigii*	Refractive Index (at 20° C)	1.4871	1.4998
		Optical Rotation	-27.2°	-28.06°
		Specific Gravity (at 20° C)	0.8722	0.8948
3.	*Lantana camera*	Refractive Index (at 30° C)	1.4896	1.5010
		Optical Rotation	-14.7°	+15.2°
		Specific Gravity (at 30° C)	0.8842	0.9100
4.	*Tagetes eracta*	Refractive Index (at 20° C)	1.4850	1.4980
		Optical Rotation	+4.90	+5.18°
		Specific Gravity (at 20° C)	0.87525	0.8842
5.	*Ocimum santum*	Refractive Index (at 20° C)	1.4891	1.5010
		Optical Rotation	-9.85	-10.01°
		Specific Gravity (at 20° C)	0.8502	0.8666

Table 53.3. Major constituents of essential oils, identified by GC

S. No.	Materials	Composition of oil
1.	*Callistemone lanceolatus*	1:8 cineole (48.6%(α-pinene (26.6%) α-terpinoil (11.2%), limonene (6.0%) p-cymene (3.1%)
2.	*Murraya koenigii*	β- caryophyllene (29.0%),β--gur junene (21.0%) β- elemene (6.9%),β - phellandrene (6.1%),
3.	*Lantana camera*	α - farmesene (30.1%),α -phellandrene (15.2%), β - Caryophyllene (8.0%),β-ocimene (3.8%), α - pinene (2.2%),
4	*Tagetes eracta*	d-limonene (29.2%), ocimene (10.9%), linalool (14.8%),nonanal (1.1%), β- phellandrene (6.6%), 1:8 cineole (4.2%),
5.	*Ocimum santum*	Methyl eugenol (12.4%), β- caryophyllene (16.1%),β-elemence (30.8%),

VARIOUS PROJECT REPORTS IN CD-ROMS

37 ALUMINIUM AND ALUMINIUM BASED INDUSTRIES Rs. 11000/-

Aluminium powder, AAC & ACSR aluminium conductors, Aluminium silicate, Aluminium utensil, Aluminium wire drawing, Aluminium paint, Aluminium ingots from scrap, Aluminium alloy & ingots, anodizing of aluminium, Aluminium chloride, Aluminium channels, aluminium rolling mill, Aluminium bottles, Aluminium foil cutting & roll making, Aluminium end caps, Aluminium door,Window, Aluminium colapsible tube, Aluminium phosphide, Aluminium ingots from bauxite, Aluminium caps, Aluminium furniture & hardware, aluminium beverage cans, Aluminium cans for capacitors, Aluminium & Aluminium alloys from aluminium scraps to make utensils,(induction furnace melted),Aluminium hot & cold rolling mill (aluminium sheets & circles), Anodic aluminium labels, aluminium slugs & circles, Aluminium printing plate for offset printing machine, Aluminium foils, Aluminium wire and rods, Brass and aluminium hinges, Hard anodizing on aluminium, Pilfer proof caps, Piston assembly (Aluminium alloy), Pressure die casting Al., Paper coated al.wire, Pressure cooker.

14 POTATO AND POTATO BASED PROJECTS (14 PROJECT REPORTS) Rs. 8500/-

Alcohol from potatoes, Dextrose powder from potatoes, Frozen finger chips, I M F L (whisky) from potatoes, Liquid glucose, Potato chips/waffers, Potato powder (automatic plant), Potato starch, Potato chips, Potato and onion flakes, Potable beer (alcoholic) based on potato & barley/malt, Potato powder, Sago seeds (saboo dana), Vodka from potatoes

21 BAKERY & ALLIED PROJECTS Rs. 7500/-

Automatic bread and biscuit unit, Automatic biscuit plant, Baking powder, Biscuit unit (pineapple) automatic pineapple biscuit making plant, Bread plant, bakery unit (rusk, Pastries,Bread, Buns cake, toffee, etc. confectionery industry, Confectionery industry (toffee & candy), Chocolate, Custard powder, Candy hard boiled, icing sugar, Jelly powder, Lecithin (soya based), Mithai/halwai (sweet & namkeen), Milk powder & ghee, Mini flour mill (maize, sorghum, millet), Namkeen industry (bhujia, Chana chur etc.), Potato chips/waffers, Roller flour mill (mini flour mill), Yeast from molasses.

5 POWER PLANT PROJECTS Rs. 11000/- (THERMAL, HYDRO, SOLAR, WIND ENERGY AND LIGNITE COAL BASED)

Power plant (thermal), Power plant from lignite coal, Power plant (hydro based), Solar power plant, Wind energy power project (capacity: 10 mw).

12 MOSQUITOES PREVENTIVE PROJECTS (COILS, MATS,LIQUIDS, AGARBATTI, NETS, SPRAY ETC.) Rs. 7500/-

Mosquito coils using eucalyptus leaves, Mosquito coils and mats, allethrin mosquito repellent oil, Mosquito repellent mats, aerosol & mosquito repellent spray (baygon, hit, Mortein type), pest control, Allethrin mosquito mat recharger, Mosquito net, mosquito larva destroyer, Mosquito repellent oil, Mosquito coil agar batti (incense sticks), Mosquito & flies repellent agarbatti (incense sticks)

10 MOLASSES BASED LUCRATIVE PROJECTS Rs. 11000/-

Animal feed (cattle, Poultry, sheep or pig),(liquid feed) (molasses based), Acetic acid from molasses, Absolute/neutral alcohol (purified ethyl alcohol)from sugar cane juice or molasses, Citric acid from molasses, Country liquor from molasses, Ethanol (biofuel) from molasses, Industrial alcohol (rectified spirit), Oxalic acid from molasses, Octanol (octyl alcohol) from molasses, yeast from molasses.'

24 FRUITS/VEG. & ALLIED FOOD DEHYDRATION PROJECTS Rs. 11000/-

Banana powder, Curcumin & turmeric oil from turmeric, Dehydration of jack fruit, Dehydration of figs by sun drying method, dehydration of onion and garlic, Desiccated coconut powder, Dry ginger powder and oleoresin, Dry ginger (ginger powder), Onions & onion powder, Egg powder, Fruit juice powder, Fruits and vegetable dehydration, Glucose-d powder, Garlic flakes and powder (dehydrated), Grape dehydration, Instant food, Mango powder, mustard powder, Milk powder & ghee, Potato powder, Turmeric powder (edible grade), Tamarind juice powder, Tomato powder, yeast dry powder from maize.

PROFITABLE NEW 35 INDUSTRIES Rs. 11000/-

Aluminium ingots from bauxite, Ayurvedic dant manjan (red colour - dabur type), Angora rabbit wool, Aluminium powder, Aluminium Foils, Besan plant, Bee keeping, Corn/maize oil, Cotton yarn, corn flakes, Detergent cake & powder, Dairy farming, Dehulled sesame seeds, Dairy products, Dry ginger (ginger powder), Egg powder, Fish farming, Fruit juices bottling plant, Fruits and vegetable dehydration, Goat farming, Honey processing and packaging, Mango processing & canning (mango pulp), Neem oil from seeds, Packed coconut water, Peanut butter, Pappad plant (automatic), Potato and onion flakes, Plastic buttons (by injection moulding methods), Potato powder, Pickles, Processed food, Rabbit farming, Sanitary napkins, Tamarind kernel powder, Tamarind juice powder.

ENGINEERS INDIA RESEARCH INSTITUTE Mobile : 9811437895
4449, Nai Sarak, Main Road, Delhi - 110 006 (INDIA) Ph./Fax : 91-11- 23918117, 23916431, 23840361